The Sage Dictionary of
Social Research Methods

Compiled and edited
by
Victor Jupp

 SAGE Publications

London ● Thousand Oaks ● New Delhi

First published 2006

The format of this dictionary was originated by Eugene McLaughlin and John Muncie and was first used in the *SAGE Dictionary of Criminology* (Sage, May 2001).

SAGE Publications Ltd
1 Oliver's Yard
55 City Road
London EC1Y 1SP

SAGE Publications Inc.
2455 Teller Road
Thousand Oaks, California 91320

SAGE Publications India Pvt Ltd
B-42, Panchsheel Enclave
Post Box 4109
New Delhi 110 017

British Library Cataloguing in Publication data

A catalogue record for this book is available
from the British Library

ISBN13 978 0 7619 6297 7   ISBN13 978 0 7619 6298 4 (pbk)
ISBN10 0 7619 6297 2   ISBN10 0 7619 6298 0 (pbk)

Library of Congress Control Number 2005923706

Typeset by C&M Digitals (P) Ltd., Chennai, India
Printed on paper from sustainable resources
Printed in Great Britain by Athenaeum Press, Gateshead

The Sage Dictionary of Social Research Methods

Contents

List of Contributors

Editor

Victor Jupp, Northumbria University, UK

Project Administrator

Susan Doberman, Northumbria University, UK

Administrative Support

Angela Brady, graduate, Northumbria University, UK
David Doberman, graduate, Warwick University, UK
Rachael Beth Moss, graduate, Northumbria University, UK

International Advisory Board

Martin Bulmer, University of Surrey, UK
Amanda Coffey, Cardiff University, UK
Norman Denzin, University of Illinois, USA
Nigel Gilbert, University of Surrey, UK
Martyn Hammersley, The Open University, UK
Yvonna Lincoln, Texas A&M University, USA
Jonathan Potter, Loughborough University, UK
Catherine Kohler Riessman, Boston University, USA
Clive Seale, Brunel University, UK
David de Vaus, La Trobe University, Australia

Contributors

Lee Barron, Northumbria University, UK
Russell W. Belk, Northwestern University, USA

Roy Boyne, University of Durham, UK
Angela Brady, Northumbria University, UK
David Brockington, University of Plymouth, UK
Martin Bulmer, University of Surrey, UK
John Bynner, University of London, UK
David Byrne, University of Durham, UK
Paul Bywaters, Coventry University, UK
Ellis Cashmore, Staffordshire University, UK
Amanda Coffey, Cardiff University, UK
Anthony Columbo, Coventry University, UK
Louise Corti, University of Essex, UK
Iain Crow, University of Sheffield, UK
Julia Davidson, University of Westminster, UK
Pamela Davies, Northumbria University, UK
Martyn Denscombe, De Montfort University, UK
Derek Edwards, Loughborough University, UK
Nigel G. Fielding, University of Surrey, UK
Uwe Flick, University of Applied Sciences, Berlin, Germany
Jeremy J. Foster, Manchester Metropolitan University, UK
Sally French, The Open University, UK
Philip Gardner, Cambridge University, UK
Jeanette Garwood, Leeds Metropolitan University, UK
Maureen Gillman, Northumbria University, UK
Luca Greco, University of Paris III (Sorbonne Nouvelle), France
Martyn Hammersley, The Open University, UK
Jamie Harding, Northumbria University, UK
Rom Harré, Georgetown University, USA
Alexa Hepburn, Loughborough University, UK
Claire Hewson, Bolton Institute, UK
Dick Hobbs, University of Durham, UK
Mark Israel, Flinders University, Australia
David Jary, University of Birmingham, UK
Victor Jupp, Northumbria University, UK
Vince Keddie, Department for Education and Skills, UK
Aidan Kelly, University of East London, UK
Robert V. Kozinets, Northwestern University, USA
Richard Lampard, University of Warwick, UK
Gayle Letherby, Plymouth University, UK
Curtis Le Baron, Brigham Young University, Utah, USA
Ana Lopes, University of East London, UK
Eugene McLaughlin, City University, UK
Craig McLean, University of Newcastle upon Tyne, UK
Bernd Marcus, Chemintz University, Germany
Steve Miles, Liverpool University, UK
David L. Morgan, Portland State University, USA
Rachael Beth Moss, University of Liverpool, UK

George Moyser, University of Vermont, USA
John Muncie, The Open University, UK
John Newton, Northumbria University, UK
Paul Oliver, University of Huddersfield, UK
Geoff Payne, formerly University of Plymouth, UK
Sarah Pink, Loughborough University, UK
Helen Poole, Coventry University, UK
Jonathan Potter, Loughborough University, UK
Paul E. Pye, University of Teesside, UK
Deborah Reed-Danahay, University of Texas at Arlington, USA
Karl-Heinz Renner, University of Bamburg, Germany
Catherine Kohler Riessman, Boston University, USA
Lyn Richards, Director, Research Services, QSR, Australia
Margaret Rowe, Northumbria University, UK
Andrew Rutherford, University of Keele, UK
Roger Sapsford, University of Teesside, UK
Mark N.K. Saunders, Oxford Brookes University, UK
Thomas A. Schwandt, University of Illinois, USA
John Scott, University of Essex, UK
Christina Silver, University of Surrey, UK
Teresa Smallbone, Oxford Brookes University, UK
Mark J. Smith, The Open University, UK
Paul E. Spector, University of South Florida, USA
Robert A. Stallings, University of Southern California, USA
Thomas Staufenbiel, University of Osnabrueck, Germany
Graham Steventon, Coventry University, UK
Reinhard Suck, University of Osnabrueck, Germany
Maggie Sumner, University of Westminster, UK
John Swain, Northumbria University, UK
Nick Tilley, Nottingham Trent University, UK
Adelinde Uhrmacher, University of Rostock, Germany
Paul Valentine, University of East London, UK
David de Vaus, La Trobe University, Australia
Margaret Wetherell, The Open University, UK
Chris Wharton, Northumbria University, UK
Malcolm Williams, University of Plymouth, UK

Editor's Introduction

Organizing themes

Although presented in alphabetical order, the concepts covered in this Dictionary were selected on the basis of several key themes which are embraced within the term 'social research'. These are:

(1) Philosophy of science, for example issues of *ontology* (what is the essential nature of reality?) and *epistemology* (whether or how we can gain knowledge of that reality).
(2) Research paradigms, for example *positivism* (which in general terms is taken to include the scientific study of some objective social reality) and *constructionism* (which is concerned with the study of ways in which the social world is constructed through social interactions).
(3) Research designs, for example the *experiment* (the attribution of outcomes to the controlled administration of a 'treatment' to one group and not another) and *social survey* (the systematic collection of data from or about units of analysis, usually individuals, often using sampling techniques).
(4) Specific aspects of data collection, for example *participant observation* (participating in a group in a covert manner in order to study that group) and specific aspects of data analysis, for example *multivariate analysis* (a set of statistical techniques to examine the relationships between several variables).
(5) Issues to be addressed when carrying out research, for example *ethics* (what standards should be adopted, say in relation to obtaining informed consent from subjects?) and *politics and research* (the extent to which research is contributing to the oppression of certain groups in society).
(6) The role of research in terms of function, for example *policy-related research* (research to evaluate the impact of social policies) and in terms of context, for example *marketing research* (the systematic collection of data about consumers of products and services in order to make informed decisions).

Structure of the contributions

The term 'Dictionary' is used to be consistent with the Sage Publications series of Dictionaries but, as with others such as *The Sage Dictionary of Criminology* it is more encyclopaedic in nature. Each of the contributions is structured according to a standardized format. First, there is a very brief *definition* of the concept. Second, this is followed by a longer elucidation of *distinctive features*, which could include historical background, disciplinary background (for example, sociology, psychology, economics), key writers, applications (where appropriate) as well as main features. Authors were encouraged to think in terms of writing a critical and reflective essay. Therefore, for each concept, there is an *evaluation* in which authors raise some of the key issues and problems relating to the concept under consideration. The issues and problems which are raised are those chosen by each author rather than as a result of prescriptions laid down by the editor. It is the sections on distinctive features and on evaluation which give the publication its encyclopaedic character. For each entry, cross-references are made to *associated concepts* within the Dictionary. Some of these are associated by 'similarity' and 'mutuality' and others because they represent 'challenges' and 'rivalry' to the concept under consideration. The cross-references facilitate a mapping of concepts in terms of similarities and differences as described below. Finally, a brief list of *key readings* is provided.

How to use the Dictionary

The text can be used as a conventional dictionary or encyclopaedia to clarify the meaning of a term. However, more usefully it can be used in almost textbook fashion as a means of learning about the field of social research, and in the construction of an essay or dissertation, by making use of the cross-referencing provided by the *associated concepts*. The latter provide a mechanism for mapping connections between concepts in terms of similarities and differences. Associated concepts relating to any given definition have been chosen to direct the reader not solely to other concepts that share common features or underlying themes and principles but also to concepts that differ – often sharply – in terms of such features, themes and principles. The features of two of the definitions in this Dictionary can be adapted to assist in this endeavour. First, *network analysis* is a technique that examines the relationships between units of analysis. It was in part based on sociometry, a method founded upon asking children about their friendships. Network analysis is now more sophisticated and permits the examination of the strengths of relationships and the degree of density and interconnectedness of networks. By following cross-references it is possible to construct and examine networks of concepts: which concepts relate to one another, how they relate in terms of closeness, strength of relationship, similarities and differences. The second key concept is called the *constant comparative method*, which is a form of analysis in qualitative research and includes the process of minimal and maximal comparison of units of analysis in order to further understanding. Minimal comparison involves examination of cases which are as similar as possible and maximal comparison involves examination of cases which are as different as possible. This idea can be adapted to further the understanding of the territory of social research by listing the ways in which certain concepts in the network are similar and how other concepts differ. In this way the breadth and depth of social research can be uncovered.

A

ACCESS

Definition

The process of gaining and maintaining entry to a setting or social group, or of establishing working relations with individuals, in order that social research can be undertaken.

Distinctive Features

Access is part of the initial phase of social research, and is usually negotiated at the start of the research project. Access can also be conceptualized as a continuous process (Lee, 1993). Relationships may need to be renegotiated throughout the course of research. It is sometimes unclear exactly what access is required once research is under way.

There are a variety of practical and theoretical matters associated with ensuring research access. There are certainly practical issues involved in gaining entry to settings or data, and to establishing rapport with research participants. These might include formal approaches or applications (by letter or direct contact), arranging initial meetings and providing descriptions of the research for potential settings and participants. It is usually appropriate to offer reassurances of confidentiality and trust as part of initial access negotiations.

Identifying and establishing rapport with key gatekeepers or (informal) sponsors within a setting can be important to gaining and maintaining access (Hammersley and Atkinson, 1995). This can entail developing a theoretical or analytical appreciation of the setting or social group, and the relative standing of different social actors within the field. There are also occasions when access will need to be negotiated with a variety of different social actors within the setting. This can mean paying particular attention to the role(s) that the researcher adopts during social research, and the ways in which these roles are managed throughout the research encounter. This role management can include adopting certain styles of dress or personae in order to fit into the setting.

Complex and protracted access negotiations are most often associated with qualitative or ethnographic work (de Laine, 2000). However, there may be similar processes involved in gaining access to secondary data, documentary sources, or large research samples. Establishing trust and gaining a working familiarity of the research field are essential components of undertaking social research of all kinds.

Evaluation

Access is not a single event to be undertaken only at the beginning of the research process. However, advice tends to focus on the initial negotiation of access, rather than on the maintenance and renegotiation of access over time. Access is more than seeking formal permission or gaining informed consent. It is also part of a more general process of active engagement with settings and social actors, and of recognizing the need to work at ethical research relationships (Denscombe, 2002).

How much information to disclose during access negotiations is a matter for careful consideration. It may not be possible to inform potential research participants about the full extent of the research, particularly if an exploratory study is envisaged, with new research questions emerging over time. Equally, full disclosure may not be desirable, perhaps because this may jeopardize access, or potentially change the behaviour of informants. Sometimes it is easier to give a fuller account of the aims of the research once initial access has been secured and a level of rapport and trust established. However, where possible, those concerned should be told about any implications of the research from the outset. Deception should certainly be avoided.

Amanda Coffey

Associated Concepts: confidentiality, covert research, dangerous research, ethics, gatekeeper, impression management, informed consent, organizational research, participant observation, reflexivity, research bargain, unobtrusive measures, validity of measurement

Key Readings

de Laine, M. (2000) *Fieldwork, Participation and Practice: Ethics and Dilemmas in Qualitative Research*. Thousand Oaks, CA: Sage.

Denscombe, M. (2002) *Ground Rules for Good Research*. Milton Keynes: Open University Press.

Hammersley, M. and Atkinson, P. (1995) *Ethnography: Principles in Practice*. London: Routledge.

Lee, R. M. (1993) *Doing Research on Sensitive Topics*. London: Sage.

ACTION RESEARCH

Definition

Action research is a type of applied social research that aims to improve social situations through change interventions involving a process of collaboration between researchers and participants. The process is seen to be both educational and empowering. Action research should not be confused with evaluation research which attempts to measure the impact of interventions without the active collaboration of participants.

Distinctive Features

In a systematic review based on UK healthcare settings, Waterman et al. (2001) identified two distinguishing features of action research: first, the cyclic process, and second, the research partnership. The action research cycle begins with the analysis of a social situation or the identification of a problem. This is typically followed by the formulation of some kind of intervention (for example, nurses in a clinic may change the way they carry out some aspect of professional practice), which is then evaluated. The planning, action, reflection and evaluation may lead to new rounds of intervention and evaluation. The research element often focuses on the process of change and the achievement of planned objectives.

The second distinguishing feature of action research is a partnership or collaboration between the researcher(s) and the researched. In traditional research there is a clear separation between the researcher(s) and the researched, which is seen as essential to preserving objectivity. In action research, however, there is a deliberate attempt to involve participants as a way of promoting change and as a device to reduce the social distance between researchers and subjects. This involvement is felt to be both educative and empowering. As Greenwood and Levin (1998: 6) say: 'Action research aims to increase the ability of the involved community or organization members to control their own destinies more effectively and to keep improving their capacity to do so.'

It is clear that underpinning these distinguishing features are certain value commitments. The first of these is what could be called a democratizing motive, which reverses the conventional relationship between researchers and researched, which some action researchers see as elitist and exploitative. The second commitment is to participation. Drawing on a long heritage of pragmatist scholarship Peter Reason (1994) has argued that traditional social science alienates subjects from their own understandings of the world. Action research attempts to transcend this alienation through the active involvement of people in transforming organizations or social groups. The third commitment is to forms of inquiry that rely on subjective understanding. Action researchers believe that it is only through action and reflection that participants can understand their social situation and through formulation of interventions arrive at new understandings.

Evaluation

If judged by the standards of conventional academic research, action research might appear to be unscientific. The close and collaborative relationship between researchers and researched, for example, could be seen as a source of bias because the researcher is no longer independent of the research setting. The flexible design features of action research projects might also be an anathema to the mainstream social researcher. In contrast to the clear specification of research questions or hypotheses to be found in conventional empirical studies, action research is characterized by a fluid and ongoing process of formulation, implementation, adaptation and evaluation in which the identification of stages or project milestones is often difficult. Research design in action research is evolutionary rather than specified beforehand in a research protocol.

Since there is such a marked difference between conventional and action research it would probably make more sense to judge the latter on its own terms. Such a judgement would need to consider the action research process, with its emphasis on participation to bring about change and the role of reflection and self-evaluation in that process.

Evaluation should also take into account how action research aims to change the way people do things. Its outcomes are not necessarily 'findings' in the conventional sense of theoretical progress, but in terms of new practices, changed behaviour patterns or improvements in organizational processes.

Given the rapidly changing nature of organizational settings and the continuing pressure on organizational members to improve their performance it is likely that action research has a considerable contribution to make in the management of change. As Waterman et al. (2001: 57) suggest, action research has the potential to go 'beyond an analysis of the *status quo* to directly consider questions of "what might be" and "what can be"'.

John Newton

Associated Concepts: applied research, emancipatory research, evaluation research, messy research, participatory action research, policy-related research, practitioner research

Key Readings

Greenwood, D. J. and Levin, M. (1998) *Introduction to Action Research: Social Research for Social Change.* London: Sage.
Reason, P. (ed.) (1994) *Participation in Human Inquiry.* London: Sage.
Waterman, H., Tillen, D., Dickson, R. and de Koning, K. (2001) 'Action research: a systematic review and guidance for assessment', *Health Technology Assessment,* 5 (23).

ANALYSIS OF VARIANCE (ANOVA)

Definition

A set of procedures that estimate and attribute variance in a data set to different sources and determine the probability, under the null hypothesis, of obtaining the differences between the variance estimates by chance.

Distinctive Features

In ANOVA, variance attributable to differences between groups of scores is compared with an average variance attributable to differences between the scores within each group. Between-group variance is defined with respect to differences between the group means, and within-group variance is defined with respect to differences between the individual scores and their group mean. If the nature of the groups influences the scores more than chance fluctuation, then the between-group variance estimate will exceed the within-group variance estimate. If this difference between the variance estimates is sufficiently large, then the null hypothesis that all group means are equal is rejected.

The t-test compares the means of two experimental conditions. However, when there are more than two groups or conditions, more than one t-test is needed to compare all of the conditions. Unfortunately, the likelihood of obtaining a significant result by chance increases with the number of statistical tests carried out (that is, hypotheses tested). A Type 1 error is committed when the null hypothesis is rejected erroneously. Therefore, the Type 1 error rate increases with the number of statistical tests applied to any data set. ANOVA was developed to assist in the analysis of data obtained from agricultural experiments with any number of experimental conditions without any increase in Type 1 error. ANOVA procedures appropriate for an extensive variety of experimental designs are now available (e.g. Kirk, 1995).

Nevertheless, despite ANOVA being developed for use in experimental research, it may be applied to any data organized by categories. However, as with any statistical procedure, interpretation of the ANOVA results will depend upon the data collection methodology and the conformity of the data to the statistical assumptions underlying the analysis (e.g. Rutherford, 2001).

Evaluation

When regression, ANOVA and ANCOVA (analysis of covariance) are expressed in matrix algebra terms, a commonality is evident. Indeed, the same matrix algebra equation is able to summarize all three of these analyses. As regression, ANOVA and ANCOVA can be described in an identical manner, clearly they follow a common pattern. This common pattern is the GLM (general linear modelling) conception. It is said that regression, ANOVA and ANCOVA are particular instances of the GLM or that the GLM subsumes regression, ANOVA and ANCOVA. Unfortunately, the ability of the same matrix algebra equation to describe regression, ANOVA and ANCOVA has resulted in the inaccurate identification of the matrix algebra equation as the GLM. However, just as a particular language provides a means of expressing an idea, so matrix algebra provides only one notation for expressing the GLM.

Andrew Rutherford

Associated Concepts: experiment, general linear modelling, inferential statistics, multivariate analysis

Key Readings

Keppel, G., Saufley, W. H. and Tokunaga, H. (1992) *Introduction to Design and Analysis: A Student's Handbook*, 2nd edn. New York: Freeman.

Kirk, R. E. (1995) *Experimental Design: Procedures for the Behavioral Sciences*. Pacific Grove, CA: Brookes/Cole.

Rutherford, A. (2001) *Introducing ANOVA and ANCOVA: A GLM Approach*. London: Sage.

ANALYTIC INDUCTION

Definition

A research strategy of data collection and analysis which explicitly takes the deviant case as a starting point for testing models or theories developed in research. It can be characterized as a method of systematic interpretation of events, which includes the process of generating hypotheses as well as testing them. Its decisive instrument is to analyse the exception or the case that is deviant to the hypothesis.

Distinctive Features

This procedure, introduced by Znaniecki in 1934, of looking for and analysing deviant cases is applied after a preliminary theory (hypothesis, pattern or model) has been developed. Analytic induction, above all, is oriented to examining theories and knowledge by analysing or integrating negative cases.

The procedure includes the following steps: (1) a rough definition of the phenomenon to be explained is developed; (2) a hypothetical explanation of the phenomenon is formulated; (3) a case is studied in the light of this hypothesis to find out whether the hypothesis corresponds to the facts in this case; (4) if the hypothesis is not correct, either the hypothesis is reformulated or the phenomenon to be explained is redefined in a way that excludes this case. Thereafter, the researcher actively searches for negative cases to discredit the hypothesis, model or typology.

Practical certainty can be obtained after a small number of cases has been studied, but the discovery of each individual negative case by the researcher or another researcher refutes the explanation and calls for its reformulation. Each negative case calls for the redefinition of concepts and/or the reformulation of hypotheses. Further cases are studied, the phenomenon is redefined and the hypotheses are reformulated until a universal relation is established.

Evaluation

Analytic induction is not based on enumerative argumentation. As it focuses on the single deviant case to test a more or less generalized model, it is a genuinely qualitative way of assessing the stability and limitations of research findings. With its emphasis on testing theories it goes one step further than

the development of grounded theory. Three types of results are obtained with analytic induction: forms of activities (how something is done normally), accounts of self-awareness and explanations, and motivational and other reasons for specific behaviours are all analysed and presented.

Analytic induction does not start from conventional definitions or models of what is studied. As it implicitly assumes that hypotheses, theories and models are not immediately perfect, it is a strategy to refine interpretative conclusions from data. By searching for negative cases and by testing models and theories against them, it is a strategy to define their limits and to make explicit under what time, local and social conditions they are *not* valid. Therefore, analytic induction is a way to generalize and to delimit qualitative, case-based findings.

Analytic induction has been criticized as it does not – as originally intended by Znaniecki (1934) – provide a means for establishing causal laws and universals. There are question marks against the generalization of case studies and external validity in general. Nevertheless, analytic induction has its own importance as a procedure for assessing and developing analyses by the use of negative cases.

Uwe Flick

Associated Concepts: case study method, constant comparative method, deviant case analysis, grounded theory, hypothesis, induction, validity

Key Readings

Cressey, D. R. (1950) 'Criminal violations of financial trust', *American Sociological Review*, 15: 733–48.
Flick, U. (2002) *An Introduction to Qualitative Research*, 2nd edn. London: Sage.
Lincoln, Y. S. and Guba, E. G. (1985) *Naturalistic Inquiry*. London: Sage.
Znaniecki, F. (1934) *The Method of Sociology*. New York: Farrar & Rinehart.

ANTI-RACISM RESEARCH

Definition

Research that focuses on studying the belief (and social practices) that there are racial groups which have distinct physical or cultural characteristics usually, but not only, defined in negative terms.

Distinctive Features

The desire to categorize people into racial types based on physical appearance (or skin colour) has a long tradition in Western society (see Banton, 1987). Darwin's evolutionary theory of 1859 instituted the idea that there was a racial hierarchy based on different species or races with natural, discernible biological characteristics. Darwin also talked of the 'civilized races of man' exterminating and replacing the 'savage races' and was at one with Galton in demanding control of how different races breed (eugenics). For many decades, in a variety of national settings, positivist 'race scientists' researched for the genetic base of race. These investigations were originally encouraged by European colonization and the development of the European and American slave trade and reached their high point in Nazi Germany, with extensive government resources being allocated to verify scientifically the superiority of the Ayran race. However, social scientists increasingly argued that we needed to put quotation marks around the word 'race' to indicate that we are dealing with a social construction of individuals and groups, rather than an established unproblematic scientific fact (Wetherell, 1996). This rejection of the scientific validity of the concept of race opened up the possibility of more sophisticated research designs examining how and why 'race' matters.

A substantial programme of research has been carried out based on standardized social surveys and tests with the acknowledgement in the United States and the UK in the 1970s that white racism was a serious social problem. 'Racism' can be said to refer to beliefs and social practices that draw directly or indirectly on the conviction that there are racial groups which have distinct physical or cultural characteristics which are usually but not only defined in negative terms. Social scientists distinguished *racial prejudice*, which is hostile and negative attitudes towards minority races and ethnic groups, *racial stereotyping* and *racial discrimination*, defined as unjustified negative or harmful action towards minority races and ethnic groups. The conclusions were that racial prejudice and racial stereotyping premised upon notions of white superiority were widespread and pervasive in the United States and the UK. There was also evidence of racial discrimination across a variety of social and economic settings, and of *racial violence*, the most extreme form of discrimination.

Researchers realized that one problem with survey and questionnaire data was that it only provided information on the racism that people were willing to admit to. In addition, as a result of social changes, it became apparent that fewer people were willing to express overtly racist attitudes to researchers. This posed a key question: were white people becoming less prejudiced or were an increasing number of people much more knowing and therefore guarded about revealing their true sentiments on racial matters to researchers? Researchers concluded that subtle more flexible forms of racism had replaced the old-fashioned racism expressed by previous generations of respondents (McConahay et al., 1981). This is likely to be the case because in several countries the direct expression of racist views has been outlawed.

One of the key proponents of this argument is US social psychologist David Sears (see Sears, 1988; Sears et al., 1999). His work on the new racism describes a more elusive, abstract symbolic language of race that avoids blatantly negative racist statements in favour of political code words and symbols. This new racism being expressed is partly based on a view of racial discrimination as being outdated and puts the onus of achievement and equality on blacks and other minority groups.

The new racism asserts that it is black people's own deficiencies that are the cause of their problems, not the history of slavery segregation, discrimination, prejudice and racism that is assumed to have come to an end. The new racism is thought to be most obvious in white people's views on affirmative action and various social problems. Conversations on these topics are often framed by an unspoken subtext of racist attitudes and negative associations. Researchers have devised sophisticated modern racial prejudice scales to examine various covert forms of contemporary racism (see Sears et al., 1999; see also Bobo, 1999; Dovidio and Gaertner, 1998). Wetherell and Potter (1992) have argued that the modern racism approach in social psychology is limited by its dependence on the prejudicial model of racism. They argue that racism should not be narrowly equated with a particular psychological complex of feelings, thoughts and motives. Their interviews focused on how the taken-for-granted discourse of white New Zealanders rationalizes and justifies Maori disadvantage, how inequality is normalized and rendered unproblematic and conflicts subdued.

Sociologists, suspicious of the psychologizing of racism, have undertaken ethnographic case studies of community attitudes towards race or have accidentally uncovered everyday talk about race to be a central issue in the course of research. Some of the most interesting if controversial sociological studies have involved research on white racists groups (see Blee, 2002). A substantial body of sociological research findings also exists on the media and racism. Research on race and the news media, for understandable reasons, tends to concentrate on studying how visible ethnic minorities are negatively portrayed and crudely stereotyped by white-controlled media organizations. A particular focus is analysing the discourses used by sections of the news media to racialize public debate about law and order and other social problems (Law, 2002). The possibilities for researching media and racism have increased dramatically with the development of the Internet.

A separate sociological research programme has focused on analysing official data to identify racial and ethnic inequalities, most noticeably in the labour market, government agencies, housing, education, the media and criminal justice. This has concentrated minds on structural and systemic rather than individual and group dimensions of racism. In the UK context this debate received renewed focus as a result of the conclusion of the judicial inquiry into the murder of black teenager Stephen Lawrence that the murder investigation was hindered by 'institutionalized racism' within the Metropolitan Police (see Macpherson, 1999). Originally coined in 1967 by the US Black Panther Stokely Carmichael and Charles V. Hamilton, the inquiry defined institutional racism as: 'the collective failure of an organization to provide an appropriate and professional service to people because of their colour, culture, or ethnic origin. It can be seen or detected in processes, attitudes and behaviour which amount to discrimination through unwitting prejudice, ignorance, thoughtlessness and racist stereotyping which disadvantage minority ethnic people' (Macpherson, 1999: 28). This finding has provided a challenge to social scientists to develop the methodological tools to research the British government's programme of action to identify and eradicate 'institutional racism'. Given the nature of the Macpherson inquiry, it is not surprising that a considerable focus of research is on the rules, procedures and guidelines that produce discriminatory outcomes in the criminal justice system.

Evaluation

Contemporary racism takes a bewildering variety of forms and is spawning a new generation of research questions that require a rethinking of conventional methodologies. This is also generating critical writings on the ethical dilemmas associated with the *doing* of anti-racism research (Twine and Warren, 2000). Researchers need, for example, to work through how their racial and ethnic backgrounds influence the analytical lens through which they view their research subjects. There are also 'who's side are we on?' questions and the temptation to expose the views of racist respondents to advance a particular political agenda. Finally, there is the controversial question of whose racism is researched? To date the primary focus has been on the racism of lower socio-economic white groups. Researching institutional racism will require, amongst other things, accessing powerful government agencies and multinational corporations. In addition, there is also a lack of research on what we might describe as the rationales and dynamics of non-white racism.

Eugene McLaughlin

Associated Concepts: critical research, discourse analysis, discursive psychology, emancipatory research, Internet research, media analysis, official statistics, politics and social research

Key Readings

Banton, M. (1987) *Racial Theories.* Cambridge: Cambridge University Press.

Blee, K. M. (2002) *Inside Organised Racism: Women in the Hate Movement.* Berkeley, CA: University of California Press.

Bobo, L. (1999) 'Race, interests and beliefs about affirmative action', *American Behavioural Scientist*, 41 (7): 985–1003.

Dovidio, J. F. and Gaertner, S. L. (1998) 'On the nature of contemporary prejudice: the causes, consequences and challenges of aversive racism', in J. L. Eberhardt and S. T. Fiske (eds), *Confronting Racism: The Problem and the Response.* London: Sage.

Law, I. (2002) *Race in the News.* London: Palgrave.

Macpherson, Sir William (1999) *The Stephen Lawrence Inquiry.* London: TSO.

McConahay, J. B., Hardee, B. B. and Batts, V. (1981) 'Has racism declined in America? It depends upon who is asking and what is asked', *Journal of Conflict Resolution*, 25: 563–78.

Sears, D. (1988) 'Symbolic racism', in P. Katz and D. Taylor (eds), *Eliminating Racism.* New York: Plenum Press.

Sears, D., Sidanius, J. and Bobo, L. (1999) *Racialised Politics: The Debate about Racism in America.* Chicago: University of Chicago Press.

Twine, F. W. and Warren, J. W. (eds) (2000) *Racing Research and Researching Race: Methodological Dilemmas in Critical Race Studies.* New York: New York University Press.

Wetherell, M. (1996) 'Group conflict and the social psychology of racism', in M. Wetherell (ed.), *Identities, Groups and Social Issues.* London: Sage. pp. 175–234.

Wetherell, M. and Potter, J. (1992) *Mapping the Language of Racism: Discourse and the Legitimation of Exploitation.* London: Sage.

APPLIED RESEARCH

Definition

Research that focuses on the *use* of knowledge rather than the pursuit of knowledge for its own sake. A motivation behind applied research is to engage with people, organizations or interests beyond the academic discipline and for knowledge to be useful outside the context in which it was generated.

Distinctive Features

This engagement with the 'outside world' (for example, government departments, commercial organizations, pressure groups) gives applied research some distinctive characteristics. Bickman and Rog (1998), for example, argue that basic and applied research differ in purposes, context and methods. Although the differences are presented in dichotomous terms, the authors suggest that in reality they should be seen as continua. The differences of *purpose* can be described in terms of the goals of knowledge production. For the basic researcher the production of knowledge is an end in itself whereas for the applied researcher knowledge is used to further other ends or goals. For example, a basic researcher might be interested in understanding how customers make purchasing decisions with no other concern than the process of decision making itself. An applied researcher might be interested in the same kind of behaviour but be primarily concerned with how the findings of the research could be used, say, to increase the sale of certain commodities.

This points to an important difference in the *context* of applied and basic research. Applied research is often initiated by someone other than the researcher (it could be a government department, a pressure group or a commercial organization). Basic research, in contrast, is more often than not conducted by the person(s) who formulated the topic or research question in the first place. Where research is 'other initiated', the researcher may have less control over various aspects of the research process (for example, the design of the study, its scope and timeframe and, perhaps, whether the results will be made publicly available). Where research is 'self-initiated' there is greater opportunity to 'set one's own agenda' and be less constrained about how the research is managed and conducted. Even so, the standard conditions attaching to externally funded projects mean that basic researchers are also subject to a number of 'other-initiated' requirements (for example, compliance with ethical guidelines).

There are no specific research *methods* associated with either basic or applied research, but Bickman and Rog (1998) suggest that applied researchers are more likely to pay greater attention to issues of external validity. This does not imply a lack of attention to internal validity on the part of applied researchers; it is simply a matter of usefulness. Applied researchers will want to show that their results can be used to address a problem or issue in the 'real world'.

Evaluation

Different social science disciplines have engaged in applied research with different levels of enthusiasm. Some, like economics, have established a close relationship between the development of theory, techniques of measurement and statistical analysis in order to explain the workings of the economy (and other economic phenomena) which frequently inform government decision makers. Outside government, university-based economists, have a long-standing reputation for their forecasts on economic growth (Begg and Henry, 1998).

Psychology, too, has always recognized the practical application of its knowledge base. In World War II psychological assessment techniques were used to recruit pilots, and after the war returning members of the armed forces brought home emotional problems which were managed by a growing number of clinical psychologists. Today, the discipline of psychology has become institutionalized as a professional activity with a variety of applied specialisms, such as clinical, educational, forensic and industrial. Each specialism has its own conferences and peer-reviewed journals under the umbrella of the relevant national association for example, the American Psychological Association and the British Psychological Society.

Sociology, in contrast, has been slower to develop as a form of practice, though this is perhaps more the case in the UK than the United States. Even in the US, however, the President of the American Sociological Association opened his 1980 presidential address with the remark that 'the stance of our profession toward applied work ... has been one of considerable ambivalence' (Rossi, 1980: 890). Various explanations have been put forward for this stance. The 'opt out' view argues that sociologists have always seen their discipline primarily as a form of scholarship in which the subject is seen as an accumulation of literature to be learned, debated and developed. As such, sociologists have not been concerned to promote or advertise their work to others. The result, Martin Albrow has suggested, is that sociology has become something of a 'subterranean mystery' (Albrow, 2000); a craft rather than a profession. The 'sell out' view argues that sociology's identity is borne out of radicalism. The 'debunking motif' inherent in some views of the sociological enterprise has meant that sociologists have been reluctant to become embroiled in applied research because this would entail an endorsement of existing power structures and would turn sociologists into state-funded 'apparatchiks'.

These 'anti-applied' views are not completely dominant, however. A volume of essays published by the British Sociological Association called for an 'active sociology' (Payne and Cross, 1991). Its editors argued that no academic discipline can afford to become too introspective or passive towards the world outside academia. What is required, they say, is 'an applied sociology ... [which] ... will be an active participative sociology which engages with society' (1991: 2).

John Newton

Associated Concepts: action research, critical research, econometrics, evaluation research, emancipatory research, policy-related research, politics and social research, practitioner research

Key Readings

Albrow, M. (2000) Review of Steele, S. F., Scarisbrick-Hauser, A. M. and Hauser, W. J., 'Solution centred sociology: addressing problems through applied sociology', *Sociology*, 34 (3): 596–7.

Begg, I. and Henry, S. G. B. (1998) *Applied Economics and Public Policy*. Cambridge: Cambridge University Press.

Bickman, L. and Rog, D. J. (1998) *Handbook of Applied Social Research Methods*. London: Sage.

Payne, G. and Cross, M. (eds) (1991) *Sociology in Action: Applications and Opportunities for the 1990s*. London: Macmillan.

Rossi, P. H. (1980) 'The challenge and opportunities of applied social research', *American Sociological Review*, 45 (Dec.): 889–904.

AREA SAMPLING

Definition

A form of sampling in which the clusters that are selected are drawn from maps rather than listings of individuals, groups, institutions or whatever. Sometimes a further sub-sample is taken in which case the phrase multi-stage sampling is used.

Distinctive Features

With area sampling, data are collected from or about all individuals, households or other units within the selected geographical areas. Area sampling is sometimes referred to as block sampling, especially in the United States. It is also a form of cluster sampling.

Evaluation

Area sampling is used a great deal in countries where there are no adequate population lists, which are replaced instead by maps. However, the boundaries on such maps must be clearly defined and recognizable, both at the stage of sampling and at the stage of data collection. This form of sampling is not appropriate where the aim of the research is to follow a cohort of individuals over time because of the population changes within the areas that have been selected in the sample.

Victor Jupp

Associated Concepts: cluster sampling, cohort study, cross-sectional survey, longitudinal study, sampling, social survey

Key Reading

Moser, C. A. and Kalton, G. (1971) *Survey Methods in Social Investigation*. London: Heinemann.

ATLAS.ti

Definition

One of a number of Computer Assisted Qualitative Data Analysis Software (CAQDAS) programs designed to facilitate the management and analysis of qualitative data. It was originally developed as an exercise to support grounded theorizing.

Distinctive Features

Like all CAQDAS programs, Atlas.ti is a tool for facilitating analysis rather than a method in itself and therefore can feasibly be used to support a number of methodological or theoretical approaches. It supports the management and analysis of textual, audio and visual data and enables the creation of (semantic) networks to facilitate theory building processes.

As well as the code and retrieve, organizational (for example, demographic variables) and search (for example, Boolean, Proximity etc.) tools available in most CAQDAS programs, Atlas.ti provides a number of additional tools which increase flexibility and facilitate analytic development.

The code margin view is fully interactive, enabling codes and memos to be easily and quickly accessed, edited, merged, replaced and linked. Not only can codes be grouped into (for example, theoretical) families, but the new Super Families tool enables additional hierarchical collections to be created and a particular code can belong to any number of families. The Autocoding tools are also particularly flexible.

In addition to being able to directly code multi-media data, objects (for example, Excel, PowerPoint) can be embedded into rich text format (rtf.) files. These objects can then be edited in-context as the functionality of the corresponding application becomes available within Atlas.ti.

The Networking tool is extremely versatile, allowing quotations (segments of text), codes, documents and memos to be linked to each other in a variety of ways. It is also possible to create hyperlinks between quotations to, for example, track a story or sequence of events within or between data files. As a presentation tool, the Networking facility is flexible, allowing, for example, quotations to be displayed as illustrations of research findings or theoretical processes to be visualized.

The Query tool allows both simple and sophisticated interrogation of the data set.

Searches can be filtered in a variety of ways and the Supercode tool allows search expressions to be easily saved and re-run. Some of the more sophisticated search operators are based on the nature of links between codes.

A number of tools facilitate the organization and management of team projects. These include a tool to merge projects, a facility allowing shared data to be accessed by several projects ('Hermeneutic Units'), support for East Asian and right-to-left languages, easy ways to back up and move projects and XML project export.

Atlas.ti also enables the integration of quantitative and qualitative aspects of projects offering a flexible word count facility, the results of which can easily be exported to statistical or spreadsheet packages. It is also possible to import (and export) demographic information.

Evaluation

The evaluation of any CAQDAS package must take into consideration a number of factors – such as methodology, theoretical approach, type of data, size of data set, project aims and requirements. Therefore certain packages may be particularly useful for certain types of studies and researchers are advised to investigate the various options before choosing.

Atlas.ti is clearly amongst the more sophisticated options available, offering a variety of powerful and flexible means by which to explore, work with and interrogate qualitative data. As such, it enables analysis to go beyond code and retrieve processes.

Perhaps its most frequently cited advantage is that, in comparison to other CAQDAS software, Atlas.ti keeps the researcher very 'close' to the data. For instance, when navigating around coded data, if required, quotations will be illustrated in their source context – allowing easy in-context re-coding. Atlas.ti is therefore often seen by researchers as particularly well suited for 'grounded' approaches to qualitative analysis.

Atlas.ti is a multi-faceted software and the user may employ only a small proportion of the tools available for any given project. Its size and flexibility are both its advantage and its disadvantage. It can be used easily at a basic level but possibly needs a more experienced and confident researcher to make innovative use of specific tools for investigating and representing complex relationships.

Christina Silver

Associated Concepts: CAQDAS, coding, The Ethnograph, grounded theory, NUD*IST, qualitative research, QSR NVivo

Key Readings

Atlas.ti website http://www.atlasti.de/
CAQDAS Networking Project website http://caqdas. soc.surrey.ac.uk/
Coffey, A., Holbrook, B. and Atkinson P. (1996) 'Qualitative data analysis: technologies and representations', *Sociological Research Online*, 1 (1).
Fielding, N. and Lee, R. (eds) (1991, 2nd edn 1993) *Using Computers in Qualitative Research*. London: Sage.
Kelle, U. (ed.) (1995) *Computer-Aided Qualitative Data Analysis: Theory Methods and Practice*. London: Sage.
Lewins, A. (2001) 'CAQDAS: Computer Assisted Qualitative Data Analysis', in N. Gilbert, *Researching Social Life*, 2nd edn. London, Sage. pp. 302–23.
Weitzman, E. and Miles, M. (1995) *A Software Source Book: Computer Programs for Qualitative Data Analysis*. Thousand Oaks, CA: Sage.

ATTRITION

Definition

The 'wearing away' or progressive loss of data in research.

Distinctive Features

Attrition occurs when cases are lost from a sample over time or over a series of sequential processes. One form of sample attrition occurs in longitudinal research when the subjects studied drop out of the research for a variety of reasons, which can include: unwillingness of subjects to continue to participate in research, difficulties in tracing original respondents for follow-up (for example, because of change of address) and non-availability for other reasons (for example, death, serious illness). A survey of major longitudinal studies in the United States found that the average attrition rate was 17 per cent (Capaldi and Patterson, 1987, cited in Sapsford and Jupp, 1996). Therefore, quite a lot of cases may be lost.

A second sense of attrition relates to the loss of data from secondary sources in the process of collection. A commonly used example is the case of crime statistics, which are the end product of processes of decisions by victims to report crimes to the police, police decisions about recording and decisions by various agencies in the criminal justice process which may or may not result in prosecution, conviction and the imposition of a particular sentence. Using the British Crime Survey (BCS) (a random household survey of criminal victimization) as a base line, it is estimated that only 45 per cent of the crimes recorded by BCS are reported to the police, only 24 per cent are recorded as crimes, 2 per cent result in a conviction and 0.3 per cent result in a prison sentence (Home Office, 1999). Thus there is a considerable loss of data between the base source and subsequent measures.

Evaluation

The problem of attrition is not merely the problem of a reduction in sample size but, more importantly, it raises the possibility of bias. Those who 'drop out' may have particular characteristics relevant to the research aims (for examples, see Sapsford and Jupp, 1996: 9). The same point applies to the crime statistics example: certain crimes may be less likely to be reported, recorded or result in a conviction. For example, Kelly (2000), reviewing studies of attrition in rape cases, found that fewer than 1 per cent of these cases result in conviction. Researchers thus need to be aware of the problem of attrition and the threats to representativeness that can result.

Maggie Sumner

Associated Concepts: bias, cohort study, longitudinal study, official statistics

Key Readings

Capaldi, D. and Patterson, G. R. (1987) 'An approach to the problem of recruitment and retention rates for longitudinal research', *Behavioural Assessment,* 9: 169–77.

Home Office (1999) *Digest 4: Information on the Criminal Justice System in England and Wales.* London: Home Office.

Kelly, L. (2000) 'A war of attrition: recent research on rape', *Trouble and Strife,* 40 (http://www.cwasu.org/warattrition1.htm).

Nathan, G. (1999) 'A review of sample attrition and representativeness in three longitudinal surveys', *Government Statistical Service Methodology,* Series No. 13. London: Government Statistical Service.

Sapsford, R. and Jupp, V. (1996) *Data Collection and Analysis.* London: Sage.

AUDITING

Definition

A procedure whereby an independent third party systematically examines the evidence of adherence of some practice to a set of norms or standards for that practice and issues a professional opinion.

Distinctive Features

The concept and practice of auditing is manifest in several ways in the social sciences. First, in social programme evaluation, the general idea of auditing has informed the process of meta-evaluation – a third-party evaluator examines the quality of a completed evaluation against some set of standards for evaluation.

Also, a form of evaluation called programme and performance auditing is routinely performed at state and national levels. As defined by the Comptroller General of the United States (US GAO, 1994), a performance audit is 'an objective and systematic examination of evidence ... of the performance of a government organization, program, activity, or function in order to provide information to improve public accountability and facilitate decision-making'. A programme audit is a subcategory of performance auditing in which a key objective is to determine whether programme results or benefits established by the legislature or other authorizing bodies are being achieved. Evaluators of social programmes and performance auditors share a professional interest in establishing their independence and warranting the credibility of their judgements.

Second, an auditing procedure has been suggested as a means to verify the dependability and confirmability of claims made in a qualitative study (Lincoln and Guba, 1985; Schwandt and Halpern, 1988). A researcher is advised to maintain an audit trail of evidence documenting the data, processes and product (claims) of the inquiry. A third-party inquirer then examines that the audit trail can attest to the appropriateness, integrity and dependability of the inquiry process and also the extent to which claims made are reasonably grounded in the data.

Third, auditing has entered the scene of social science theory. At issue is the proliferation of audit practices in all spheres of human activity – management, education, social services, healthcare and so forth – influenced largely by the ideology of New Public Management (NPM). NPM emphasizes a programmatic restructuring of organizational life and a rationality based on performance standards, accountability and monitoring. By being submitted to formal audit procedures the work of organizations is held to be more transparent and accountable.

Evaluation

Whether auditing and evaluation are (or ought to be) comfortable bedfellows can be debated. Some observers have argued that evaluation and performance auditing differ in the ways each conceives of and accomplishes the aim of assessing value. Some of the differences noted between the two practices include the following. First, auditors address normative questions (questions of what is, in light of what should be) while evaluators are more concerned with descriptive and impact questions. Second, auditors work more independently of the auditee than evaluators do with their clients. Third, auditors are more exclusively focused on management objectives, performance and controls than evaluators. Fourth, auditors work with techniques for generating evidence and analysing data that make it possible to provide quick feedback to auditees, while evaluations often (though not always) have a longer time frame. Fifth, although both auditors and evaluators base their judgements in evidence, not on impressions, and both rely on an extensive kit of tools and techniques for generating evidence, they often make use of those tools in different ways. Finally, auditors operate under statutory authority while evaluators work as fee-for-service consultants or as university-based researchers. Other observers have argued that the practices of auditing and evaluation, although they often exist independently of one another, are being blended together as a resource pool for decision makers and managers in both public and private organizations. In this circumstance, an amalgamated picture is emerging of professional objectives (for example, placing high value on independence; strict attention to documentation of evidence), purpose (for example, combining normative, descriptive and impact questions) and methodologies (for example, making use of a wide range of techniques).

A variety of criticisms based in empirical and conceptual investigations are directed at the audit society, audit culture, or the culture of accountability as the latest manifestation of the infiltration of technological, means–end and instrumental rationality into the forms of everyday life. Auditing is viewed as an example of a key characteristic of modernity – that is, the drive for efficiency, perfection, completion and measurement that strongly shapes conceptions of knowledge, politics and ethics. For example, some scholars argue that auditing (and associated practices such as total quality management, performance indicators, league tables, results-oriented management, monitoring systems) is not simply a set of techniques but a system of values and goals that becomes inscribed in social practices thereby influencing the self-understanding of a practice and its role in society. Thus, to be audited, an organization (or practice like teaching or providing mental health care) must transform itself into an auditable commodity – auditing thus reshapes in its own image those organizations and practices which are monitored for performance (Power, 1997). Others argue that audit culture or society promotes the normative ideal that monitoring systems and accountability ought to replace the complex social-political processes entailed in the design and delivery of social and educational services and the inevitably messy give-and-take of human interactions. Still others contend that the growing influence of an audit culture contributes to the disappearance of the idea of *publicness* as traditional public service norms of citizenship, representation equality, accountability, impartiality, openness, responsiveness and justice are being marginalized or replaced by business norms like competitiveness, efficiency, productivity, profitability and consumer satisfaction.

Thomas A. Schwandt

Associated Concepts: applied research, cost–benefit analysis, critical research, evaluation research, meta-analysis, performance indicator, politics and social research, process mapping, secondary analysis, social indicators

Key Readings

Lincoln, Y. S. and Guba, E. G. (1985) *Naturalistic Inquiry*. Beverly Hills, CA: Sage.
Power, M. (1997) *The Audit Society: Rituals of Verification*. Oxford: Oxford University Press.

Schwandt, T. A. and Halpern, E. S. (1988) *Linking Auditing and Metaevaluation.* Newbury Park, CA: Sage.

US General Accounting Office (1994) *Government Auditing Standards.* Washington, DC: US General Accounting Office.

Wisler, C. (ed.) (1996) 'Evaluation and auditing: prospects for convergence', *New Directions for Evaluation,* No. 71. San Francisco, CA: Jossey–Bass.

AUTOETHNOGRAPHY

Definition

A form of self-narrative that places the self within a social context. It includes methods of research and writing that combine autobiography and ethnography. The term has a dual sense and can refer either to the ethnographic study of one's own group(s) or to autobiographical reflections that include ethnographic observations and analysis.

Distinctive Features

In autoethnography there is both self-reference and reference to culture. It is a method that combines features of life history and ethnography. The term autoethnography has been used both by qualitative researchers in the social sciences, who emphasize the connections between ethnography and autobiography, and by literary critics who are mainly concerned with the voices of ethnic autobiographers. Autoethnography can be associated with forms of the following: first, native anthropology or self-ethnography – in which those who previously were the objects of anthropological inquiry come to undertake ethnographic research themselves on their own ethnic or cultural group; second, ethnic autobiography – in which autobiographers emphasize their ethnic identity and ethnic origins in their life narrative; and third, autobiographical ethnography – a reflexive approach in which ethnographers analyse

their own subjectivity and life experiences (usually within the context of fieldwork). For literary critic Mary Louise Pratt (1992), autoethnography is a mode of self-and group representation on the part of colonial or post-colonial subjects that is informed by representations of them by others who are more dominant. In literary theory, autoethnography is frequently viewed as a form of counter-narrative.

Memoirs, life histories and other forms of self-representation are analysed as autoethnographies when they deal with topics such as transnationalism, biculturalism or other forms of border crossing, and local cultural practices. Ethnographers make use of such texts to explore these issues in the context of life experiences and cultural constructions of these. Ethnographers have also adopted the term autoethnography to label forms of self-reflexivity. For example, Arthur Bochner and Carolyn Ellis (2002) are sociologists who advocate an 'emotional sociology' that incorporates personal narrative as a method to avoid the objectification of more scientific methods of research by erasing boundaries between the self of the researcher and that of the researched. Anthropologists such as Reed-Danahay (1997) use the concept of autoethnography to analyse the uses of self-writing among anthropologists and among 'natives'.

Evaluation

Autoethnography, as a method of research and writing, requires reflective and critical approaches to understandings of social and cultural life and the relationship between the self and the social. Autoethnographic texts are most compelling when they synthesize objective (outsider) and subjective (insider) points of view, rather than privileging the latter. Because there is such a wide range of work currently labelled 'autoethnography', ranging from creative nonfiction to ethnic autobiography to the testimonials of postcolonial subjects, the task of evaluation is challenging and depends in large part on the intent of the writer/researcher. Questions are frequently raised about authenticity and voice in such texts, regarding the authority of the speaker. Personal accounts of fieldwork are, for example, often used to evoke the 'ethnographic authority' (Clifford, 1983) of the ethnographer. Autoethnography calls attention to issues of power, and can be most effective when it foregrounds the complex and nuanced relationships between researcher and researched, dominant and subordinate, in the context of individual experience and socio-cultural structures of beliefs and control.

As a method, autoethnography is frequently contrasted to 'objective' scientific or positivist methods that call for the researcher to set him- or herself apart from the object(s) of research. In ethnography, this would require a stance of distance from the self, from those who are being studied and from the social contexts of the research situation. Those who advocate an autoethnographic approach argue that reflexivity about oneself and about the research situation, that is, being aware of one's position in the context of research rather than denying it, is vital to a full understanding and is not completely at odds with forms of 'truth' or validity. Although there are variations in the degree to which autoethnographers emphasize their own experience or that of the ethnographic

context, this form of research and writing is critically evaluated on the basis of how well it synthesizes the subjective experience of participant(s) in social and cultural life and the structural conditions in which their lives take place.

Deborah Reed-Danahay

Associated Concepts: cultural research, ethnography, intellectual craftsmanship, life history interviewing, oral history, reflexivity

Key Readings

Bochner, A. P. and Ellis, C. (eds) (2002) *Ethnographically Speaking: Autoethnography, Literature, and Aesthetics.* Walnut Creek, CA: Alta Mira Press.

Clifford, James (1983) 'On ethnographic authority', *Representations*, 2: 118–46.

Pratt, M. L. (1992) *Imperial Eyes: Travel Writing and Transculturation.* London: Routledge.

Reed-Danahay, D. (ed.) (1997) *Auto/Ethnography: Rewriting the Self and the Social.* Oxford: Berg.

B

BIAS

Definition

Generally regarded as a negative feature of research, as something that can and should be avoided; occasionally the term is used in a neutral or even a positive sense, referring simply to the fact that the researcher has adopted a particular angle of vision.

Distinctive Features

Even in its negative sense, there are broader and narrower interpretations of the term. Sometimes it refers to any systematic deviation from the truth, or to some deformation of research practice that produces such deviation. Thus, quantitative researchers refer to 'measurement bias' and to 'sampling bias', by which they mean systematic failure in measurement or sampling procedures that produces erroneous results. The contrast here is with random (or haphazard) error. However, another influential usage of the term 'bias' refers to a particular source of systematic error: a tendency on the part of researchers to collect data, and/or to interpret and present these data in such a way as to favour false results that are in line with their presuppositions and/or their political and practical commitments. This may consist of a positive tendency towards a particular, but false, conclusion; or it may mean the exclusion from consideration of some set of possible conclusions that happens to include the truth.

Evaluation

'Bias' is part of a set of terms – 'validity' and 'objectivity' are others – that were once an uncontested central component of social science methodology. In recent years, however, especially under the influence of constructionism and postmodernism, there has been growing debate, especially among qualitative researchers, about the meaning and usefulness of these terms (see, for example, Lather, 1986; Kvale, 1989; Harding, 1992; Altheide and Johnson, 1994). In part, this reflects the fact that they had previously often been interpreted in ways that depended on a form of positivism that is now largely discredited. The latter presented research, when properly executed, as producing conclusions whose validity follows automatically from the 'givenness' of the data on which they are based.

On this view, the course that inquiry should take is clearly defined and, as a result, deviation from it – whether caused by prior commitments or by some other source of error – is also straightforwardly identifiable. What is required to avoid bias is for researchers to be objective; in other words, they must pursue research in the way that 'anyone' would pursue it who was committed to discovering the truth, whatever their personal characteristics or social position, appealing only to data that are observable by 'anyone'.

The influence of positivism meant that a clear distinction was not always drawn between, on the one hand, a researcher having potentially biasing commitments, for example particular political views, and, on the other, these commitments impacting negatively on the research process. In other words, researchers were (and sometimes still are) described as biased simply because they have commitments pertaining to the topic on which research is being carried out. This follows from the false assumption that, in order to be objective, a researcher must strip away all his or her assumptions until the bedrock of empirical givens is reached, and then build up true knowledge from that foundation solely by logical means. Modern philosophy of science has rendered this view indefensible.

It is worth pointing out, however, that, in effect, some of the critics of the concepts of truth, objectivity and bias have taken over this idea. They rely on it in their denial that research can ever be unbiased (see, for example, Gitlin et al., 1989). If we adopt a more realistic conception of what objectivity and bias involve, this sceptical conclusion can be avoided. Nevertheless, it must be recognized that, once we abandon positivism, error becomes much more difficult to identify. Given that there is no bedrock of absolute givens, and no method that guarantees valid findings, what constitutes systematic deviation from the rational pursuit of inquiry (that is, bias) is not always clear. In the course of inquiry about any topic, we necessarily take other matters for granted; and in the absence of a foundation of absolute givens these can only be matters about which we believe our knowledge to be sound but less than absolutely certain. If we did not make such assumptions, we would have no ground at all on which to stand, and we would indeed lapse into a thoroughgoing scepticism. Judgements have to be made, then, about the validity of presuppositions; but in the absence of any prospect of absolute proof. Where, previously, procedural error was thought to be a matter of logic, it now becomes deviance from communal judgements about what is and is not reasonable behaviour in pursuit of knowledge in the relevant context, with these judgements being open to dispute and to subsequent revision.

So, while all research is not necessarily biased, there is always the potential for bias. Furthermore, some of this will be non-culpable, in the sense that the researcher could not have known that what was being relied on was erroneous or dysfunctional. At the same time, some systematic error *will* be culpable, in that researchers were in a position to recognize that an assumption on which they

were relying had an unacceptable chance of being wrong and might therefore lead them astray. In short, they did not take the proper methodological precautions to avoid error, for example by assessing the relative validity of alternative interpretations.

In conclusion, then, while the abandonment of positivism requires us to recognize that research will inevitably be affected by the personal and social characteristics of the researcher, and that this can be of positive value as well as a source of systematic error, it does not require us to give up the guiding principle of objectivity: in other words, the commitment to avoiding bias.

Martyn Hammersley

Associated Concepts: autoethnography, constructionism, error, measurement, positivism, postmodernism, qualitative research, quantitative research, validity

Key Readings

Altheide, D. L. and Johnson, J. M. (1994) 'Criteria for assessing interpretive validity in qualitative research', in N. K. Denzin and Y. S. Lincoln (eds), *Handbook of Qualitative Research*. Thousand Oaks, CA: Sage. pp. 485–99.

Gitlin, A. D., Siegel, M. and Boru, K. (1989) 'The politics of method: from Leftist ethnography to educative research', *International Journal of Qualitative Studies in Education*, 2 (3): 237–53.

Hammersley, M. and Gomm, R. (2000) 'Bias in social research', in M. Hammersley (ed.), *Taking Sides in Social Research*. London: Routledge. ch. 6.

Harding, S. (1992) 'After the neutrality ideal: science, politics and "strong objectivity"', *Social Research*, 59 (3): 568–87.

Kvale, S. (ed.) (1989) *Validity Issues in Qualitative Research*. Stockholm: Students Literature.

Lather, P. (1986) 'Issues of validity in openly ideological research', *Interchange*, 17 (4): 63–84.

C

CAQDAS

Definition

Software specifically designed for qualitative research, supporting detailed exploration, coding and analysis of textual and other non-numerical data. The acronym is for 'Computer Assisted Qualitative Data Analysis Software'. Such software is more commonly referred to simply as 'QDA software' or 'qualitative software'.

Distinctive Features

QDA programs vary widely in functions. A checklist of the primary tools currently available in one or more packages is as follows. First, importing text files, sometimes writing them in the program, sometimes also accessing associated pictorial, tape or tabular data. Usually these files are in plain text, though recent programs allow formatting and rich text appearance. Second, coding passages of text or non-textual material, as user-created categories, and managing the categories (adding, deleting, merging their coding, ordering them in index systems), sometimes storing weightings for codes. Third, accessing data coded at a topic, reporting and sometimes re-contextualizing coded segments and in some programs also coding this text on to further categories. Fourth, automating coding and generation of codes, usually by text search. Some programs automate coding by document outline and some support command scripts for automating other processes.

Other features include: support for dynamic data (that is, documents can be edited from within the project software, whilst still maintaining the integrity of coding and other pointers); categorizing records or parts of records by demographic and other attributes, to inform subsequent analyses; editing memos, notes and reports, which may be available for coding and searching; filtering and grouping documents or categories; text searching (sometimes with wild cards, sometimes storing finds as coded data); graphical modelling tools for displaying and exploring theories and relationships (semantic networks or free-form drawings), whose items are live to the data.

Evaluation

QDA software appeared in the 1980s, long after programs for statistical analysis, and took longer to become normalized. Qualitative records are complex and understood in context, by methods emphasizing interpretative processes, rather than mechanical ones. Early programs based on the manual methods of coding and retrieval were often rejected as adding technological challenges to an already unsatisfactory method of exploring data. Since then, the range and user-friendliness of tools has increased, as have the number of programs and rate of revision. Use of QDA software is expected or required across many disciplines, and software clearly supports qualitative methods of access and exploration of data not possible by manual means.

Lyn Richards

Associated Concepts: Atlas.ti, coding, The Ethnograph, NUD*IST, QSR NVivo, qualitative research, SPSS

Key Readings

Any print descriptions of programs are necessarily out of date; use websites for current information. A central website is provided by the UK-based program carrying the CAQDAS acronym (http://caqdas.soc.surrey.ac.uk/).

Alexa, M. and Zuell, C. (1999) *A Review of Software for Text Analysis*. Spezial Band 5, Mannheim: ZUMA.

Bazeley, P. (2002) 'Computerized data analysis for mixed methods research', in A. Tashakkori and C. Teddlie (eds), *Handbook of Mixed Methods for the Social and Behavioural Sciences*. Thousand Oaks, CA: Sage.

Richards, L. and Richards, T. (1994) 'Using computers in qualitative analysis', in Norman K. Denzin and Yvonna S. Lincoln (eds), *Handbook of Qualitative Research*. Thousand Oaks, CA: Sage.

Weitzman, E. and Miles, M. B. (1995) *Computer Programs for Qualitative Data Analysis*. Thousand Oaks, CA: Sage.

CASE STUDY METHOD

Definition

An approach that uses in-depth investigation of one or more examples of a current social phenomenon, utilizing a variety of sources of data. A 'case' can be an individual person, an event, or a social activity, group, organization or institution.

Distinctive Features

A major feature of the case study, according to Hakim (2000), is its flexibility. It can range from a simple narrative description to a very rigorous study achieving experimental isolation by the selection of cases on the basis of the presence or absence of key factors rather than the use of random assignment. A case study can involve a single case (for example, a community study or a 'socio-biography' of a member of a deviant sub-culture) or a number (possibly quite large) of cases (for example, in the analysis of the conflict behaviour of different types of work groups).

The main thrust of a case study can be descriptive, exploratory or explanatory (Yin, 1984). Exploratory case studies may provide initial analysis of a phenomenon that will then be systematically explored in other studies, possibly by the use of another approach, such as a sample survey. Or they may follow on from survey work to provide a more detailed account of particular findings. A descriptive study will attempt to provide a full portrayal of the case or cases being studied. An explanatory case study will attempt to provide an account of what caused a particular phenomenon observed in the study.

Case studies have a key place in policy research. They are frequently undertaken to provide examples of good practice in the delivery of a specific policy or programme, or they may be undertaken as part of an evaluation project, providing examples of the impact of a policy. In these, and other instances, a key factor affecting the success of the study will be the criteria for selection of the cases to be studied. For the results to be persuasive they will normally need to be based on cases that provide a report of the operation of the policy in a range of settings. There may, however, be occasion to test the policy in a 'critical-case' setting, which presents the most difficult circumstances for it to succeed.

Evaluation

The main criticism of the case study method is that in most circumstances the individual cases are not sufficiently representative to permit generalization to other situations. Efforts to overcome this perceived weakness include increasing the number of cases so as to improve their representativeness, and provide for comparative analysis within the case study (Bryman, 1988). But, as Yin (1984) argues, this issue affects other methods as well. How is it possible to generalize from an individual experiment? In both instances the generalization involves the statement of a theoretical proposition, which in turn will be tested through the use of further case studies and other methods. This, for example, is often the use of case studies in the study of organizations, where organizational theory has been developed on the basis of one or a small number of cases. The depth and rigour of the analysis will be the crucial issue here. Where negative or critical cases are used to test and develop theories, the term *analytic induction* is sometimes used.

As was noted above, case studies are frequently exploratory in nature and are linked with other methods. In these instances the case study may be viewed less as a vehicle for generalization than as a form of pilot study. Also, in policy research it may be not necessary to have numerous cases in order to identify the negative impact of a phenomenon, policy or programme. The main factor here will be whether the criteria for the selection of the case or cases will provide a robust test.

Note

The above material does not represent the views of the Department of Education and Skills, UK.

Vince Keddie

Associated Concepts: analytic induction, community study method, evaluation research, exploratory research, good practice studies, policy-related research, validity of generalization

Key Readings

Bryman, A. (1988) *Quantity and Quality in Social Research.* London: Unwin Hyman.
Hakim, C. (2000) *Research Design.* London: Routledge.
Yin, Robert K. (1984) *Case Study Research: Design and Methods.* Beverly Hills, CA: Sage.

CASIC

Definition

Acronym for Computer Assisted Survey Information Collection. The term encompasses the technological developments which swept through data collection in professional social survey research organizations during the last 15 years of the twentieth century, particularly in North America and Western Europe.

Distinctive Features

In professional survey research organizations, surveys are now normally conducted by interviewers using portable laptop computers, into which the survey questionnaire has been programmed using a package such as BLAISE, now the standard for public sector surveys. Such programs take the interviewer through the survey questions from screen to screen, according to the rules for the routing of questions programmed into the questionnaire. The interviewer sees one question at a time, then is taken to the next question to be asked of the respondent, determined by the program. Very complex questions can be asked, with specific thresholds (for example, on income, savings, state benefits and financial circumstances generally). Unlike the traditional social survey, however, there is no paper copy of the questionnaire for the interviewer; the whole process is electronic. At the end of the process, data is downloaded to the survey organization for editing and analysis, usually remotely from the interviewer's home. Such editing and analysis is typically carried out by software packages such as SPSS.

The first type of CASIC instrument was CATI (Computer Assisted Telephone Interviewing), carried out from central locations with interviewers sitting at IT consoles, scrolling though a CASIC questionnaire as they asked the questions. The interviewer did not leave the office. With the availability of relatively lightweight portable computers, the development of CAPI (Computer Assisted Personal Interviewing) became possible, which is the most common mode of delivering CASIC questionnaires in large survey organizations today. There are other forms, such as CASI (Computer Assisted Self Interviewing), where (perhaps for one section of a survey) the portable is turned around and respondents fill in the section themselves, according to instructions which appear on the screen in front of them. This is particularly suitable for ensuring a better response on private or confidential matters.

Evaluation

CASIC has facilitated a greater degree of technical complexity in the survey data collection process. Survey researchers are trained to write questionnaires in programs such as BLAISE, which means that all interviewers administer them in a standardized fashion, thereby reducing error emanating from the interview process.

CASIC programmes are also being developed for Web surveys, although this mode of research faces many more challenges in relation to sampling.

Martin Bulmer

Associated Concepts: coding, interview, questionnaire, social survey, SPSS

Key Reading

Couper, M. (1988) *Computer Assisted Survey Information Collection.* New York: Wiley.

CAUSAL MODEL

Definition

A representation of a set of relationships in which the causal connections between several variables are examined simultaneously.

Distinctive Features

Causal models can take several forms and may be used at different stages in research.

For example, a pictorial model is a way of portraying possible relationships between several variables and in this sense should be treated as an integrated set of hypotheses which are worthy of further investigation. Lines are drawn between variables to indicate potential relationships and when arrowheads are added they indicate causal direction. The production of such pictorial models, no matter now crude, can form part of exploratory research and they subsequently act as guides to further inquiry. Their shape and content can be based on theorizing, previous research findings or, sometimes, hunches.

Models can also take the form of a statistical equation. An example is the multiple regression equation whereby values of a dependent variable (say, income) are predicted from the values of several independent variables (say, terminal age of education, number of qualifications, father's social class). A residual term is usually included in the equation to represent the degree of variation in the dependent variable which cannot be explained by the combination of independent variables. The multiple regression model is founded on the assumptions that all variables are linear and that the effects of all the independent variables add up. This is known as *additivity*.

A third form of model is a graphic representation of relationships between variables. Lines between the variables indicate relationships, arrowheads indicate causal direction, but further, scores are added to the lines to provide numeric representations of the strength of relationship between paths of variables when all other variables are held constant. An example is a path diagram, based on path analysis in which path coefficients provide the numeric value of strength of relationship. Although they are related, path analysis has one big advantage over ordinary multiple regression analysis, namely that it is possible to examine direct and indirect pathways to a dependent variable and therefore calculate the direct and indirect effects which independent variables have on the dependent variable.

Evaluation

Unlike exploratory pictorial models, those based on multiple regression and on path analysis are concerned with testing a theoretical model against the data. They seek to assess the degree of 'fit' between model and data. Their value over individual hypotheses is that, out of recognition of the complexity of the social world, they can look at the effects of several variables simultaneously. However, such models cannot by themselves demonstrate causality. The notion of causality is very much an in-built assumption and inferences about causal direction come not from statistical analysis but from the researcher him- or herself.

A much more fundamental critique is that social science research should not be founded on the principle of causality. This critique comes from those who work within a different paradigm, especially one that seeks explanation-by-understanding.

Victor Jupp

Associated Concepts: causality, exploratory research, hunting (snooping and fishing), hypothesis, path analysis

Key Readings

Blalock, H. (1961) *Causal Inferences in Non-experimental Research*. Chapel Hill, NC: University of Carolina Press.
Sapsford, R. and Jupp, V. (1996) *Data Collection and Analysis*. London: Sage.

CAUSALITY

Definition

A complicated concept that seems to have its source in a relatively simple experience common even for very small children: that actions of particular kinds bring about particular sorts of result. Note that what is involved here is not just a singular event, but a recurrent experience. And on the basis of that experience it may be concluded (almost certainly falsely) that doing A will always produce B or (more circumspectly) that it often produces B. Even the character of this simple form of causation has been the subject of much, largely unresolved, philosophical dispute. However, the complexities are multiplied when we extend the meaning of 'causality' to refer to situations involving feedback processes, and/or where we are concerned with how factors cause outcomes that themselves involve human action.

Distinctive Features

Researchers have varied in their attitudes towards the concept of causality. In recent times, many of those engaged in quantitative research have aimed at producing causal knowledge, while recognizing that establishing a correlation between two or more variables can never demonstrate with absolute certainty that they are causally related. The ways in which quantitative researchers have sought to deal with this problem have included path analysis, where correlations are interpreted in terms of a structural model that is designed to identify possible causal relationships, for example on the basis of temporal ordering and sometimes also a theoretical rationale. Along with this, various precautions are taken to avoid designating as causal what are in fact spurious relationships generated by associations between some extraneous factor and both the independent and dependent variables.

Qualitative researchers have varied in their attitudes towards causation. Some have argued that in observing patterns of social interaction causal relationships can be directly perceived and documented. This might seem to involve a form of naive realism, of the same kind that confuses correlation with causation. As Hume argued: while we may see events follow one another, we do not see that they *must* do so. However, a more sophisticated version of this argument would rely on the idea that, even if there is a sense in which we cannot eyeball the causal link between actions and events, the 'inference' to such links will in many cases be beyond reasonable doubt – in the sense that it would be questionable only if we were prepared to doubt much of what we routinely take to be knowledge about the world.

Evaluation

Other qualitative researchers have denied that causality operates in the social realm, arguing that the task of research is, instead, to understand the meanings which are constructed by participants in it. And this links to the arguments of some philosophers that human actions must be understood in terms of reasons rather than causes (see, for example, Peters, 1958). In part, this is a reaction against what is seen as the determinism that is implicit in the notion of causality: the idea that the actions of human beings are simply a product of the various causal factors operating on them. Such determinism is opposed on two grounds. First, it is argued that it is at odds with our experience of frequently *choosing* to act in one way or another. Secondly, determinism is opposed on ethical grounds. Some see it as encouraging the treatment of people as objects, as manipulable – a view that is often believed to serve the interests of the powerful. Others argue that it makes people no longer responsible for their actions, and thereby legitimates unethical behaviour. It should be said, though, that most qualitative researchers find it difficult to avoid the use of words and phrases that seem to carry at least some sort of causal import: for instance, the verbs 'influence', 'shape' and 'structure'. A further complication is that the reasons people give for their behaviour often involve reference to putative causal relationships.

Many social scientists have insisted on the multi-causal character of human social life: that what happens is always a product of *many* factors. Some quantitative researchers have sought to deal with this by measuring the relative contributions of different factors, reconciling themselves to the discovery of causal laws that are *probabilistic* in character; in other words, laws that indicate the likelihood that one type of event will cause another, rather

than establishing relationships that occur *whenever* given conditions are met. Some of those with a more qualitative orientation have rejected this approach, insisting that universalistic laws can be identified, notably through analytic induction or via some form of comparative analysis (see, for example, Ragin, 1987). Here the aim, often, is to identify the necessary and sufficient conditions for some type of event happening.

It has also occasionally been argued that the sequence and pacing of the impact of causal factors needs to be taken into account in any analysis: that the same set of factors operating in a different order, or at a different pace, will produce different outcomes (Becker, 1998). Such thinking is close to that of many historians (and, interestingly, also to that of epidemiologists), who distinguish between different ways that causal factors can operate: for example, as an underlying or predisposing factor, or as a trigger stimulating a particular sort of outcome. Here, the focus is usually more idiographic than nomothetic; in other words, the aim is to explain why some particular event happened when it did, rather than to develop or test a theory about what causes what across many situations. Even so, any identification of a causal relationship carries implications about what would and would not happen in other situations; this so-called 'counterfactuality' is essential to the distinction between correlation or sequence, on the one hand, and causation, on the other.

The concept of causality is a difficult one, then, but it is one on which most social research cannot avoid relying.

Martyn Hammersley

Associated Concepts: analytic induction, causal model, correlation, hypothesis, idiographic, nomothetic, path analysis, positivism

Key Readings

Abbott, A. (1998) 'The causal devolution', *Sociological Methods and Research*, 27 (2): 148–81.

Becker, H. S. (1998) *Tricks of the Trade*. Chicago: University of Chicago Press.

Hage, J. and Meeker, B. F. (1988) *Social Causality*. London: Unwin Hyman.

MacIver, R. M. (1942) *Social Causation*. New York: Harper and Row.

McKim, V. R. and Turner, S. P. (eds) (1997) *Causality in Crisis: Statistical Methods and the Search for Causal Knowledge in the Social Sciences*. Notre Dame, IN: University of Notre Dame Press.

Peters, R. S. (1958) *The Concept of Motivation*. London: Routledge & Kegan Paul.

Ragin, C. C. (1987) *The Comparative Method*. Berkeley, CA: University of California Press.

Taylor, R. (1967) 'Causation', in P. Edwards (ed.), *The Encyclopaedia of Philosophy*. New York: Macmillan. p. 127.

CENSUS

Definition

A census can have two meanings. One is an attempt to collect data from every member of the population being studied rather than choosing a sample. The other is a specific form of social survey organized by governments with the aim of collecting information from every household in the country. Government censuses are organized at regular intervals – most commonly every ten years – with the information collected affecting political structures and social policies.

Distinctive Features

Taking the first meaning of a census, some populations can be easily identified, such as every delegate to the United Nations or every athlete who competed at the most recent Olympic Games. However, censuses can also be taken of less obvious groups. Research that collected data from every person entering a specified supermarket between 2 pm and 4 pm on a specified day would be a form of census.

Governments, particularly those of Europe and North America, have collected information about their population through censuses for several centuries. A census was first conducted in Sweden in 1749, in the United States of America in 1790 and in the United Kingdom in 1801. The key purpose of the Census in the United States is to divide the 435 seats in the House of Representatives fairly between the fifty states, based on the size of their population. However, there are also other purposes: for example, to allocate funds to geographical areas and to identify groups in need of services. In the UK, the link to political representation is not so direct, although the boundaries of parliamentary constituencies are periodically reviewed in the light of changing population figures. Census data are used primarily for social purposes, particularly to determine the level of funding allocated by central government to local authorities.

The UK Census collects data by sending one form to every household. In 2001, there were a number of questions for one person to answer on behalf of the household and 35 to be completed by each individual. The 2000 Census in the USA used two forms: a short one consisting of seven questions was sent to most households, while a longer one was used in approximately one in six cases.

Evaluation

A census with a 100 per cent response rate has an advantage over a sample in that there are no concerns as to whether the people who take part are representative of the population. However, if not everybody responds to the census, there remains a difficulty in seeking to establish whether the non-respondents would have given different information, or expressed different opinions, to the people who took part.

Government censuses internationally tend to have response rates of over 95 per cent. However, the 2000 Census in the USA achieved a response rate of only 67 per cent, although this was an improvement on the 65 per cent achieved in the 1990 Census. This was the first time that the response rate had risen from one census to the next, possibly as a result of a programme of advertising, promotions and special events emphasizing the importance of taking part. The Census Bureau undertook a coverage measurement survey and, on the basis of this, decided not to adjust the census figures.

The UK census has traditionally achieved a higher response rate – over 97 per cent of the population is believed to have been covered by the 1991 Census. However, non-response was not evenly spread between different geographical areas and different groups: in some cities, over 20 per cent of all young males were believed to have been missed. A Census Validation Survey did not establish the extent and distribution of the under-enumeration.

Similar problems emerged with the 2001 UK Census, but there were better techniques in place to try to overcome them. This time approximately one million people were thought to have been missed by the official count. From previous census and other publicly available data it again became clear that young men were particularly likely to have been missed by the count, but so were other groups, such as older women.

Attempts were made to correct the 2001 data through the Census Coverage Survey. A sample of approximately 300,000 households was taken from areas that were stratified by an index estimating the number of 'hard to count' groups. Information was collected by interview, which offered more opportunity to establish whether people had been accidentally excluded than had been the case with the original self-completion form. Interviewers were instructed to make as many calls as was necessary to contact a household member. The differences between the data revealed by the Census Coverage Survey and that obtained in corresponding areas by the Census was used to 'impute' the number and type of households missing from the Census nationally.

The 'imputing' of individuals to add to the Census data has caused some unease and is symptomatic of the increasing difficulties in conducting such surveys in Western countries,

with their increasingly mobile populations. However, these difficulties are relatively small when compared to the situation in other countries, where a national census would be an impossible undertaking. A condition of conducting a comprehensive population survey is that at least a large majority of people can be found at any one time, with resources available to pay enumerators to collect the data and research staff to analyse it. These conditions are clearly not met in countries where there is severe poverty, war or internal conflict.

Jamie Harding

Associated Concepts: bias, data archives, empiricism, error, official statistics, quantitative research, secondary analysis, social survey

Key Readings

Periera, R. (2002) 'The Census Coverage Survey – the key elements of a one number census', *Population Trends,* 108: 16–31 at http://www.statistics.gov.uk/articles/population_trends/censuscoverage_pt108.pdf

US Census Bureau (2002) *Census 2000 Basics*. US Department of Commerce at: http://www.census.gov/mso/www/c2000basics/00Basics.pdf

de Vaus, D. (2002) *Surveys in Social Research,* 5th edn. London: Routledge.

CHI-SQUARE TEST

Definition

A statistical test of significance which is used to compare observed frequencies with expected frequencies.

Distinctive Features

The chi-square χ^2 test is used for analysing data where one has counted the frequency (number of cases or respondents) in different categories. For example, one might have recorded the number of men and the number of women who have died within a certain period from lung cancer. There are two variables, 'sex' and 'cause of death'. Both are category variables, as people are divided into mutually exclusive groups or categories. In this example, each variable has two levels; sex has the levels of 'male' and 'female' and cause of death has the levels 'from lung cancer' and 'not from lung cancer'. (There can be more than two levels of a variable: if one had 'death from lung cancer', 'death from other cancers', 'death from any other cause' there would be three levels of the cause of death variable.)

When the observed frequencies have been obtained, it is possible to construct a cross-tabulation or contingency table like this:

Cause of death

Sex	From lung cancer	Not from lung cancer
Male		
Female		

The entries in each cell of the table would be the number of cases, so the number of males who died from lung cancer would be entered in the top left cell.

The researcher is usually concerned with whether there is a relationship between the two variables, for example, whether there is a relationship between sex and likelihood of dying from lung cancer. The two-sample chi-square test is used to answer such a question.

The test involves calculating the frequencies, known as the expected frequencies, which would be found if there were no relationship between the variables and comparing them with the observed frequencies. If the difference between the expected and the observed frequencies is sufficiently large, it can be concluded that there is a relationship between the variables.

It is important not to confuse the two-sample chi-square with the one-sample chi-square, which is used if one has a single categorical variable and has measured the frequency of some event at each level of that variable. For example, suppose one has recorded the number of road accidents on each day of the week over a six-month period. 'Day of the week' is a categorical variable with seven levels (one for each day). One might ask whether accidents are related to days. If there were no relationship between accident frequency and day, the total number of accidents would be divided equally between the days. The one-sample chi-square is used to test whether the observed frequencies differ from what would be expected if the variables were unrelated.

For the chi-square test to be valid, the entries in the cells have to be independent which means no respondent or case can occur in more than one cell of the table. So N, the total number of cases in the table, must equal the number of participants. (If one has repeated measures, the McNemar test may be appropriate.)

It is commonly stated that for the test to be valid the expected frequencies in the cells of the table must be 5 or more in at least 20 per cent of the cells. (But some authorities say this is not essential.) To meet this requirement, one may be able to merge rows or columns or have to collect more data.

With a 2 × 2 contingency table, Yates' correction for continuity can be applied in calculating chi-square but many authors do not recommend it.

Evaluation

The chi-square test is a valuable tool for analysing frequency data, but is restricted to studying no more than two variables at a time. When there are three or more categorical variables, it is necessary to use more complex procedures such as log-linear analysis.

Jeremy J. Foster

Associated Concepts: coding, correlation, descriptive statistics, log-linear analysis, variable analysis

Key Readings

Howell, D. C. (2002) *Statistical Methods for Psychology*, 5th edn. Pacific Grove, CA: Duxbury.

Tabachnick, B. G. and Fidell, L. S. (1996) *Using Multivariate Statistics*. New York: HarperCollins.

CLUSTER ANALYSIS

Definition

A group of statistical algorithms used to classify objects on the basis of their similarity with respect to a set of attributes. Objects can be persons, groups or any other entities of interest for the social sciences. Attributes, for example traits of persons or leisure preferences of socio-cultural groups, are measured so that every object can be described by a profile that represents the respective values of an object on these attributes. Cluster analyses generate a numerical classification or taxonomy that comprises groups or 'clusters' of objects in such a way that profile differences between objects within a cluster are minimized and profile differences between clusters are maximized.

Distinctive Features

Cluster analytic techniques are used in many different sciences whenever objects are to be classified. Carrying out a cluster analysis involves the following main steps:

(1) Object attributes, for example personality traits of individuals, that seem to be relevant for a given theory must be selected.

(2) To calculate (dis)similarity between the objects on these traits an adequate measure must be chosen, depending on the attributes' measurement level and theoretical considerations.

(3) The calculated (dis)similarities between the objects serve as a starting point for running a cluster algorithm. Agglomerative-hierarchical cluster methods, for example Ward's algorithm that is recommended for interval-scaled variables, start with the finest possible classification in which each single object forms one cluster. They then proceed to fuse objects into fewer and fewer clusters until all objects are grouped into one large cluster. Divisive-hierarchical algorithms start the other way round, that is, they begin with all objects in one cluster. Non-hierarchical procedures start with a predetermined number of clusters, for example one based on hypotheses or some pre-specified classification. Probabilistic techniques like latent class analysis do not assign objects deterministically into clusters but yield different assignment probabilities for each object within each cluster or latent class. Probabilistic methods differ from hierarchical and non-hierarchical algorithms in their underlying statistical assumptions (see Rost and Langeheine, 1997).

(4) Several suggestions exist to determine the number of clusters when using hierarchical algorithms that do not end with the 'correct' numerical classification. A common rule when using Ward's algorithm is to consider the increase in error sum of squares after each fusion step. That number of clusters, say for example four, can be chosen after which a sharp increase in error sum of squares results in the next step, that is when the four are fused into three clusters. However, determination of a cluster solution based on this criterion is usually not that unequivocal, so that additional criteria should be used (see Everitt et al., 2001).

(5) Once a certain cluster solution is selected, it should not be accepted at face value but evaluated against different criteria, for example concerning its replicability across different algorithms and samples.

Evaluation

A single best strategy for carrying out a cluster analysis does not exist, since there are no definite rules for selecting the 'right' attributes, similarity measures, cluster algorithms and for determining the correct number of clusters. However, certain strategies have proven to be more valuable under certain conditions. Facing this relative indeterminacy, it is essential to replicate and validate a cluster solution using different criteria and methods. In this context, the interpretability and usefulness of a cluster solution should also be considered.

Karl-Heinz Renner

Associated Concepts: discriminant function analysis, factor analysis, multivariate analysis, quantitative research, validity

Key Readings

Bailey, K. D. (1994) *Typologies and Taxonomies: An Introduction to Classification Techniques.* London: Sage.
Everitt, B. S., Landau, S. and Leese, M. (2001) *Cluster Analysis.* London: Arnold.
Rost, J. and Langeheine, R. (eds) (1997) *Applications of Latent Trait and Latent Class Models in the Social Sciences.* Münster: Waxmann.

CLUSTER SAMPLING

Definition

A method of survey sampling which selects clusters such as groups defined by area of residence, organizational membership or other group-defining characteristics.

Distinctive Features

Cluster sampling is often used where a complete list of subjects is impossible or impractical to construct. Cluster sampling is a two- (or more) stage process whereby clusters of individual units are first defined and selected and then samples of individual units are taken from each of the defined clusters. Large-scale household surveys may involve multi-stage cluster sampling where regions are determined, then areas within regions randomly selected, then several levels of smaller areas, then finally households within the smallest area. For example, a study may define a number of towns typical of the different types of towns found in a nation-state and then conduct a random sample from the registered residents in each town. In some survey research designs all members in a cluster chosen at the final stage will be studied, for example, all children in a class chosen for inclusion in the study.

Evaluation

Random sampling is an ideal standard that it is often not possible to attain because of practical and ethical issues. Cluster sampling may be justified on pragmatic (including cost) grounds, especially where the consequences of erroneous inferences are considered to be slight. They may also be justified theoretically where relationships between those in selected clusters are characteristics of the cluster that may influence the individual subject (as in multi-level or structural effects).

The major problem of cluster sampling is that the sample does not fully represent the population from which it is drawn. It is generally the case that individuals within the clusters are more like each other than those outside their cluster. Thus, cluster sampling reduces and thus does not fully represent the variety that would be found in a true random sample. In multi-stage sampling the larger the number of higher level units sampled the more representative the final sample will be of the population.

Aidan Kelly

Associated Concepts: area sampling, probability (random) sampling, sampling, social survey, stratified sampling

Key Readings

Barnett, V. (1991) *Sample Survey: Principles and Methods.* London: Edward Arnold.
Kish, L. (1965) *Survey Sampling.* New York: Wiley.

CODING

Definition

The process by which observations recorded in the course of social research – typically in a social survey questionnaire – are transformed from raw data into categories and classifications, which then become the subject of quantitative data analysis. Coding involves the act of measurement, for in classifying answers to a question, one is trying to measure the underlying social variable which the survey question intends to tap.

Distinctive Features

In professional social survey research many survey questions are asked in fixed-choice format, the answers to which are pre-coded into categories. The respondent's answer is assigned by the interviewer to one of these categories when their response is given. Other questions, often of a more complex kind, may be coded after the interview by office coders, working from a coding frame, which sets out the rules according to which answers are to be classified. This involves knowledge of the range of responses possible, and for more complex issues, like the measurement of social class, reliance upon other classifications as the building blocks for the major coding decisions. Thus in the case of social class, occupation is commonly used in the UK as the basis for assigning a person to a particular social class, and this relies upon the official Classification of Occupations to determine the occupation, industry and employment status of the person concerned.

Coding is a neglected topic in social research, and deserves more attention. Bateson argues that it should be approached in terms of *data construction*, and questions asked about how the researcher is constructing the phenomenon being studied. Questions of the validity of measurement are also critical in scrutinizing the results of coding. The wider topic of measurement error is closely linked to the efficacy of coding.

Evaluation

Coding is an issue for other types of research than social survey research. For example, in all the forms of qualitative research (such as observation, analysis of documents and texts, ethnographic interviews, collection of trace or unobtrusive measures) there is a need to categorize or segment the data. Typically this is done *after* data collection and in the pursuit of theory *formation* rather than theory testing. There is increasing interest in software packages for the analysis of qualitative data, which involves the use of coding. In all forms of research the risk is that the researcher imposes inappropriate and invalid categories and codes on the data.

Martin Bulmer

Associated Concepts: CAQDAS, measurement, operationalization, qualitative data archives, qualitative research, quantitative research

Key Readings

Bateson, N. (1984) *Data Construction in Social Surveys*. London: Unwin Hyman.
Rose, D. (2003) *A Researcher's Guide to the National Statistics Socio-economic Classification*. London: Sage.

COHORT STUDY

Definition

Prospective cohort studies re-investigate groups of people who share some social characteristic.

Distinctive Features

Cohort study takes its name from two intellectual traditions. Cohorts were Roman army units of about 600 men. The medical profession adopted this classical reference to describe studies of groups of patients undergoing particular treatments, and it is here that the term is most frequently encountered today. In both cases, the common theme is how many survivors there were.

Although there are more complicated cohort designs, the best cohort study design in health research started with two matched groups of people. After initial assessment, the experimental group received a measurable treatment: their medical outcomes were followed through repeated tests, preferably until patients were healed. The other, 'control', group did not receive the treatment: any emerging differences could plausibly be attributed to the effects of the treatment. Cohort studies thus combine the core characteristics of an experiment (although not all intervening effects can be controlled by matching the two groups) with those of the longitudinal study, in which claims of causality may be justified by showing that one thing occurs before another (the treatment *causes* recovery because it happens first).

Whereas medical researchers mainly use the term cohort study, social scientists see cohort studies as a special case of longitudinal studies, trend studies or time series often using these labels interchangeably. The methods are actually similar. Medical usage usually involves stronger notions of causality, whereas social science usage is more exploratory, historical and involves more variables in its explanatory model. Cohort and longitudinal studies usually re-study the same people: trend studies and time series collect quantitative, often socio-economic, data from a series of different samples over time. The terminology used owes more to conventions of academic disciplines than essential differences.

The greater popularity of cohort studies among doctors is partly due to the simplicity of the core design. It is easily explained, and used with simple statistical techniques. It also suffers less from one of the key problems of sociological and psychological cohort studies, maintaining continued participation of the sample.

In medical research this is less problematic. The length of cohort studies is often shorter than the life-long perspective of many social science projects, so there is less chance of people dropping out. It is in patients' self-interest to continue treatment, because of the implied promise of improved health. In social science research, the benefits are less obvious. In health research, not only do hospitals provide regular supplies of patients as potential recruits, but back-up facilities for keeping track of samples are already in place in the form of hospital administrative personnel and medical records, whereas social science projects are usually set up from scratch with more limited funds. Those running health studies – doctors – have high social status, whereas the patient role has low status: patients are more likely to comply with a medical study than are the general public dealing with mere academic social scientists. This may explain why most of the larger and better-known social science cohort studies, like the National Child Development Study (NCDS) in theUK, had their origins in public health.

Variations on the core design include retrospective (or historical) designs, where records are used to construct a sample whose members share prior common characteristics. For example, the Australian Gulf War Veterans Health Study (almost uniquely successful in recruiting every veteran and all but two of the matched control group) was established a decade after the conflict. Concurrent or prospective studies use larger samples with no control group, sometimes adding new members as required: the US Multicenter AIDS Cohort Study started with 4954 men in 1985, adding another 668 between 1987 and 1991.

Evaluation

The key attraction of cohort studies is the time component, enabling interactions of variables to be better understood than in single point studies like the one-off (cross-sectional) survey (Davies, 1987). While a time series study based on successive independent samples is cheaper and easier to organize (for example, the British General Election Studies, the Social Attitudes Surveys, the Labour Force

Survey), variation in findings may in part be attributable to sampling. Time series studies are, however, much better than comparing respondents of different ages within a single sample: this can produce long-term seriously misleading results, such as the false picture of social mobility drawn by the Nuffield College study (Payne and Roberts, 2002).

Apart from high costs, the disadvantage of the prospective cohort study is waiting for data. Studies of how childhood experience impacts on adult disease risk or social outcome involve waiting literally a lifetime. Meanwhile, researchers change their priorities and improved research techniques (or medical treatments) become available. After 50 years in which it had to abandon its Northern Ireland element, and having been run by three entirely different organizations using six different data collection agencies, the NCDS (Bynner and Parsons, 1997) retains only two-thirds of its original sample (not surprisingly, the frequent absence of systematic associations being reported for the NCDS data is beginning to raise doubts about its quality).

The attrition rate, the loss of participants during the study, is a major defect. The Aberdeen Birth Cohort Study of people born in 1921 had contact with only six in ten of its sample 70 years later. If those who drop out have different social characteristics from those who remain, any findings will not be applicable to the general population.

Geoff Payne

Associated Concepts: attrition, causality, cross-sectional survey, experiment, longitudinal study, one-shot design, panel study, prospective study, retrospective study

Key Readings

Bynner, J. and Parsons, S. (1997) *It Doesn't Get Any Better*. London: Basic Skills Agency.
Davies, R. (1987) 'The limitations of cross sectional analysis', in R. Crouchley (ed.), *Longitudinal Data Analysis*. Aldershot: Avebury. pp. 1–15.

Marmot, M. and Wilkinson, R. (1999) *Social Determinants of Health*. Oxford: Oxford University Press.
Payne, G. and Roberts, J. (2002) 'Opening and closing the gates: recent developments in British male social mobility', *Sociological Research Online*, 6 (4).
Ruspini, E. (2002) *An Introduction to Longitudinal Research*. London: Routledge.

COMMUNITY STUDY METHOD

Definition

An approach that uses a range of research strategies and methods to study communities in a holistic manner, usually with the close involvement – and sometimes participation – of researchers in those communities.

Distinctive Features

The community study method has its roots in social anthropology and was subsequently at the heart of the work of the Chicago School of Sociology in the 1920s and 1930s. The Chicagoans studied a whole range of social issues, especially those which were crime-based, but in the context of the community. Their research used statistics to map social conditions in Chicago but also complemented this with a range of qualitative methods – such as participant observation, life history interviews and documentary analysis – to capture the subjective experiences of life in the Chicagoan communities. The method was also central to the study of politics and power in middle America in the 1950s, for example in the work of Lynds and Lloyd Warner, and also to examine the effects of urban decline on working class family life in the East End of London. In the twenty-first century there has been a revitalization of interest in the community via the communitarianism movement and also participatory action research (PAR).

A key feature of the community study method is a holistic approach, that is, there is an assumption that the groups or communities are more than or different from the sum of their parts. Therefore it is necessary to study the community in totality. A wide range of methods is used, mainly but not exclusively qualitative in nature. Methods include participant observation, interviews, life histories, documents. More recently the use of videos, small area statistics and modelling techniques have been used.

Evaluation

A number of issues surround the community study method. Some of these are practical issues of research design and data collection, for example, how to gain access, how to avoid marginality and how to study communities in a holistic manner when they are divided and when there are conflicts between sections of the community – acceptance by one section can involve rejection by another.

There are also contentions and disputes about the concept of 'community' in itself. For some, it is much more sensible and realistic to think about social networks rather than community. The notion of social networks is viewed as being much more valid in a fragmented and postmodern social world.

Victor Jupp

Associated Concepts: access, covert research, cultural research, ethnography, fieldwork, network analysis, methodological pluralism, participatory action research

Key Readings

Bell, C. and Newby, H. (1971) *Community Studies*. London: Allen & Unwin.

Bulmer, M. (1984) *The Chicago School of Sociology*. Chicago: University of Chicago Press.

Crow, G. and Allan, G. (1994) *Community Life*. Hemel Hempstead: Harvester Wheatsheaf.

Wellman, B. and Berkowitz, S. D. (eds) (1988) *Social Structures: A Network Approach*. Cambridge: Cambridge University Press.

Whyte, W. F. (1988) *Learning from the Field*. Beverly Hills, CA: Sage.

COMPARATIVE METHOD

Definition

The selection and analysis of cases that are similar in known ways and differ in other ways, with a view to formulating or testing hypotheses.

Distinctive Features

The comparative method is reflected in different research styles. For example, the use of quasi-experimental designs to evaluate policy initiatives involves the comparison of the two groups or areas, one of which receives the policy initiative whilst the other does not. The two groups are compared before and after the introduction of the initiative with regard to the feature at which the policy is aimed. This two-way comparison (of two groups on a before–after basis) facilitates some evaluation of the effectiveness of the policy initiative. The comparative method in social surveys is illustrated by the way in which categories of people in a sample (for example, men and women: old and young) are compared in terms of their having or not having an attribute (for example, a scale which measures 'fear of crime'). Qualitative, ethnographic work emphasizes the development of generalizations and of grounded theory by the systematic comparison of cases in terms of their similarities and their differences. The cases which are compared include interactions, social meanings, contexts, social actions and cultural groups. Because this is a continuous, rather than a once-and-for-all activity, it is sometimes referred to as the constant comparative method. Other methods to use comparison include content analysis (the comparison of documents), historical analysis (comparison of time periods) and analysis of official statistics (comparison of areas, groups or time period in terms of social indicators). Comparison permeates different stages of research. For example, in research design it is illustrated in the ways in which samples are selected for study so as to compare sub-sets on some variables while holding others constant. At the analysis stage different areas of social groups can be compared on a variable at the same point in time (cross-sectional analysis) or the same areas of groups can be compared on a variable at different points in time (longitudinal analysis). Sometimes comparison takes place after publication of results, for example, in examining the conclusions of projects from different parts of the world to consider how different societies deal with domestic disputes.

Evaluation

Comparison is an essential part of research methodology. It involves deliberately seeking or anticipating comparisons between sets of observations. Without comparison with a base-line or against a control group it is not possible to reach plausible and credible conclusions. However, this requires the clear establishment of a base-line and the ability to control for factors that the researcher does not wish to vary.

Victor Jupp

Associated Concepts: constant comparative method, content analysis, cross-sectional survey, secondary analysis, longitudinal study, quasi-experiment

Key Readings

Bryman, A. (2004) *Social Research Methods,* 2nd edn. Oxford: Oxford University Press.
Hopkin, J. (2002) 'Comparative methods', in D. Marsh and D. Stoker (eds), *Theory and Method in Political Science,* 2nd edn. London: Palgrave. pp. 249–67.
Kennett, P. (1973/2001) *Comparative Social Policy: Theory and Research.* Milton Keynes: Open University Press.
OEyen, E. (ed.) (1990) *Comparative Methodology: Theory and Practice in International Social Research.* London: Sage.

COMPOSITE MEASUREMENT

Definition

Measurement of an unobservable variable or construct by means of aggregating scores on several observable variables into an overall score. Composite scores can be computed either by using simple sums or averages or by performing transformations on the original variables.

Distinctive Features

Single indicators are usually insufficient to provide researchers with satisfactorily reliable and valid measures of complex theoretical constructs. It is therefore often necessary to combine multiple indicators of the same construct into a composite. Examples of such composites include scores on psychological tests made up of multiple items, measures of socio-economic status composed of various observable indicators, or the consumer price index based on a weighted combination of prices of various goods – to name only a few.

If the single indicators are scored on the same scale and can be assumed to be of roughly equal relevance, as, for example, in most psychological tests, it is often possible to simply compute the sum or arithmetic mean of the raw scores as the composite score. If scales are identical but the significance across indicators is not (for example, combining counts of more or less severe crimes into an index of criminal conduct), a weighted combination may be more appropriate. Furthermore, if the individual items are measured on different scales (for example, protocols of behavioural observations and teacher ratings of aggressiveness combined into an index of aggressive behaviour), it is necessary to transform the single item scores into comparable measurement units before a composite score can be computed.

The next steps in the development of composite measures are to assess how the single indicators are related to each other and how the composite relates to outside variables. The use of multiple indicators is a necessary precondition for performing the former task but not a sufficient one. Structural analyses provide the researcher with the information to decide which of the single variables are adequate and which should rather be dropped from the composite. Further evidence on the construct and criterion-related validity of inferences based on the measure may then be obtained from external validation studies.

Evaluation

Composite measures usually yield more desirable psychometric properties than single indicators. However, in deciding which indicators should be retained for the final composite, the test constructor may be faced with a dilemma: highly intercorrelated indicators lead to homogeneous measures with a relatively unequivocal meaning. On the other hand, higher correlations with outside variables can often be obtained by combining only weakly correlated variables (cf. Ghiselli et al., 1981). Thus, there is some trade-off between construct validity and the goal of predicting external criteria. It is possible to distinguish between observed indicators as effects of constructs (for example, behaviour as a manifestation of a personality trait) and indicators as causes of the construct (for example, education, income etc. as determinants of socio-economic status), and it is also possible to demonstrate that high intercorrelations between indicators are desirable only in the former case. To summarize, every decision in the construction of a composite measure should be guided by careful theoretical considerations but also be informed by additional empirical analyses.

Bernd Marcus

Associated Concepts: factor analysis, indicator, measurement, multiple indicators, performance indicator, quantitative research, reliability, scaling, validity

Key Readings

Ghiselli, E. E., Campbell, J. P. and Zedeck, S. (1981) Measurement Theory for the Behavioral Sciences. San Francisco, CA: Freeman.

Nunnally, J. C. and Bernstein, I. H. (1994) Psychometric Theory, 3rd edn. New York: McGraw–Hill.

CONFIDENTIALITY

Definition

The principle that information about participants in research is private and should only be revealed with their consent.

Distinctive Features

When people allow researchers to investigate them, they often negotiate terms for their agreement. Participants in research may, for example, consent on the basis that the information obtained about them will be used only by the researchers and only in particular ways. The information is private and is voluntarily offered to the researcher in confidence in exchange for possibly not very much direct benefit. While social science research participants might be hurt by insensitive data collection, often a more significant danger is posed by what happens to data *after* it has been collected.

In general, three different arguments are used to justify maintaining confidentiality. *Consequentialist* arguments examine the results of an ethical practice and may consider what would happen if the practice did not exist. So, interviewees might be reluctant to reveal secrets to social scientists if they thought that the information might be freely disseminated to third parties. Researchers who break confidences might not only make it more difficult for themselves to continue researching but, by damaging the possibility that potential participants will trust researchers, might also disrupt the work of other social scientists.

The second justification for confidentiality is *rights-based*. Beauchamp and Childress (2001) argued that our right to privacy rests on the principle of respect for autonomy. While some matters cannot or should not be concealed, people should have the right, as far as is possible, to decide what will happen to them. In research, they should be able to maintain secrets, deciding who knows what about them. Finally, *fidelity-based* arguments rest on the view that researchers owe loyalty to the bonds and promises associated with research. By offering a promise of secrecy, researchers offer to give allegiance and agree at minimum to keep silent or possibly even to do more to guard a confidence.

In some research projects, negotiations around confidentiality may be fairly straightforward. Some researchers operate in relatively predictable contexts where standardized assurances may be included in a covering letter with a questionnaire. However, other work takes place in informal and unpredictable environments, where agreements need to be negotiated with individuals and groups and renegotiated during the course of lengthy fieldwork. A further complication may arise if the participant has commercial interests to protect and the resources and expertise to ensure that these protections are stipulated in any agreement. However, obligations of confidentiality cannot be considered absolute and in some situations – such as when researchers uncover gross injustice – researchers might contemplate disclosing information received under an implied or explicit assurance of confidentiality.

In some cases, researchers may be forced by government officials or courts to disclose data, breaching assurances of confidentiality. There are two kinds of measures that can be taken to preserve confidentiality. The first is methodological, the second legal. Researchers have acted to protect the confidentiality of research participants and their activities either by not recording names and other data at all, or by removing names and identifying details of sources from confidential data at the earliest possible stage. These precautions offer the advantage of helping guard data against theft or improper disclosure by other members of a research team. Some researchers have reported sending files out of the jurisdiction, and avoiding using the mail or telephone system so that data could not be intercepted.

In qualitative research, identifiers such as names, geographical clues and vernacular terms can also be removed in the writing up stage. However, it can be difficult to hide the identity of some people from themselves, their peers, investigative journalists or officials. In quantitative research, practices of stripping data of individual identifiers may be compromised by improved capacities to manipulate multiple, linked data sets. While a survey might not include individual names or other unique identifiers, it may include sufficient identifying attributes to allow a person's identity and/or various sensitive attributes to be inferred. There are two major statistical ways to disguise or conceal the identities of individuals whose attributes are reported in data sets. The first involves altering the data and the second requires restricting access to the data (Brady et al., 2001). Data alteration may allow data to be disseminated more broadly, but may affect the confidence that people can place on particular aspects of the data. Conversely, restricting access may create inconveniences and limit the pool of researchers that can use the data, but generally permits access to greater data detail.

Evaluation

Researchers should evaluate their position in relation to the law. Some researchers in the United States, Canada and Australia have received statutory protection for specific kinds of data. Even without statutory protection, researchers *have* refused to reveal information to courts (McLaughlin, 1999). The reasons for their decisions and the point at which they decided they could no longer cooperate with the legal system varied considerably. Picou undertook a longitudinal study of the social impact of the 1989 Exxon Valdez oil tanker disaster. Exxon subpoenaed his files but Picou (1996) persuaded the court to restrict access to data used for published papers to an expert sociologist retained by Exxon who was only to use the data for statistical analysis. In Canada, a Master's student investigating the death of AIDS patients was subpoenaed by the Vancouver Coroner to appear at an inquest. Ogden won his case on the basis that the information had been obtained in confidence, confidentiality was essential to the research relationship, that the research was socially valuable and that the harm of breaching confidentiality outweighed the benefit to be gained by disclosure (Palys and Lowman, 2001). Of course, researchers may be vulnerable if they refuse to disclose information where ordered by a court. In 1972, a Harvard political scientist, Samuel Popkin, spent eight days in jail while an American sociology graduate student, Rik Scarce, spent 159 days in jail in 1993.

Mark Israel

Associated Concepts: access, covert research, data archives, ethics, exploitative research, gatekeeper, informed consent, politics and social research, research bargain

Key Readings

Beauchamp, T. L. and Childress, J. F. (2001) *Principles of Biomedical Ethics,* 5th edn. New York: Oxford University Press.

Brady, H. E., Grand, S. A., Powell, M. A. and Schink, W. (2001) 'Access and confidentiality issues with administrative data', in M. Ver Ploeg, R. A. Moffitt and C. F. Citro (eds), *Studies of Welfare Populations: Data Collection and Research Issues.* Washington, DC: National Academy of Sciences. pp. 220–74.

McLaughlin, R. H. (1999) 'From the field to the courthouse: should social science research be privileged?', *Law and Social Inquiry,* 24 (4): 927–65.

Palys, T. and Lowman, J. (2001) 'Social research with eyes wide shut: the limited confidentiality dilemma', *Canadian Journal of Criminology,* 43 (2): 255–67.

Picou, J. S. (1996) 'Compelled disclosure of scholarly research: some comments on high stakes litigation', *Law and Contemporary Problems,* 59 (3): 149–58.

CONSTANT COMPARATIVE METHOD

Definition

Part of the methodology developed by Glaser and Strauss (1967) for building grounded theories from collecting and analysing empirical data. It stresses that comparing all the data throughout the analytic process is the most elucidating way to knowledge.

Distinctive Features

Glaser (1969) suggests the 'constant comparative method' as a procedure for interpreting empirical material. It basically consists of four stages: '(1) comparing incidents applicable to each category, (2) integrating categories and their properties, (3) delimiting the theory, and (4) writing the theory' (Glaser, 1969: 220). It is similar to the procedures suggested in later versions of grounded theory by Strauss and Corbin (1990), but puts more emphasis than these on interpretation and comparison than on (open, axial and selective) coding. For Glaser, the systematic circularity of this process is an essential feature. 'Although this method is a continuous growth process – each stage after a time transforms itself into the next – previous stages remain in operation throughout the analysis and provide continuous development to the following stage until the analysis is terminated' (Glaser, 1969: 220). This procedure becomes a method of *constant* comparison when interpreters take care that they compare codes over and over again with codes and classifications that have already been made. Material that has already been coded is not 'done with' after its classification but is continually integrated into the further process of comparison.

The constant comparative method has been a starting point for more recent developments. Several authors suggest the minimal and maximal contrasting of individual cases for a comparative interpretation of interviews or biographies (see Flick, 2002 for an overview). The cases are structured according to reconstructive criteria in order to develop a typology from such interviews. Biographies with maximal similarities are classified as groups, which are labelled as empirical types in the further proceeding. For each type, specific everyday situations are distilled from the material and analysed across the individual cases. Developing ideal types and comparing them with real types (of existing cases) is another elaboration of the constant comparative method. This strategy includes the following steps: after reconstructing and contrasting the cases with one another, types are constructed; then, 'pure' cases are tracked down. Compared to these ideal types of processes, the understanding of the individual case can be made more systematic: after constructing further types, this process comes to an end by structure-understanding that is the understanding of relationships pointing beyond the individual case. The main instruments are the *minimal* comparison of cases, which are as similar as possible, and the *maximal* comparison of cases, which are as different as possible. They are compared for differences and correspondences. The comparisons become more and more concrete with respect to the range of issues included in the empirical material. The endpoints of this range receive special attention in the maximal comparison, whereas its centre is focused in the minimal comparison.

Evaluation

The constant comparative method, contrasting cases and developing a typology from contrasting cases represent three ways to generalization in qualitative research. Generalization here is the gradual transfer of findings from case studies and their context to more general and abstract relations, for example a typology. In the process of building grounded theories, these methods are as important as, for example, theoretical sampling.

Uwe Flick

Associated Concepts: case study method, comparative method, grounded theory, theoretical sampling

Key Readings

Flick, U. (2002) *An Introduction to Qualitative Research,* 2nd edn. London: Sage.
Glaser, B. G. (1969) 'The constant comparative method of qualitative analysis', in G. J. McCall and J. L. Simmons (eds), *Issues in Participant Observation.* Reading: Addison–Wesley. pp. 216–28.
Glaser, B. G. and Strauss, A. L. (1967) *The Discovery of Grounded Theory: Strategies for Qualitative Research.* New York: Aldine.
Strauss, A. L. and Corbin, J. (1990) *Basics of Qualitative Research.* London: Sage.

CONSTRUCTIONISM

Definition

A perspective that considers facts, descriptions and other features of 'objective reality' to be inescapably contingent and rhetorical. This is a more recent formulation of constructionism (without the 'social') which follows the traditional view of social constructionism as a perspective wherein people are seen as produced (constructed) through social interaction rather than through genetic programming and biological maturation.

Distinctive Features

There are a number of different traditions of constructionist thought. In feminist theory there are arguments for the constructed rather than essential nature of gender categories. In educational research constructionism describes a theory that emphasizes the activity of the learner in constructing knowledge. In sociology Berger and Luckmann's hugely influential book from 1966, *The Social Construction of Society,* emphasized the way people experience reality through different constructions.

Gergen (1999) distinguishes between some of the different constructionisms that have developed in psychology:

Constructivism has been used to describe the work of thinkers such as Jean Piaget and George Kelly. There is a strong emphasis on the constructions as something mental (like images or pictures) produced through interaction with objects or some features of the external world.

Social constructivism has been used for work where the constructions are something mental, as with constructivism, but they are generated as much through social relationships and conversation as through interaction with objects. Lev Vygotsky and Jerome Bruner are key exponents of this perspective. Another variant of social constructivism comes in the form of social representations theory, developed by Serge Moscovici. Its emphasis is on mental representations and how these are used to construct reality.

Social constructionism is distinct again for giving a central role to discourse in the construction of self and the world. Gergen (1994) usefully highlights some basic assumptions for a social constructionist science. These include the following. First, the terms we use to describe ourselves and our worlds are not dictated by their objects. Second, the terms through which we understand the world and ourselves are social artefacts, produced over historic time through exchanges between people within cultures. Third, any account of the world or self is sustained not by its objective validity but by social processes. Finally, language derives its significance in human affairs from the way it functions within relationships.

A major impetus behind modern constructionism comes from sociology of scientific knowledge (SSK) where a series of highly detailed studies of various scientific and engineering controversies highlighted the contingency of scientific facts and technological artefacts. In contrast to standard views of science, SSK researchers suggested that the products of scientists are fabricated through social interaction between specific individuals in accordance with ad hoc criteria in idiosyncratic circumstances in which scientists work in an opportunistic manner.

Potter (1996) has attempted to systematize the field of constructionist thinking in discourse analysis, sociology of scientific knowledge and post-structuralism. He focuses on constructionism as a practical position that highlights particular research topics. Rather than searching for a fundamental philosophical justification, the idea of discourse

constructing the world rather than *reflecting* directs the researcher towards studying how descriptions are made to seem objective and independent of their producer, and how they are used in particular actions. Potter reviews a range of procedures through which descriptions can be made objective, including:

(1) *Category entitlements.* Descriptions are constructed as coming from a category that is credible or knowledgeable in a way that is relevant to the claim.

(2) *Stake inoculation.* Descriptions are constructed as coming from someone whose stake in that talk is counter to what you would expect when making the claim. 'I used to be sceptical, but experience of [the death penalty/workers' cooperatives/alien abduction/etc.] leads me to think ...'

(3) *Corroboration and consensus.* Descriptions are constructed as corroborated by an independent witness (preferably from an appropriate category) and/or something that everyone agrees on. 'Two or three other people started to look scared ...'

(4) *Active voicing.* Descriptions are constructed using quotations and reports of thoughts to present the views and impressions of others as corroborating, or to show the vivid or unexpected nature of what is described. 'Karen turned to me and said "What the hell's that?"'

The general point is that descriptions of things or people are construct*ed* (how are accounts built?) and construct*ive* (how do accounts build the world?). Potter has developed this line of argument as a major feature of discursive psychology that treats all descriptions as constructions *oriented to action*. Edwards, Ashmore and Potter (1995) have generated considerable debate in defending a radical version of constructionism.

Evaluation

Critics of constructionism tend to be concerned that it denies the 'real' – whether this is 'inner' reality of the unconscious, of phenomenological experience, of the essence of gender or of cognitive processes; or 'outer' reality – of social structures, institutions and inequalities. The former critiques tend to come from psychoanalysis, psychologists taking a traditional cognitivist approach and critical psychologists embracing critical realism. The latter critiques tend to come from various forms of structural sociology, including Marxism.

The value of constructionism lies in its recognition of the way in which objects enter into social life through descriptions and in focusing research on topics that previously had seemed natural, objective or universal.

Alexa Hepburn

Associated Concepts: deconstruction, discourse analysis, discursive psychology, phenomenology, realism, relativism

Key Readings

Edwards, D., Ashmore, M. and Potter, J. (1995) 'Death and furniture: the rhetoric, politics and theology of bottom line arguments against relativism', *History of the Human Sciences*, 8: 25–49.
Gergen, K. J. (1994) *Realities and Relationships: Soundings in Social Construction*. Cambridge, MA: Harvard University Press.
Gergen, K. J. (1999) *An Invitation to Social Construction*. London: Sage.
Potter, J. (1996) *Representing Reality: Discourse, Rhetoric and Social Construction*. London: Sage.

CONTENT ANALYSIS

Definition

A method of analysing the contents of documents that uses quantitative measures of the frequency of appearance of particular elements in the text. The number of times that a particular item is used, and the number of contexts in which it appears, are used as measures of the significance of particular ideas or meanings in the document.

Distinctive Features

Content analysis was used as a way of studying the contents of newspapers and it was developed most systematically during the 1940s in a series of studies on political propaganda in the mass media. Under the direction of Harold Lasswell, this research aimed to uncover the intentions and interests behind particular media products and to show how these intentions and interests shaped the presentation of information and ideas in the media. They aimed to show, for example, how newspaper and radio presentation of information about wartime events could produce a distinctive message, or set of messages, that would have the effect of producing particular attitudes and preferences among the members of the audience. Content analysis formed a part, therefore, of a particular model of mass media production and effects in which it was combined with the survey analysis of readers and audiences. Over the following decades, content analysis was systematized as a distinctive formal method, separate from these particular assumptions, that could be used as a step in the analysis of any kind of documentary source.

In content analysis, the contents of a document are analysed by the frequency with which particular categories of meaning are used. The aim is to identify clear and coherent categories that highlight salient aspects of the message conveyed and to use objective and reliable methods of calculating their relative significance in the overall message. The categories used will vary from study to study, according to the nature of the material and the theoretical presuppositions of the researcher. Categories in content analysis will, therefore, include such diverse things as positive, negative and neutral expressions concerning political parties, women, medical treatment, asylum seekers, God and street crime. Very often, the aim is to devise categories that grasp favourable or unfavourable attitudes or representations of these. For each category, the particular words, phrases or images that exemplify it must then be specified. The researcher takes the frequency with which the words, phrases and images appear as indicators of the salience of the category of meaning.

Holsti (1969) has said that such sets of categories must meet the formal criteria of comprehensiveness, exhaustiveness, mutual exclusiveness and independence. The compilation of a set of categories depends upon the range of materials from which they are selected. Content analysis must aim to cover as wide a range of relevant sources as possible. A set of categories must be exhaustive in that they allow every relevant item to be classified into one of the categories; and the categories must be mutually exclusive in that it is not possible to classify any item into more than one category. These criteria reduce the ambiguity of classification. The criterion of independence means that the classification of any one item must not affect the classification of any others. Each classification decision is taken on its own terms.

Once the initial categories have been chosen and the principles of classification have been decided, it is possible to apply them to a particular discourse or set of documents and to generate a quantitative picture of the range of meanings conveyed in the document.

Evaluation

Although content analysis is built around the construction and use of objective and reliable procedures, the validity of its conclusions are no more unambiguous than those of more qualitative approaches. The meaning of a particular word, phrase, or image depends upon its context. A simple word, such as 'freedom', can mean any of a large number of different things depending on the context and the time at which it appears. Any judgement of context relies on a body of background knowledge and assumptions.

Content analysis discloses, at best, the 'internal' meaning of a document: it discloses the meaning that the text would convey to a reader who employed reading techniques similar to those used by the researcher. For most readers and audiences this is not the case. Audience research has shown that people see, hear and read documents in a variety of

complex ways – they may read them more or less superficially, they see them in the light of what they have been told by other people, and they very often hear only what they want to hear. For this reason, the actually *received messages* among readers and audiences may be very different from the message disclosed by a piece of content analysis. Content analysis may disclose the range of possible received messages, rather than specifying any one as *the* message.

Nor can content analysis give a completely valid picture of the *intended message*. Producers of documents have their own agendas and concerns, shaping their intentions and interests, and the original inspiration behind content analysis was to disclose the effects of producer intentions. The process of production of a document, however, is a social process in which many different agents are involved – each with their own intentions – and in which the process itself has a logic and momentum that ensures that the final, internal meaning of the document cannot simply be taken as an expression of the intentions of a particular group of producers.

Content analysis, therefore, is a useful and important tool of documentary analysis, providing objective and rigorous methods for investigating social meanings. Its results, however, correspond neither to the intended nor to the received messages of the document, and it must be used with caution.

John Scott

Associated Concepts: coding, diary, document analysis, media analysis, quantitative research, textual analysis

Key Readings

Berelson, B. (1952/1971) *Content Analysis on Communication Research.* New York: Hafner.

Holsti, O. R. (1969) *Content Analysis for the Social Sciences and Humanities.* Reading: MA: Addison–Wesley.

Weber, R. P. (1990) *Basic Content Analysis,* 2nd edn. Beverly Hills, CA: Sage.

CONVERSATION ANALYSIS

Definition

The detailed study of the methods used by participants to achieve social practices such as greetings, giving directions and telling stories in a variety of contexts (formal, informal). The term 'conversation' does not refer so much to a given type of speech (a genre) as to the idea of 'talk-in-interaction' as a social activity.

Distinctive Features

As a field of research, conversation analysis emerged in the 1960s and 1970s in the United States and evolved from the work of a group of sociologists drawing inspiration from ethnomethodologist Harold Garfinkel.

Conversation analysts use audio and/or video recordings of carefully transcribed talk-in-interaction. Recording and transcribing data drawn from 'natural' situations (that is, without intervention by the researcher) is a methodological advantage for social studies. It guarantees a more reliable corpus than note taking, enables the analyst to study the same fragment over and over and makes it easier to share interpretations with other researchers. There are no a priori categories or hypotheses involved in the process of analysing the conversational data since they are themselves 'research-generating'. Contrary to other social sciences with an exogenous approach of context, conversation analysis uses an endogenous approach. In this respect, it is not because an interaction takes place in a hospital or a tribunal that it should be interpreted as necessarily 'formal'. Rather, it is the participants' behaviours (and not the decision of the analysts) within this specific interaction that will set off particular elements of the context. This only becomes relevant for its interpretation if some of its features have a bearing on the structure of the interaction (size and ordering of turns, type of sequence ...).

Analytical inquiry of corpora tries to account for what has occurred in a conversation by reconstructing the members' perspectives in terms of questions such as 'What's going on?' and 'Why that now?'. Then, after locating a structurally recurring phenomenon in the conversation, the analyst will collect the same phenomenon in the whole corpus and possibly also in other contexts.

Harvey Sacks (who died prematurely in 1975) is considered the founding father of this field. In his lectures at Irvine and UCLA (1964–1972) and his collaborative research with Goffman, then Garfinkel, Schlegoff and Jefferson, he developed a radically empirical approach to the study of social behaviour in context, which had relevance to the whole field of sociology.

In the field of conversation analysis, conversation is a way of approaching social order. Conversation is far from the apparently unorganized and random object it might seem at first. It is a locus for social interaction where speaker-change recurs (or occurs), parties talk at a time; transitions with no gap and no overlap are common. This orderliness is exhibited by speakers according to what has been described by Sacks, Schlegoff and Jefferson (1974) as *turn-taking organization*. Turn is the fundamental unit of description in conversation analysis. It can be defined as the length of time a speaker holds the floor. Length and turn constructional units are constantly negotiated by speakers as they interact. A turn can be anything from any audible sound, to a single word, a clause, a sentence, a narrative. Another feature of this type of organization is projectability. Through the turn-taking system, hearers can detect *first possible completion* of the current speaker's turn. This point is called *transition relevant place*, that is the moment at which change of speaker may take place. Turn-allocational techniques centre around three options:

(1) a current speaker may select a next speaker (for example, asking a question);
(2) if (1) is not used, then parties may self-select in starting to talk;
(3) if (2) is not used, then the current speaker may continue to talk.

One fundamental kind of sequential organization is constituted by adjacency pairs (question/answer, greeting/greeting, offer/acceptance ...) with the following features (Schegloff and Sacks, 1973):

(a) the sequence is composed of two adjacency turns issued by two different speakers;

(b) given the first, the second is expectable (*conditional relevance rule*);

(c) when the second part is missing (for example, the answer in the 'question/answer' pair), its absence is pointed out by one of the speakers;

(d) this mechanism provides a frame for interpretation: by producing a second pair, speakers display their understanding of what the first pair is actually doing.

In adjacency pairs, the second pair often presents two alternative courses of action (for example, invitation/acceptance or refusal). *Preference* is the term that researchers have chosen to indicate the series of possibilities where the unmarked alternative, usually short and simple (for example, 'yes'), is referred to as 'preferred'; whereas the 'dispreferred' alternative can be marked by pauses, hesitations, excuses, mitigations and justifications.

Preference is also at work in repairs performed by speakers when they detect a problem concerning speaking, hearing or understanding during a conversation. Schlegoff, Jefferson and Sacks (1977) have noticed that speakers (in certain situations) tend to prefer 'self-repair' versus 'other-repair'. So that when a speaker notices a trouble source in the other speaker's turn, he may have recourse (rather than directly using repair) to 'repair initiations' such as 'What?', 'You mean X?', 'Do what?', generating a self-repair in the next turn of the addressee.

Evaluation

Conversation analysis is currently applied in a range of disciplines sharing an interest in social interaction (anthropology, linguistics, psychology); with interesting issues concerning methodology (use of video technology, ethnographic fieldwork, quantification) and

analysis (cognition in context, communication disorders, work organization; grammar in interaction).

Luca Greco

Associated Concepts: constructionism, empiricism, ethnomethodology, grounded theory, hermeneutics, interpretive repertoires, narrative analysis, phenomenology, videography

Key Readings

Atkinson, J. M. and Heritage, J. (eds) (1984) *Structures of Social Action.* Cambridge: Cambridge University Press.

Sacks, H. ([1964–72] 1992) *Lectures on Conversation* (2 vols) (ed. by Gail Jefferson, with an introduction of Emmanuel A. Schegloff). Oxford: Basil Blackwell.

Sacks, H., Schegloff, E. A. and Jefferson, G. (1974) 'A simplest systematics for the organisation of turn-taking for conversation', *Language*, 50: 696–735.

Schegloff, E. A. and Sacks, H. (1973) 'Opening up closings', *Semiotica*, 8: 289–327.

Schegloff, E. A., Jefferson, G. and Sacks, H. (1977) 'The preference for self-correction in the organisation of repair in conversation', *Language*, 53: 361–82.

CORRELATION

Definition

Correlation refers to the linear relationship between two variables. The correlation coefficient is a measure of the association between two numerical variables, usually denoted as x and y. It is a symmetrical relationship: if x is correlated with y, y is correlated with x.

Distinctive Features

The value of the correlation coefficient lies between +1 and −1. A positive coefficient indicates that a high value of x tends to be associated with a high value of y and a negative coefficient indicates that as the value of x increases the value of y is likely to decrease. A coefficient of +1 is a perfect positive correlation between x and y, while a coefficient of −1 is a perfect negative correlation (sometimes referred to as an inverse correlation). A coefficient of 0 means that there is no relationship between the two variables.

The Pearson product moment correlation coefficient (r) is calculated for data that are at the interval level of measurement at least. The correlation coefficient is calculated by the formula

$$r = \frac{\sum(x - \bar{x})(y - \bar{y})}{\sqrt{\sum(x - \bar{x})^2 \sum(y - \bar{y})^2}}$$

The size of the resulting coefficient gives some indication of the strength of the association. Its statistical significance can be read from a book of statistical tables or, if the number of pairs is greater than 100, by using the standard error of r. The degrees of freedom equal the number of pairs minus two. Where the data are at the ordinal level of measurement, Spearman's rank order correlation (rho) can be used.

Where a data set containing a number of variables is involved, it is possible to compute a correlation matrix showing the correlation coefficients of every suitable variable with every other suitable variable. When examining the significance levels of a large matrix, however, the researcher needs to remember that some coefficients are likely to be statistically significant by chance.

If the correlation coefficient is squared it gives the proportion of the variance of one variable that is 'explained' by the other variable. Since a proportion multiplied by 100 gives a percentage, this enables one to know what percentage of y is explained by x. Thus, if $r = 0.64$, then $r^2 = 0.41$, and we can say that 41 per cent of the variation in y is explained

by x, but this should not be interpreted as meaning that 41 per cent of y is *caused* by x.

Evaluation

Correlation does not indicate causality. This means that x may cause y, or y may cause x, or both may be caused by another, intervening variable (z), or by a set of other variables $(z_1, z_2, \dots z_k)$. The influence of an intervening variable can be controlled for by computing a partial correlation coefficient.

In addition to calculating the correlation coefficient, it is also advisable to view a scatter diagram to gain a better appreciation of any relationship, or its absence. Sometimes other information about the units can explain a correlation or the lack of it (For example, a trend with time, or correlations between subgroups rather than individual units.) There may be a *linear* relationship between variables, where change in one variable takes place at the same rate as change in another variable. Alternatively, there may be a *curvilinear* relationship, in which the rates of change between variables varies. For example, people are more likely to need medical attention when they are very young and very old than at other times in their lives. If one were to plot a scatter diagram of medical contact with age this would show a relationship that is higher at the two extremes than in the middle. Such a relationship would yield a very low or negligible correlation coefficient, but would be more apparent from a scatter plot. Truncation of one variable (that is, only measuring a small part of the possible range) will reduce the correlation. Lack of correlation may be misleading for this reason.

Small samples cannot detect low correlations. Large samples may enable low correlations to be detected. A low correlation only indicates a slight relationship, but if it is significant it shows that there is an association. If a coefficient is not statistically significant it may be due to chance, and should not be interpreted.

Care should be taken not to assume that a correlation between units such as geographical locations means that a similar correlation applies to the individuals within those areas. This is the ecological fallacy.

Iain Crow

Associated Concepts: causality, descriptive statistics, ecological fallacy, hypothesis, inferential statistics

Key Readings

Fielding, J. and Gilbert, N. (2000) 'Interval data: correlation and regression', in *Understanding Social Statistics*. London: Sage. ch. 8.

Norusis, M. J. (1992) 'Measuring linear association', in *SPSS for Windows, Base System User's Guide, Release 5.0*. Chicago: SPSS Inc. ch. 17.

Pallant, J. (2001) 'Correlation', in *SPSS Survival Manual*. Milton Keynes: Open University Press. ch. 11.

COST–BENEFIT ANALYSIS

Definition

Also known as cost-effectiveness analysis, cost–benefit analysis involves a comparison of the cost of inputs of an intervention or initiative, with the outputs and outcomes of that intervention. It is used in all areas of strategic decision making. The focus here is on cost–benefit analysis by public bodies rather than commercial enterprises.

Features

Cost–benefit analysis is typically employed in applied research, especially evaluations, in order to inform an organization's decisions on resource allocation between varying options. Accordingly, cost–benefit analysis often forms the basis of best-practice or best-value guides for central government agencies such as the police. For example, evaluations of the use of forensic evidence in police investigations have often balanced the costs of achieving a forensic identification with the likelihood of a 'positive' outcome, such as an arrest.

In the UK the importance of cost–benefit analysis has increased significantly in recent years as a result of three major factors: first, central government control of certain public agencies has increased; secondly and related to this, there has been an impetus to allocate scarce resources effectively; and thirdly, there has been a move towards evidence-based approaches to social interventions allowing for such analysis to be made.

Agencies within the UK criminal justice system have been particularly concerned with such analysis because it has been increasingly subject to central government control and research. Most importantly perhaps, increases in crime rates have resulted in increasing costs throughout the system. Costs of criminal justice inputs such as police service strength, prison numbers and the use of community penalties, must ultimately be balanced against the effects on crime rates. In this way, agencies and organizations are able to make informed decisions about how best to employ scarce resources.

Evaluation

Typically, cost–benefit analysis allows for comparison between the inputs and outputs/outcomes of an initiative but without taking into account any of the processes that occur in between, or external factors that may impact on a research project. Furthermore, it may fail to acknowledge any negative impact or unmeasured positive impact that an initiative may have. For example, cost–benefit analysis of expensive high-visibility policing operations may reveal a temporary and spatial benefit to crime rates (the police deter offenders in that area whilst they are present), but may ignore the fact that offenders are displaced, that police are removed from other (potentially beneficial) duties, or positive impacts on the public's confidence in the police and reductions in the fear of crime.

It is therefore implicit that cost–benefit analysis in all areas of research is used only as part of a wider evaluation of the impacts of a project. Nevertheless, in an age of accountability, it is important to be able to demonstrate that public funds are being deployed wisely and effectively.

Helen Poole

Associated Concepts: applied research, auditing, evaluation research, good practice studies, organizational research, performance indicator, process mapping

Key Readings

Dhiri, S. and Brand, S. (1999) *Analysis of Cost and Benefits: Guidance for Evaluators.* (Crime Reduction Programme Guidance Note 1.) London: Home Office.

Laycock, G. (2002) 'Methodological issues in working with policy advisers and practitioners', in N. Tilley (ed.), *Analysis for Crime Prevention.* Devon: Willan.

COVARIANCE

Definition

A condition where two measures vary together, such as the level of educational attainment and income. In general language, this might also be referred to as *association* or *correlation*. In the case where the analysis is conducted on a random sample, covariation can be tested statistically to determine the probability that an observed relationship is not real but the product of random chance in the sample. Additionally, an assortment of measures of association exist that estimate the degree of covariance, the selection of which depends upon certain parameters of the measures under study. The most common parameter that affects the measure of covariance is the level of measurement of the two variables. Note that the presence of covariance, in the absence of solid theory and/or research design, does not imply the presence of a causal relationship.

Distinctive Features

Three basic types of covariance exist. Positive covariance exists where as one variable increases in value, the second variable increases in value as well. Negative covariance is where two variables tend to decrease in value together. Null covariance is the state of observed independence between two variables. Note that the observation of independence in a sample might not reflect the reality in the population. Furthermore, if the underlying relationship between two variables is not linear, measures assuming linearity might estimate no relationship.

There are two general tests of covariance. One establishes the existence of a relationship observed in a sample of a larger population, while the other estimates the strength of this association. Assuming the presence of a random probability sample, it makes sense to discuss the first before moving on to the second. Basic analysis of covariance simply establishes the existence of a relationship, which is necessary before considering the strength of an observed relationship. It is common to employ a chi-square test (χ^2) when the level of measurement of the variables under study is either nominal or ordinal. For interval, ratio and other continuous measures, the F test or t-test are used to test for significance.

Once the existence of a relationship has been established (or in cases where one has access to the universe under study), one moves on to estimate the strength of the relationship. Again, the particular measure employed is a function of the level of analysis of the underlying variables. Yule's Q is a basic test for nominal data; under certain circumstances it is advisable to employ Lamda. With ordinal data, Gamma and Tau are commonly employed to estimate the strength of association, while Pearson's r is common to estimate relationships at the interval level.

Evaluation

One limitation of most statistical estimates of covariance is that they are restricted to the particular properties of the two variables under analysis. Comparisons across different paired sets of variables are difficult, as most estimations of covariance are dependent upon the scale of measurement for the constituent variables. It is possible to sidestep this problem in multivariate regression models by comparing the beta coefficient for several independent variables, which is standardized by measuring the change in the standard deviation of the dependent variable for every one standard deviation in the independent variables.

David Brockington

Associated Concepts: causality, correlation, descriptive statistics, inferential statistics, measurement, multivariate analysis, probability (random) sampling, variable analysis

Key Readings

Schroeder, L. D., Sjoquist, D. L. and Stephan, P. E. (1986) *Understanding Regression Analysis: An Introductory Guide.* Sage Series in Quantitative Applications in the Social Sciences. London: Sage.

Wildt, A. R. and Ahtola, O. T. (1978) *Analysis of Covariance.* Sage Series in Quantitative Applications in the Social Sciences. London: Sage.

COVERING-LAW MODEL OF EXPLANATION

Definition

(Also known as 'deductive–nomological explanation' or D–N), a model of scientific explanation particularly associated with the philosophers Carl Hempel and (in a more particular form) Karl Popper. According to this model, the defining feature of a scientific explanation rests on the operation of general scientific laws and particular 'initial condition statements' (together known as the *explanans*) which logically entail the phenomenon thus explained (the *explanandum*).

Distinctive Features

The basic D-N model is as follows:

(1) law(s);
(2) statement(s) of particular initial conditions, which point to the applicability of the chosen law(s) to the case in hand;
(3) the phenomenon explained (and predicted), that is as the outcome, as a deduction from, the above.

The laws involved are couched as *universal conditional statements*: 'For any *a*, if *a*, then *b*'. For example, 'Water heated at the pressure at sea level boils at 100 °C'.

Whilst the D-N model thus identifies science as involving deterministic laws, 'probabilistic laws' (inductive–statistical or I-S model – asserting 'if *a*, then a certain probability of *b*') can also be accommodated as can 'functional explanations' (involving self-regulating systems) in some forms.

A crucial distinction made on the basis of the model is between scientific and non-scientific prediction: rather than being unconditional, scientific prediction is conditional on the occurrence of the relevant initial conditions. The model is proposed as providing a unified account of the role of explanation, prediction and test in science, based on a suggested 'logical symmetry' of explanation and prediction.

Evaluation

Criticism of the covering-law model has focused particularly on its claims to provide a universal, defining model of scientific explanation. There is now general acceptance that subsumption under empirical 'covering laws' is a sufficient or a necessary condition for satisfactory scientific explanation. Is, using Boyle's Law, a change in the pressure of a gas *explained* by a change in volume? Explanation usually depends on an associated theoretical embeddedness for laws and often causal assumptions beyond mere 'constant conjunction'. Also, successful claims to explanation can be formulated without these always being dependent on empirically observable regularities or straightforwardly the basis of prediction. One suggestion made (for example, in 'scientific realism' as outlined by Bhaskar, 1978) is that scientific explanation instead involves the identification of underlying causal 'powers' or 'mechanisms' that may not be associated with straightforward empirical covering laws or allow prediction. For example, while Darwinian theory provides a highly important explanatory account of biological evolution this is couched in terms of general mechanisms (for example, 'natural selection'), which do not predict particular variations or new species.

In the social sciences in particular (not least in historiography, in relation to which Hempel especially argued for his model) it is apparent that significant kinds of explanation exist which have cogency and validity but are dependent neither on covering law nor on general mechanisms. These include 'intentional explanations' (a person's reasons for undertaking a specifiable course of action) and 'particular historical explanations' (for example, 'the Danes plundered England before they settled') and also, at least in some versions (for example, where conscious design is involved) 'functional explanations'.

Thus, while the covering-law model may be seen as adequately portraying one form of scientific explanation there is no widespread acceptance that it provides an adequate overall model of physical science, or still less, of the range of explanatory modes (especially modes of 'meaningful understanding and interpretation') employed in the social sciences and humanities (see Wright, 1971). However, 'ideal types' (for example, 'rational action', 'perfect competition'), as heuristic aids to explanation or as parts of formal theory, allow exploration of the factors involved in empirical 'departures' from these 'idealized' forms and may be seen as providing, as

for Max Weber, a half-way house between (and blending of) explanation by covering laws and more particular explanations.

For all the controversies, explanation and prediction in terms of covering laws (whether deterministic or statistical) remains a strong feature of the practical world of science. In social science, for example, even in the conspicuous absence of a body of agreed universal laws, hypothesis testing (including the testing of 'null hypotheses' and 'causal modelling') can be seen as an explicit or implicit use of the covering-law model.

David Jary

Associated Concepts: causal model, causality, falsification, hypothesis, hypothetico-deductive model, ideal type, positivism, realism

Key Readings

Bhaskar, R. (1978) *A Realist Theory of Science*, 2nd edn. Hemel Hempstead: Harvester.

Hempel, C. (1965) *Aspects of Scientific Explanation*. New York: Free Press.

Popper, K. (1934, English translation, 1959) *The Logic of Scientific Discovery*. London: Hutchinson.

Wright, G. von (1971) *Explanation and Understanding*. London: Routledge & Kegan Paul.

COVERT RESEARCH

Definition

Research that is undertaken without the consent or knowledge of respondents. This type of social research is most strongly associated with participant observational work where a researcher joins a group or organization assuming a covert role in order to observe first hand the functioning and daily life of the group.

Distinctive Features

Covert research has a strong tradition in sociological and criminological work. Early ethnographers such as Whyte (1943) wished to explore the social world using naturalistic techniques in the same way that anthropologists have sought to understand different cultures through first-hand experience.

Covert observation has been used with difficult-to-access or deviant groups. Gaining access can be difficult. This is often achieved through a key informant who is a part of the group or organization and may know the real purpose of the researcher's presence, and such a person can act as a gatekeeper allowing access to participants and events. Adopting a believable and acceptable role with the group can also be problematic, and sometimes researchers choose to covertly observe an organization that they are already a part of. A good example of this is Holdaway's (1983) account of police work conducted covertly while he worked as a police officer. Managing the role and developing a successful exiting strategy are also important issues, given that the researcher's presence is built around deceit and close relationships may be established during the fieldwork with participants. There is also a danger that researchers become too immersed in the group they are studying and lose objectivity. Further, there are practical difficulties associated with data recording and researchers must recall events and informal conversations at a later time or carry a concealed tape or video recorder.

Evaluation

Covert observational research can provide a rich account of experience and context. However, relatively little covert research is undertaken by social scientists as it is time-consuming. Given the high cost of fieldwork and doubts about the validity (which are often misplaced) of such research, key funding bodies are reluctant to support this type of work.

Ethnographers' claims to capture the fabric and reality of life through covert observational methods have been criticized. The difficulty is one of accurately interpreting events and successfully translating these events into academic writing, what Pearson (1993) has referred to as *'the requirement to carry the narrative back home'* (p. xvii). The problem is that the 'reality' may be lost in the researcher's interpretation.

Covert research is ethically problematic as it transgresses ethical codes of conduct such as those produced by the American Sociological Association, British Sociological Association and the Social Research Association. One of the key ethical principles in research is that of informed consent, the understanding that those participating in research should be fully informed about its nature and purpose before they agree to participate. Indeed some researchers gain written consent. Covert researchers cannot gain informed consent from participants as the work is based upon deceit and dependent for its success upon participants being unaware of the researcher's real role. Those conducting this type of research would argue that this is justified given what the research adds to our understanding of the complexities of the social world.

Julia Davidson

Associated Concepts: access, dangerous fieldwork, ethnography, fieldwork, gatekeeper, informed consent, naturalistic data, organizational research, participant observation, validity of measurement

Key Readings

Bryman, A. (2001) *Social Research Methods.* Oxford: Oxford University Press.

Hammersley, M. and Atkinson, P. (1995) *Ethnography: Principles in Practice.* London: Routledge.

Hobbs, D. and May, T. (eds) (1993) *Interpreting the Field: Accounts of Ethnography.* Oxford: Clarendon Press.

Holdaway, S. (1983) *Inside the British Police.* Oxford: Blackwell.

Norris, C. (1993) 'Some ethical considerations on field work with the police', in D. Hobbs and T. May (eds), *Interpreting* the Field: Accounts of Ethnography. Oxford: Clarendon Press.

Pearson, G. (1993) 'Talking a good fight: authenticity and distance in the ethnographer's craft', in D. Hobbs and T. May (eds), Interpreting the Field: Accounts of Ethnography. Oxford: Clarendon Press.

Whyte, W. (1943) Street Corner Society. Chicago: University of Chicago Press.

CRITICAL ETHNOGRAPHY

Definition

Studies of social practices and cultural institutions which specifically aim to be critical of the taken-for-granted social, economic, cultural and political assumptions and concepts (e.g., family, work, self, agency, power, conflict, race, class, gender) of Western, liberal, middle-class, industrialist, capitalist societies.

Distinctive Features

Critical ethnographies are focused, theorized studies that aim to change awareness of specific social institutions or practices, or of life itself. They may engage in ideology critique or demystification, showing, for example, interests hidden behind, or vested in, cultural meanings and practices or revealing forms of domination or power. They may employ the technique of juxtaposing Western practice against the 'other' practice in order to probe and make problematic understandings assumed in each. Theoretical sources for critique are multiple and include ideas drawn from cultural Marxism, critical theory of the Frankfurt School, praxis theory, cultural studies, feminist studies, racialized and queer epistemologies, and the broad postmodern critique of advanced capitalist societies. Some examples of the rich variety of studies informed by these different and sometimes overlapping theoretical frameworks include Paul Willis's Learning to Labour; Peter McLaren's Schooling as a Ritual Performance; Jean Comaroff's Body of Power, Spirit of Resistance: The Culture and History of a South African People; Michael Taussig's Shaminism, Colonialism and the Wild Man; Michelle Fine and Lois Weiss's The Unknown City; Kathleen Stewart's A Space on the Side of the Road. While difficult to characterize in terms of a single set of features, critical ethnographies in the main are marked by several shared dispositions: a disavowal of the model of ethnographer as detached, neutral participant observer; a focus on specific practices and institutions more so than holistic portraits of an entire culture; an emancipatory versus a solely descriptive intent; and a self-referential form of reflexivity that aims to criticize the ethnographer's own production of an account. This last feature may perhaps be the most telling for what constitutes a critical ethnographic investigation. Critical social science, in general, aims to integrate theory and practice in such a way that individuals and groups become aware of the contradictions and distortions in their belief systems and social practices and are motivated to change those beliefs and practices. A critical theoretical approach to social investigation links hermeneutic (interpretive) and explanatory interests to normative concerns. However, this approach is never innocent; it is never merely a theory 'about' the world. Because critical social scientists assume that their very ways of theorizing the world constitute the ways we access the world (theories provide the categories through which we think about and experience the world), they interrogate (and frequently disrupt and decentre) their way of theorizing by means of reflexive critique.

Evaluation

Critical ethnographers argue that conditions of social, economic and political inequality, false ideology and distorted self-understanding are real characteristics of society. They claim they can document and re-present these morally unacceptable conditions. Yet, they also acknowledge that all social inquirers participate in regimes of power/knowledge – they are part of formal modern institutions that exercise power through the production and management of knowledge about society. Thus, critical ethnography, particularly in its encounter with postmodern insights regarding deconstructing the social construction and production of knowledge, is a rich site for examining the meaning, limits and authority of social theorizing.

Thomas A. Schwandt

Associated Concepts: critical research, ethnography, emancipatory research, hermeneutics, postmodernism, reflexivity, value-free research

Key Readings

Carspecken, P. F. (2002) 'The hidden history of praxis theory within critical ethnography and the criticalism/postmodernism problematic', in Y. Zou and E. T. Trueba (eds), *Ethnography and Schools.* Lanham, MD: Rowman & Littlefield.

Kincheloe, J. and McLaren, P. L. (2000) 'Rethinking critical theory and qualitative research', in N. K. Denzin and Y. S. Lincoln (eds), *Handbook of Qualitative Research* 2nd edn. Thousand Oaks, CA: Sage.

Levinson, B., Foley, D. and Holland, D. (eds) (1996) *The Cultural Production of the Educated Person: Critical Ethnographies of Schooling and Local Practice.* Albany, NY: State University of New York Press.

Marcus, G. E. (1998) *Ethnography Through Thick and Thin.* Princeton, NJ: Princeton University Press.

Marcus, G. E. and Fischer, M. M. J. (1986) *Anthropology as Cultural Critique.* Chicago: University of Chicago Press.

CRITICAL RESEARCH

Definition

A generic term usually applied to any research that challenges those conventional knowledge bases and methodologies – whether quantitative or qualitative – that make claims of scientific objectivity. Rather, critical social research attempts to reveal the socio-historical specificity of knowledge and to shed light on how particular knowledges reproduce structural relations of inequality and oppression.

Distinctive Features

Critical social research, in the sense of offering critiques of social order, has a long history encompassing the likes of Aristotle, Socrates, Hobbes and Marx. It is currently evident in the work of a wide variety of social critics, including Marxists, feminists and post-structuralists and is often 'hailed' through attaching the adjective of 'critical' to any number of existing disciplines or methodologies, as in 'critical sociology', 'critical discourse analysis', 'critical anthropology', 'critical psychiatry', 'critical criminology', 'critical ethnography' and so on. Yet, unlike other methodological traditions, the defining characteristics of a critical approach have rarely been spelt out. Its key features remain elusive, though they are generally understood to involve a critique of conventional research agendas and methodologies by pointing out their (frequently hidden) ideological and oppressive nature. Its intent is to expose enduring structures of power and domination, to deconstruct the discourses and narratives that support them and to work as advocates for social justice.

The term 'critical theory' is widely associated with the Frankfurt Institute for Social Research founded in 1922. In particular, members of the 'Frankfurt School' – such as Adorno, Marcuse and Horkheimer – provided a damning critique of scientism and rationalism by revealing the significance of values and beliefs as key constituents of culture. Technical and one-dimensional forms of reason had subverted and eclipsed critical reasoning about moral and political values. So, they argued, it was precisely the ethos of value neutrality, so revered by academics in 1930s Germany, that had created the moral vacuum to be filled by fascism. The solution lay in reconnecting reason with questions of ethics, nature and morality. Value neutrality was a dangerous illusion, to be avoided at all costs.

This emergent critical paradigm was further developed by the fracturing of mainstream paradigms in the social sciences associated with the civil rights, student protest, anti-war, counter-culture and feminist movements of the 1960s. Empirical science, structural functionalism and notions of a 'common value system' came to be increasingly critiqued as the tools of a 'power elite'. Notions of scientific neutrality, especially when practised through American corporate and military policies, were condemned as little more than a convenient cover for systematic forms of control at home and subversion abroad. Orthodox social scientists were singled out as mere 'technicians of power' (Gouldner, 1971). The time had come, as Howard Becker put it, to ask 'Whose side are we on?'.

At this time a related research style evolved which was designed to sustain social criticism and to facilitate radical social change. Lehmann and Young (1974), for example, talk explicitly of a 'conflict methodology' in which the research agenda is shifted from the powerless (the usual subjects of conventional research) to exposing the exploitations and scandals of the powerful. Research as exposé and as advocacy for the powerless becomes indivisible. Critical social research would not, however, claim any one direct political affiliation. Rather, it is committed to delving beyond surface appearances in order to reveal oppressive and discriminatory social processes and structures and thereby suggests ways in which the oppressive can be challenged through praxis (Harvey, 1990). In this senses it is less a specific method and more a theoretical, empirical, reflexive and engaged process informed by various 'standpoint' commitments to social justice and human rights (Hudson, 2000).

Evaluation

Critical social research does not occupy a single well-defined space. It is theoretically and methodologically diverse. Its meaning is probably only captured through the particular disciplines within which, or against which, it works. As a result, it has been condemned as an 'empty rhetorical shell' (Hammersley, 1995). It does, however, continually remind us that social research should not, indeed cannot, stand on the sidelines of society. Research is a value-laden activity, from the choice of research subject and the questions to investigate through to the interpretations and publication of results. Critical research is not afraid to reveal its theoretical, political and ideological underpinnings. It actively engages with and challenges dominant assumptions and 'taken for granted' ways of knowing. Its 'critical' credentials are especially clear when it is employed to reveal the hidden agendas, partialities and limitations of 'official' research and when it is part of an ongoing process of, and advocacy for, radical social change. As a result it is always likely to suffer from mainstream political arguments that attempt to discredit it as subjective, over-politicized and thus not 'real research'. It is no surprise that it is consistently denied any significant research funding.

John Muncie

Associated Concepts: critical ethnography, deconstruction, emancipatory research, feminist research, standpoint research, politics and social research, value-free research

Key Readings

Gouldner, A. (1971) *The Coming Crisis of Western Sociology.* London: Heinemann.

Hammersley, M. (1995) *The Politics of Social Research.* London: Sage.

Harvey, L. (1990) *Critical Social Research.* London: Sage.

Hudson, B. (2000) 'Critical reflection as research methodology', in V. Jupp, P. Davies and P. Francis (eds), *Doing Criminological Research.* London: Sage. pp. 175–92.

Lehmann, T. and Young, T. R. (1974) 'From conflict theory to conflict methodology: an emerging paradigm for sociology', *Sociological Inquiry,* 44: 15–28.

CROSS-SECTIONAL SURVEY

Definition

Any collection of data from a sample of individuals (or groups) at a particular point in time as a basis for inferring the characteristics of the population from which the sample comes. A cross-sectional survey of a population can be one-off or repeated at regular intervals thereby providing a means of 'monitoring' changes in the population in response to societal and policy change. A population census is in effect a 'bench mark' social survey in which all population members form the sample.

Distinctive Features

Cross-sectional sample surveys are described as 'descriptive' or 'analytic' depending on whether the prime purpose is to provide descriptive estimates of the population's parameters or to test hypotheses about the relationships between the variables encompassed by it. Analytic surveys build into the design a wide range of variables to which statistical models can be applied. Such approaches require fairly strong assumptions about temporal sequencing, which the data are often unable to support. There is always the problem of 'endogeneity', whereby it is uncertain when investigating the relationship between two variables, such as educational attainment and educational aspirations, as to which one is a function of (or causing) the other. However, hypothesized causal relationships that are not borne out by survey data provide a basis for falsification of hypotheses. For example, if we hypothesize that girls are discriminated against compared with boys in relation to certain occupational opportunities, and the survey shows no relationship between gender and occupational opportunity, then the hypothesis falls.

Effective surveys of a population need to be based on a sample that is drawn on strict probability lines, that is to say, each sample member has a known probability of being selected. Designs can range from simple random samples of a population identified from a sampling frame, for example, Social Security registers, to a 'multi-stage, disproportionately, stratified clustered' sample in which sub-samples of the main sample may be boosted for certain purposes and the data collected in from whole groups of individuals in a limited number of locations rather than across the country as a whole. Another common type of design dispenses with the probability sampling principle and simply constructs the sample from individuals selected purposefully to meet certain quotas considered important to the subject matter of the survey, such as gender, social class, educational level, type of housing and so on. Because such samples are selected on non-random principles, it is not strictly possible to estimate the standard error of the sample for them and consequently the generalizability of the survey results is limited to this extent.

Evaluation

Social surveys are powerful tools in social science that offer a quick and efficient means of collecting information about a range of variables in a sub-sample of the population. However, to do this effectively is expensive, because of the time and cost involved in drawing up sampling frames, selecting a sample and then carrying out the fieldwork. Much survey work, however, is not conducted to these demanding standards and is typically done on a one-off basis by students for dissertation purposes or for organizations who want quick snap-shots of particular groups of people, such as employees or local residents and so on. In these instances, the generalizations drawn from the survey data are often difficult to sustain. Nevertheless, the results do provide basic descriptions of the people involved in the survey, which gives some indication of the prevalence of behaviours and attitudes in the particular group.

John Bynner

Associated Concepts: census, cluster sampling, cohort study, falsification, hypothesis, longitudinal study, panel study, probability (random) sampling, quota sampling

Key Readings

Hoinville, G. and Jowell, R. (1978) *Survey Research Practice*. London: Heinemann.

Kish, L. (1995) *Survey Sampling*. New York: Wiley.

Moser, C. A. and Kalton, G. (1971) *Survey Methods in Social Investigations*. London: Heinemann.

Oppenheim, A. N. (1992) *Questionnaire Design, Interviewing and Attitude Measurement*. New York: Basic Books.

de Vaus, D. (2002) *Surveys in Social Research*, 5th edn. London: Routledge.

CULTURAL RESEARCH

Definition

A cross-disciplinary endeavour that applies a range of methods concerned with researching the ways in which social groups express their place in the world and hence the 'meaning' of culture in all its diverse forms.

Distinctive Features

The impact and meaning of culture has long been an issue that has fascinated, and to a degree, mystified, researchers from a wide range of disciplines including Sociology, Cultural Studies, Politics, Economics, Human Geography and the Humanities. Cultural research is concerned with the properties associated with a concept, namely culture, that is constantly being revised by courtesy of the fact it is itself the product of on-going social change. But at the heart of what cultural research seeks to find out is the way in which societies or groups see the world and their part in that world and, perhaps most pertinently, how such groups express their place in that world. In this sense, culture is the 'production and circulation of meaning' and cultural research is the study of how that meaning in all its diverse forms is constructed.

A key issue lying at the heart of the production of meaning is undoubtedly the relationship between high culture and popular culture. Cultural research is disparate in that its subject matters are extremely diverse, ranging from the historical relevance of the works of Beethoven to the everyday consumption of soap operas to the impact of museums on social exclusion. Cultural research can span from the almost entirely abstract discussions as to the impact of globalization to highly focused policy-oriented analyses of art gallery provision in a local community.

Cultural researchers deploy many of the skills associated with social research more generally, from ethnographic methods to large-scale quantitative research. But they may equally use the skills associated with, say, the art historian or the expert in heritage or museum studies. At the policy end of the spectrum cultural research has become increasingly interested in the social agenda and in particular questions of social inclusion and urban regeneration. Such approaches have tended to favour a more quantitative approach. This may involve large-scale questionnaires on cultural attendance and attitudes or the collection of secondary data illustrating the impact of cultural investment on employment. At the other end of the spectrum many cultural researchers are concerned with how texts produce meaning, through, for example, advertising, and have therefore deployed a semiotic analysis.

Cultural research should not be assumed to be a by-product or off-shoot of Cultural Studies. Indeed, many cultural researchers would disassociate themselves from what they wrongly or rightly perceive to be the lack of a method or methodology in Cultural Studies (Gray, 2003). In this sense, cultural research has no discernible disciplinary identity. It does not subscribe to a specific methodological dogma or disciplinary agenda, but is rather a collection of diverse approaches to a range of broadly related phenomena.

Evaluation

The distinctiveness of cultural research as an approach in its own right continues to be undermined by its apparently disparate nature. Despite the richness of a multi-disciplinary perspective, cultural researchers remain in a constant battle to establish the worthiness of an area of research that does not necessarily fit very neatly into traditional academic disciplinary boundaries. This lack of a disciplinary identity exacerbates a situation in which cultural research is not apparently collected in a coherent or systematic fashion.

Meanwhile, public policy makes particular demands of its research to the extent that there is a danger that the outcome of such research will be trimmed to suit those demands. There is a particular concern to establish the economic value of the cultural or arts sector, and to construct dispassionate economic impact studies, but as authors such as Johnson and Thomas (2001: 215) have suggested, 'there is also a need to pursue an altogether wider research agenda on the economic effects of the arts. This agenda would focus more on the measurement and valuation of the impact of the activities of the arts sector on the enjoyment, appreciation and human capital of participants.'

At a policy level cultural researchers often find themselves in the position of having to 'prove the case for culture' through quantitative data that can make an immediate policy impact. Cultural researchers are therefore in danger of finding that their own creativity is increasingly hamstrung by a policy-oriented agenda. This tendency to research the wrong things for the wrong reasons may mean cultural research will continue in its struggle to establish a coherent identity. An over-reliance on quantitative data is a particular concern because, by its very nature, culture is a multi-faceted phenomenon that demands a more triangulated approach.

In many respects cultural research finds itself in a difficult position – unaccepted by the academic mainstream both for its supposed deficiencies in methodological rigour and for an alleged lack of a genuine academic tradition. Nonetheless, cultural research can be said to be making genuine in-roads on both counts. As long as cultural researchers can convince policy makers and funders alike of the validity of their work, as well as the benefit of a more sophisticated and long-sighted approach, then there is no reason why such progress cannot continue apace.

Steven Miles

Associated Concepts: media analysis, methodological pluralism, policy-related research, qualitative research, quantitative research, visual methods

Key Readings

Alasuutari, P. (1995) *Researching Culture: Qualitative Method and Cultural Studies.* London: Sage.

Gray, A. (2003) *Research Practice for Cultural Studies.* London: Sage.

Johnson, P. and Thomas, B. (2001) 'Assessing the economic impact of the Arts', in S. Selwood (ed.), *The UK Cultural Sector: Profile and Policy Issues.* London: Policy Studies Institute. pp. 202–16.

D

DANGEROUS FIELDWORK

Definition

Forms of data collection in which there is a risk to the physical or mental well-being of the researcher.

Distinctive Features

Fieldwork can be dangerous in a number of ways, and danger may be an accidental or deliberate aspect of life in the field. When researchers enter the field they enter places, spaces and cultures that are not their own, and this makes the fieldworker vulnerable due to unfamiliar hazards that can emerge naturally. The field itself can throw up dangerous physical obstacles and hazards, particularly if the setting is especially removed from the kind of comforts and bourgeois sensibilities that most academics take for granted. For similar reasons the fieldworker runs the risk of behaving inappropriately, or of using language that is foreign and generally offensive to indigenous sensibilities. This latter category can render the fieldworker vulnerable to anger or attempted retribution by populations who are subjected to the fieldworker's gaze, or those on the periphery of that gaze.

Researching transgressive fields can also be dangerous, for as part of immersion in the field the fieldworker may become implicated in illegal behaviour, or may even be required to participate in crime, and so becoming vulnerable to police action. Similarly, carrying out fieldwork on illegal activity can result in the researcher being suspected of being an informant or agent of regulatory or law enforcement organizations. Indeed, few fieldworkers working with criminals have not at some time been accused of 'working with the other side', and this clearly places the fieldworker at risk from coercion or retribution. Researching law enforcement itself can also be dangerous, as the researcher may be exploring activity that is corrupt, illegal or morally ambiguous. The danger here is similar to that posed by other deviant groups who need to reduce the possibility of negative consequences, either deliberate or otherwise emerging from the data. In transgressive fields the researcher needs to build up empathy and trust with individuals in the field. Whether based upon overt or covert tactics, acceptable language, appearance and a range of indigenously based cultural competencies need to be acquired in order to reduce danger to manageable levels.

In addition, the object of certain types of fieldwork is more dangerous than others. For instance, researching essentially dangerous jobs, pastimes, sports or hobbies places the fieldworker at a similar level of risk to that posed to indigenous participants. However, if the fieldworker is new to the endeavour, or is incompetent or less than expert in an activity that may be either central or peripheral to the investigation, danger is increased. In such settings danger is an integral part of the research and the fieldworker, who may or may not possess the necessary competencies, will in effect be researching danger.

However, the cultural and physical contexts within which certain fields reside can also be dangerous, even if the object of the research is not in itself hazardous. For instance, carrying out a study of an urban school, nursery or social work department may produce few, if any, obviously dangerous occurrences that are integral to the targeted setting. However, the fieldworker, in order to contextualize these activities, will face the ethnographic realities of living in the area, travelling to work, shopping and drinking in local pubs, and generally experiencing day-to-day pressures. In this respect even the most competent fieldworker is likely to face those hazards and dangers that are everyday realities for inner city residents.

Evaluation

While the dangers of fieldwork should never be ignored, it is important to remember that the fieldworker has volunteered for the task, and will eventually leave the field, unlike the subjects of the research who experience the daily rigours of the field as a permanent lived reality. Consequently, while a consideration of personal safety in the field should always be given a high priority, the reflexive researcher will acknowledge both the temporary nature of being in harm's way, and attempt via the experience of fieldwork to extract some notion of life in its permanent shadow.

Dick Hobbs

Associated Concepts: access, confidentiality, covert research, fieldwork, exploitative research, impression management, participant observation, research bargain

Key Readings

Coffey, A. (1999) *The Ethnographic Self*. London: Sage.
Ferrell, J. and Haamm, M. (1998) *Ethnography at the Edge*. Boston, MA: Northeastern University Press.
Hobbs, D. (2001) 'Ethnography and the study of deviance', in P. Atkinson, A. Coffey, S. Delamont, J. Lofland and L. Lofland (eds), *Handbook of Ethnography*. London: Sage. pp. 204–19.
Lee-Treweek, G. and Linkogle, S. (eds) (2000) *Research Methods, Danger and Ethics*. London, Routledge.

DATA

Definition

Data are observations about the social world. Data, the plural of datum, can be quantitative or qualitative in nature. The initial view of the concept of data tends to be numerical, but qualitative data, for example descriptions of interactions, are also common in social science. Marsh (1988: 42) points out that 'data ... is [sic] produced, not given'; that is, researchers choose what to call data, it is not just 'there' to be 'found'.

Distinctive Features

When data take the form of variables, they can be discrete or continuous. Discrete data describe single properties, they are not continuous in nature; legal offences (larceny, assault, homicide), types of household (nuclear family, extended family, friends or individual) and environmental hazard types (acid rain, oil spills, agricultural chemicals) are all examples of discrete data. A datum from one of these discrete groups will have one of these properties. Continuous data are composed of properties that can be measured, such as infant body weight, time to complete anagrams, or distance covered by racing snails during ten minutes. At least theoretically, these continuous data can be measured to the level of minute units, for example milligrams for infants, milliseconds for anagram solving, and millimetres for racing snails.

In addition to 'variable', a further important concept is that of attribute. Attributes are 'word categories', and they generate non-numerical data. The category of legal offence can have the labels such as those given above. They cannot have numbers meaningfully given to them, as they are not measures with numerical values. However, once a number has been assigned to a category it can be very tempting to subject the data set to inferential statistical analysis. This temptation should be resisted, since the results of such analysis are generally meaningless. For example, on a Likert scale question on fear of crime, analysed by gender of respondent, women could produce a mean value of 3.48, and men a score of 3.12, and this difference could be statistically significant, but meaningless. It would be possible to investigate the relationship of gender to fear of crime, however, by using a chi-square analysis, where each category forms a column, and male and female form the rows, with the number of participants responding within each category each contributing a datum.

Evaluation

Data can also be qualitative in a far wider sense, for example interview transcriptions, letters to newspapers, minutes of public meetings, television advertisements, television interviews, videos of children playing, or in school classes, street art, graffiti, CCTV footage, and Internet sites.

Data can be raw, and unprocessed, such as an interview transcription or survey scripts, or they can be processed, such as summary data from questionnaires or the average of reaction times for different experimental conditions in an experiment. Data can also be things that others have not noticed as important, or pre-designed into a study, as in the case of trace and unobtrusive methods. For example, data can be the number of tram or bus tickets sold on a particular route, before and after a crime reduction intervention, or the wear of floor coverings at an exhibition as an indicator of the relative popularity of exhibits.

The general goal in collecting data is the idea of being able to analyse them in some way after their collection. Therefore the kind of data collected will be dictated by the kind of analysis the researcher is able to undertake, whether with the help of others, or alone (Robson, 2002). One of the most unfortunate outcomes for inexperienced researchers is the collection of data that cannot be analysed.

Jeanette Garwood

Associated Concepts: chi-square test, data archives, diary, indicator, Internet research, measurement, qualitative research, quantitative research, trace measures, unobtrusive measures, variable analysis

Key Readings

Marsh, C. (1988) *Exploring Data: An Introduction to Data Analysis for Social Scientists.* Cambridge: Polity Press.
Robson, C. (2002) *Real World Research,* 2nd edn. Oxford: Blackwell.

DATA ARCHIVES

Definition

Data archives are resource centres that acquire, store and disseminate digital data for secondary analysis for both research and teaching. Their prime function is to ensure long-term preservation and future usability of the data they hold.

Distinctive Features

Data archiving is a method of conserving expensive resources and ensuring that their research potential is fully exploited. Unless preserved and documented for further research, data that have often been collected at significant expense, with substantial expertise and involving respondents' contributions may later exist only in a small number of reports that analyse only a fraction of the research potential of the data. Within a very short space of time the data files are likely to be lost or become obsolete as technology evolves.

The data archiving movement began in the 1960s within a number of key social science departments in the United States which stored original data of survey interviews. The movement spread across Europe and in 1967 a UK data archive (UKDA) was established by the UK Social Science Research Council. In the late 1970s many national archives joined wider professional organizations such as the International Association of Social Science Information Service and Technology (IAS-SIST), established to promote networks of data services for the social sciences and to foster cooperation on key archival strategies, procedures and technologies.

The first data archives collected data of specific interest to quantitative researchers in the social sciences. In the 1960s these were largely opinion poll or election data, but as the trend for large-scale surveys grew, by the late 1970s the UKDA began to acquire major government surveys and censuses. Because of their large sample sizes and the richness of the information collected, these surveys represent major research resources. Examples of major British government series include the General Household Survey and the Labour Force Survey. In the United States, key government survey series include the Survey of Income and Program Participation, the Current Population Survey and the National Health Interview Survey.

By the 1990s the UKDA collection had grown to thousands of data sets spanning a wide range of data sources. Well-known UK-based academic large-scale survey series include the British Social Attitudes Survey and the British Household Panel Survey. In the United States, the General Social Survey, the Panel Study of Income Dynamics and the National Longitudinal Survey of 1972 are examples of long-running survey series. Major cross-national series include the World Values and European Values Surveys and the International Social Survey Program Series.

In the 1990s the research community recognized the needs of qualitative researchers

by funding the Qualitative Data Archive (Qualidata) at the University of Essex, UK, in 1994. In 1995 a history data service was established, devoted to the archiving and dissemination of a broad range of historical data. More recently, in 2003, the UK Economic and Social Data Service (ESDS) was established to provide a long-term and integrated strategy for preserving, processing and disseminating all types of social science data with an enhanced focus on supporting and training users.

Typically, social science data archives acquire a significant range of data relating to society, both historical and contemporary, from sources including surveys, censuses, registers and aggregate statistics.

Data archives typically collect numeric data, which can then be analysed with the use of statistical software. Numeric data result when textual information (such as answers to survey questions) has been coded or they may represent individual or aggregated quantities, for instance earned income. The demand for access to digital texts, images and audiovisual material has meant that material, from in-depth interviews and field notes to recorded interviews, as well as the open-ended survey questions, is now available for computer analysis.

Finally, data sets from across the world are available through national data archives' reciprocal arrangements with other national data archives.

A key concern for a data archive is to ensure that the materials they acquire are suitable for informed use and meet demand. All materials deposited are selected, evaluated and must meet certain criteria, such as being documented to a minimum standard. Acquisitions policies should be flexible and responsive to changes in both data and information needs of the research communities and in the rapid changing climate of technology.

It is the responsibility of data archives to keep up with technological advances, by monitoring hardware and software developments and migrating their collection accordingly. When technology changes, the data in their holdings are technically transformed to remain readable in the new environment. Computer programs are maintained to allow data to be easily transformed from an in-house standard to the various formats required by users.

Data processing activities include first checking and validating, for example examining numeric data values and checking that the risk of identifying individuals is minimal. Second, metadata (data about data) are produced with the aim of producing high-quality finding aids and providing good user documentation. Metadata cover information describing the study and the data, and for numeric data, files creating variable and value labels. A systematic catalogue record is created for all studies, detailing an overview of the study, the size and content of the data set, its availability and terms and conditions of access. User guides contain further information on how the data were collected, the original questionnaires and how to use the data.

Evaluation

Data supplied by data archives can be used for reporting of statistics, such as basic frequency counts, and for more in-depth secondary analysis. Secondary analysis strengthens scientific inquiry, avoids duplication of data collection and opens up methods of data collection and measurement. Re-using archived data enables new users to: ask new questions of old data; undertake comparative research, replication or restudy; inform research design and promote methodological advancement. Finally, data can provide significant resources for training in research and substantive learning.

Users typically request data in a particular format, such as a statistical or word processing package. These days, data can be accessed via instant Web download facilities or can be dispatched on portable media such as CD-ROM. The twenty-first century has seen a move towards sophisticated online analysis tools, where users can search and analyse data via a Web browser, such as Nesstar. Users are typically required to be registered

and sign an agreement to the effect that they will not attempt to identify individuals when carrying out analyses.

Louise Corti

Associated Concepts: census, confidentiality, official statistics, qualitative data archives, qualitative research, secondary analysis, SPSS

Key Readings

ESDS website (December 2003) (Online): www.esds.ac.uk/

IASSIST website (December 2003) (Online): http://datalib.library.ualberta.ca/iassist/

ICPSR (December 2003) Guide to Social Science Data Preparation and Archiving,

ICPSR website (Online): www.icpsr.umich.edu/access/dpm.html

Ryssevik, J. and Musgrave, S. (2001) 'The social science dream machine: resource discovery, analysis, and delivery on the Web', *Social Science Computing Review*, 19 (2): 163–74.

DECISION-MAKING RESEARCH

Definition

A process whereby the context, background and dynamics of political decisions are analysed. Practically it seeks to understand how and why a particular legislative proposal or government policy has come to fruition.

Distinctive Features

Key characteristics of this type of research include its varied nature in addition to the various possible strategies that are afforded to the researcher. One could, for example, decide to conduct elite interviews, analyse official documents and public records, or study the political biographies of the relevant decision makers (although the latter would involve waiting until the diaries of the decision maker are published, which may be several decades after the event, or which may indeed never happen).

A clear example of this type of approach can be seen in decision making in the European Union. If one were to research the EU's Common Fisheries Policy (CFP), it would immediately become apparent that the decision-making process is wide and diverse. Policy is not solely initiated by the institutions of the EU. Rather, decision making takes place within and between a complex web of inter-connected institutions and stakeholders at the EU (supranational), national and sub-national levels. In order to overcome this complexity, researchers are often required to make certain methodological choices, for instance selecting one level of analysis in preference to another.

Such choices have caused controversies within the academic community. For inter-governmental (sometimes termed state-centric) scholars such as Andrew Moravcsik, the primary focus for decision making must be the nation-state. In many respects this type of research strongly mirrors classical realism, although there are several marked differences between the two. The main thrust of the inter-governmental argument, however, is that political decisions taken to integrate within the EU are solely the preserve of the member states. At times of history-making decisions, such as the signing of the Maastricht Treaty, the principal decisions are taken by the member states. Accordingly, controversies surrounding the CFP could ultimately be resolved by individual EU members. Should it be to the taste of a particular member state government to withdraw from the policy, then it would be free to do so. When undertaking decision-making research, therefore, the researcher should primarily focus on the bargains reached between individual states, particularly in the Council of Ministers.

Many scholars, however, refute the notion that individual countries drive the decision-making process. A contra stance to the inter-governmental view of the decision-making process is that the institutions of the EU drive the policy agenda. This line of argument is most strongly enunciated in the supranational writings of Ernst Haas (neo-functionalism)

and the institutionalist writings of Paul Pierson (historical institutionalism). These scholars argue that legislative decisions are strongly influenced by the main EU institutions, which include the Commission, the Council of Ministers (and the Council), the Parliament and the European Court of Justice. As soon as these institutions were created, they began to assume powers that the individual member states had not envis-aged. Consequently, they have gradually assumed greater competence in legislative proposals and policy initiation. In terms of fisheries policy, which is now under the exclusive competence of the EU, the decision-making powers of member states have now been largely emasculated, resulting in an inability on the part of individual states to set the policy agenda.

Although not yet fully developed, one could make the case that the decision-making process is highly influenced by sub-state groupings in the form of pressure groups, or even by transnational alliances. The former may include European regions; the latter may include pressure groups. Because of the nature of the EU, many regional representa-tives or pressure groups can simply bypass a member state and lobby the Commission directly. The clearest example of this type of research has been forwarded by Gary Marks, Liesbet Hooghe and Kermit Blank with their writings on multi-level governance. Decision-making is but one of a number of processes in Europeanization, which also includes policy initiation, implementation and adjudi-cation. The decision-making process is said to take place in a highly fragmented environ-ment in which individual states, EU institu-tions, pressure groups and sub-national levels of government all play an important role. Decisions on fisheries policy could therefore be described as occurring in an environment that includes all four of the major institutions, in which all 25 member states are repre-sented, as well as including the lobbying of individual regions and various pressure groups. As this arena is so eclectic, it tends to be less elegant than intergovernmental or state-centric research approaches.

Methodological choices need to be made by the researcher depending on the decision-making perspective that the researcher deems to be most convincing. An intergovernmental researcher may interview elites in a particular national government; a supranational scholar by contrast may conduct elite interviews in the Commission or Parliament. Furthermore, a multi-level governance scholar may decide to conduct interviews in a combination of the two in addition to speaking to pressure groups and representatives of sub-national governments. At this moment, however, there is no clear consensus on how one can best study the decision-making process in both the EU and international context.

Evaluation

Clearly all of the particular research strategies outlined above have merit. A problem that they all face to a greater or lesser degree, however, is that of access, which is a problem encountered by most scholars of contemporary life. It could be the case that a contemporary political scientist or sociologist will simply be unable to fully understand the real motives underlying decisions that are made by politicians. A historian, relieved of the baggage of everyday controversies when the relevant embargo on official documents has elapsed, may be better able to comprehend why particular decisions were made at a given point.

Craig McLean

Associated Concepts: access, document analysis, elite interviewing, historical analysis, mixed-methods research, policy-related research, process mapping

Key Readings

Haas, E. B. (1968) *The Uniting of Europe: Political, Social and Economic Forces.* Stanford, CA: Stanford University Press.
Marks, G., Hooghe, L. and Blank, K. (1996) 'European integration from the 1980s: state-centric v. multi-level governance', *Journal of Common Market Studies*, 34 (3): 341–78.
Moravcsik, A. (1999) *The Choice for Europe: Social Purpose and State Power from Messina to Maastricht.* London: UCL Press.
Pierson, P. (1996) 'The path to European integration: a historical institutionalist analysis', *Comparative Political Studies*, 29 (2): 123–63.

DECONSTRUCTION

Definition

A style of thought developed by the French philosopher Jacques Derrida. On the one hand, Derrida argues against the philosophico-metaphysical tradition for its presupposition of pure transcendence. On the other hand, he also argues against the non-philosophical (empiricist) tradition of the human and social sciences for failing to acknowledge the necessity of a momentary transcendence. Deconstruction, then, is the inscription of the 'beyond' of the transcendental into the empirical, and is thus the inscription of absence into presence by arguing that subjects and objects are a play of *traces* (present-absence).

Distinctive Features

Deconstruction provides a complex response to some of the major twentieth-Century strands in philosophy and social theory, notably phenomenology, psychoanalysis and structuralism. Philosophers and social theorists have traditionally assumed an epistemology that involves the presence of a transcendent individual subjectivity and a universal objectivity. Hence language becomes the medium or tool that represents and defines both the inner and outer worlds. On this traditional view, language is secondary to the things it defines, like 'thoughts' and 'objects'.

By contrast, deconstruction 'is' the disruption of all metaphysical-ontological questions beginning 'What is ... ?' The paradox of this opening definition is that, by deconstruction's standards, it would have to disrupt itself. But the event of this disruption would be that this paradox is the definition of definition itself. On the one hand, it is because of deconstruction that we can define; on the other hand, it is because of deconstruction that any 'definition' is thus a violent reduction (simplification of complexity) of the very term it attempts to define. Thus, we cannot begin with a 'definition' of deconstruction – because we have already begun; we are already enmeshed in complexity and difference.

Derrida's work seems to condemn this move of the definition as the familiar 'metaphysical' move towards an unattainable origin. He suggests that any starting point will be complex or multiple – undecidable, an 'originary trace'. The attempt to assign some simple origin, e.g. God, humanness, to this complexity is itself a *secondary* move, an invention that occurs in *response* to that complexity. For example, for Derrida the 'person' is not an origin, rather it arises out of the very attempt to assign a simple origin to some primordial complexity.

When Derrida refers to language he does so with respect to its 'play' – the 'problem of language' (Derrida, 1974: 6) arises in *not* seeing it as a game whose play of differences involves a necessary and originary absence. But presence and absence of what? Derrida's work shows that the history of metaphysics has been a history of the privilege of presence over absence (the presence of *subjec*tivity and *objec*tivity – and all other privileged terms in a binary opposition) – what Derrida calls 'logocentrism'. Derrida's main task has always been the deconstruction of the logocentrism intrinsic in metaphysics.

To give a brief example, Derrida's (1988) analysis of Austin and Searle develops three interconnected arguments related to the 'signature', the 'event' and the 'context'. Austin used the notion of the utterance-origin to suggest that we can refer to the person who does the actual uttering, in both verbal and written utterances. For verbal utterances it is simply by being the person who does the uttering. In written utterances however, the source is confirmed via the person's signature. Thus, the signature signifies a person's presence (and therefore the presence of their intentions) in their absence.

Derrida argues, however, that the repetition (iterability) of the signature implies that it can both be imitated and imitates itself. The signature is neither entirely inside nor outside of the text that it is supposed to be authenticating, but rather it is on the edge of the text. This suggests that the 'origin' of the text (and therefore the author's intentions) is never fully present within it. This non-presence, this absence of the origin and its intentions, is part of the structure of language.

Derrida also suggests that both Austin and Searle erase things from their analyses of context – the 'parasitic', 'fictional', 'non-serious', 'abnormal', 'absence' (mainly of intentions) – the 'infelicities' of speech acts. The reason they do this is because they are seeking 'ideal' contexts, but Derrida argues that this 'deprives such theory of precisely what it claims for itself: seriousness, scientificity, truth, philosophical value etc.' (Derrida, 1988: 72). If context were to be determinable – as Austin and Searle want it to be – then it could only be fully known to itself. Only when it is realized that the context is undecidable and can never be fully known, as Derrida suggests, does it become possible to at least *begin* to understand how to understand it.

For researchers wanting to adopt a deconstructive stance the task would be to apply Derrida's rather esoteric thought to practical issues of analysis. The issue of analysing is inseparable from *what it is that we think we are analysing* – a participant's thoughts or intentions, a social context, or a piece of text? Deconstruction would always take the latter: we are first and foremost enmeshed in textual traces. A necessary and originary absence (of *subjec*tivity and *objec*tivity etc.) is the consequence of this beginning.

So what would a deconstructive analysis look like? Deconstruction, among other things, is the demonstration of certain paradoxes, contradictions, or 'aporias' of language. For Derrida, these contradictions are not simply a contingent aspect of language, but are necessary for language to function at all. An example here would be to take the binary opposition of necessary/contingent itself: if the thought of contingency is central to the deconstruction of metaphysical eternal and infinite necessity, then we can say that the thought of contingency is a 'necessary contingency'. That is, if that which is necessary is contingency, then the necessary is never simply necessary; and likewise, because if it is contingency that is necessary (as it must be), then the contingency is never simply contingent. Deconstruction is not the deconstruction of metaphysics as if metaphysics existed prior to its deconstruction; rather, metaphysics can only exist through this deconstruction.

So we can surmise that to deconstruct is to inhabit with no fixed assumptions about the unchanging presence or absence of subjectivity and objectivity. So we analyse texts rather than the presumed subjectivity or objectivity of that which lies behind the text. This means that, like Derrida, we need to work from inside the text – where we are now, these texts in front of us, and we need to be sensitive to the production of features of context, culture and history that re-create meaningful utterances. But we cannot assume in advance that we know what these things 'are' – to do this is to completely overlook them. In addition, if we want a textual analysis that escapes the closures of metaphysical language we need to think of language in terms of its *function* rather than its mere *presence*. And we need a non-cognitive approach to semiotics and analysis – grammatology replaces semiology.

Evaluation

Deconstruction is *neither* theory nor method in the traditional sense of these words; rather it is the process of calling into question the stability of binary oppositions such as theory/method, invoking the value of plurality or multiplicity. However, this often leads to the criticism that we are left with no grounds upon which to make a decision – crucial moral distinctions such as that between right and wrong, good and evil, will be blurred.

Jurgen Habermas raises a typical example of this type of criticism. He claims that deconstruction 'levels' the crucial distinction between philosophy and literature. Derrida's (1998) response to this type of criticism would be that he sees decisions and responsibilities as things that arise out of plurality and complexity. Only in the context of this undecideability can any decision be taken.

Similarly, previous attempts at incorporating deconstruction into critical approaches in psychology typically bypass the more radically anti-foundationalist features of a Derridean deconstruction, and the sense in which it provides a resource for showing us that identities and realities can be constituted in order to be recognizable as not constituted.

Alexa Hepburn

Associated Concepts: constructionism, discourse analysis, epistemology

Key Readings

Bennington, G. (2000) *Interrupting Derrida*. London: Routledge.
Derrida, J. (1974) *Of Grammatology* (trans. G. C. Spivak) Baltimore, MD: The Johns Hopkins University Press.
Derrida, J. (1978) *Writing and Difference* (trans. A. Bass). London: Routledge.
Derrida, J. (1982) *Margins of Philosophy* (trans. A. Bass). London: Prentice-Hall.
Derrida, J. (1988) *Monolingualism of the Other, or the Prosthesis of Origin* (trans. P. Mensah). Stanford, CA: Stanford University Press.
Hepburn, A. (1999) 'Derrida and psychology: deconstruction and its abuses in critical and discursive psychologies', *Theory and Psychology*, 9 (5): 641–67.

DEDUCTION

See Hypothetico-Deductive Model

DEMOGRAPHY

Definition

The study of population structure, processes and change, with analyses of fertility, nuptiality, mortality and migration featuring prominently. The tools used in demographic analyses include simple but effective mathematical techniques, some specific to demography, alongside more sophisticated, generic forms of statistical analysis (Rowland, 2003; Hinde, 1998).

Demographic research uses data from censuses, surveys, vital registration systems and population registers. While demographic analyses of official statistics are often macro-level, micro-level demographic analyses are equally significant, with retrospective surveys and longitudinal studies being particularly valuable sources of micro-level life history data.

Distinctive Features

When examining phenomena such as fertility and mortality, rates are an important tool. Age is central to demographic research, hence the use of age-specific rates is often appropriate, with measures such as the total period fertility rate and life expectancy being summaries of such rates across a range of ages. In demography, the term standardization usually refers to the process of adjusting data to take account of age structure, to facilitate meaningful comparisons between different populations.

The life table is a key demographic tool, consisting of a set of values (rates, numbers of cases, etc.) for a succession of age categories. The life table for a particular period (for example, a year) contains the age-specific mortality rates for that period and further columns of figures corresponding to a hypothetical cohort of people experiencing those rates (for example, the proportion of the cohort surviving to each age, the life expectancies of cohort members who reach that age, etc.). More generally, a life table can be applied to any process that ends in something equivalent to a 'death', for example, the dissolution of first marriages.

Demographic methods for examining such processes are referred to as survival analysis techniques. One such technique is the proportional hazards model. Cox's semi-parametric version of this technique builds upon the life table, concentrating on variations between population sub-groups in the risk of some event, as opposed to variation over time in the underlying hazard rate (risk) for the whole population (Trussell et al., 1992).

In addition to more sophisticated event history analysis techniques (for example, for the analysis of repeated events) and other recently developed statistical methods (for example, multi-level models), demographers frequently utilize standard statistical techniques (regression, logistic regression, etc.), as well as relatively simple measures (for example, sex ratios, parity progression ratios). They also create measures and techniques for specific demographic purposes, for example the historical back-projection technique used by Wrigley and Schofield (1989) and, more generally, techniques used for forward population projections and forecasts.

Evaluation

Good demographic research often involves the application of sophisticated mathematical or statistical techniques to high quality, appropriately structured survey data. However, demographic processes have economic, social, cultural and psychological dimensions, thus theoretical accounts of such processes may draw upon various disciplines. Additionally, many contemporary demographers recognize the value of qualitative data (for example, in relation to processes involving decision making).

In countries such as the UK and the United States, the availability of microdata from recent Censuses has opened up new research horizons. However, the coverage and quality of data available for population research are uneven; population data for many less-developed countries remain limited, notwithstanding international endeavours like the

Demographic and Health Surveys, and historical demographic research often relies on the availability of parish registers and tax-related returns.

Richard Lampard

Associated Concepts: causal model, census, cohort study, forecasting, longitudinal study, multivariate analysis, official statistics, prospective study, retrospective study

Key Readings

Hinde, A. (1998) *Demographic Methods.* London: Arnold.

Rowland, D. T. (2003) *Demographic Methods and Concepts.* Oxford: Oxford University Press.

Trussell, J., Hankinson, R. and Tilton, J. (eds) (1992) *Demographic Applications of Event History Analysis.* Oxford: Clarendon Press.

Wrigley, E. A. and Schofield, R. S. (1989) *The Population History of England, 1541–1871: A Reconstruction.* Cambridge: Cambridge University Press.

DESCRIPTIVE STATISTICS

Definition

Basic statistical methods, and measures derived from them, which summarize large sets of data so that descriptive statements can be made about individuals, social groups and societies. Sometimes descriptive statistics are contrasted with inferential statistics. The latter are estimates of features of a population (say indicators of multiple deprivation) derived from a sample of that population.

Distinctive Features

Descriptive statistics are used to describe individuals, social groups and societies on key variables. Variables relating to individuals can include type of personality, attitudinal disposition and level of intelligence. Key variables with which to describe groups or societies include social indicators about education, social class, ethnicity, gender and demographic structure.

Sometimes descriptive data are derived from primary sources, for example social surveys conducted by a researcher for his or her own purposes. Alternatively, data can be derived from secondary sources and applied and adjusted to the researcher's aims. These can include official statistics collected by government departments as an aid to decision making. Data archives also provide important sources of secondary data.

In the main, analysis using descriptive statistics is one-variable or univariate as opposed to multivariate. Multivariate analysis looks at the relationship between several variables simultaneously, often with a view to constructing or testing causal models. By contrast, univariate analysis seeks to describe individuals or social groups using one variable at a time. This can be done by a frequency distribution which counts the number of people in social class categories or the number who answer survey questions in a particular way. The frequency in each category can be converted to a percentage which provides a standardized basis for comparison between categories and also between individuals or social collectives. Frequency distributions can be portrayed visually as bar charts or pie charts.

Other descriptive statistics include measures of central tendency or average (means, medians and modes) and measures of dispersion (standard deviation and variance). The latter indicate how closely scores are bunched around an average and, therefore, tell us about the overall shape of a frequency distribution for any given variable.

Evaluation

The use of descriptive statistics alone puts limitations on any analysis. Such statistics facilitate the description of an individual, group or society on a range of variables. They also allow 'mapping', for example in examining the social

66

and geographical distribution of crime rates in a city. However, descriptive statistics do not by themselves provide an analysis in terms of relationships between two or more variables, as in a causal model or any form of multivariate analysis. In this sense they cannot capture the complexity of the social world. Nevertheless, the examination of descriptive statistics is a vital preliminary stage in such advanced analyses in terms, say, of deciding which variables to include in a causal model or assessing whether certain statistical characteristics can be assumed (for example, whether values are normally distributed).

There is a further critique which can be levelled at the use of descriptive statistics, one which applies to quantification and statistical analyses in general. This relates to the fundamental epistemological question of whether it is possible to measure the dimensions of individuals' psyches or features of the social world.

Victor Jupp

Associated Concepts: causal model, data, epistemology, hunting (snooping and fishing), inferential statistics, measurement, multivariate analysis, qualitative research, quantitative research, variable analysis

Key Readings

Black, T. R. (2001) *Understanding Social Science Research*, 2nd edn. London: Sage.
Blaikie, N. (2003) *Analysing Quantitative Data*. London: Sage.
Diamond, I. and Jeffries, J. (2000) *Beginning Statistics: An Introduction for Social Scientists*. London: Sage.

DEVIANT CASE ANALYSIS

Definition

The examination, in conversation analysis (CA), of examples that do not seem to fit whatever rule or pattern of conversational interaction is currently being proposed.

Distinctive Features

Conversation analysis (CA) involves listening to recordings of talk-in-interaction, alongside transcriptions, looking for robust patterns of social interaction. In particular, CA looks for rules of conversational sequencing, such as in 'adjacency pairs', invitation–refusal sequences, story-prefacing and so on. Deviant case analysis is a procedure for checking the validity and generality of whatever phenomena emerge from that inductive method. It bears comparison to hypothesis testing and falsification, as general methodological principles (cf. Mitchell, 1983). However, it has special features that make it an essential ingredient in CA.

In CA, rules of conversational sequencing are not statistically observed regularities, nor are they causal connections between one event (or turn-type) and another. Rather, they are normative patterns, in the sense that they are demonstrably used, and oriented to, by conversational participants. This means that exceptions to a conversational rule or pattern are not simple phenomena to spot, such as by using a content coding scheme of some kind. For example, it is a normative matter that greetings will be reciprocated, questions answered, invitations responded to, and so on. However, when such expectable second turns are absent, we are not forced to alter the analysis. Rather, norms are typically observed in the breach (Garfinkel, 1967), in that absences or other non-normative responses are heard and responded to as such.

What makes a case 'deviant' is not merely that it contains an oriented-to breach of some conversational norm. Rather, it is a case that seems to disconfirm the developing analysis, which will already recognize the normative status of the rule or pattern being identified. Yet the importance of deviant cases, beyond their serious status as potential disconfirmations, is that they are often examples that do turn out to demonstrate participants' normative orientations.

Stephen Clayman and Douglas Maynard (1995) define three uses of deviant cases in CA:

(1) deviant cases may turn out, upon analysis, to instantiate the same normative orientations as are proposed for the standard cases;

(2) a new analysis may be proposed that now takes full account of both the (apparently) deviant cases, and also the main set;

(3) a deviant case may turn out to exhibit a different kind of order in its own right, such that it properly belongs in a different collection.

The classic example of the second type, where a revised analysis is proposed, is an early CA study by Emanuel Schegloff (1968), on the ways in which telephone conversations routinely begin. Using a corpus of 500 examples, Schegloff had proposed a 'distribution rule for first utterances', to the effect that the person answering the call is, expectably, first to speak. One case was found to deviate from the rule. This led to a questioning and radical revision of what the rule proposed. Rather than proposing a rule in which call answerers make first turns, which might be considered first parts of a greeting exchange (for example, 'hello', answered by 'hello'), a revised rule could be proposed which accounted for all 500 cases. This was the summons–answer sequence, in which the first utterance of 'hello' (or whatever) was now understood as the second part of a different kind of pair, the answer to the summons, which was the phone ringing.

Evaluation

Deviant case analysis bears comparison to hypothesis testing, but the basic procedure remains inductive, what conversation analysts call 'unmotivated looking' (Psathas, 1995). There need be no hypothesis prior to, nor as a criterion for, data collection. Nor do we have to endorse induction, or empiricism, as general philosophical theories of knowledge and perception. Rather, induction and

deviant case analysis are matters of research policy and practice. As such, deviant case analysis provides an essential corrective to the tendency to look for confirming examples. Its special relevance in CA lies in the nature of its phenomena as normatively oriented-to, rather than frequent or causal, patterns of social interaction.

Derek Edwards

Associated Concepts: analytic induction, causality, constructionism, conversation analysis, discursive psychology, epistemology, hypothesis, induction, interpretive repertoires, transcription

Key Readings

Clayman, S. E. and Maynard, D. (1995) 'Ethnomethodology and conversation analysis', in P. ten Have and G. Psathas (eds), *Situated Order: Studies in the Social Organization of Talk and Embodied Activities*. Washington, DC: University Press of America. pp. 1–30.

Garfinkel, H. (1967) *Studies in Ethnomethodology*. Englewood Cliffs, NJ: Prentice Hall.

Mitchell, J. C. (1983) 'Case and situational analysis', *Sociological Review*, 50 (3): 273–88.

Psathas, G. (1995) *Conversation Analysis: The Study of Talk-in-Interaction*. London and Beverly Hills, CA: Sage.

Schegloff, E. A. (1968) 'Sequencing in conversational openings', *American Anthropologist*, 70: 1075–95.

DIARY

Definition

A document, generally written for personal use rather than for publication, that records events and ideas related to the particular experiences of the author. Researchers may sometimes commission the writing of diaries related to specific events and ideas as a way of acquiring relevant data.

Distinctive Features

The keeping of diaries is closely related to the growth of literacy and to a cultural orientation towards self-inspection and reflexivity. In Britain it was not until after the Reformation that diary keeping became at all common. Among the wealthier and more literate classes, diaries (as against account books and other forms of memoranda) began to be produced in large numbers from the second half of the seventeenth century. The best known – largely because they were eventually published – are those of John Evelyn and Samuel Pepys. Both wrote mainly about public affairs, though Pepys does describe aspects of his private life, and they seem to have been cast as memoirs, political commentaries and autobiographies. Because of their greater literacy and their greater concern for religious self-reflection, clergymen were prolific diarists, and many clerical diaries have also survived through publication. Prominent examples are those of Josselin, Woodforde, Kilvert, Fox and Wesley. The everyday diaries of 'ordinary' people – often little more than appointments books – are common, but rarely survive in a form suitable for research use. Many contemporary diaries are electronic. They are kept on computer and may be stored in specialist programs that combine diaries with address books, contact lists and e-mail facilities. For large numbers of people, the everyday paper diary is being replaced by a handheld electronic device.

Diaries are often assumed to be written spontaneously and contemporaneously with the events that they describe. Typically, the diarist is assumed to write his or her diary at the end of each day, so giving an insight into the immediate subjectivity of his or her experience. However, a diary account – like any account – is the outcome of a continuous, ongoing reflection. It is written at various times, is edited and rewritten periodically, and is likely to be compiled in the light of some larger goal or intention.

Some sociologists have solicited the production of diaries geared to their research interests. Respondents are asked to keep a diary for a specified period and are given a greater or lesser amount of guidance on what events and ideas are to be included in the diary. Such diaries differ from the more spontaneously produced diaries, but they are more likely to contain relevant and usable data. Researchers into time budgeting have often used this method.

Evaluation

A diary cannot be used as a reliable source in social research unless the conditions of its production are considered. Even when they have not been written for publication, diaries may be written with other people in mind: the author invariably considers the possible readers and shapes his or her material accordingly. Indeed, some diaries are produced with publication (and posterity) explicitly in mind. This is a particular issue where diaries have been solicited or commissioned by researchers.

Many diaries do not survive the deaths of their authors or are not likely to be made available to researchers. This problem has been given a new dimension by the growth of electronic diaries as these are rarely archived and so no running record is retained. It is extremely difficult to get an adequate sample of naturally occurring diaries covering issues of interest to a social researcher.

John Scott

Associated Concepts: content analysis, discourse analysis, document analysis, historical analysis, qualitative data archives, secondary analysis, trace measures, unobtrusive measures

Key Readings

Allport, G. W. (1942) *The Use of Personal Documents in Psychological Science*. New York: Social Science Research Council.
Fothergill, R. A. (1974) *Private Chronicles*. Oxford: Oxford University Press.

Matthews, W. (1950/1967) *British Diaries*. Gloucester, MA: P. Smith.

Ponsonby, A. (1923) *English Diaries*. London: Methuen.

DISABILITY RESEARCH

Definition

The examination of structural, environmental and attitudinal barriers to full participation and citizenship experienced by people with impairments, and the resistance by disabled people and their supporters to institutional discrimination.

Distinctive Features

Disability has generally been defined in an individualistic, medicalized way as an internal condition of the individual, and most research on disability reflects this orientation. Many disabled people, on the other hand, view disability in terms of social, physical and attitudinal barriers which could be removed if only the political will to do so were present.

Disability research has developed in two related directions: participatory and emancipatory approaches. Participatory approaches have developed from general qualitative methodology, often by non-disabled researchers who wish to break down the traditional hierarchical researcher–researched relationship. This can be seen, for instance, in the referral to people who are the subjects of the research as 'co-researchers' or 'research participants'. General characteristics of participatory methodology include the following:

(1) The research aims to reflect, explore and disseminate the views, feelings and experiences of research participants from their viewpoint.

(2) Participation, however, goes further to include the involvement of research participants in the design, conduct and evaluation of the actual research process.

(3) Participatory research is research with, rather than on, people.

(4) The research process is itself seen as a process of change, most often characterized as a process of empowerment.

(5) The research can also be a process of change through influencing, for instance, professional policy and practices, by reflecting the opinions of service users.

Emancipatory research, in the area of disability at least, has its roots in the growth of the Disabled People's Movement and the development of a social model of disability. The emancipatory paradigm takes the adoption of a social model of disability as the basis for research production. It can be argued that emancipatory research, unlike participatory research, is not a research methodology as such, but rather part of the struggle of disabled people to control the decision-making processes that shape their lives and to achieve full citizenship. Changing the social relations and conditions of research can be seen as part of the wider struggle to remove all forms of oppression and discrimination in the pursuit of an inclusive society.

Emancipatory research goes further than participatory research by aiming to change the social relations of research production, with disabled people taking complete control of the research process. Although certain features of participatory and emancipatory research may overlap, one common confusion is the equating of emancipatory research with the qualitative paradigm. There is no reason inherent within the nature of emancipatory research why it should adopt a qualitative methodology, as long as the research agenda is generated by disabled people themselves. For instance, emancipatory research into the housing stock and, in particular, accessibility of housing for disabled people is likely to take the form of a quantitative survey to produce statistics to influence housing policies. Participatory and emancipatory are, therefore, two distinct, though by no means incompatible, research paradigms. There are shared beliefs within the two paradigms, but the differences also need to be recognized.

In general, disability research continues to be developed both in terms of the methodology adopted, for example narrative approaches, and in terms of the arenas of social life examined, for example childhood and sexuality.

Evaluation

Key questions need to be addressed in an evaluation of disability research. First, does the research promote disabled people's control over the decision-making processes that shape their lives? The question can be directed at the decision-making processes within the research, and the empowerment of the participants through their involvement in research. Consideration of the effectiveness of the research in relation to this question hinges crucially on the constraints over control. Ultimately, the question can only be answered by disabled people themselves. A second question is: does the research address the concerns of disabled people themselves? This question can be addressed in relation to the disabled research participants, but also to the broader population of disabled people. In terms of emancipatory intentions, a key question is: does the research support disabled people in their struggle against oppression and the removal of barriers to equal opportunities and a full participatory democracy for all? This, of course, is the most difficult question to answer. Whether research can deliver anything in terms of contributing to the transformative process required by the emancipatory paradigm remains an open question (Barnes, 2003). Questions of the connection between research and social change underpin fundamental controversies in current debates in disability research.

John Swain and Sally French

Associated Concepts: anti-racism research, critical research, emancipatory research, ethnography, participatory action research, politics and social research, practitioner research, qualitative research, value-free research

Key Readings

Barnes, C. (2003) 'What a difference a decade makes: reflections on doing "emancipatory" disability research', *Disability and Society*, 18 (1): 3–18.

Barnes, C. and Mercer, G. (eds) (1997) *Doing Disability Research*. Leeds: The Disability Press.

Moore, M., Beazley, S. and Maelzer, J. (1998) *Researching Disability Issues*. Milton Keynes: Open University Press.

Oliver, M. (1992) 'Changing the social relations of research production', *Disability, Handicap and Society*, 7 (2): 101–15.

DISASTER RESEARCH

Definition

The study of the behaviour of individuals and the actions of groups and large-scale organizations as they attempt to deal with extreme, life-threatening events.

Distinctive Features

The wide range of events studied, the diversity of disciplines involved and the variety of different research methods employed are features of disaster research. Sudden-onset events causing widespread physical destruction and social disruption, such as tornadoes, hurricanes and floods, have been most frequently studied. So-called man-made or technological disasters, such as nuclear reactor accidents, massive power outages and airline disasters, have received increasing attention. More recently chronic events involving mass deprivation, such as drought and mass starvation as well as conflict situations such as civil wars, ethnic cleansing and acts of terrorism, have become subjects for some researchers.

Disaster research is a multi-disciplinary endeavour carried out independently by researchers trained in different disciplines. Disciplines represented include sociology, geography, political science, anthropology, psychology and social psychology, public administration and management science. As one might expect, both the topics studied and the methods employed to study them are diverse. The field is most closely identified with the case study method, focusing on individual and organizational actions just before, during and immediately after the onset of disasters. Qualitative or field methods such as depth interviewing and, where opportunities present themselves, non-participant observation, are commonly used in these studies. Survey research methods are used to study pre-disaster behaviour, such as household and organizational preparedness and responses to warnings and predictions, as well as post-disaster adjustments and recovery. Content analysis has been employed in studying organizational records and news media coverage of disasters. More recently it has been used in studies of the popular culture of disasters. Secondary data on a variety of social indicators have been used in statistical analyses of the long-term consequences of disasters. Historiographic methods have been employed to study a few early disasters using both archival and privately held documents. Disaster research using surveys with panel and longitudinal designs as well as controlled experiments under laboratory conditions are rare, but there are notable examples of both in the literature. In general, methods used in disaster research reflect those extant in the disciplines in which researchers have been trained.

Although studies of how individuals and organizations react in the short term to the actual onset of disasters remain common, increasing attention in recent years has been devoted to studies of longer-term adjustments such as mitigation, the physical and social changes made during periods of normalcy with the intent of reducing losses in future disasters, particularly economic costs. Newer research foci include examination of vulnerability and the vulnerable in disasters, especially along lines of class, ethnicity and gender. Studies of the role of women in disasters in particular have become increasingly more common. Studies of the popular culture of disasters, a topic of intermittent interest throughout the history of the field, have become more frequent and have dealt with subjects such as disaster humour, images of disasters in films, and disaster memorials.

Evaluation

Several unresolved issues currently confront researchers in this field, some long-standing but others of more recent origin. Most fundamental is the issue of the appropriate subject matter and boundaries of the field itself. The seemingly esoteric question 'What is a disaster?' is actually about what types of events should be studied and for what purpose. There is increasing enthusiasm for viewing disasters not as 'acts of God' or 'acts of nature' but as centrally and primarily involving human agency, that is, as the consequences of prior human decisions and actions; for including as disasters harmful chronic conditions and undesirable long-term trends; and for seeing governments as not only part of the solution to problems of disasters but also as one of the causes of disasters.

Related to this are issues of the appropriate theoretical framework for disaster research and, although still mostly latent and unrecognized, of the proper balance between researchers' roles as detached, unbiased observers and as experts whose special insights create a moral obligation to actively participate in the amelioration of the unwanted consequences of disasters. Most disaster research over the years has been atheoretical. Although some researchers recently have attempted to develop the concept of sustainability, borrowed from environmental studies, into an overarching theoretical framework, one that might also facilitate more cross-disciplinary research, most disaster research remains loosely grounded in the theoretical traditions of the disciplines noted above.

These recent developments within the field have been overrun by current events. The terrorist attacks in the United States in

2001 have created new theoretical, method-ological, and practical challenges. It is no longer possible to exclude acts of violence in their various forms from the definition of dis-aster. Disaster research is increasingly sub-ject to centralized screening processes aimed at reducing duplication of both qualitative field studies and survey research instru-ments. These challenges also include the increasing scrutiny of all research by institu-tional review boards concerned with the use of human subjects.

There remains a disparity between the world's disasters and the world of disaster research. While a majority of disasters, including the severest of them, occur in developing countries, the vast bulk of disaster studies have been conducted in a relatively small number of industrialized nations. This disparity primarily reflects the current con-centration of disaster researchers in a handful of developed countries.

Ethical questions such as 'Disaster research for whom?' and, 'Disaster research to what end?' are raised by some of these recent devel-opments but remain little discussed. Traditionally, disaster research either explicitly or implicitly has been a vehicle for improving the quality of emergency services provided by governments and nonprofit organizations. This 'top-down' philosophy is reflected in the proliferation of university-based degree programmes in emergency management. Increasing attention to categories of people who are especially vulnerable in disasters has been accompanied by the rise of a competing philosophy. A 'grass roots' strategy is implied, one that would empower those especially vul-nerable in disasters – women, the poor, indige-nous populations – enabling them to improve their overall situation.

Robert A. Stallings

Associated Concepts: case study method, content analyses, ethics, fieldwork, GIS, lon-gitudinal study, politics and social research, sensitive research, social indicators

Key Readings

Drabek, T. E. (1986) *Human System Responses to Disaster: An Inventory of Sociological Findings*. New York: Springer-Verlag.

Quarantelli, E. L. (eds) (1998) *What Is a Disaster? Perspectives on the Question*. London and New York: Routledge.

Perry, R. W. and Quarantelli, E. L. (eds) (2004) *What Is a Disaster? New Perspectives on Old Questions*. Philadelphia, PA: Xlibris.

Stallings, R. A. (ed.) (2002) *Methods of Disaster Research*. Philadelphia, PA: Xlibris.

Tierney, K. J., Lindell, M. K. and Perry, R. W. (2001) *Facing the Unexpected: Disaster Preparedness and Response in the United States*. Washington, DC: Joseph Henry Press.

Wisner, B., Blaikie, P., Cannon, T. and Davis, I. (2003) *At Risk: Natural Hazards, People's Vulnerability and Disasters*, 2nd edn. London: Routledge.

DISASTROUS RESEARCH

Definition

Research that is either not accomplished or is low in validity.

Distinctive Features

There may be several reasons for the non-completion of a research project. For example, access to the research field or to the research subjects may be denied by gatekeepers. Also, the nature of the research topic may be such that it becomes too dangerous to continue with fieldwork. Even where a project is completed its findings and conclusions may not enter the public domain because of promises made to the research subjects via a research bargain, or because sponsors of research refuse to sanc-tion publication as a result of not being happy with conclusions or because they see them as a threat to their interests.

Research can be low in validity because of issues of measurement, explanation or generalization. Measurement validity refers to the extent to which a researcher measures what he or she intends to. Where a researcher uses a faulty measure or one that fails to capture the full extent of the concept under consideration the findings will be low in validity. Even if the measures can be trusted it is possible that the researcher may fail to provide an adequate explanation by not including all relevant variables or by falsely treating correlations between variables as sufficient evidence of a causal relationship. This is the issue of validity of explanation, or internal validity. Even where reasonably valid conclusions have been reached they will be specific to the subjects and the contexts under consideration. However, researchers typically aim to generalize and make wider claims. Where such wider claims are not justified the research will be low in validity of generalization, or external validity. This may be because the research subjects are not typical or representative of the wider population about which researchers wish conclusions to be made.

Evaluation

The above issues underline the importance of decision making about research in order to anticipate, as far as possible, the potential problems of carrying out and publishing research and the various threats to the validity of conclusions. No research is perfect in execution and validity is always relative. Decision making about research is about trade-offs between the strengths and weaknesses of different research strategies and designs in order to maximize the likelihood of accomplishing research and maximizing the validity of its findings.

Victor Jupp

Associated Concepts: access, dangerous fieldwork, gatekeeper, politics and social research, validity

Key Reading

Jupp, V. R. (1996) *Methods of Criminological Research*. London: Routledge. ch. 5.

DISCOURSE ANALYSIS

Definition

Detailed exploration of political, personal, media or academic 'talk' and 'writing' about a subject, designed to reveal how knowledges are organized, carried and reproduced in particular ways and through particular institutional practices.

Distinctive Features

Discourse analysis is a generic term covering a heterogeneous number of theoretical approaches and analytical constructs. It derives, in the main, from linguistics, semiotics, social psychology, cultural studies and post-structural social theory. It is primarily a qualitative method of 'reading' texts, conversations and documents which explores the connections between language, communication, knowledge, power and social practices. In short, it focuses upon the meaning and structure (whether overt or hidden) of acts of communication in context.

Numerous types of discourse-based research can be identified. For example, a branch of linguistics might be concerned with providing systematic accounts of conversational exchanges in particular settings, whilst some areas of psychology might explore the effect of discourse structure on recall and memory. However, the broad appeal of discourse analysis to social researchers lies in its ability to reveal how institutions and individual subjects are formed, produced, given meaning, constructed and represented through particular configurations of knowledge. Potter and Wetherell (1994) identify three key concerns which characterize the research practice of discourse analysis:

(1) locating talk and texts as social practices;
(2) identifying processes of action, construction and variability;
(3) recognizing the rhetorical or argumentative organization of talk and texts.

Much of this derives from the work of Foucault (1972) and his 'archaeology' of the knowledges, 'interpretive repertoires' and practices of medicine. He used the concept of discourse to counter positivist and scientific claims to the 'truth' and to identify the mechanisms whereby some versions of 'truth' come to be accepted and internalized, whilst other readings are marginalized, discredited or discarded. Power is realized not through overt coercion but by a steady acceptance by all that a coherent text underlies all apparent contradictions and paradoxes. Discourses are 'practices which form the objects of which they speak' (Foucault, 1972: 49). Through interacting with text/talk we interpret experience through structures already available to us and in doing so lend those structures a solidity and normality which is difficult to move outside of (Mills, 1997). In different ways all of us are regularly addressed by discourses that position and place us. They remind us of who we are and what might be expected of us in different social situations. Neither do discourses operate in isolation. At one and the same time we may be positioned as a customer, a citizen, a consumer, a member of the public, a taxpayer, a worker, a public service user and so on. Neither are our subject positions fixed and stable. In turn this raises the questions of contradiction and contestation. Whilst Foucault's analysis tends to disempower the subject as a passive recipient of discourse, some Marxist and feminist scholars have identified the negotiated, contingent and dynamic nature of discursive activity. Discourses can also be refused, contested and critiqued (Mills, 1997).

The revealing of how text and talk produce identifiable subject positions is one of the basic skills of the discourse analyst. Data may be collected from any number of sources from legal statutes and media reports to diaries and personal testimonies. Identifying

their explicit and implicit discourses can be achieved in a number of ways. For example, in deconstructing policy documents the researcher might ask:

- What are the conditions out of which this text emerged? What are the social, cultural and political conditions which made this text possible?
- What traces of other texts (intertextuality) are evident in the text?
- How consistent, contradictory or coherent is the text? How are contradictions managed?
- How are people, objects and thought categorized? Who and what are included/excluded?
- Who and what are viewed as normal, natural and common sense?
- Are there any gaps, silences or 'absent presences'?
- What is presented as legitimate/illegitimate?
- Who are assumed to be the primary readers of the text? What assumptions are being made about the audience?
- What are the likely social effects of the text?
- What alternative readings might be made by different social groups?

These questions force the researcher to look beyond the immediate message of a text to reveal how it produces and disseminates particular ways of knowing. Importantly this does not simply end at a level of identifying multiple interpretations but in gaining insights into how some discourses come to be taken as more legitimate than others. In other words, discourses not only have tangible material effects, but can be contested and resisted by counter discourses and social practices.

Evaluation

It is easier to trace the theoretical underpinnings of discourse analysis than to identify and describe the formal processes of actually carrying out such research. This is partly due to the often intuitive and reflexive nature of the skills involved. How then do we know that one 'reading' is to be preferred over another? Discourse analysts would respond by arguing that no social research can ever be fixed and objective. A single 'true' reading of social realities, by whatever method, is an impossibility. Discourse analysis is then just as valid as any other. Moreover, despite such concerns over the relativity of this knowledge, the process of producing a reading allows us to discuss, compare and challenge multiple readings and the processes through which they were arrived at. The methodology of discourse analysis then emphasizes the importance of being reflexive and open to competing knowledge claims. The avoidance of formulaic analyses and commitment to be open to the new insights that a particular text/talk might provide remain vital. The importance of this method will remain in its linking of methodological challenges about how we acquire knowledge to epistemological challenges about the nature of knowledge itself. It will continue to play an important role in encouraging critical readings not only of conventional research methods but also of established modes of understanding.

John Muncie

Associated Concepts: constructionism, conversation analysis, critical research, deconstruction, discursive psychology, epistemology, interpretive repertoires, postmodernism, textual analysis

Key Readings

Foucault, M. (1972) *The Archaeology of Knowledge.* London: Tavistock.
Mills, S. (1997) *Discourse.* London: Routledge.
Phillips, N. and Hardy, C. (2002) *Discourse Analysis.* London: Sage.
Potter, J. and Wetherell, M. (1994) 'Analysing discourse', in A. Bryman and R. Burgess (eds), *Analysing Qualitative Data.* London: Routledge.
Wetherell, M., Taylor, S. and Yates, S. (eds) (2001) *Discourse Theory and Practice.* London: Sage.

DISCRIMINANT FUNCTION ANALYSIS

Definition

A form of multivariate analysis which uses a number of independent variables, measured at interval level, to predict the category or group to which a person might belong.

Distinctive Features

The discriminant function is a multiple regression equation in which category or group membership is treated as the dependent variable. It is also a categorical variable whereas the independent or predictor variables are measured on an interval scale. For example, if the research aim is to predict voting preference in terms of either Republican or Democrat the dependent variable will be treated as having only two values (say, Republican = 1, Democrat = 0). A range of independent variables will then be introduced to discriminate between those voting Republican and those voting Democrat. The analysis can also indicate the relative importance of different independent variables in predicting category or group membership. Discriminant function analysis (DFA) can be used where the dependent variable involves more than two categories.

Some researchers use DFA as an alternative to multiple regression to predict the values of a discriminating variable, especially where there is interest in the explanatory power of a categorical variable such as gender. For example, assume that the aim is to predict respondents' incomes from social class, occupational status, level of educational qualifications and gender. The analysis can proceed by using the discriminant function to predict gender from social class, occupational status and level of educational qualifications. The percentage explained by the combination of these variables will be given by R-squared. If income is subsequently introduced into the equation and there is a significant increase in R-squared this would indicate that income is an important variable and that men and women differ in terms of income when the other variables have been allowed for.

Evaluation

The value of discriminant function analysis is that it can incorporate categorical variables as dependent variables in multivariate analysis. The limitations relate to statistical assumptions which must be met: for example, the discriminating variables must be on an interval scale and also it is assumed that groups being studied are drawn from populations within which the discriminating variables are normally distributed.

Logistic regression analysis is sometimes used as an alternative to DFA because it requires fewer assumptions. It also predicts dichotomous or categorical variables, but this is usually in the form of whether something will occur, for example whether individuals with particular characteristics are likely to graduate or offend.

Victor Jupp

Associated Concepts: causal model, general linear model, hypothesis, hunting (snooping and fishing), log-linear analysis, prediction, SPSS

Key Readings

Byrne, D. (2002) *Interpreting Quantitative Data.* London: Sage.
Sapsford, R. and Jupp, V. (1996) *Data Collection and Analyses.* London: Sage.

DISCURSIVE PSYCHOLOGY

Definition

A strand of discourse analysis developed out of the work of Billig (1996), Potter and Wetherell (1987) and Edwards and Potter (1992) as an alternative to the type of psychology that uses cognitive theories and experimental methods. Most specifically, discursive psychology is a research perspective that considers psychology as an object *in* and *for* interaction. More generally, it is a distinct form of discourse analysis in its own right.

Distinctive Features

Discursive psychology (DP) focuses on how psychology is used by people in everyday and institutional settings as a part of descriptions, constructions and orientations. It asks what psychological categories and constructions are used *for*, and studies the *practices* in which they are used. Rather than trying to explain actions as a consequence of inner entities and processes (cognitivism) it focuses on their role in performing actions through talk and texts. While theory and method in cognitive psychology presume an out-there reality that provides input to cognitive operations, discursive psychology focuses on the way both 'reality' and 'mind' are constructed by people conceptually, in language, in the course of their execution of various practical tasks (Edwards, 1997; Potter, 1996).

Take the example of scripts. In cognitive psychology scripts are mentally encoded templates that guide action in situationally appropriate ways. In DP the topic becomes how script formulations are used by people themselves in situated discourse to perform particular actions (for example, to present a speaker as acting in a normative manner or, conversely, as driven by specific psychological dispositions). The orderliness (or not) of what someone has done can be constructed *in* the interaction for the purposes *of* the interaction. Rather than scripts existing as cognitively represented entities driving interaction, then, in discursive terms they are inseparable from action, bound up with the practical and moral world of accountability (Edwards, 1997).

Consider the following example from a relationship counselling session, where 'Connie' is characterizing the solidity of her marriage (in contrast to the disruption caused by her partner's recent affair):

1   *Counsellor:*   Whe:n: (.) before you moved over
                    here how was
2   the marriage.
3   (0.4)
4   *Connie:*   ↑O↓h. (0.2) I– (.) to me: all alo:ng,
                    (.)right
5   up to now, (0.2) my marriage was
                    rock solid.
6   (0.8) Rock solid.= We had argu-
                    ments like
7   everybody else had arguments,
                    (0.4) buthh (0.2)
8   to me there was no major problems.
                    (Edwards, 1997: 154)

Note the way having arguments is here script formulated as characteristic of all marriages (and thereby discountable as an explanation of the *specific* problems that led this couple to counselling).

The theoretical and analytic development of DP enables it to do justice to the status of practices as practices. That is, it focuses on the way discourse is oriented to action, situated and co-constructed in stretches of interaction, and given sense through the categories and formulations of participants.

DP's analytic approach is guided by three broad themes:

(1) *Discourse is situated.* Discourse is (a) *occasioned* in the conversation analytic sense; that is, talk and texts are reflexively related to their position in interaction (Hutchby and Wooffitt, 1998) and (b) rhetorically oriented, often designed to counter actual or potential alternative versions (Billig, 1991).

(2) *Discourse is action-oriented.* DP focuses on how discourse is involved in actions and practices as people do their jobs, live their relationships, relate as professionals and clients and so on.

(3) *Discourse is constructed.* DP asks two kinds of constructionist question: (a) how is discourse itself constructed out of metaphors, rhetorical devices, categories, interpretative repertoires and so on? and (b) how is discourse used to construct versions of the world in the service of particular activities?

Take the script example above. Connie's description of her marriage uses particular terms (3a) to construct a version of the marriage that presents it as unexceptional (3b). This description is delivered in response to a question in a counselling session (1a) and works to counter her husband's account of their marriage having long-standing problems (1b). Overall, it helps construct her partner as to blame for the marriage problems and as the one who may need to change in response to counselling (2).

Evaluation

DP is a relatively new social science perspective. Its success has come from the provision of a rigorous way of working with records of interaction (rather than the output measures and variable relations that are the staple of more traditional social and cognitive psychology). It has been particularly successful in explicating interaction in complex multi-party settings, whether everyday or institutional.

There is some controversy over whether DP will complement or supplant more traditional forms of psychology. There is live debate over its relation to, for example, perspectives such as psychoanalysis (Billig, 1999). Currently most clarity results from pressing a thoroughgoing DP perspective and seeing where more traditional psychological notions are required. Its success in providing rich analyses of classically individual, private notions such as emotion suggests that it can be developed further.

Questions arise as to the relation of DP to conversation analysis. Do the two perspectives complement one another, or is there important conflict between their conceptualization of the nature of cognition? There is no clear resolution to this question at present (see Te Molder and Potter, 2004).

A recent theme in DP has been the development of a discursive psychology of institutions. This is focused on the role of psychological categories and orientations to do specific institutional business. For example, how do a caller and a child protection officer collaboratively use psychological constructions in performing important tasks at the start of calls to a child protection helpline (Potter and Hepburn, 2003)?

Jonathan Potter

Associated Concepts: constructionism, conversation analysis, discourse analysis, interpretive repertoires, naturalistic data, reflexivity

Key Readings

Billig, M. (1991) *Ideologies and Beliefs.* London: Sage.

Billig, M. (1996) *Arguing and Thinking: A Rhetorical Approach to Social Psychology*, 2nd edn. Cambridge: Cambridge University Press.

Billig, M. (1999) *Freudian Repression: Conversation Creating the Unconscious.* Cambridge: Cambridge University Press.

Edwards, D. (1997) *Discourse and Cognition.* London and Beverly Hills, CA: Sage.

Edwards, D. and Potter, J. (1992) *Discursive Psychology.* London: Sage.

Hutchby, I. and Wooffitt, R. (1998) *Conversation Analysis: Principles, Practices and Applications.* Cambridge: Polity Press.

Potter, J. (1996) *Representing Reality: Discourse, Rhetoric and Social Construction.* London: Sage.

Potter, J. and Hepburn, A. (2003) 'I'm a bit concerned – early actions and psychological constructions in a child protection helpline', *Research on Language and Social Interaction*, 36: 197–240.

Potter, J. and Wetherell, M. (1987) *Discourse and Social Psychology: Beyond Attitudes and Behaviour.* London: Sage.

Te Molder, H. and Potter, J. (eds) (2004) *Talk and Cognition: Discourse, Mind and Social Interaction.* Cambridge: Cambridge University Press.

DOCUMENT ANALYSIS

Definition

The detailed examination of documents produced across a wide range of social practices, taking a variety of forms from the written word to the visual image. The significance of the documents may be located in the historical circumstances of production, in their circulation and reception of the item and also the social functions, interpretations, effects and uses that may be associated with them.

Distinctive Features

A wide range of documents is available to the social researcher. Personal items such as diaries, letters, *aide-mémoires*, shopping lists and photographs produced as part of everyday existence may form a *private documentary* record, evidence of the way lives are lived and how the social world is engaged with by individuals and social groups at different times and in different places. Life is usually recorded by a birth certificate, accompanied by a passport or identity card and may be concluded by a death certificate. Although involving intensely personal meanings, these documents are produced by or on behalf of the state and like so much documentary material the information carried there is part of *public documentation*.

Places of work, commercial and public organizations and educational institutions are amongst the many economic, social and cultural organizations that produce documents that are of interest to research. These may range, for example, from contracts of employment to till receipts and records of educational achievement and offer information about people's lives, work and leisure and the social and economic relations they enter into.

The continuing development of technology and the recent expansion of telecommunications and the mass media have added to the amount and number of forms that documents take, from the hand production of written and visual documentation to the mechanical production of printed material and reproduction of mass media documents. Although document analysis is usually of the written word other forms of communication must be accounted for (Prior, 2003: 5). Radio, cinema and television generate a prolific twenty-first century display of visual, textual, oral and sonic document forms. As with all documents, these have a variety of social functions, including information, leisure and social control functions. A television advertisement, for example, is a ubiquitous example of a mass media document, loaded with commercial and social information, styles, ideas, attitudes, values, persuasions and ideologies and circulated widely, through multiple broadcasts and receptions. Internet websites represent commercial, governmental, educational and other organizational interests and exist alongside personal websites and individually managed 'blogs', the frequently updated web journals, that make up the pages of virtual documentation. So there is a wide range of documents out there waiting to be analysed, and the social researcher will pose questions about document availability and reasons for retention but will also recognize that not all social facts have been documented and that not all documents are available to research.

Evaluation

A series of essential criteria is applied to the analysis of documents. Questions about the document's authenticity, credibility, representativeness and meaning are the usual starting points (Scott, 1990). Establishing the authentic nature of a document, that it was produced by the author or authorizing body ascribed to it, leads into wider issues of the nature and circumstances of the document's production. An exploration of the encoding process, the procedure of selection and putting into place the words, images or other elements that make up the content of the document is important not least in a consideration of any meaning the document may come to have (Hall, 2001). The credibility of the document as evidence hinges on the truth and accuracy of its reference and how widely it represents the phenomena the researcher is investigating. For example, questions of authenticity regarding an inscription on a public building or monument commemorating a historical event may be few but questions of why, how and whose interest the document serves may be many.

A content analysis of documents will tend towards a systematic and enumerative approach in order to quantify the frequency of elements within documents (such as words or images) or the quantity of similar types of document. Typically, this kind of analysis is concerned with the manifest content of a document and is usually associated with the positivist tradition of social research. Textual analysis on the other hand is usually thought of as being part of the qualitative and interpretivist tradition. Here emphasis is less on the amount and frequency of occurrences and more on interpreting the meaning the document might have. Semiology, the study of signs, identifies words and especially images as signs that offer complex meanings or significations beyond the surface of the text. Linguistic analysis explores the use and meaning of words and phrases. The analysis of a television advertisement as a social document might require both enumerative and textual analysis to give an indication of its frequency and potency.

Further areas of inquiry investigate document interpretation, recognizing that different people will interpret or 'decode' documents in various ways which may be different to the producer's or 'encoder's' intentions. Documents may have an effect, change or reinforce a belief, attitude or form of behaviour, but in certain circumstances the recipient of the document message may choose to use the message for other purposes. For example, the health warning appearing on a packet of cigarettes may provide a wealth of documentary information and make an unambiguous statement about the nature of the product, but this message might be interpreted by the user and acted upon in a variety of ways. This is often characterized as a 'field of action', an area of activity centred on the document, where the document message as intended by the producer may become diffuse amongst a social group or may be interpreted and reinterpreted through discussion and use (Prior, 2003: 2). The cutting, pasting and reassembling of electronic documents through computer technology is a good example of the latter.

Chris Wharton

Associated Concepts: content analysis, discourse analysis, diary, idiographic, netnography, qualitative data archives, textual analysis, unobtrusive measures

Key Readings

Hall, S. (2001) 'Encoding/decoding', in M. G. Durham and D. M. Kellner (eds), *Media and Cultural Studies Keyworks*. Oxford: Blackwell.

Prior, L. (2003) *Using Documents in Social Research*. London: Sage.

Scott, J. (1990) *A Matter of Record*. Cambridge: Polity Press.

E

ECOLOGICAL FALLACY

Definition

The failure to distinguish between a correlation where the unit of analysis is indivisible (for example, an individual person) and one where the statistical object is a group or area.

Distinctive Features

An ecological correlation exists where the researcher is interested in the prevalence of a particular phenomenon in a group or area. Ecological correlations are often used because data about individuals are not available, and mounting a study to collect such data would be costly. However, the researcher should not then make inferences about the behaviour of individuals based on the ecological data. For example, there may be a positive correlation between levels of unemployment in police force areas and the crime rate in those areas. This is not, however, the same as comparing unemployment and offending amongst a number of individuals. To confuse the two types of correlation is an ecological fallacy. (For further comment on this example see Farrington et al., 1986). While a relationship may be found between the levels of unemployment and the levels of crime in police force areas, it does not follow that if individuals in those areas were sampled a correlation would necessarily be found between levels of unemployment and levels of offending for the individuals in the samples.

Evaluation

The dangers of drawing conclusions about individuals based on ecological correlations were highlighted by a number of studies during the 1930s in the United States. These have been considered in an article in the *American Sociological Review* which demonstrated the mathematical relationship between ecological and individual correlations (Robinson, 1950). Robinson explains that while individual correlation and ecological correlation both depend on the within-areas individual correlations, they do so in different ways:

> The individual correlation depends upon the *internal* frequencies of the within-areas individual correlations, while the ecological correlation depends on the *marginal* frequencies of the within-areas individual correlations. ... The within-areas marginal frequencies which determine the percentages from which the ecological correlation is computed do not fix the internal frequencies which determine the individual correlation. Thus, there need be no correspondence between the individual correlation and the ecological correlation. (Robinson, 1950: 354)

The size of ecological correlations is affected by the number of sub-areas. For example, the size of an ecological correlation can depend on whether the unit involved is a county, a city, a district and so on. The size of the ecological correlation between two variables for a county may be affected by the fact that the correlation for the county is based on correlations for local authorities within those counties.

The danger of confusing individual and aggregate data is noted (again by Farrington, 1992) in discussing trends in juvenile delinquency. It is pointed out that whereas a great deal is known about correlates of juvenile offending based on studies of individuals, it is aggregate variables relating to neighbourhoods, such as measures of social disorganization, that are most useful in explaining variations in regional or national delinquency rates. The two should not, however, be confused. Another example can be found in a study in which two American researchers reported that the greater the airtime devoted to country music, the greater the white suicide rate (Stack and Gundlach, 1992). The study was based on data for 49 metropolitan areas in the United States. Although further analysis of the data showed that the association was independent of divorce rates, poverty and gun availability, because the data were based on metropolitan area rates, it does not necessarily follow that individual people who listen to country music more than others are more likely to commit suicide than those who listen to it less. Even were such an individual level correlation to be found, this does not mean that listening to country music *causes* people to commit suicide; consideration also needs to be given to the possibility that the suicidally inclined find solace in listening to country music.

Iain Crow

Associated Concepts: causality, correlation, qualitative research, variable analysis

Key Readings

Farrington, D. P. (1992) 'Trends in English juvenile delinquency and their explanation', *International Journal of Comparative and Applied Criminal Justice*, 16 (2): 151–63.
Farrington, D. P., Gallagher, B., Morley, L., St Ledger, R. J. and West, D. J. (1986) 'Unemployment, school leaving and crime', *British Journal of Criminology*, 26 (4): 335–56.

Robinson, W. S. (1950) 'Ecological correlation and the behaviour of individuals', *American Sociological Review*, 15: 351–7.
Stack, S. and Gundlach, J. (1992) 'The effect of country music on suicide', *Social Forces*, 71 (1): 211–18.

ECONOMETRICS

Definition

The study of economic theory, and the application of economic principles using a mathematical or statistical approach.

Distinctive Features

Traditional classic econometric analysis comprises a number of steps.

Step 1 Stating a hypothesis. The hypothesis can be based upon theory and/or empirical findings. It can be a result of intuition, questions arising from prior reading or work-based findings. However, the aim of econometrics is to address the hypothesis utilizing a quantitative analysis as opposed to a qualitative approach.

Step 2 Stating any prior assumptions about the hypothesis in a mathematical form. Once we have stated the hypothesis we need to give it form. In econometrics this is based around the use of mathematical equations.

Step 3 Specifying the nature of the econometric model. Specifying assumptions about our hypothesis, using equations, assumes that we can exactly model the phenomena we are studying. The complex interrelationships, which exist in the most simplest of economic phenomena, make this assumption highly questionable. Therefore in order to accommodate this we derive an econometric model which allows us to introduce these imperfections into the study. This is done by adding an error term to the equations used in the model.

Step 4 Data collection. Data collection in econometrics is vital for success. Success does not solely mean gaining results from our analysis which support the hypothesis. Success here should be read in broader terms, that is, having confidence in the results, and in the validity and meaning of the conclusions. Econometrics tends to be based upon large amounts of data, although considerable breakthroughs in theory and principles have been found using small data sets. The general rule is 'bigger is better'.

Step 5 Utilization of statistical/mathematical procedures aimed at answering the hypothesis. Once the data have been collected an analysis has to be undertaken. The two most popular forms of analysis in econometrics are multiple regression and time series analysis. However, there are other techniques, and the researcher should strategically choose in advance which techniques are best suited to answer the hypothesis, and the level of confidence required. In the main, econometric models are multivariate models.

Step 6 Utilization of findings. This is for the purposes of forecasting, adding to knowledge or theory and formulating or evaluating policy. In this respect there can be differences between econometrics and other disciplines. Some disciplines are only concerned with finding out whether there is a relationship between the dependent variable and the independent variable(s), and the nature of that relationship. Econometrics takes this further by utilizing this information and predicting events, which may follow as a result of it.

Evaluation

This model of econometrics is known as the classical model. Alternative models or approaches do exist. Wojciech, Charemza and Deadman (1992) highlight the shortcomings of the classical model and suggest a range of alternative approaches which are in line with the evolution of complementary disciplines such as mathematics and statistics and the development of computer hardware and software.

Whatever the type of approach chosen to perform an econometric analysis there are a number of issues that need to be considered. First, there is the question of whether it is possible to reduce economic phenomena to a mathematical or statistical form which reflects reality. Second, there is the issue of whether it is possible to adapt the mathematical form into an econometric model ready for testing. Simply adding an error term to an equation may be viewed as a rather naive approach in attempting to construct an econometric model. Third, there are general research issues regarding the ability to gather data, whether samples are representative and whether results are generalizable. Econometrics places a good deal of importance on the ability of a derived model to accurately forecast and predict what will happen in the future given a certain set of circumstances. The validity of forecasts and predictions is very much dependent on whether these questions and issues can be addressed successfully.

Paul E. Pye

Associated Concepts: causal model, forecasting, hypothesis, modelling, multivariate analysis, prediction, quantitative research, regression analysis, SPSS, time series design

Key Readings

Carter Hill, R., Griffiths, W.E. and George, G. (2001) *Undergraduate Econometrics*, 2nd edn. New York: Wiley.
Maddala, G. S. (2001) *Introduction to Econometrics*, 3rd edn. New York: Wiley.
Wojciech, W., Charemza, W. and Deadman, D. F. (1992) *New Directions in Econometric Practice: General to Specific Modelling, Cointegration and Vector Autoregression*. Aldershot: Edward Elgar.

ELITE INTERVIEWING

Definition

The use of interviews to study those at the 'top' of any stratification system, be it in sport, academia, social status, religion, beauty or whatever. In practice, however, elite research focuses mainly on political and economic notables. The study of elites touches on some of the major and perennial issues of social analysis. The views and activities of generals, businessmen, politicians and church leaders have been of concern to social thinkers since the earliest days of Western thought.

Distinctive Features

The study of elites exhibits a considerable diversity of research techniques, reflecting the many substantive purposes such study serves, as well as the wide range of evidence elites typically generate. These include written and printed materials, such as speeches, diaries and autobiographies. There are also behavioural data, such as voting records, secretarial diaries and judicial decisions. Then there are the much-used personal and biographical statistics in standard publications. However, a further source is now used quite frequently – the personal interview. Of course, this is not always a viable option. Elites can pose considerable problems of access for scholars even in relatively open cultural milieux.

Where elite interviewing is possible, its value will depend on the particular research objectives. In some cases, interviewing would be laboriously inefficient, such as for questions of elite social composition, where published sources would normally be better. In other cases, elite interviews may serve only in a secondary role, for example, to gain access to private documents. But certainly there are times when interviewing can be appropriately used as the principal means of inquiry.

There are three broad needs that face-to-face contact can help fulfil. Above all, through interviewing, elites may provide first-hand information about their personal backgrounds, outlooks and motivations. Secondly, interviews might also be undertaken where the elites serve as experts. It is often the case that such individuals have unique experiences as 'insiders', enabling them to comment upon events or evidence, provide interpretations and suggest fruitful lines of further inquiry. Thirdly, elites may serve as gatekeepers who, formally or informally, control access to needed data sources. These may be official records, internal reports, or even other individuals. Interviewing the person at the top may simply be aimed at gaining institutional rapport and 'unlocking the door'.

Elite interviewing requires careful preparation. First, the specific individuals must be located and selected. This may be problematic even in 'open' milieux. Furthermore, there is an array of varied selection procedures (for example, positional, reputational, decisional), each with its own well-known virtues and faults. Often, however, the elite may be readily identifiable, and simply be 'important' individuals worth studying.

Gaining quality access to particular individuals once selected can also pose problems. In part it is, again, a matter of the relevant elite and legal milieu. It also depends on the image of the potential interviewer, the research project or even of the host institution or social science in general. Often, one help can be some link with the interviewer that the interviewee values. Perceived ideological, social or even sartorial or gender similarities may also have the same effect. On the other hand, links and similarities can handicap the interviewer as a neutral 'outsider'.

Access is also influenced by the research agenda, some agendas being very sensitive in particular circumstances or to particular elites. This may lead to outright (and revealing) refusals or to a reduced level of cooperativeness that may not be immediately apparent. In general, it is a cost–benefit situation where the interviewees especially weigh the pluses and the minuses of the exchange. Such considerations bear on the selection and preparation of the interviewer. In some instances, professional interviewers have been successfully employed. More typically, however, the researcher acts as interviewer because of the substantive and technical demands of the situation.

This means that, even for the scholar–interviewer, there is a heavy premium upon personal prior preparation. He or she will be assumed to be, within limits, an expert by the elite respondent. This entails familiarization with the values, terminology and significant reference points likely to be used by respondents. Without this capacity to demonstrate familiarity, valuable data gathering opportunities may be lost and, not least, trust and rapport may be compromised. In general, sound preparation will always be rewarded and poor preparation revealed.

Elite interviews, as noted, potentially serve varied purposes. They may also take varied forms. Some, for example, involve lengthy in-depth encounters over a period of several meetings while others are brief one-offs. Equally, the format may differ according to the degree of structure or standardization employed – the order in which topics are raised, the way specific questions are asked, and whether closed or open-ended responses are allowed. Some are fully structured, while others have limited, or almost no, structure.

Evaluation

The choice as to type of interview is a matter of weighing different considerations. Issues need to be raised, such as whether the end-product of the study is to emphasize the qualitative and particular, or the quantitative and general; technically, how much control the researcher is willing to cede to the interviewee, and how much procrustean structure the latter will tolerate; practically, whether the needed interviews will be very numerous. In general, considerations tend to militate against the fully structured interview. It is precisely because elite individuals are important repositories of expertise, with unique experiences, and often-sophisticated intellectual capacities, that many scholars find less structured formats are generally preferable. Here, the researcher can define the agenda in broad terms, but the respondents are allowed scope to respond to its constituent parts in *their* own particular terms. Interviews also tend to be one-offs. The typical elite individual has a very demanding schedule that rarely permits extended discussion, although surprisingly many make themselves available. Only exceptionally, such as for retired elites, is time not a pressing issue.

The most important ingredient for the success of elite interviewing is trust and rapport. Usually this requires a stance of empathetic neutrality but, on occasion, a challenging style may be needed to get some respondents to open up. However, scholars (unlike media interviewers) have few sanctions at their disposal, and hence threatening stances can mean failure. In general, experience shows that elite interviews can be highly variable in quality, ranging from the unproductive and uninformative to the essential and highly insightful. It is a matter of using interviewing appropriately, preparing well and being aware of the relevant problems.

George Moyser

Associated Concepts: access, decision-making research, elite selection, ethnographic interviewing, gatekeeper, interview, politics and social research, research bargain

Key Readings

Dexter, L. A. (1970) *Elite and Specialized Interviewing*. Evanston, IL: Northwestern University Press.

Field, G. L. and Highley, J. (1980) *Elitism*. London: Routledge & Kegan Paul.

Marcus, G. E. (ed.) (1983) *Elites: Ethnographic Issues*. Albuquerque, NM: University of New Mexico Press.

Moyser, G. and Wagstaffe, M. (eds) (1987) *Research Methods for Elite Studies*. London: Allen & Unwin.

Parry, G. (1969) *Political Elites*. London: Allen & Unwin.

ELITE SELECTION

Definition

A form of research which seeks to identify and select elite individuals in social groupings, communities, organizations and society as a whole in order to address a range of questions, for example, about their social networks, their influence and their power.

Distinctive Features

Social theorists have long recognized that human society manifests a fundamental inequality in the way that it is organized. Whether from differences of ability or from such collective social imperatives as the need for authority, there is an observed tendency for society to produce individuals who are especially influential, dominant or noteworthy – 'top people' in their chosen sphere. Various classical theorists, such as Pareto, Mosca and Michels have argued that these individuals constitute a single elite group with a certain collective self-consciousness, ideological coherence and commonality of action. As such, the elite would form a particularly dominant element in society. Much analysis, therefore, has been done to test these views empirically.

Today, theorists tend to recognize that there can be many elite groups, one for each sphere of social action, in education, sport, the arts, even criminal activity. These have all received some attention – social celebrities and the glitterati as elites, for example. But, following the classical tradition, most attention is still reserved for those elites who have the greatest potential influence over society as a whole – top individuals in government, the economy and military affairs (Putnam, 1976; Scott, 1990). How are they recruited, renewed and replaced? What are their views and social backgrounds? What influences do they exert in shaping the goals of society, in maintaining and integrating society? Above all, to what extent do these individuals form a unified elite, tied together through social and ideological networks, and capable of being a 'power elite' or a 'ruling class' for the rest of society?

To answer such questions, particular elite individuals must first be identified and then selected for further analysis. But as substantive questions of influences and power are involved, there has been considerable disagreement about the appropriate selection methods to be used. In the debate, three generic methodological approaches have emerged, each reflecting different views about the nature of power and how it should be located and observed. Theory and method, in other words, are here closely interwoven.

Selection by position A common view of modern societies is that power is institutionalized – it is a function of formal offices within certain social institutions. The powerful, then, are those individuals who occupy key positions in government, party committees, commercial and industrial corporations and public bureaucracies. On this basis, the members of the elite are identified and selected by determining which formal offices are powerful. Such decisions can be difficult, particularly at the margins and in relatively 'closed' societies and sub-cultures (see Moyser and Wagstaffe, 1987). But, in general, information is often available that can make the process relatively straightforward. As a result, positional analysis is commonly used as a selection method (see Mills, 1954, for example). It is not, however, uncontroversial. Even in modern societies, power is not always solely a function of formal office, but also of other less tangible factors as suggested by the phenomenon of the *eminence grise*, the person of 'real' power behind the façade of the throne. As a result, individuals may be selected into the elite who should be excluded, and other individuals left out who should be included.

Selection by reputation To try to remedy such problems, selection by reputation has been employed, using a method originated by Hunter (1953). This approach treats power as being potentially either formal or informal. For Hunter, therefore, the elite is best uncovered by the broader notion of reputation than by institutional position. The method centrally involves a set of expert judges who select the elite by their general reputation of power. The elites are then, in turn, asked to nominate others for inclusion. One key potential weakness of this method is the reliance it places on the views of the judges. This may be ill-informed, confused or even deliberately biased about the structure of power. Some researchers have indeed found that different panels of judges produce different lists of elite individuals.

Selection by decision making A third selection method focuses on the analysis of particular decisions, or events, on the view that the essence of power is the capacity to make the tough big decisions. As developed by Dahl (1961), its advantage is the recognition that an individual's scope of power may be circumcised or limited to a particular arena. Hence, the possibility arises of many different elite groups rather than one that is all-embracing. However, this method may tend systematically to underplay the latter possibility, producing an overly fragmented view of the elite by linking power too closely to involvement in particular disparate decisions. It also has to face the problem that one 'face' of power is the capacity to prevent issues coming up for decisions (as with judges), which might produce a different list of elites.

Evaluation

In recognition that none of the above seems to be adequate in itself, researchers such as Presthus (1964), for example, have combined selection methods employing two of them together. One approach is to start with positional analysis and augment it with reputational selection. This is known as the 'snowball' technique. Individuals are initially selected by position. Then they become the judges who nominate additional individuals by reputation. Those who receive multiple nominations in turn offer names until the process is complete, or too few names are added to justify continuation. The technique

also can be used to gauge the reputation of the original positional elites or even, conceivably, to de-select them.

There is no single method for elite selection that is free of criticism. Each is associated with certain substantive views of power, and each could arguably produce different results. In this situation, it would perhaps seem most appropriate to rely on a combination, or *synthetic* approach. This might be the closest one can get to the idea of a neutral technique in which the choice of a particular selection method keeps open what the findings about the elite in question will turn out to be.

George Moyser

Associated Concepts: access, critical research, decision-making research, messy research, mixed-methods research, organizational research, snowball sampling, triangulation

Key Readings

Dahl, R. A. (1961) *Who Governs?* Yale: Yale University Press.
Mills, C. Wright (1954) *The Power Elite*. New York: Oxford University Press.
Moyser, G. and Wagstaffe, M. (1987) *Research Methods For Elite Studies*. London: Allen & Unwin.
Presthus, R. V. (1964) *Men at the Top: A Study in Community Power*. New York: Oxford University Press.
Putnam, R. D. (1976) *The Comparative Study of Political Elites*. Englewood Cliffs, NJ: Prentice Hall.
Scott, J. (1990) *The Sociology of Elites*. Cheltenham: Edward Elgar Publishing.

EMANCIPATORY RESEARCH

Definition

Research that seeks to empower the subjects of social inquiry. It is now commonly recognized that power is a fundamental aspect of all research relationships. Traditional research processes have been criticized for their objectification of respondents. One response has been to argue for an emancipatory research process: one which recognizes this power imbalance in research and aims to empower respondents through research.

Distinctive Features

Traditional research processes argued for the objective and value-free production of knowledge: a 'scientific' social science. From this perspective the research process is value-free, coherent and orderly – in fact 'hygenic' (Stanley and Wise, 1993; Kelly et al., 1994). Amongst other criticisms of this approach is the viewpoint that power is a fundamental aspect of all research relationships. It is useful here to draw on the work of Giddens (1985), who argues that power is in one way or another an aspect of all relationships and makes the distinction between two types of resources involved in power – control of material resources (for example, money, time research 'tools') and control of authoritative resources (for example, as in holding the status of researcher). Within research it is usually the researchers who have the time, resources and skills to conduct methodological work, to make sense of experience and locate individuals' experiences in historical and social contexts. The researcher usually has control over, for example, the construction of the questionnaire, the order in which the questions are asked in a qualitative interview, the frequency and timing of visits to a research site, and thus holds the associated status that this brings. Furthermore, it is the researcher who is more often than not responsible for the final analysis and presentation of the data. Thus, researchers 'take away the words' of respondents and have the power of editorship. So, it is important to acknowledge that researchers often have the objective balance of power throughout the research project and have control of both the material and authoritative resources. With all of this in mind, Stacey (1991: 144) argues that 'elements of inequality, exploitation, and even betrayal are endemic to [research]'.

This leads some to argue that researchers should be aware of the power that they hold and should make themselves vulnerable and try to equalize their relationships with respondents which would allow for empowerment through research (for example, Stanley and Wise, 1993). This may involve including respondents in the construction of the research design, investment of the researchers' self and life experience in research encounters and involving respondents in the checking of data before the final presentation of the research report. Although considered less often in methodological literature, issues of power and empowerment within research teams are also important to consider if the aim is for an empowering research experience for all (Kelly et al., 1994).

Evaluation

Issues of power are complex within research. As suggested above, there is an assumption that the researcher is always in control of the research situation and is the one who holds the balance of power, but it is often more complicated than this in reality. It is important not to over-passify research respondents, not least by assuming that they are always vulnerable within research. Some respondents do not feel disempowered by either their life experience or by the research relationship and it may be patronizing of the researcher to assume that the respondent needs to be empowered by the process. Also, research relationships are fluid and jointly constructed and at times during the research process it is the researcher who might feel vulnerable and/or at a disadvantage. This may be the case when researching individuals who are older, more experienced, more knowledgeable and/or when undertaking research with people with sexist, racist, homophobic (and so on) views and attitudes (for example, Collins, 1998). In addition to the emotional danger suggested here it is important to also acknowledge that research can be physically dangerous for researchers.

Even when aiming for an emancipatory research process it is an illusion to think that, in anything short of a fully participatory research project, respondents can have anything approaching 'equal' knowledge (about what is going on) to the researcher. It may also be simplistic to assume that an approach which includes the respondents at all levels is ultimately empowering for respondents. 'Participatory' research can entail disparate levels of input from research respondents at different stages of the research process and some may not wish this type of involvement. Thus, there may be a tension between the desire to give respondents a voice and the making of knowledge, not least because individuals may not necessarily possess the knowledge (or have the desire) to explain everything about their lives. Arguably, equalizing relationships within research could also be seen to be exploitative in that it could encourage isolated individuals to come forward and reveal aspects of their experience that they later regret. Furthermore, making people feel powerful within the research process does not necessarily change the emotional and material circumstances of their lives.

Gayle Letherby

Associated Concepts: anti-racism research, critical research, dangerous fieldwork, disability research, disaster research, exploitative research, feminist research, participatory action research, politics and social research

Key Readings

Collins, P. (1998) 'Negotiated selves: reflections on "unstructured" interviewing', *Sociological Research Online*, 3 (3) www.socresonline.org.uk/socresonline/3/3/4.html

Giddens, A. (1985) *The Nation State and Violence*. Cambridge: Polity Press.

Hunter, F. (1953) *Community Power Structure: A Study of Decision Makers*. Chapel Hill: University of North Carolina.

Kelly, L., Burton, S. and Regan, L. (1994) 'Researching women's lives or studying women's oppression? Reflections on what constitutes feminist research', in M. Maynard and J. Purvis (eds), *Researching Women's Lives from a Feminist Perspective*. London: Taylor and Francis.

Stacey, J. (1991) 'Can there be a feminist ethnography?', in S. B. Gluck and D. Patai (eds), *Women's Words, Women's Words, Women's Words: The Feminist Practice of Oral History*. New York: Routledge.

Stanley, L. and Wise, S. (1993) *Breaking Out Again: Feminist Ontology and Epistemology*. London: Routledge.

EMPIRICISM

Definition

Empiricism began as a philosophical doctrine in the seventeenth century in the writings of Locke, Berkeley and Hume. In the twentieth century it had an enormous influence on scientific method and was the basis of logical positivism (itself sometimes called logical empiricism) (Gillies, 1993: 17–21).

Distinctive Features

In empiricism knowledge is only validated through sense experience, or in more recent versions through the surrogates of scientific instrumentation (which in the social sciences would include survey questionnaires and interview data). Its importance to scientific method in the natural and social sciences lies in the centrality of emphasis placed on empirical hypothesis testing. Thus if we formulate a hypothesis such as 'industrialization leads to worker alienation', this is only meaningful if it can be verified empirically; anything less is metaphysical speculation. Moreover empiricists (unlike realists) eschew claims of causal necessity, because (after Hume) it is maintained that although event A may precede event B in time, we cannot be sure A brought about B. In social science this principle is exemplified by the social survey where the strength and direction of association between variables is expressed, but no necessary function claimed.

In the nineteenth and early twentieth centuries empiricism was a radical and even liberating movement for philosophy of science, providing a demarcation between meaningful (that is, testable) scientific statements and philosophical speculation (Philips, 1987: 39). Testability allowed adjudication between scientific theories and thus for progress to be demonstrated. The approach was enormously influential in mid-twentieth century social science, particularly in the United States and especially in the survey and experimental approaches pioneered by the 'Columbia School' (Oakley, 2000: 168). Large-scale longitudinal experiments were set up to demonstrate whether or not social programmes had worked and there were clear criteria about what counted as 'working'. Yet ironically whilst empiricist methods were reaching their zenith in US social science, in philosophy of the natural sciences empiricism (specifically logical positivism) was undergoing a two-pronged attack from the philosopher Karl Popper (Popper, 1959).

The first part of Popper's argument concerned the criterion of meaningfulness in empiricism. Testability in empiricism requires an observation language (to describe those things observed) quite separate from a theoretical language. The problem is that the descriptions themselves must be the result of prior cognitive processes. Thus in science, according to Popper, there are no statements about the way the world is that are theoretically neutral. An observation language therefore cannot be successfully differentiated from a theoretical one.

Popper's second and more famous criticism was of the verification principle. For empiricists a hypothesis was verified if there was positive empirical evidence to confirm it. This raises the question of whether further positive evidence increases the level of corroboration. Popper maintained that it did not. No matter how many confirming instances are observed there is no certainty of truth, but just one disconfirming instance will falsify the hypotheses. On the basis of this (quite correct) logical reasoning Popper built an alternative falsificationist philosophy of science, itself the subject of sharp criticism later (see Lakatos and Musgrave, 1970 for a review of this debate).

Falsification requires a clear criterion of what counts as a falsification of a hypothesis, a condition usually only obtaining in chemistry or physics and usually in the laboratory. The social sciences are mostly not based on laboratory experiments, but rely on data generated from experiments in open or semi-open systems, survey data or interpretive data. In the first two cases such data are probabilistic and thus are dependent on inductive reasoning, that is, that the characteristics of a properly constructed sample can be inferred to a population. Nevertheless, technical difficulties and the problems of operationalization aside, it might be claimed that a sample from a defined population is immune from Popper's critique, because the researcher does not intend claiming that all xs are ys, merely that a percentage of xs are ys. The degree of corroboration is a function of the strength of association.

In the social survey the emphasis on probability and variable analysis has been a lasting legacy of empiricism and is retained in other non-empiricist approaches such as realism. However, Popper's first objection has more telling implications. As Pawson points out (1989: 39–41), most variables in social science are derived from unobserved latent constructs (for example, class, ethnicity etc). In other words they require prior theorizing, the data do not 'speak for themselves' but are the result of a selection process that will contain both theoretical and empirical elements. Most social researchers accept this position nowadays and this has resulted in modified and more sophisticated versions of empiricism. It is, for example, accepted that there may be hidden variables that are producing (causing) something to happen, but as Hubert Blalock has argued (1961: 10), by definition these cannot be observed or measured. The best that can be done is to note covariation and that x and y vary together in a predictable way. According to this version of empiricism, embraced by most statisticians, the ability to successfully predict outcomes obviates the requirement to demonstrate causality beyond statistical association.

Evaluation

The influence of empiricism remains strong in the social survey, though arguably this is more to do with the emphasis on the centrality of measurement, associational techniques and statistical testing than adherence to a philosophical doctrine. Empiricism, in the form of positivism, has long been the subject of criticism in social science, usually by interpretivists who associate it with (what they see as) an inappropriate use of the methods of science to study the social world (Williams, 2000: 87–104). Yet ironically something much closer to the spirit of nineteenth-century empiricism is found in just those interpretivist approaches that prioritize the experiences of actors in the generation of theory (Bryman, 1988: 119). Grounded theory in particular proceeds from a close observation of the social world to systematically build theory, whilst phenomenological approaches seek to bracket off the researcher's prior constructs in favour of concepts generated by those studied. In each, something like an 'observation language' is used to describe actions and events prior to their being theorized.

Malcolm Williams

Associated Concepts: falsification, grounded theory, methodology, ontology, phenomenology, positivism, postmodernism, realism, relativism, subjectivity

Key Readings

Blalock, H. (1961) *Causal Inference in Nonexperimental Research*. Chapel Hill, NC: University of North Carolina Press.

Bryman, A. (1988) *Quantity and Quality in Social Research*. London: Routledge.

Gillies, D. (1993) *Philosophy of Science in the Twentieth Century*. Oxford: Blackwell.

Lakatos, I. and Musgrave, A. (eds) (1970) *Criticism and the Growth of Knowledge*. Cambridge: Cambridge University Press.

Oakley, A. (2000) *Experiments in Knowing: Gender and Method in the Social Sciences*. Cambridge: Polity Press.

Pawson, R. (1989) *A Measure for Measures: A Manifesto for Empirical Sociology*. London: Routledge.

Philips, D. (1987) *Philosophy, Science and Social Inquiry: Contemporary Methodological Controversies in Social Science and Related Applied Fields of Research*. Oxford: Pergamon.

Popper, K. R. (1959) *The Logic of Scientific Discovery*. London: Routledge.

Williams, M. (2000) *Science and Social Science: An Introduction*. London: Routledge.

EPISTEMOLOGY

Definition

A field of philosophy concerned with the possibility, nature, sources and limits of human knowledge.

Distinctive Features

As distinct from ontology (the study of the essential nature of reality), epistemology is concerned with whether or how we can have knowledge of reality: questions that have concerned philosophers since, at least, the Ancient Greeks. Criteria for what counts as knowledge (rather than mere belief) normally include reference to truth and to the justification for it. A lucky guess that happens to be true might not count.

Historically, a central epistemological debate has been between empiricism and rationalism. Empiricism holds that knowledge derives from the external world, albeit mediated through sensory perception. Valid knowledge is based a posteriori upon the 'facts' derived from systematic observations and reflection upon them: inductive reasoning from observational data allows the formulation of general laws, which can be tested and verified through further observation. One criticism is that this provides no guarantee of truth, since it is always possible that future observations will not provide verification of a theory. 'Fallibilism' or 'falsificationalism'

(Popper, 1959) suggests that, whilst the truth is inherently uncertain, it is possible to know and discard what is false. Thus, knowledge is always provisional, consisting of 'falsifiable conjectures': those conjectures that stand up to empirical testing can be regarded as nearer the truth than those that do not. For Popper, what distinguishes scientific knowledge is that it specifies the empirical criteria upon which it could be shown to be false (hence he attacked Marxism as unscientific).

Rationalism is the view that human rationality and cognitive processes make ontological knowledge possible through logical deduction from a priori principles. Knowledge is not limited to observable phenomena but encompasses a deeper reality which underpins observable appearances. This is an idea that goes back to Plato. More recently, some forms of structuralism (for example, the work of Levi-Strauss) are predicated upon the view that there are deeper causal structures which are not capable of direct empirical observation, but nevertheless underpin cognition as well as language and human society.

To the extent that rationalism locates knowledge in the rationality of the knowing subject, rather than external phenomena, it can be considered as a form of idealism. Some forms of idealism go further and maintain that knowledge of reality is only available through perceptual or theoretical grids, so, strictly speaking, there can be no evidence of any ontological reality outside of those perceptions. The assumption of any intrinsic ability to grasp the true nature of reality thus can also be seen as questionable. 'Reality' cannot be known independently of our perceptions and assumptions: it is a construction of the knower. Constructivism underpins a range of perspectives in the social sciences, including symbolic interactionism, phenomenology, post-structuralism, postmodernism and some forms of feminism. These are predicated on the idea that knowledge is contextual and that it varies over time and space and between social groups. All knowledge is viewed as an outcome of the conditions of its construction: epistemology, in effect, gives way to hermeneutics.

Critical realism ('transcendental realism' and sometimes just 'realism'), associated particularly with the work of Bhaskar (e.g. 1975), derives from a critique of both empiricism and idealism. Critical realism accepts epistemological relativism (knowledge is always context-bound) but argues for recognition of a reality which exists independently of human activity and which should properly be the object of inquiry. Such inquiry is not limited to what is observable (as it is for empiricists), although this is important, but should be directed towards an understanding of the deeper causal structures which shape not only reality itself but also the context and meaning of human perceptions. Critical realism thus re-asserts the importance of ontology and criteria of truth and suggests (in contrast to postmodernism) that some forms of knowledge may have more validity than others. Weber's concept of *verstehen* has been put forward as exemplifying this type of approach.

Evaluation

The possibility of certain knowledge has increasingly been questioned both within philosophy and by scholars from other disciplines, who draw attention to the social contexts of knowledge production as well as the philosophical problems. A number of influential writers on the sociology of science in the 1960s and 1970s pointed out that the reality of science is much messier than is suggested by either empiricism or fallibilism. Claims about the unique rationality of science are seen to be reflections of conventional assumptions which are also (particularly in the work of Michel Foucault) seen as inextricably intertwined with the exercise of power, 'disqualifying' other knowledges. This latter point has also been argued by feminists who point to the ways in which women have been construed as irrational and to the marginalization of women as producers of knowledge and as objects of inquiry. However, there is no single feminist epistemology: rather feminists have adopted a variety of epistemologies which Harding (1991) characterizes as empiricism, standpointism (which has much in common with critical realism, see Cain, 1990) and postmodernism: there is no one feminist epistemology.

Constructivist epistemologies, particularly postmodernism, accept and even celebrate the existence of multiple 'knowledges' and methods. However, a frequent criticism of these approaches, from critical realists in particular, concerns the danger of a slide into complete relativism in which there are no epistemological criteria of truth or for judging between different knowledges. Thus contemporary epistemological debates continue to be characterized by contestation, many of the arguments reflecting much older arguments in philosophy.

Maggie Sumner

Associated Concepts: constructionism, empiricism, falsification, hermeneutics, hypothetico-deductive model, induction, ontology, phenomenology, positivism, rationalism, realism, *Verstehen*.

Key Readings

Bhaskar, R. (1975) *A Realist Theory of Science*. Leeds: Leeds Books.

Cain, M. (1990) 'Realist philosophy and standpoint epistemologies: feminist criminology as a successor science', in L. Gelsthorpe and A. Morris (eds), *Feminist Perspectives in Criminology*. Milton Keynes: Open University Press. pp. 124–40.

Harding, S. (1991) *Whose Science? Whose Knowledge?* Milton Keynes: Open University Press.

Popper, K. (1959) *The Logic of Scientific Discovery*. London: Routledge.

Williams, M. and May, T. (1996) *Introduction to the Philosophy of Social Research*. London: UCL Press.

ERROR

Definition

In general, error denotes the deviation of an empirical observation from a true or optimal result. In an experiment variation in a dependent variable which cannot be accounted for by the values of the independent variable(s) is regarded as error. It can be caused by the observation and the measuring equipment, by the experimental design, by the data processing techniques, by variables not included in the investigation, or any kind of random effects.

Distinctive Features

A major distinction is between systematic and random error. A systematic error or bias is a shift of the results common to all individual data points. For example when body weights are sampled from fully dressed children then the weight of the clothes is a systematic error.

In statistics, error denotes the difference between a true value of a parameter and an approximation to that value; mostly it is called sampling error. For example, the difference between an expectation (that is, a population mean) and a sample mean is a point in question.

For mathematical reasons the difference is in most cases expressed as a quadratic deviation. The best thing to happen is that the expectation of this quadratic difference depends on the sample size in such a way that the limit is zero for increasing sample size. If in the above example we are granted a true random sample then

$$E(M-\mu)^2 = \sigma^2/N \qquad (1)$$

where M is the sample mean (regarded as a random variable because the sample is random) of a sample of size N taken from the random variable X whose expectation is and variance is σ^2. (E is the expectation operator). For most other parameters of random variables similar laws obtain. Equation (1) contains two messages – one good, one bad. The good thing is that error can be kept as low as is necessary by increasing the sample size (this is called consistency). The bad thing is that the increase of precision is rather slow. Put another way, to halve the statistical error requires four times the sample size.

Moreover, one has to consider the possibility of bias. The sample may be biased in some way; the sampled population may not be identical with the target population. The expectation of the squared deviation of an estimator, say T, of some parameter θ can be shown to fulfil:

$$E(T-\theta)^2 = E(T-E\,T)^2 + (E\,T-\theta)^2 \qquad (2)$$

The left-hand side of Equation 2 is called the mean square error. The first term on the right of Equation 2 is the variance of the estimator (that is, Equation(1) in case of the sample mean), the second is the square of the bias. While the first usually approaches zero with increasing N, the second does not. The only way to keep bias small lies with the choice of the estimator T, or with the experimental design, in particular with the chosen method of sampling.

Evaluation

If one proposes a theoretical model for a set of data then usually there will be some discrepancy between model and data. To mend this fact an 'error term' is introduced. This move, however, is meaningless unless this error term behaves appropriately. Conditions pertinent to this situation are, for example, expectation zero, or variance independent of values of other variables involved in the model (homoscedasticity), or normal distribution. Above all, the error term should be sufficiently small compared to the main terms (with high probability). Numerous statistical techniques such as the least squares method are based on error minimization.

Reinhard Suck and Thomas Staufenbiel

Associated Concepts: bias, estimation, inferential statistics

Key Reading

Stuart, A., Ord, K. J. and Arnold, S. (1999) *Kendall's Advanced Theory of Statistics: Classical Inference and the Linear Model.* New York: Oxford University Press.

ESTIMATION

Definition

Statistical estimation is the process of inferring the true value of a variable in the population from a sample drawn from that population.

Distinctive Features

Many problems in social research require the estimation of some unknown quantity. For example, we might wish to know the proportion of voters favouring candidate A or the effect of an anti-smoking commercial on the attitude of adolescents. We can gather the relevant data (approval ratings) from a sample of subjects (voters). Based on the sample results, we can look for a 'best guess' for the true value in the population (of all voters). Statistical estimation is concerned with this problem of inferring a population parameter from a sample statistic.

More formally, we assume that a random sample of N observations X_1, X_2, ..., X_N is selected from the population. We denote the unknown population parameter as θ and the point estimator as T. The observations and T as a function of the X_i are random variables. The probability distribution of the estimator is called the sampling distribution of T, its standard deviation being the standard error SE_T. We will first discuss some of the properties a good estimator should possess.

An estimator is said to be *unbiased* if the expected value of the estimator is equal to the parameter, $E(T) = \theta$. It can be shown that the sample arithmetic mean $M = \Sigma_i(X_i)/N$ is an unbiased estimator of the population mean μ, $E(M) = \mu$. On the other hand, the variance $S^2 = \Sigma_i(X_i-M)^2/N$ of a random sample is not an unbiased estimator of the population variance σ^2. The bias is $E(S^2) - \sigma^2 = -\sigma^2/N$ and can easily be removed by using $s^2 = \Sigma_i(X_i - M)^2/(N-1)$ instead of S^2.

Efficiency denotes the accuracy of the estimation, which corresponds to the variance of the sampling distribution of T. The smaller the standard error of the estimator SE_T, the more efficient is T in the estimation of θ. Commonly the efficiency of T is evaluated by comparing it with another unbiased estimator T'. The relative efficiency of T is then defined as $SE_{T'}/SE_T$. In a normally distributed population the sample mean and median Md are both unbiased estimators of μ, but M is more efficient than Md. If the distributions are not normal, this relation can be reversed.

A third criterion for evaluating estimators is *consistency*. An estimator is consistent when the variance of the sampling distribution tends towards 0 with increasing sample size. The sample mean and many other statistics are consistent estimators. The probability that they come close to their population counterparts increases with larger sample sizes.

The last property of an estimator to be considered here is *sufficiency*. T is said to be sufficient if it makes use of all the information available in the sample. This is true of the sample mean or variance as in their computation they take into account all X_i. The median, mode or range on the other hand are statistics, which do not depend on all observations and are therefore not sufficient estimators.

There is another approach called *interval estimation*. It consists of determining an interval, which contains the parameter θ with a given probability. Its advantage compared to point estimation is that the length of the interval quantifies the precision of the estimation. For example, the 95 per cent confidence interval around the mean of a larger sample taken from a normally distributed population is given by $M 1 \pm 1.96 \times SE_M$. The probability that this confidence interval contains θ is 0.95.

There are a number of general methods that produce estimates which possess many of the above mentioned desirable properties. Two widely used methods of estimation are *least squares* and *maximum likelihood estimation*. For example in multiple regression a variable Y is regressed on a set of k predictors X_i by means of the linear model $Y = \beta_0 + \beta_1 X_1 + \dots + \beta_k X_k + E$. The beta weights β_i are (ordinary) least squares estimates that minimize E^2. If the statistical assumptions are met, these weights are unbiased, consistent, sufficient and the most efficient estimators.

Evaluation

Statistics derived from samples are used to estimate population parameters. How good these estimates are depends on how the sample has been drawn, in particular the size of the sample and the degree to which it is representative of the population. Representativeness can be improved by stratification of the sample.

Thomas Staufenbiel and Reinhard Suck

Associated Concepts: bias, error, inferential statistics, prediction, probability (random) sampling, stratified sampling

Key Reading

Stuart, A., Ord, K. J. and Arnold, S. (1999) *Kendall's Advanced Theory of Statistics: Classical Inference and the Linear Model.* New York: Oxford University Press.

ETHICS

Definition

A field of moral philosophy dealing with the standards by which behaviour should be regulated. In terms of the ethical issues faced by social researchers, most learned societies and relevant professional bodies publish codes of ethics which provide rules, standards or guidance on what is and is not acceptable practice.

Distinctive Features

Research is generally justified in terms of the search for new or better knowledge, which is regarded as a social good or benefit. Ethical problems in research arise from the tensions between this objective and the rights and interests of individuals and groups which may be affected. Research is not carried out in a social vacuum and there are a number of groups with a direct interest in it. Most obviously, these groups include those who commission and fund research, who have their own agendas in determining what should be studied. They may sometimes have a vested interest in research that will produce the findings they want or is quick and cheap, rather than high quality, or an interest in publicizing welcome results and playing down results that are less happy from their point of view. A second group is the wider research community, which has an interest in not jeopardizing future research by allowing research activity to get a bad name. A third group is those who may be affected directly or indirectly by policies formulated on the basis of research findings. Finally, but far from least, there are those who participate directly in the research as providers of the data which the researcher seeks. Here the researcher must balance the need to obtain valid data against the rights of individuals and groups to privacy and autonomy.

Much of the debate on the ethics of social research has been concerned with these last issues, the relationship between researcher and researched. One basic principle is that research should not bring harm to respondents, but longer-term consequences of research participation are not always easily calculated. A second fundamental principle of ethical social research is that of informed consent, which respects the right of people to know that they are being researched, the purposes of the research and what will be expected of them. People can then consent or not. There are issues here, of course, about who can give informed consent: the most obvious issue relates to children and the age at which they can be considered capable of giving valid consent (in practice, most codes of practice regard parental consent as necessary for people under 16). Related problems can occur in a variety of situations in which the validity of consent is questionable, for example where gatekeepers of research access have considerable power over potential participants so that people may be fearful of the consequences of non-participation (for example, in institutions such as prisons). The principle of informed consent would also suggest that covert research is not acceptable, nor is concealment of the researcher's real

purposes or any other form of deception. A related principle is that of respect for the right to privacy: researchers should not intrude on privacy to any greater degree than is required by the research. There are particular issues here in relation to intrusive questions and particularly questions on sensitive issues, such as sexual behaviour or illegal activity. There are also legal aspects to this, in terms of data protection legislation. A fourth key principle of ethical practice is confidentiality, providing assurance that the information collected will be used only for research purposes. Generally, this goes together with assurances of anonymity: that is the individual will not be identifiable from the way in which the findings are presented.

Evaluation

Discussions of the ethics of social research frequently focus upon highly problematic pieces of work, one of the most widely discussed of which is Humphreys (1970) and, in particular, his use of covert observation (see Bryman, 2001: 477 for a brief description). However, ethical dilemmas arise in all social research and are not confined to specific cases.

Because ethical dilemmas are endemic to social research, the publication of guidelines has been an important activity for both learned societies of academic researchers, for example, the American Sociological Association, British Psychological Society, and professional associations, for example, in the UK, the Social Research Association and the Market Research Society; and these cover both qualitative research and the collection of statistical data. All of the guidelines mentioned are available via the Internet, using search engines.

However, these guidelines are just that. They are not mandatory. There is some disagreement among social researchers about the extent to which ethical principles are near absolute values that should never be infringed. It can be argued that it is sometimes impossible to do research without infringing ethical principles to some degree: for example, where access to certain groups might be impossible without some degree of deception about the researcher's real purposes or where explaining those purposes might affect the validity of the responses. It would follow that the researcher must make some personal moral judgements about the right balance between the need to know and the rights of others.

Maggie Sumner

Associated Concepts: access, confidentiality, gatekeepers, informed consent, validity

Key Readings

Barnes, J. A. (1979) *Who Should Know What?* Harmondsworth: Penguin.

Bryman, A. (2001) *Social Research Methods.* Oxford: Oxford University Press.

Bulmer, M. (ed.) (1982) *Social Research Ethics.* London: Macmillan.

Bulmer, M. (2001) 'The ethics of social research', in N. Gilbert (ed.), *Researching Social Life.* London: Sage. pp. 45–57.

Homan, R. (1991) *The Ethics of Social Research.* London: Pearson Education.

Humphreys, J. (1970) *The Tea Room Trade: Impersonal Sex in Public Places.* Chicago: Aldine.

Punch, M. (1994) 'Politics and ethics in qualitative research', in N. K. Denzin and Y. S. Lincoln (eds), *Handbook of Qualitative Research.* London: Sage. pp. 83–97.

THE ETHNOGRAPH (VERSION 5.0)

Definition

One of a number of Computer Assisted Qualitative Data Analysis Software (CAQDAS) programs designed to facilitate the management and analysis of qualitative data. Originally developed in 1985 by the sociologist John Seidel, it is now marketed through Qualis Research Associates.

Distinctive Features

Like all CAQDAS programs, The Ethnograph is a tool for facilitating analysis rather than a method in itself and therefore can feasibly be used to support a number of methodological or theoretical approaches. However, it is only possible to work directly with textual data when using The Ethnograph.

The Ethnograph facilitates the qualitative data analysis process in a number of key ways, enabling the researcher to: create and manage data files; code data according to user-defined conceptual themes and group codes into families; organize data according to demographic information; note analytic thoughts as they occur; and having coded, search the data set in a number of ways. In addition, the code mapping function visually represents how data have been coded using a margin view visible whilst coding.

Textual data can be pasted direct from a word processing application into The Ethnograph where it will be automatically formatted, or previously saved data files can be imported. In addition, it is possible to transcribe data directly into the editor window and the spell check function facilitates this process.

As well as being able to apply factual variables to whole data files (for example, interview transcripts), The Ethnograph includes powerful organizational autocoding tools for structured data. In focus group data, for example, if formatted correctly, upon file import each speaker-section will be automatically coded. It is then easy to apply demographic variables to those coded segments.

At any stage coded data can be retrieved and reviewed, allowing the researcher to focus on a particular code, or group of codes, in isolation from the rest of the data set.

The search tool interrogates the dataset using standard Boolean operators to assist investigating relationships between codes and/or factual variables. It provides easy ways to filter searches based on, for example, a particular speaker in focus group data, or a particular file, to which a particular or combination of variables applies.

Clearly labelled output following a search is usually given in the form of segments for each data file and also displays other codes present in the retrieved data. The segments can then be printed and saved for importation as data to be re-analysed.

The memo tool is versatile, whereby all memos (whether attached to a line of text, a data file, or the project) can be viewed together or sorted and retrieved according to a number of attributes.

Evaluation

The evaluation of any CAQDAS package must take into consideration a number of factors – including methodological and theoretical approach, type of data, size of data set, project aims and requirements and certain practicalities. Therefore, certain packages may be particularly useful for certain types of studies and researchers are advised to investigate the various options before choosing.

The Ethnograph is a package designed to handle small to medium-sized data sets in the application of a few basic tasks of qualitative data analysis. Its attractiveness lies in its relative simplicity compared to other more sophisticated CAQDAS software. It is fairly easy to learn and therefore may be particularly useful for teaching students. The software manual is very well written and provides methodological and step-by-step help.

It lacks tools such as a text search (across the whole data set) function, and the broader range of sophisticated search facilities and visual networking and modelling tools available in some CAQDAS packages. However, many software users claim that the basic coding, clearly labelled, flexible retrieval and memoing tools are all they have time to use and that a lot of analytic work is anyway conducted outside the software and away from the computer.

The Ethnograph may have some compatibility problems with some operating systems (W2000, WME, XP). Users should check compatibility with their system before installing the software.

Christina Silver

Associated Concepts: Atlas.ti, CAQDAS, coding, NUD*IST, qualitative research, QSR NVivo

Key Readings

The CAQDAS Networking Project website http://caqdas.soc.surrey.ac.uk/
The Ethnograph website http://www.qualis research.com
Fielding, N. and Lee, R. (eds) (1991, 2nd edn. 1993) *Using Computers in Qualitative Research*. London: Sage.
Kelle, U. (ed.) (1995) *Computer-Aided Qualitative Data Analysis: Theory Methods and Practice*. London: Sage.
Weitzman, E. and Miles, M. (1995) *A Software Source Book: Computer Programs for Qualitative Data Analysis*. Thousand Oaks, CA: Sage.

ETHNOGRAPHIC INTERVIEWING

Definition

A form of interviewing conducted in the context of a relationship with interviewees with whom the researcher has, through an ongoing presence, established relations of rapport and respect sufficient for a genuine 'meeting of minds' and that enable a mutual exploration of the meanings the interviewee applies to their social world (Heyl, 2001).

Distinctive Features

Ethnographic interviewing originated in cultural anthropology, hence its emphasis on duration and frequency of contact, on the quality of the relationship with respondents, and on the meaning of actions and events to respondents. These emphases are consistent with ethnography's aim to 'grasp the native's point of view' (Malinowski, 1922: 25).

Ethnographic interviews are normally conducted in unstructured, in-depth format with people from a particular culture, or who share particular experiences. As well as anthropology, the method is practised in fields including sociology, education, and psychology. What distinguishes it *procedurally* from other in-depth interviews is the centrality of rapport based on relatively long-term contact, the investment of time in each round of interviewing and the kind of openness on the researcher's part that stimulates an even-handed relationship. Thus, a key feature is the idea that the researcher is there to learn from the respondent rather than impose an external frame of reference, epitomized in Spradley's (1979: 34) representation of the researcher's posture as being that 'I want to know what you know in the way that you know it ... Will you become my teacher and help me understand?' This means that, more than other methods, interviewees are empowered to shape the interview's content and even the focus of the research, and that the interviews can elicit strong emotions. A supplementary feature is the frequent interest in documenting interviewees' culture in their own language (Spradley, 1979: 24). Life history interviews can be seen as a form of ethnographic interview as they often share these emphases.

Spradley (1979) offers perhaps the most systematic treatment of the method. He devotes detailed attention to criteria for 'locating' informants, and suggests what makes a 'good' informant (see also Johnson, 1990). He tracks the interview's stages step-by-step, from explaining the project and interview to asking questions, turn-taking in talk, and various devices that facilitate communication. He discusses documenting the interviews (not simply a matter of audio recording), advises on question design, profiles appropriate types of (anthropological) analysis (domain, taxonomic, componential) and discusses writing up. While attuned to concerns about the status of ethnographic interview data that have latterly become prominent, some find Spradley's approach rather rigid.

Ethnographic interviews are distinguished from other types of interview *analytically* by their focus on cultural meanings. The early practice of ethnographic interviewing was premised on the 'naturalistic' convention that, if rapport was achieved, full and frank response would be forthcoming. There was also an assumption that research subjects had unique insight into their own culture. These premises, necessary to a belief that ethnography can produce objective knowledge, can no longer be unproblematically accepted. Indeed, the analytic tradition with which sociological ethnography is most often associated – symbolic interactionism – itself contained the seeds of a more sophisticated perspective on ethnographic interviews in its vision of them as sites of emergent interaction. Cultural anthropology, too, traced a path away from positivist assumptions during the 1980s and 1990s (Behar, 1996). Key texts on ethnographic interview methods that accommodate the new perspectives include Kvale's (1996) stage-based approach (with epistemological and ethical concerns arising at each stage), Holstein and Gubrium's (1995) 'active interview' approach (where, for example, interviewers attune to signs of perspectival shifts by interviewees) and Mishler's (1986) power-oriented distinction between three types of interviewer/interviewee relationship (informants and reporters; research collaborators, learners/actors and advocates).

Evaluation

Consistent with ethnography more generally, ethnographic interviewing raises many epistemological and ethical issues. Prominent are concerns about the relationship between researcher and research 'subjects', and about the status of the accounts offered in interviews. These concerns are inter-related and, as well as arising from epistemological debates, they have been animated by revelations about the early fieldwork that gave rise to some of the principles of ethnography and exemplars of its methods. Sexual relationships sometimes developed between researchers and 'the natives', and there is also testimony that data from ethnographic interviews could sometimes be called to account because subjects guessed what interpretation researchers favoured and 'fed them' what they wanted to hear (Freeman, 1998). Such contingencies may not be common but suggest the need to take into account the motives both of researcher and subject when interpreting the data from ethnographic interviews. As Heyl (2001: 370) observes, while there are now many competing perspectives on ethnographic interviewing (see, e.g., Mishler, 1986; Kvale, 1996; Reinharz, 1992), there is agreement about its high level goals – to 'listen well and respectfully', to be aware of the researcher's role in 'the co-construction of meaning during the interview process', to be aware of how ongoing relationships and social context affect the interview process, and 'to recognize that dialogue is discovery and only partial knowledge will ever be attained'. A reflexive posture is necessary when conducting and analysing ethnographic interviews. That can, indeed, be regarded as affirming the centrality the method has, since its origin, placed on the relationship between interviewer and interviewee.

Nigel G. Fielding

Associated Concepts: cultural research, epistemology, ethics, ethnography, intersubjective understanding, interview, life history interviewing, naturalistic data, reflexivity, *Verstehen*

Key Readings

Behar, R. (1996) *The Vulnerable Observer*. Boston, MA: Beacon Press.

Freeman, D. (1998) *The Fateful Hoaxing of Margaret Mead*. Boulder, CO: Westview.

Heyl, B. (2001) 'Ethnographic interviewing', in P. Atkinson, A. Coffey, S. Delamont, J. Lofland (eds), *Handbook of Ethnography*. London: Sage. pp. 368–83.

Holstein, J. and Gubrium, J. (1995) *The Active Interview*. Thousand Oaks, CA: Sage.

Johnson, J. (1990) *Selecting Ethnographic Informants*. London: Sage.

Kvale, S. (1996) *InterViews*. London: Sage.

Malinowski, B. (1922) *Argonauts of the Western Pacific*. London: Routledge.

Mishler, E. (1986) *Research Interviewing: Context and Narrative*. Cambridge, MA: Harvard University Press.

Reinharz, S. (1992) *Feminist Methods in Social Research*. New York: Oxford University Press.

Spradley, J. (1979) *The Ethnographic Interview*. New York: Holt Rinehart.

ETHNOGRAPHY

Definition

A research method located in the practice of both sociologists and anthropologists, and which should be regarded as the product of a cocktail of methodologies that share the assumption that personal engagement with the subject is the key to understanding a particular culture or social setting. Participant observation is the most common component of this cocktail, but interviews, conversational and discourse analysis, documentary analysis, film and photography, life histories all have their place in the ethnographer's repertoire. Description resides at the core of ethnography, and however this description is constructed it is the intense meaning of social life from the everyday perspective of group members that is sought.

Distinctive Features

Closely linked with, but actually the product of, various forms of fieldwork, ethnography is a particularly valuable resource for researchers seeking to unpack cultures or social settings that are hidden or difficult to locate. For instance, the researcher may seek to understand the culture of places and spaces such as the factory, or the school, or alternatively the ethnographer may be interested in processes such as childhood, ageing, sexuality or death. Whatever the focus of the ethnographer, the method is marked out by the intensity of the relationship between the researcher and the field, and in particular, the researcher and his/her informants. The latter is, of course, a natural bona fide resident of the social setting that is being studied, while the researcher is to varying extents an outsider whose motivation for being there is research-led.

Ethnography is based on the assumption that every social group is distinctive in its own right, and in order to explore this distinction researchers must engage with the group on its own ground. With participant observation at the core of ethnographic research, this requires the ethnographer to adopt a role within the setting being studied that enables a smooth blending with the rules, codes and expectations of the locals, and that is pragmatic, serving the instrumental objectives of the study. Ethnographers have found roles for themselves in a multitude of formal institutions such as schools, the police, factories, churches, prisons and businesses. They have also negotiated roles within a wide range of settings and cultures such as street gangs and poor neighbourhoods. All of these fieldwork settings require the construction of a practical and convincing role or 'front' that enables data to be gleaned with a varying degree of personal impact on the field setting. Strategically this involves varying levels of involvement from complete observer, where the researcher remains unobtrusive and observes the group in action, through to the complete participant who is a full member of the social group, and is fully involved in the group's activities (see Gold, 1958 for a full discussion of his four-part model of the ethnographer's role).

When ethnographers totally adopt, in the eyes of their critics, the culture of the researched, they are often accused of 'going native', or becoming one of the researched group. The accusation here is that during fieldwork the ethnographer has abandoned the role of researcher and forgotten the research task at hand, the disadvantage being that the academic product, the ethnography, requires a measure of distance through which theoretical work can emerge.

The adopted role may be covert or overt, and both carry advantages and disadvantages. The adoption of a covert role often enables access to fields that would otherwise be closed, and can enable a relatively unimpeded, albeit intense and stressful immersion in a given culture. Inevitably the covert role has been criticized on ethical grounds, and the names of certain writers will forever be associated with so called 'unethical' research. For instance, in his illuminating and controversial study of male sexuality, Humphreys adopted the role of 'Watch Queen' in male public toilets that were being used for sexual activity.

This role enabled access to the social setting while serving a useful purpose for those he was attempting to observe. As Humphreys himself acknowledges, an overt strategy would have resulted in failure. Many ethnographers, however, retain both overt and covert strategies, for social life generally demands a degree of reticence regarding our motives at the best of times, and researchers are no exception. Therefore, in gaining access and maintaining a role in the field, will all or none of the group know the ethnographer's identity, or the reason for her or his presence?

Ethnographers typically collect data in the form of field notes and seek to induce analysis by way of appreciation. Appreciation is at the heart of any ethnographic analysis, which utilizes categories made up of description, interviews, documents or visual presentation as appreciative cues and exemplars. From this ethnographic description, theory is derived from applying various interpretive techniques which are based upon presenting a convincing account of the observer's understanding the particular social rules of the culture (Glaser and Strauss, 1967).

Evaluation

Ethnography is an extremely broad church, and the range of methodological stances adopted by ethnographers extend across theoretical, political and technological divides (see Atkinson et al., 2001).

Ethnography is an ideal method for deriving meaning from social lives that otherwise might go hidden or unnoticed. As a method it is intense and often makes considerable personal demands upon the researcher. But as an academic product, the output of ethnography can be a vivid document with human resonance impossible to recreate by the application of other methodologies.

Dick Hobbs

Associated Concepts: access, autoethnography, critical ethnography, cultural research, ethnographic interviewing, fieldwork, idiographic, microethnography, netnography, participant observation, qualitative research, videography

Key Readings

Atkinson, P., Coffey, A., Delamont, S., Lofland, J. and Lofland, L. (eds) (2001) *Handbook of Ethnography*. London: Sage.

Glaser, B. and Strauss, A. (1967) *The Discovery of Grounded Theory*. Chicago: Aldine.

Gold, R. (1958) 'Roles in sociological field observations', *Social Forces*, 36: 217–23.

Humphreys, L. (1970) *Tearoom Trade*. Chicago: Aldine.

ETHNOMETHODOLOGY

Definition

An approach to studying the social world developed by Harold Garfinkel in the early 1950s which focuses on how social order is created, ongoingly, in and through the practices by which people make sense of what others are doing, and display that understanding through their actions. In doing so it recommends a re-specification of the focus of sociological inquiry, away from a concern with explaining the causes, development and/or effects of social processes or institutions.

Distinctive Features

Garfinkel started from a problem which he detected in efforts to create a theoretically informed scientific sociology in the United States in the late 1940s and early 1950s. The dominant theoretical framework at this time was Parsons's social theory. This focused on 'the problem of order', and Parsons explained the orderliness of social action as produced by the socialization of actors into the values and norms characteristic of their society. However, Garfinkel raised questions about this theory by noting that values and norms do not include instructions for their own application. From this he drew the radical conclusion that, as a result, they cannot provide a scientific explanation for behaviour. Instead, values and norms must be seen as constructs that are used by actors to account for what they and others do. Moreover, other explanatory resources used by conventional forms of sociology, such as the notion of interests, have much the same status.

Contrary to the way in which ethnomethodology is sometimes understood, Garfinkel's response to this problem was to try to find a more rigorous, scientific basis for the study of human social life. He did this by redefining the focus of the sociological project, drawing on phenomenology. He argued that the orderliness of social life must be a product of collective human activity: of our ability to interpret situations and act on those interpretations. Moreover, we do this despite the fact that there are always many different ways of interpreting any scene. We 'read' the behaviour of others for what it tells us about how they understand a situation, what they are intending to do, and we act on the basis of those 'readings'. Furthermore, in acting we indicate to others *our* understandings, and they will in turn act on the basis of *their* understanding of *us*; and so on.

In this way, social situations are self-organizing: their character is created continuously in and through the actions that make them up. But how is it possible for actors to read one another's behaviour in this way and thereby to coordinate their actions? Garfinkel's answer to this question is that, in making sense of the situations they face, ordinary people engage in practical reasoning that is *methodical* in character. If it were not, others would not be able to understand it, and the social world would not be intelligible. And he claims that it follows from this that what social scientists should be focusing on, if they are interested in the problem of social order, are the methods employed by actors in the practical reasoning through which they continuously constitute, and simultaneously display the orderliness of, the social world. This is his re-specified focus for sociological inquiry.

Ethnomethodology has inspired a range of different kinds of research. The best known is conversation analysis. This is concerned with documenting how people who are engaged in talk-in-action coordinate and construct it in an orderly fashion. For example, there has been investigation of the ways in which certain types of utterance, such as questions, make relevant other types of utterance, such as answers; and how the production of, or failure to produce, the succeeding action is monitored and responded to. There has also been a body of work, significantly different in character, and carried out by a later generation of Garfinkel's students, that is devoted to documenting work practices. Here the emphasis is on the details of how particular kinds of work – notably but not exclusively that of natural scientists and mathematicians – gets done and how what is produced is tied to the processes of its production (see Lynch, 1993).

Evaluation

There has been a great deal of criticism of ethnomethodology, much of it misdirected because based on a false understanding of the nature and rationale of the enterprise. There are, though, some problems which it faces. Indeed, these can be discerned in internal criticisms of each version of ethnomethodological analysis by those committed to others. For example, Lynch and Bogen (1994) criticize the work of Sacks, the founder of conversation analysis, for a 'primitive empiricism' that does not take account of the constitutive character of social scientific inquiry itself. And it is true that conversation analysis entails a rather restrictive conception of what can and cannot be studied scientifically. At the same time, though, ethnomethodological studies of work do not display the impressive cumulation of knowledge that is one of the most attractive features of conversation analysis. Furthermore, abandonment of any distinction between the orientation of science and that of other sorts of activity – which is characteristic, for example, of the work of Lynch – leads to doubts about the nature of the whole enterprise, given Garfinkel's original project. Finally, it must be noted that the cost of re-specifying the focus of social inquiry in ethnomethodological terms is considerable: it means that social scientists cannot address many of the questions that they have previously been interested in, many of which relate to pressing social problems.

Martyn Hammersley

Associated Concepts: causality, conversation analysis, covering-law model of explanation, hermeneutics, methodology, phenomenology, positivism

Key Readings

Heritage, J. (1984) *Garfinkel and Ethnomethodology.* Cambridge: Polity Press.
Hutchby, I. and Wooffitt, R. (1998) *Conversation Analysis: Principles, Practices and Applications.* Cambridge: Polity Press.
Lynch, M. (1993) *Scientific Practice and Ordinary Action.* Cambridge: Cambridge University Press.
Lynch, M. and Bogen, D. (1994) 'Harvey Sacks's primitive natural science', *Theory, Culture and Society*, 11: 65–104.

EVALUATION RESEARCH

Definition

The systematic identification and assessment of effects generated by treatments, programmes, policies, practices and products.

Distinctive Features

Formal evaluations are conducted for various reasons: to inform policy and practice, to inform resource allocation, to hold policy makers accountable, to inform consumers and to inform decisions about programme and policy continuation.

Social policies and programmes have been a major focus of evaluation research. Social policies and programmes comprise theories that the introduction of some new measure or policy will bring about an alteration in a regularity that would be observed in the absence of that policy or programme. In most cases the policy or programme begins with some pattern of events, behaviours or conditions that are considered undesirable or problematic. The purpose of the policy or programme is then to alter that pattern to reduce or remove the problem. A given pattern of school failure, crime, cancer, road accidents, or unemployment might, for example, comprise the presenting problem. The policy or programme will then be concerned with reducing or removing some pattern of school failures, crime, cancer, road accidents or unemployment. In a few cases programmes and policies attempt to pre-empt problems that might otherwise be expected, for example in relation to pollution, crime or traffic congestion. In such cases the aim of the policy or programme is to avert the emergence of a problematic pattern that would otherwise be expected. Evaluations of policies and programmes comprise tests of the policy and programme theories. Where products are being evaluated rather than policies or programmes, the theory being tested is that the product enables users better to achieve their objectives.

There are many methodological approaches to evaluation, largely reflecting the methodological divisions in the social sciences more generally. Qualitative and quantitative methods are used singly and in combination. 'Constructivists' stress qualitative methods and construe programmes as constituted in and through the negotiations of stakeholders, including programme architects, deliverers and participants. 'Experimentalists' stress quantitative methods and construe programmes as variables to be isolated with effects to be observed. 'Theory-driven' evaluators use both quantitative and qualitative methods and fall into various camps, all advocating that programmes theories be identified and tested. Evaluations using 'theories of change' or 'programme logic' methods explicate the chains of events presumed in programmes and test their presence in practice. Other theory-driven evaluation theorists stress the inherently normative character of evaluation. 'Realists' emphasize the presence of various layers of social reality that need to be understood in programmes and also stress generative accounts of causal forces, whose release through programmes needs to be grasped to make sense of outcome patterns produced.

Evaluation

There have been some sharp debates over evaluation methodology, in particular between experimentalists and realists. 'Experimentalists' attempt to hold all other conditions bar programme or policy presence constant and to measure the difference made by the programme in relation to the problematic event, behaviour or condition being targeted. At best this is achieved by randomized controlled trials (RCTs). RCTs are deemed to achieve 'internal validity' – the conclusive association of the treatment with the effect. They allocate subjects randomly to experimental and control conditions and compare the changes in each before and after the introduction of the treatment to the experimental group. RCTs are concerned to rule out any factor other than the policy or programme for any change observed in the experimental group. Replication is undertaken in the interests of trying to achieve 'external validity' – the generalization of findings to populations beyond those sampled for experimental purposes. Meta-evaluations aggregate findings from series of experimental studies to achieve large sample sizes that enable conclusions to be drawn with greater confidence. The Campbell Collaboration conducts 'systematic reviews' of suites of rigorous evaluations, favouring those that are or that approximate RCTs in order to draw out dependable findings.

Realists stress the importance of understanding 'mechanisms' – the causal forces released or inhibited by programmes; 'contexts' – the conditions necessary for mechanisms to be activated; and 'outcomes' – the changes in regularity brought about by the activation of the mechanisms in the contextual conditions in which the policy or practice is introduced. Programmes and policies tend to trigger multiple mechanisms and to operate in multiple contexts, with varying and changing outcomes. The products of realist evaluations are tested suites of context–mechanism–outcome pattern configurations (CMOCs). As in theory in the natural sciences, CMOC theories are not proven. Efforts to test them however promise generalized middle range theories that become ever stronger as they are further tested. The stronger theories have greater truth-content and hence are more dependable as premises for action. The theories embodied in policies and programmes include not only those of policy makers. Practitioners and participants will also hold programme theories that can usefully be articulated and tested. Social science may yield yet further conjectures about the ways in which programmes activate changes in causal mechanisms. For realists, evaluation review involves canvassing any available research that can be brought together to yield tests of realist programme theory. There is no a priori preference for experiments. Indeed, realists are sceptical of experiments that disregard mechanisms and the contextual conditions for their activation.

Whilst experimentalists take definitions of programmes, projects, policies and intervention measures at face value and attempt to isolate their associated changes in the problem patterns at issue, realists are more concerned with the ways in which underlying causal mechanisms come to be activated by measures introduced, in ways often not acknowledged or recognized by programme designers and in contingent ways according to context. Experimentalists try to establish what works and what does not work. Realists try to establish what works for whom, in what circumstances and how.

Nick Tilley

Associated Concepts: applied research, auditing, experiment, field experiment, messy research, meta-analysis, policy-related research, process mapping, quasi-experiments

Key Readings

Campbell, D. and Russo, J. (1999) *Social Experimentation*. Thousand Oaks, CA: Sage.
Chelimisky, E. and Shadish, W. (1997) *Evaluation for the 21st Century*. Thousand Oaks, CA: Sage.
Mark, M., Henry, G. and Julnes, G. (2000) *Evaluation*. San Francico, CA: Jossey-Bass.
Pawson, R. and Tilley, N. (1997) *Realistic Evaluation*. London: Sage.

EXPERIMENT

Definition

A research design used to draw causal inferences regarding the impact of a treatment variable on an outcome variable.

Distinctive Features

An experiment normally involves the randomized allocation of cases to experimental and control groups, exposing only the experimental group to a treatment whilst controlling the influence of extraneous factors. Analysis seeks to determine whether the experimental group changes significantly, over time, on the outcome variable in comparison with the control group that is not exposed to the experimental treatment. The classic experimental design focuses on two variables: the treatment variable (also called the intervention or the independent variable) and the outcome variable (also called the dependent variable). Its purpose is to evaluate whether the treatment variable has a causal impact on the outcome variable. This is achieved with five key design elements. First, there is a time dimension in which cases are (normally) measured on the outcome variable at least twice – once at the beginning and once at the end of the experiment. Second, the design uses at least two groups of cases (the experimental and control groups). Third, cases are normally randomly allocated to these groups at the beginning of the experiment to ensure that the two groups are initially equivalent. The two groups are then measured on the outcome variable. Fourth, the treatment variable is selectively administered to the groups – the experimental group is exposed to the treatment and the control group is denied it. Fifth, apart from this differential exposure the experiences of the two groups should be identical throughout the experiment. Finally, at some point after the treatment(s) have been administered, the two groups are re-measured on the outcome variable. The amount of change between the beginning and end of the experiment is computed for both groups. If the amount of change in the experimental group is significantly different from that in the control group this difference is attributed to the causal impact of the treatment or intervention. This conclusion is drawn because the two groups should have been identical to begin with and, with the exception of the treatment, have been exposed to identical conditions throughout the experiment. As the treatment is the only difference between the groups any differences between the groups at the end of the experiment are attributed to the causal impact of the treatment.

The settings in which experiments are conducted vary from laboratories to real-life social settings. Laboratory settings have the advantage of being able to control many of the extraneous factors and can help ensure that both the experimental and control groups have the same experiences throughout the experiment. However, because of concerns about artificiality and the fact that many social experiments last for extended periods, laboratory experiments are not widely used in social research. Real-life experiments involve either field experiments or natural quasi-experiments. Field experiments are conducted in real-life settings but retain many of the essential features of the classic experimental design. In a field experiment the investigator creates experimental and control groups through the randomized allocation of

participants to particular experimental interventions. The investigator actively intervenes and exposes particular experimental groups to specific interventions. An example of a field experiment is the New Jersey income maintenance experiment which provided different levels of guaranteed income to different groups to explore the impact on various behaviours (Orr, 1999).

The natural or quasi-experiment takes advantage of 'naturally' occurring events rather than the active intervention by an investigator. For example, an investigator, knowing that gambling is about to be legalized in a particular city could obtain measures of family well-being before and after the legislative change. A control group could be obtained by selecting a similar city where gambling remained illegal and examining whether family well-being changed more in one city than the other. The difficulty with this type of design is that it can be difficult to match the 'experimental' and 'control' groups and to eliminate the influence of other external changes.

Evaluation

Generally speaking, the experimental design has been seen as providing a more powerful way than non-experimental designs to uncover causal relationships. However, it encounters important shortcomings in social research.

One difficulty arises from practical and ethical considerations. It is frequently neither ethical nor feasible to intervene in people's lives to see what happens. Experiments can also face methodological shortcomings. While experiments provide a powerful way of identifying the causal impact of an intervention this comes at a cost. By removing the influence of all other factors through random allocation to experimental and control groups the experiment has only a limited capacity to arrive at explanations as to why one factor has the effect it does. Nor is it a good way of building a picture of how a set of factors produce a particular outcome. Experiments typically focus on the impact of just one or two factors.

A number of factors can threaten the internal validity of experimental results because they can create changes in the outcome independently of the experimental intervention. This makes it difficult to evaluate the extent to which change is due to the intervention. Such factors include the influence of other events occurring during the experimental period (the history effect), change due to participants growing older (maturation effect) and change due simply to being selected for and participating in an experiment (selection and testing effects). Experiments can also be afflicted by measuring instruments becoming less appropriate over the course of the experiment – especially in experiments where maturational change is likely (instrument decay effect). Change over the course of an experiment can also be attributed to the statistical phenomenon of regression to the mean and to experimental drop-out. Control groups can minimize the impact of these problems. Since both experimental and control groups should be affected equally by most of these issues, it is possible to isolate the influence of the experimental intervention by focusing, not on the absolute amount of change, but on differences in the levels of change between the experimental and control groups.

While it can be difficult to implement the classic experimental design in social research it is nevertheless a useful model to bear in mind when designing research. The logic of the design is useful and can inform the development of less rigorous, quasi-experimental designs.

David de Vaus

Associated Concepts: causality, ethics, evaluation research, field experiment, hypothesis, informed consent, messy research, quasi-experiment, validity

Key Readings

Campbell, Donald T. and Stanley, Julian C. (1963) *Experimental and Quasi-Experimental Designs for Research*. Chicago: Rand McNally.

Orr, Larry (1999) *Social Experiments: Evaluating Public Programs with Experimental Methods*. Thousand Oaks, CA: Sage.

de Vaus, D. (2001) *Research Design in Social Research*. London: Sage.

EXPLOITATIVE RESEARCH

Definition

Social research often involves an intrusion into people's lives and ethical guidelines exist (for example within universities or from professional organizations) to try to ensure that individuals are not exploited in any way during the research process. However, historically and to date there are examples of research that exploits respondents physically, emotionally, sexually and so on.

Distinctive Features

Defining the ethics of social research is complicated; social research is a dynamic social and human process that often involves an intrusion into people's lives. Researchers have a responsibility to their respondents and need to ensure that the design, process and delivery of the product of research is ethical and not exploitative. Universities and professional organizations produce ethical guidelines for researchers and increasingly researchers have to present reports on their method and approach to internal and external ethics committees. The potentiality for harm caused by taking part in research may be more obviously evident in medical or psychological experiments, but exploitation of respondents is possible in all social research. For example, a researcher may ask respondents to divulge views that are considered by many to be deviant and/or may be asking respondents to revisit events and experiences that make them distressed. It is possible to argue that if respondents freely agree to be part of research then they have some responsibility for the relationship. However, researchers who study people who are (arguably) particularly vulnerable (for example children, intellectually disabled adults) and who undertake covert research – that takes place without the knowledge or consent of those being studied – need to think even more carefully about the possible exploitative aspects of the research process. In addition, although a researcher – through their own reflexive practice and adherence to ethical guidelines – may collect the data in an ethically sound, non-exploitative way the way, the findings are used (which is not always within the researcher's control) may still negatively affect respondents.

Although not often considered within research reports and ethical guidelines, the research process can also be exploitative of members of the research team: for example, research staff are often employed on short-term, insecure contracts and there is much anecdotal evidence of abuse of power with research teams.

Evaluation

In the second half of the twentieth century theorists and researchers began to argue that doing sociology (and we could add all social science) is inevitably a political endeavour. Shulamit Reinharz (1983: 95) compared traditional research to rape, where researchers 'take, hit and run' and 'intrude into their subjects' privacy, disrupt their perceptions, utilize false pretences, manipulate the relationship, and give little or nothing in return'. Historically there are many examples of researchers exploiting respondents physically, emotionally and sexually in order to get the 'results' that they want.

Yet, it is important to note that even within research that aims to be non-exploitative the researcher usually has control over the research process from design through to analysis and so holds the objective balance of power. Thus, as Judith Stacey (1991: 144) argues, 'elements of inequality, exploitation, and even betrayal are endemic to [research]'. Having said this, we need also to be aware that researchers are not always 'all powerful' and that research may place the researcher in physical, emotional and sexual danger also.

Feminists and others have argued that in order to be ethically sound and non-exploitative research should be 'for' rather than 'of' the people being studied. Oakley (2000) gives an example of a research project that could be described as 'research of women' rather than 'research for women'. She cites a large research project on the social origins of depression and notes that the study resulted in a convincing explanation of the relationship between women's depression and their oppression. But there was no concern with whether or how women defined themselves as depressed, but only with how the state of women's mental health could be exposed and fit into a system of classification developed by a profession of 'experts' on mental health (psychiatrists). Also, the researchers did not begin with a desire to study the situation of women or set out to give women a chance to understand their experience as determined by the social structure of the society in which they lived. The primary aim of the data was to study depression and women were selected as respondents because they are easier (and therefore cheaper) to interview, being more likely than men to be at home and therefore available during the day.

The response of some researchers to this is to argue that researchers should not aim to represent the 'other' (that is, should not undertake research with people unlike themselves) in order to limit the possibilities of exploitation. However, there are problems here, not least because academia is not representative of all groups (for example, in relation to gender, ethnicity, age, dis/ability), which could mean that the experience of some groups remains unconsidered.

Gayle Letherby

Associated Concepts: confidentiality, covert research, disability research, emancipatory research, ethics, feminist research, informed consent, politics and social research, sensitive research

Key Readings

Homan, R. (1991) *The Ethics of Social Research*. London: Longman.

Kimmel, A. J. (1988) *Ethics and Values in Applied Social Research*. London: Sage.

Oakley, A. (2000) *Experiments in Knowing: Gender and Method in the Social Sciences*. Cambridge: Polity Press.

Reinharz, S. (1983) 'Experiential research: a contribution to feminist theory', in G. Bowles and R. D. Klein (eds), *Theories of Women's Studies*. London: Routledge.

Stacey, J. (1991) 'Can there be a feminist ethnography?', in S. B. Gluck and D. Patai (eds), *Women's Words, Women's Words, Women's Words: The Feminist Practice of Oral History*. New York: Routledge.

EXPLORATORY RESEARCH

Definition

Exploratory research is a methodological approach that is primarily concerned with discovery and with generating or building theory. In a pure sense, all research is exploratory. In the social sciences exploratory research is wedded to the notion of exploration and the researcher as explorer. In this context exploration might be thought of as a perspective, 'a state of mind, a special personal orientation' (Stebbins, 2001: 30) toward approaching and carrying out social inquiry.

Distinctive Features

In presenting social inquiry in the above way, Stebbins draws on C. Wright Mills's 'On Intellectual Craftsmanship' (Mills, 1959: 195–226). This seminal description of the lifestyle of the social scientist as explorer is a rich and detailed account of how to do exploratory research. Stebbins also develops the notion of 'concatenated exploration' (2001: 12) to emphasize how exploration refers to the overall approach to data collection, not only at the beginning but also throughout the research. The exploratory researcher does not approach their project according to any set formula. She/he will be flexible and pragmatic yet will engage in a broad and thorough form of research. Those engaged in exploratory research are concerned with the development of theory from data in a process of continuous discovery. Thus, exploratory research leads to what Glaser and Strauss (1967) appeal for in *The Discovery of Grounded Theory*, that is 'a rhetoric of generation' (1967: 18), where exploration is best interpreted as exploration for discovery. This specifically differs from exploration simply as investigation, which is rather too general a meaning for exploratory research in social science, and from exploration as innovation, which is in contrast, rather too narrow and focused. Instead, exploration constitutes a distinct form of discovery.

Evaluation

Exploratory research suffers from some fundamental misrepresentations and misunderstandings. Exploratory research is often seen rather simplistically as one initial stage in the developmental process of conducting a systematic research inquiry. In this sense exploratory research has become synonymous with the notion of 'feasibility study' or 'pilot study', both of which imply a prior or sequential stage in a research programme and thus a limited appreciation of exploration. It is also misleading to use exploration as a synonym for qualitative research. Although it can involve qualitative inquiry, this reading narrows the meaning of exploratory research and undermines the notion of exploratory research as being concerned with the development of theory from data.

Aside from misrepresenting exploratory research through using inappropriate shorthand synonyms there are further issues that relate to the poor understanding of exploration. Exploratory research as exploration-for-discovery is perhaps the most appropriate sense of exploration to convey here. Two other senses are referred to above – investigative and innovative. Neither of these forms of exploration properly represents exploratory research in the social sciences. However, further contentious issues arise from the confusion that often emerges surrounding exploratory research as a distinct form of discovery. The tendency in social sciences toward verification of theory incumbent with deductive and confirmatory procedures is sometimes used as a platform to discredit generation of theory through exploratory research. Confirmatory research has distinctly different goals to scientific exploration in the social sciences. The goal of the former is to test hypotheses. The quality of the research design is key in turning the hypothetical into the conclusive so that generalizability follows. In crude terms confirmatory research is valid, reliable and representative, it settles and confirms where exploratory research allegedly remains inconclusive, messy and vague. For those who remain to be persuaded that such criticisms are unfair and inappropriate, the associated concept of 'grounded theory' is called upon to counter such criticisms. Credibility, plausibility and trustworthiness are hallmarks of Glaser and Strauss's exposition of grounded theory, which as noted above, is in itself an appeal for exploratory research.

Pamela Davies

Associated Concepts: grounded theory, hunting (snooping and fishing), hypothetico-deductive model, intellectual craftsmanship, methodology

Key Readings

Glaser, B. G. and Strauss, A. L. (1967) *The Discovery of Grounded Theory: Strategies for Qualitative Research*. London: Sage.

Mills, C. Wright (1959) *The Sociological Imagination*. Harmondsworth: Penguin.

Stebbins, R. A. (2001) *Exploratory Research in the Social Sciences*. London: Sage.

EXTENDING SOCIAL RESEARCH

Definition

An approach which involves the researcher making findings available for implementation of policy and practice and being involved in such implementation rather than solely concerned with the design and completion of research.

Distinctive Features

The current emphasis on the usefulness of social research is nothing new. Indeed, some argue that the current momentum and level of activity associated with the idea of evidence-based policy (or evidence-based practice) is unprecedented, certainly in the UK. However, despite these and other motivations for enhancing the impact of social science research on the social world it examines, models of the social research process still commonly end at the point when findings are reported and this leads to others suggesting that social research has little impact on public policy.

Extending Social Research (see Letherby and Bywaters, forthcoming 2006) questions this end point and its associated apoliticism. From this perspective the research process is extended to encompass the tasks of making findings available, and their application and implementation in policy and practice; these elements are seen as an integral part of the research process, as much part of the responsibility of the researcher as setting the aims and deciding the methods, rather than detached activities which take place after the research has been completed.

Extending Social Research thus extends the boundaries of the traditional 'design, funding, access, fieldwork, analysis and output' model of research and involves not only a further stage – continued involvement and further developments – but also involves at every aspect of the process a reconsideration of what is meant by the research product(s).

Traditionally and to date, this is largely thought to be the research report and the presentations and publications that we write. Extending Social Research argues for the process to include active engagement with the impact of research. This goes far beyond reporting findings as clearly as possible or making recommendations for policy makers or practitioners to consider. This way of thinking about research has an influence throughout the process, from the way research is set up, the process of engagement with funders, collaborators and respondents throughout the research programme and the way researchers engage with processes of information giving, application and implementation. Extending Social Research influences every stage, includes further work for and with research funders and respondents, and necessitates not only a revision of the traditional research model but a challenge to many accepted and expected academic working practices.

Evaluation

Such is the current emphasis on evidence-based policy and practice that it may be necessary to justify the charge that currently most accounts of the research process end with the production of a report. Most, if not all, research funders require that bids include more or less detailed accounts of how findings are going to be made known. However, this expectation amongst funders is at odds with standard accounts of the research process taught to successive generations of social science students. The final stage of producing 'outputs' is usually described by teachers and authors as 'writing up' 'giving talks' or 'reporting and presenting the findings'.

Some texts and some models do clearly identify the issue of the impact of social research as an issue for the research process: that is, those that attempt to develop action and/or emancipatory research approaches. And even those not adopting these models sometimes explicitly address the issue of impact. For example, Darlington and Scott (2002: 177) include an Epilogue entitled

'From research to practice, programs and politics' in which they argue that researchers can and should be influential in 'determining the impact of their study'. However, here too there is a clear distinction drawn between the researchers' role and that of 'managers, policy makers and practitioners' (p. 177) and the focus is on the task of making recommendations, a language which itself reinforces the sense of distance between researcher and application. In their conclusion, Dartington and Scott (p. 188) recognize that 'research is rarely a linear process and it often takes the researcher down unexpected pathways'. The impact of the research may start very early on, and be an aspect of the research itself, even in studies that are not thought of as 'political'. Extending Social Research does not suggest that the researchers' engagement with the political aspects of research and the research process is unique but that all researchers (not just those engaged in explicitly identified 'action'/'political' research) have a responsibility to engage with the political aspects of the research process and the political potential of the work they do.

However, Extending Social Research is not always easy. For example, the closeness that it necessitates with funders, collaborators and respondents may prove difficult when researchers have difficult things to say and/or don't deliver findings that funders expected or hoped for. Furthermore, despite the concern of academic research funders to promote applied and practice-based research, other academic pressures, including the need to secure further research money and publishing research findings, means that time spent on Extending Social Research can feel like time wasted. This means that, for some, applied and practice-based research is somewhat of a poor relation and a distinct type of research apart from more theoretically informed traditional research.

Gayle Letherby and Paul Bywaters

Associated Concepts: action research, applied research, emancipatory research, exploitative research, policy-related research, politics and social research, research design, writing research

Key Readings

Darlington, Y. and Scott, D. (2002) *Qualitative Research in Practice: Stories from the Field.* Milton Keynes: Open University Press.

Hood, S., Mayall, B. and Oliver, S. (eds) (1999) *Critical Issues in Social Research.* Milton Keynes: Open University Press.

Letherby, G. (2003) *Feminist Research in Theory and Practice.* Milton Keynes: Open University Press.

Letherby, G. and Bywaters, P. (2006) *Extending Social Research: Application, Implementation and Publication.* Milton Keynes: Open University Press.

FACTOR ANALYSIS

Definition

A set of procedures used to simplify complex sets of quantitative data by analysing the correlations between variables to reveal the small number of factors which can explain the correlations.

Distinctive Features

Factor analysis is used to reveal the mathematical constructs underlying the responses to a set of variables such as tests or questionnaire items. So it has clarified the nature of intelligence and personality, and can indicate, for example, whether a questionnaire that claims to measure stress at work is measuring a single dimension.

Exploratory factor analysis is employed to identify the main constructs that will explain the intercorrelation matrix, a table showing the responses to each variable correlated with the responses to every other variable. Confirmatory factor analysis is where one tests whether hypothesized factor loadings fit an observed intercorrelation matrix.

A component or a factor explains the variance in the intercorrelation matrix, and the amount of variance explained is the eigenvalue for the factor. An aim in factor analysis is to obtain simple structure. This means that if there are two or more factors, each factor should have high correlations with a few variables and the remaining correlations should be close to zero. (If there is only one factor, all the correlations between the factor and the variables should be high.)

The outcome of factor analysis depends on the variables that have been measured, the respondents who yielded the data and the method of factor analysis used. When planning to carry out factor analysis there need to be at least 100 respondents and twice as many respondents as there are variables. The respondents should be heterogeneous on the variables being studied because if they are not the correlations between variables will be low. The correlations should be linear, and this can be seen if scatterplots are examined.

In exploratory factor analysis, one usually begins with a principal components analysis which yields a set of uncorrelated components. The aim of factor analysis is to explain the correlation matrix with as few factors as possible. The number to extract can be determined from a scree plot or by examining the eigenvalues of the principal components analysis. Factor analysis is then run with the number of factors set to the value obtained from the principal components analysis. Usually one allows rotation of factors, using a method such as Varimax.

There can be advantages in having oblique or correlated factors, which are obtained if one uses a procedure such as Oblimin. In deciding whether to use orthogonal or oblique factor rotation, one can apply orthogonal rotation and see whether it provides a simple structure solution.

Communality is the proportion of the variance in each variable which the factors explain. A factor loading is the correlation of a variable with a factor. A loading of 0.3 or more is frequently taken as meaningful when interpreting a factor. The naming of factors is a subjective process: one examines the variables with high loadings on the factor and selects a name that summarizes the content of these variables.

Evaluation

Factor analysis is of great value in elucidating sets of correlational data, but it is a group of procedures so the researcher has to decide which ones to use and these decisions will affect the outcome. It is a mistake to suppose that carrying out factor analysis is like arithmetic in that there is one 'right' answer, and all others are 'wrong'. Factor naming is an entirely subjective procedure.

Modern computer packages allow one to perform in a few seconds a factor analysis that would have taken many hours of hand computation. But this means that it may be used inappropriately. Researchers should refer to one of the texts on multivariate analysis to ensure the data are suitable for factor analysis to be applied and for guidance on which of the many procedures available to use.

Jeremy J. Foster

Associated Concepts: composite measurement, correlation, quantitative research, scaling, SPSS

Key Readings

Kline, P. (1994) *An Easy Guide to Factor Analysis*. London: Routledge.
Tabachnick, B. G. and Fidell, L. S. (1996) *Using Multivariate Statistics*. New York: HarperCollins.

FALSIFICATION

Definition

The empirical refutation of a scientific hypothesis or proposed law. In a general sense, the empirical confirmation or falsification of propositions is a routine aim in many areas of social science. In a stricter sense (as associated especially with the philosopher Karl Popper, 1934/1959), the falsification and the 'falsifiability' of propositions is advanced as providing a superior criterion of science ('falsificationism') than 'verification' and 'verifiability' (science as verified or potentially verifiable knowledge – the 'verification principle') as in logical positivism.

Distinctive Features

According to Popper, given the ever-present possibility of new and potentially refuting evidence, an inductive universal generalization can never be finally verified, whereas a single non-supporting ('falsifying') occurrence *can* refute a hypothesis. Thus, a single black swan refutes the general hypothesis that 'all swans are white'. On this view, science is best defined in terms of the 'falsifiability', rather than the 'verifiability', of its theories and hypotheses. This also has the merit of acknowledging the essential provisionality of scientific knowledge.

For Popper, the 'falsifiability' of a discipline's propositions provides the decisive *criterion of demarcation* between science and non-science. A virtue of the viewpoint is that in recognizing the importance of hypotheses and theories in science, and of changes in scientific knowledge, it also captures the 'critical spirit' of science. Hence, this position is sometimes also referred to by Popper as *critical rationalism*.

A related feature of falsificationism or critical rationalism, according to Popper, is its encouragement of bold hypotheses since the more unexpected the initial conjecture or prediction, the more severe the tests, and the more powerful will be the explanatory contribution to science where these hypotheses withstand falsification (in Popper's terms, receive 'corroboration').

Evaluation

Although it has attracted (and still finds) a good deal of support among social scientists and also in social policy circles (and is regarded as counting especially against 'unfalsifiable' social theories such as Marxism and Freudianism), critics of falsificationism challenge its cogency on a number of counts:

(1) that 'the facts' which are put forward as the basis of the 'independent' test of theories and hypotheses are themselves 'theory-laden' – experiments (including their instrumentation), for example, are both constituted *by* and interpreted *using* theories;

(2) in practice, in science, and contrary to the position that can be termed *naive falsificationism*, it transpires that a single refutation is rarely decisive since successful theories are not lightly discarded;

(3) the attempt (see Lakatos and Musgrave, 1970) to replace naive falsificationism with a *sophisticated falsificationism*, in which an overall judgement is made between progressive and degenerating scientific research programmes, fails to overcome the problems of falsificationism, for if no single observation is decisive and scientific research programmes are rejected and accepted holistically, falsification no longer provides a clearcut rule of thumb in the day-to-day procedures of science, or any clear overall demarcation between science and nonscience.

For many commentators (notably Feyerabend, 1971), the procedures suggested as mandatory for science by falsificationists simply fail to fit the past and present activities of science, and if used strictly would be likely to cripple it. What Feyerabend most objected to was the 'over-rationalized' and dogmatic character of Popper's account of science and his claims for a single 'scientific method'.

Where does this leave 'falsification'? As Blaug (1980: 42) has remarked: 'once granted that completely certain knowledge is denied to us there is nothing uncomfortable about the profoundly theoretical nature of our way of looking at facts about the real world'. In practice (and at odds with claims for 'incommensurability' and 'relativism') 'facts'

are often independent of particular theories and 'falsification' often serves well enough as a pragmatic approach. However, this is a long way from the claims associated with 'falsification*ism*'.

David Jary

Associated Concepts: covering-law model of explanation, hypothesis, hypothetico-deductive model, positivism, realism

Key Readings

Blaug, M. (1980) *The Methodology of Economics or How Economists Explain.* Cambridge: Cambridge University Press.

Feyerabend, P. (1971) *Against Method.* London: New Left Books.

Lakatos, I. and Musgrave, A. (1970) *Criticism and the Growth of Knowledge.* Cambridge: Cambridge University Press.

Popper, K. (1934, English trans., 1959) *The Logic of Scientific Discovery.* London: Hutchinson.

FEMINIST RESEARCH

Definition

What makes research 'feminist' is a contentious question. A view of feminist research as 'on, by and for' women has been seen as problematic and debates have focused upon whether feminist research can be defined through a distinctive choice of topic, methods, methodology or epistemology.

Distinctive Features

The term 'feminism' encompasses a variety of strands of thought. However, feminists can be said to share recognition of the significance of gender in the organization of social life, of asymmetries of power in gender relations and a political commitment to revealing and negating women's subordination. Since the 1970s, feminists have engaged in a critique of 'malestream' assumptions in research across a range of social science (and other) disciplines. Historically, social (and also natural) science and research had been largely carried out by men and focused upon men, representing the resulting knowledge as universal and objective. Thus conventional science had ignored the issue of gender and had ignored or marginalized women, (mis)representing women through stereotypical assumptions (for example, casting women as 'irrational' or 'emotional' in contrast to the rationality and objectivity claimed for scientific knowledge). Beyond critique, there has been much less agreement between feminists about what the characteristics of feminist research might and should be.

The idea current in the early 1980s that feminist research should be on, by and *for* women has come to be seen as problematic. Recognizing the significance of gender may make it important to study men as gendered beings who play an important role in women's lives. Nor is feminist research confined to research *by* women, since not all women are feminists. The important characteristic of feminist research therefore seemed to be that it is research *for* women (for example, Duelli Klein, 1983), although there are different interpretations of what this might mean. It does mean that there is an explicit political dimension to feminist research, but there are debates about whether this implies distinctive approaches to method (and, although qualitative methods, especially depth interviewing, have often been preferred, in practice, feminist research has used a variety of methods, including quantitative), methodology and epistemology.

An initial response to the critique of masculinist science was an argument for the adoption of non-sexist research practice, for example the avoidance of sexist language (for example, using the term 'men' to include women) and avoiding generalizing to women from findings based on men. 'Adding women in' would, on this view, lead to 'better' science by producing a more complete knowledge of reality. However, it is an approach that leaves unquestioned the methodological

and epistemological foundations of conventional science. This approach corresponds with what Harding (1991) calls 'feminist empiricism', which she contrasts with 'standpoint feminism' and 'postmodern feminism', both of which present greater challenges to conventional science.

For many feminists, the issue was not about 'adding women in', but rather of developing a more appropriate approach to researching for women. Research agendas needed to start from women's experiences, asking questions relevant to women's real lives, including those private and personal aspects marginalized in 'malestream' research (recognizing that the personal is political). Hence, feminists stressed the importance of recognizing subjectivity, not only that of the 'researched' (as recognized in the phenomenological tradition) but also that of the researcher. The claims of science to 'objectivity' were questioned, together with the associated idea of the researcher as a detached observer of social life, as if the researcher's own personal biography and involvement do not impinge upon the production of knowledge. The conventional view of the detached, objective researcher was recognized as leading to a view of research as a one-way process, in which those who are researched are treated as objects: such research involves an exercise of (abusive) power which was seen as ethically and politically inappropriate to feminist research. Women should be treated as 'knowers' and as experts in their own lives. Knowledge could thus be viewed as a co-production between researcher and researched, based on relationships of reciprocity and shared experience.

Standpoint feminism takes the view that research is necessarily a political act: knowledge is necessarily produced in particular contexts and from particular perspectives. Women 'know' from their particular experiences and their knowledge must be regarded as valid knowledge. Some have gone further to argue that women's knowledge is not merely different from the knowledge produced by masculinist science, but is actually 'better' knowledge: women (like other oppressed groups) have both to 'know' from the perspective of their oppressors (who have power to define the world) *and* know from their own perspective (knowledge which has hitherto been excluded or subordinated). Standpointism holds that feminist research carried out on this basis provides a new 'successor' science.

There are a number of problems with standpointism. One is that, if knowledge is necessarily produced from particular standpoints, then why should women be seen as having particular access to 'truth'? Secondly, there are problems about whether there is a 'women's standpoint': as black feminists in particular have pointed out, 'women' are not a unitary category and women's experiences are fragmented by racial, generational and other differences such as sexual orientation. Postmodern feminists argue that these criticisms mean that, inevitably, notions of absolute truth must be abandoned: rather there must be recognition of a multiplicity of relative 'truths' from the diverse experiences of women (and men). As with postmodernism in general, this seems to slide into epistemological relativism. However, some writers (for example, Cain, 1986; Stanley and Wise, 1993), whilst accepting that knowledge is fractured amongst a multiplicity of standpoints, have argued a case for a (modified) 'successor science', which holds out the possibility of 'better' knowledge (though not absolute truth) produced through personal and theoretical reflexivity about the assumptions and frameworks utilized in research. As Cain (1986) points out, this is a position close to epistemological realism.

Evaluation

Criticisms of feminist research hinge around its overtly political stance, the rejection of objectivity and issues about the relationship between method and experience. However, it could be replied that all research is produced from particular standpoints and that feminists endeavour to make their standpoints explicit. Thus, an explicit political orientation and recognition of the problems of 'objectivity' does not mean that theoretical and intellectual

rigour is abandoned. Rather, the aim is to produce good and useful knowledge (Cain, 1986) on the basis of engagement with epistemological and methodological issues, which are core to debates in social research more generally.

Maggie Sumner

Associated Concepts: anti-racism research, critical research, emancipatory research, epistemology, intellectual craftsmanship, politics and social research, postmodernism, realism, relativism, standpoint research

Key Readings

Cain, M. (1986) 'Realism, feminism, methodology and law', *International Journal of Sociology of Law*, 14: 255–67.

Duelli Klein, R. (1983) 'How to do what we want to do: thoughts about feminist methodology', in G. Bowles and R. Duelli Klein (eds), *Theories of Women's Studies*. London: Routledge. pp. 88–104.

Harding, S. (1991) *Whose Science? Whose Knowledge?* Milton Keynes: Open University Press.

Letherby, G. (2003) *Feminist Research in Theory and Practice*. Milton Keynes: Open University Press.

Stanley, L. and Wise, S. (eds) (1993) *Breaking Out Again: Feminist Ontology and Epistemology*. London: Routledge.

FIELD EXPERIMENT

Definition

An experiment conducted outside the laboratory, in a 'natural' setting.

Distinctive Features

Field experiments are contrasted with laboratory experiments. Laboratory experiments are conducted in closed, controlled conditions. Field experiments are conducted in open, natural settings. Field and laboratory experiments are undertaken both in the physical and social sciences. Laboratory experiments attempt to create conditions in which hypotheses about causal powers can be tested in idealized conditions conducive for their expression. Field experiments are sometimes conducted where laboratory experiments cannot be undertaken because of the nature of the phenomena being examined, for example in relation to many issues in climatology. Field experiments are also conducted where the potential application of laboratory-based findings to natural conditions is important, for example in trials of medical treatments applied to real, human patients as against non-human animals in laboratories.

In the social sciences, the scope for laboratory experimentation is more limited than in the natural sciences, with the exception of some areas of psychology. Hence field experiments are quite common. Field experiments are especially important in evaluation research, where the effects of new policies and practices are in question.

Evaluation

Achieving the control applied in laboratories in field settings is highly problematic. In an effort to isolate the effects of a given treatment, random assignment to experimental and control conditions is often attempted. The only difference for the experimental group comprises the treatment applied, and a comparison of changes in the experimental and control groups is made in the expectation that this will reveal the independent effects of the treatment. Random assignment, however, is often not practicable, especially where communities are the focus of intervention or where treatment groups cannot be isolated from experimental ones. Random allocation promises a method of achieving internal validity. It does not deal with many threats to external validity. Populations from which random allocation is made to treatment or control are always spatio-temporally specific and generalizations to other populations have to assume similarity in all relevant

respects. This is often unreasonable, and partially explains quite frequent variations in findings from study to study.

Field experiments do not always attempt random assignment. In both the physical and social sciences they may also use observational and quasi-experimental methods. At best, they aim to identify and explain variations according to theoretically specified sub-groups.

Nick Tilley

Associated Concepts: applied research, causality, evaluation research, experiment, hypothesis, quasi-experiment, validity

Key Readings

Campbell, D. and Russo, J. (1999) *Social Experimentation.* Thousand Oaks, CA: Sage.

Robson, C. (2001) *Real World Research.* Oxford: Blackwell.

FIELDWORK

Definition

The research practice of engaging with the worlds of others in order to study them at close quarters. This is carried out in order that the fieldworker can gain an understanding of the everyday operations and mechanisms of a particular way of life, and the meanings that members of that culture attribute to these everyday occurrences.

Distinctive Features

The natural playing out of cultural life is the object of the fieldworker's trade, and this can only be achieved by making close observations from within an environment that is natural to the observed rather than to the observer. To varying extents the fieldworker is a stranger in the field, working in an alien environment, and the extent of the strangeness experienced by the fieldworker will vary according to the specific culture under study, and the background of the fieldworker. Strangeness and distance are distinct features of nineteenth-century social anthropology, where the racial and colonial context within which researchers practiced made any sharing of perspective with the studied population at best extremely unlikely. With fieldworkers working at such a distance from their informants, native cultures were usually regarded as exotic, essentially inferior and in decline. The collection of data often constituted the amassing of cultural artefacts, with the fieldworker remaining remote from the realities of the everyday lives of the natives (Wax, 1972).

As anthropologists developed a more self-conscious approach during the 1930s and 1940s, the degree of participation in the lives and cultures of the studied population increased. This process was paralleled in sociology via the influence of the Chicago School, which combined the theoretical rigours of European theory and classical anthropology with a concern for engaging with the social problems of a rapidly evolving urban setting. Chicago's fieldworkers, if they were not already part of the culture they were studying (for instance, Nils Anderson used his former-membership of hobohemia to study transient workers), became members and associates of groups that were then subjected to close scrutiny filtered through the experience of the fieldworker The Chicago fieldwork tradition, typified by Robert Park's exhortation to his students to 'go get the seat of your pants dirty in real research', has proved to be as enduring as it is has been evocative. With echoes of Henry Mayhew's journalistic journeys into nineteenth-century London, and the campaigning writing of Jacob Riis and Lincoln Steffens, fieldwork-based studies of hobos, dancehalls, street gangs and slums laid the basis for a rich research tradition that was later joined by studies of drug users, jazz musicians and a multitude of occupations, social groups and cultures. The aura that surrounds the Chicago School as iconically urban, gritty and soaked in the dangerous mystique of the city as a social laboratory, often ignores other more mundane complementary methodologies and concerns of Chicago's sociologists. Yet although the Chicago School did indeed utilize a wide range of methodologies, their fieldwork-based studies have an enduring quality that has inspired generations of fieldworkers (see Deegan, 2001).

Evaluation

The close involvement of fieldworkers in the lives of their subjects poses a myriad of ethical problems and in many examples of fieldwork it is the researcher's proximity to problematic, ambiguous or outright criminal behaviour that constitutes the core of the issue (Hobbs, 2001). Although the roles adopted by fieldworkers can vary enormously, common to all is an academically contrived attempt to advantageously situate the researcher in order that he or she might address a social setting and the culture of those who naturally reside there.

The shapes, patterns and trajectories of action observed and experienced in the field are recorded as field notes, which are usually taken as soon as possible after the observed action (Emerson et al., 2001). Field notes are the immediate products of fieldwork, and consist of observations and reflections that are representative of time spent in the field. Consequently, field notes are selective accounts which, when accumulated over a period of time, will form the core of an academically framed account of a culture. It is via field notes that fieldworkers will seek to construct 'thick description' (Geertz, 1973), which will enable cultural interpretation to take place, and the methodologies applied by fieldworkers have had to evolve with the settings they study, and new fields are constantly emerging (Hess, 2001).

Fieldwork constitutes deliberate attempts at understanding a culture, and the utility of fieldwork has enabled a window onto disparate social worlds that would otherwise have remained hidden or obscured. The evolution of fieldwork from an archaeological enterprise linked closely to the rigours of colonial rule, into an interpretive device where the fieldworker is an essential component in the action has been a richly productive process for the social sciences.

Dick Hobbs

Associated Concepts: access, cultural research, ethics, ethnography, naturalistic data, participant observation, qualitative research, thick description

Key Readings

Deegan, M. (2001) 'The Chicago School of Ethnography', in P. Atkinson, A. Coffey, S. Delamont, J. Lofland and L. Lofland (eds), *Handbook of Ethnography.* London: Sage. pp. 11–25.

Emerson, R., Fretz, R. and Shaw, L. (2001) 'Participant observation and fieldnotes', in P. Atkinson, A. Coffey, S. Delamont, J. Lofland and L. Lofland (eds), *Handbook of Ethnography.* London: Sage. pp. 352–68.

Geertz, C. (1973) *The Interpretation of Cultures: Selected Essays.* New York: Basic Books.

Hess, D. (2001) 'Ethnography and the development of science and technology studies', in P. Atkinson, A. Coffey, S. Delamont, J. Lofland and L. Lofland (eds), *Handbook of Ethnography.* London: Sage. pp. 246–57.

Hobbs, D. (2001) 'Ethnography and the study of deviance', in P. Atkinson, A. Coffey, S. Delamont, J. Lofland and L. Lofland (eds) (2001) *Handbook of Ethnography.* London: Sage. pp. 204–19.

Wax, M. (1972) 'Tenting with Malinowski', *American Sociological Review*, 37: 1–13.

FOCUS GROUP

Definition

A method for collecting qualitative data through a group interview on a topic chosen by the researcher. A focus group typically consists of a tape-recorded discussion among six to eight participants who are interviewed by a moderator.

Distinctive Features

As a method for collecting qualitative data, focus groups emphasize learning about the thoughts and experiences of others. When the participants in a group interview share an interest in the discussion topic, their interaction can provide information about how they relate to the topic and to each other. The group dynamics in these participant-centred conversations allow researchers to hear how people explore the discussion topic. Hence, the most effective focus groups consist of participants who are just as interested in the topic as the researchers are, which helps to produce a free-flowing exchange.

When the participants are mutually interested in the discussion, their conversation often takes the form of sharing and comparing thoughts about the topic. That is, they share their experiences and thoughts, while also comparing their own contributions to what others have said. This process of sharing and comparing is especially useful for hearing and understanding a range of responses on a research topic. The best focus groups thus not only provide data on *what* the participants think but also explicit insights into *why* they think the way they do.

One particularly powerful strategy in focus group research is to bring together participants with a common background with regard to the discussion topic. This homogeneous group composition makes it easier for the participants to engage in sharing and comparing, especially on topics that may involve what others consider to be deviant behaviour. For example, a group of women who are commercial sex workers can discuss aspects of their lives that they would ordinarily keep secret from most other people. Because homogeneous focus groups can discuss topics that might be considered taboo in other contexts, they are a popular method for research in areas such as substance abuse, family violence and sexual behaviour. It is important to note, however, that this strength depends on careful recruitment procedures to ensure a group composition where the participants share a common set of experiences or beliefs with regard to the discussion topic.

Another advantage of creating groups where the participants share similar interests or experiences is an increased ability to carry on their own conversation, with less active guidance from the moderator. Such groups are frequently termed 'less structured' since the participants are free to pursue their own interests in their own ways. This style of focus group is especially useful for exploratory research where the goal is to learn the participants' perspectives. It is less useful, however, when the research team has a strong set of predetermined objectives. In that case, a 'more structured' approach would emphasize the role of the moderator as a discussion leader, who would use a fixed set of research questions to guide the group's conversation.

Taken together, these two dimensions of 'group composition' and 'interview structure' generate a variety of research design options for focus groups. This flexibility makes it possible to use focus groups for a wide range of purposes throughout the social sciences.

Evaluation

Compared to other qualitative methods, it is the interaction around a predetermined topic that makes focus groups unique. Although individual qualitative interviews also concentrate on well-defined topics, they do not provide the group interaction that is the source of data in focus groups. In particular, the process of sharing and comparing in focus groups often leads the participants themselves to explore the topic in ways that the researcher did not anticipate. Compared to participant observation as a means of collecting qualitative data, focus groups have the advantage of providing concentrated observations on the topics that are of most interest to the researcher. In particular, a focus group

with questions that generate lively exchanges can provide information about a range of experiences and opinions that might be difficult to observe outside such a discussion.

Focus groups also have a set of corresponding weaknesses, which lead to situations where other methods of collecting data would be preferable. Individual rather than group interviews would be preferable when there is a need for greater depth and detail about personal experiences or beliefs, because one-on-one conversations allow more time to generate richer narratives. Collecting qualitative data through participant observation would be preferred over focus groups when there is a need to understand behaviour in context. In addition, focus groups and other types of interviews provide only verbal and self-report data, so they are no substitute for observing how people actually behave in realistic settings. Finally, focus groups typically follow other qualitative methods in relying on small, purposefully chosen samples that generate theoretical insights, which makes survey research preferable for studies that require generalizability.

In just two decades, focus groups have moved from being almost unknown in the social sciences to become a popular method for collecting qualitative data. This widespread use clearly demonstrates their value. At the same time, however, this relative newness also means that focus groups have substantial, unexplored potential. This suggests a future for focus groups that builds on well-established procedures at the same time as it uncovers new uses for this method.

David L. Morgan

Associated Concepts: ethnographic interviews, marketing research, purposive sampling, qualitative research

Key Readings

Barbour, R. S. and Kitzinger, J. (1999) *Developing Focus Group Research.* Thousand Oaks, CA: Sage.

Krueger, R. A. and Casey, M. A. (2000) *Focus Groups: A Practical Guide for Applied Research*, 3rd edn. Thousand Oaks, CA: Sage.

Morgan, D. L. (1997) *Focus Groups as Qualitative Research*, 2nd edn. Volume 16 in the Sage Publications series on Qualitative Research Methods, Thousand Oaks, CA: Sage.

Morgan, D. L. and Krueger, R. A. (1998) *The Focus Group Kit* (6 vols). Thousand Oaks, CA: Sage.

FORECASTING

Definition

The process through which a forecast is derived. A forecast is the estimate of a value or condition in a future time period, for example, next year's level of inflation, expected demand for a product or service in 2010, whether a patient will develop chronic heart disease, students' examination results for the next semester.

Distinctive Features

All forecasts, and thereby forecasting, work on the basis that history will repeat itself, and that it will continue to do so. In addition to this, forecasting is also involved with looking at the cause and effect relationship that may exist between the independent variables and the dependent variable. Multiple regression, time series analysis econometrics and operational research methods are examples of some of the statistical techniques available. Qualitative methods such as focus groups, and the Delhi experiment might also be used to produce forecasts.

Forecasting can range from the very simple to the very complex; it depends upon what question you are attempting to answer. There are many ways to derive a forecast, none is superior to any another, and it is a matter of getting the right tool for the right job. However, the process involved in forecasting remains the same, and it is in essence based upon the scientific school of inquiry.

The forecasting process is one of:

(1) defining the problem;
(2) reviewing the information on the phenomena to be looked at;
(3) formulating a hypothesis, and research strategy (quantitative, qualitative or both) in order to address the hypothesis;
(4) gathering data;
(5) analysing the results;
(6) taking a decision as to whether to accept or reject the hypothesis;
(7) forecasting into the future as a result of this decision.

Evaluation

Does history repeat itself? Does the past impact on the future? To a certain extent the answer to these questions is yes. For example, the level of sales a company makes in previous time periods will have an effect on the demand for its products. This may be due to spares and replacements to maintain the product, high levels of customer satisfaction with the product, brand loyalty and other market features such as monopoly of supply. There are events, however, which may cause a 'blip' in history. These blips cannot be planned for, and do not occur with any degree of regularity. For example, the attack on the World Trade Centre had a devastating effect on the airline industry. Any previous forecasts as to the number of aeroplanes required to meet passenger demand had to be seriously downgraded. Indeed a number of airline companies went into liquidation due to existing market conditions and the general public's decision not to fly.

However, rail and coach business within the United States increased considerably as a direct result. Their forecasts of demand had to be revised significantly upwards.

A good deal of care and attention must be given when establishing a cause and effect model. Social phenomena are particularly complex and make forecasting all that more difficult. This problem is made more complex by the fact that most of the statistical techniques used assume linear relationships between the variables. In reality this is not necessarily so.

Paul E. Pye

Associated Concepts: causal model, econometrics, focus group, hypothesis, modelling, multiple regression, operational research management, prediction, SPSS, time series design

Key Readings

DeLurgio, S. A. (1998) *Forecasting Principles and Applications.* New York: Irwin/McGraw–Hill.

Makridakis, S. (1998) *Forecasting: Methods and Applications,* 3rd edn. New York: Wiley.

Wright, G. and Goodwin, P. (1998) *Forecasting with Judgment.* New York: Wiley.

Yaffee, R. A. (2000) *Introduction to Time Series Analysis and Forecasting.* London: Academic Press.

G

GARBOLOGY

Definition

In the narrow sense, garbology is the study of the contents of garbage cans (or dustbins) in order to make some assertions about the lifestyle of those who deposit garbage of different kinds. In a wider sense, it is the study of all materials discarded by individuals or groups, or within communities and societies in order to uncover social and cultural forms.

Distinctive Features

The study of waste products has roots in archaeology but more recently it has become associated with those who are concerned with ecological and 'green' issues. In the social sciences it has not developed a strong presence. However, where it has been employed it has been linked to the arguments for unobtrusive, trace or non-reactive measures. The problem of reactivity, for example in asking individuals questions or observing them, is that those individuals may respond or act in particular ways as a result of being studied. They may manage the impressions they give or respond in what they believe to be socially desirable ways. So, for example, in a questionnaire study of drinking habits it is likely that people will understate the amount they consume, especially if they are heavy drinkers. A non-reactive way of collecting data could involve counting the number of empty bottles in their garbage cans or examining discarded supermarket till receipts to see how much alcohol they buy.

Evaluation

The use of such trace measures is valuable in studying sensitive topics, such as excessive alcohol consumption, where reactivity is likely to be high. It is also a quick and cheap way of collecting data. However, there is the problem of making valid inferences about forms of behaviour from an examination of waste or other traces. For example, vodka bottles found in a dustbin may have been deposited by alcoholics drinking in a nearby park and not by the resident to whom the dustbin belongs. Garbology is an intriguing and innovative form of research but is unlikely to generate measures that are sufficiently strong by themselves. It is perhaps best used in triangulation with other methods of research.

Victor Jupp

Associated Concepts: covert research, trace measures, triangulation, unobtrusive measures, validity of measurement

Key Readings

Garwood, J., Rogerson, M. and Pease, K. (2002) 'Sneaky measurement of crime and disorder', in V. Jupp, P. Davies and P. Francis (eds), Doing Criminological Research. London: Sage. pp. 157–67.

Webb, E. J., Campbell, D. T., Schwartz, R. D. and Sechrest, L. (2000) Unobtrusive Measures, rev. edn. London: Sage.

GATEKEEPER

Definition

The person who controls research access. For example, the top manager or senior executive in an organization, or the person within a group or community who makes the final decision as to whether to allow the researcher access to undertake the research.

Distinctive Features

Gaining access to undertake social research is often problematic. Friends, contacts and colleagues and others may be willing to vouch for a researcher and the value of the research and act as research sponsors. However, unless permission has been granted by a gatekeeper from within the group, community or organization in which it is planned to undertake the research, it is unlikely that access will be allowed in practice.

Gatekeepers for research in formal organizations such as firms, schools, political parties and the like are normally senior managers or executives within that organization's hierarchy. In addition, employee representatives such as trade union officials may also act as gatekeepers within firms. The seniority of such people means that they control both the researcher's physical access to the organization and influence the degree of support the researcher is given subsequently by others within that organization (Saunders et al., 2003).

It is more difficult to ascertain who the gatekeepers are for research in other settings, such as those involving communities, gangs and less formal groups. Such people often take on the dual role of research sponsor and gatekeeper, both vouching for the researcher and the value of their research and controlling access to the group (Bryman, 2001). A key characteristic of such gatekeepers is the high degree of respect they command within their group.

Evaluation

Before allowing access, gatekeepers need to be convinced of the value of the research. Even if they are convinced of this, they may not be willing to engage in such additional and voluntary activities due to the time and resources involved, the sensitivity of the research topic or because of concerns about confidentiality. Gatekeepers often have different views to researchers regarding the amount of time for which it is reasonable for their colleagues to be involved in research, those issues that are sensitive, as well as issues of confidentiality. It is therefore important that these are recognized and taken into consideration when negotiating access (Saunders et al., 2003).

In order to help secure a gatekeeper's support, the researcher may offer something in return for granting access. Within formal organizations this is commonplace, often taking the form of a summary report of the research findings or an opportunity to influence the research to ensure that it incorporates issues that are pertinent to the organization (Buchanan et al., 1988). For less formal groups, such bargains are more varied due to the diverse and often informal nature of these research settings. It should be noted that some writers on research methods do not recommend this approach to securing gatekeeper support (Bryman, 2001).

Mark N. K. Saunders

Associated Concepts: access, confidentiality, covert research, ethics, organizational research, research bargain

Key Readings

Bryman, A. (2001) *Social Research Methods.* Oxford: Oxford University Press.

Buchanan, D., Boddy, D. and McCalman, J. (1988) 'Getting in, getting on, getting out, and getting back', in A. Bryman (ed.), *Doing Research in Organisations.* London: Routledge. pp. 53–67.

Saunders, M. N. K., Lewis, P. and Thornhill, A. (2003) *Research Methods for Business Students*, 3rd edn. Harlow: Financial Times/Prentice Hall.

GENERAL LINEAR MODELLING

Definition

The implementation of a set of procedures that attempts to accommodate data on a random dependent variable in terms of a linear combination of fixed and/or random variables (the model) plus a random variable (the error).

Distinctive Features

The general linear modelling (GLM) conception is that data may be accommodated in terms of a model plus error, as illustrated below,

$$\text{data} = \text{model} + \text{error} \qquad (1)$$

The model Equation 1 is a representation of our understanding or hypotheses about the data. The error component is an explicit recognition that there are other influences on the data. These influences are presumed to be unique for each subject in each experimental condition and include anything and everything not controlled in the experiment or study. The relative size of the model and error components is used to judge how well the model accommodates the data.

The term general in GLM simply refers to the ability to accommodate variables that represent both quantitative distinctions that represent continuous measures, as in regression analysis, and categorical distinctions that represent experimental conditions, as in ANOVA. This feature is emphasized in ANCOVA, where variables representing both quantitative and categorical distinctions are employed in the same GLM.

GLMs can be described as being linear with respect to both their parameters and predictor variables. Linear in the parameters means no parameter is multiplied or divided by another, nor is any parameter above the first power. Linear in the predictor variables also means no variable is multiplied or divided by another, nor is any above the first

power. However, there are ways around the variable requirement. The GLM described by Equation (2) is linear with respect to both parameters and variables.

$$Y_i = \beta_0 + \beta_1 X_i + \varepsilon_i \qquad (2)$$

However, the equation

$$Y_i = \beta_0 + \beta_1^2 X_i + \varepsilon_i \qquad (3)$$

is linear with respect to the variables, but not to the parameters, as β_1 has been raised to the second power. Linearity with respect to the parameters also would be violated if any parameters were multiplied or divided by other parameters or appeared as exponents. In contrast, the equation

$$Y_i = \beta_0 + \beta_1 X_i^2 + \varepsilon_i \qquad (4)$$

is linear with respect to the parameters, but not with respect to the variables, as X_i^2 is X_i raised to the second power. However, it is very simple to define $Z_i = X_i^2$ and to substitute Z_i in place of X_i^2. Therefore, models such as described by Equation (4) continue to be termed linear, whereas such as those described by Equation (3) do not. In short, linearity is presumed to apply only to the parameters. Models that are not linear with respect to their parameters are described specifically as nonlinear. As a result, models can be assumed to be linear, unless specified otherwise, and frequently the term linear is omitted.

Traditionally, the label *linear modelling* was applied exclusively to regression analyses. However, as regression, ANOVA and ANCOVA are particular instances of the GLM, it should be no surprise that consideration of the processes involved in applying these techniques reveals any differences to be more apparent than real. McCullagh and Nelder (1989) distinguish four processes in linear modelling: (1) model selection, (2) parameter estimation, (3) model checking and (4) the prediction of future values. While such a framework is useful heuristically, McCullagh and Nelder acknowledge that in reality these four linear modelling processes are not so distinct and that the whole, or parts, of the sequence may be iterated before a model finally is selected and summarized.

Usually, prediction is understood as the forecast of new, or independent, values with respect to a new data sample using the GLM already selected. However, McCullagh and Nelder also include a more general account of prediction, where the values fitted by the GLM (graphically, the values intersected by the GLM line or hyperplane) are taken as instances of prediction and part of the GLM summary. As these fitted values are often called predicted values, the distinction between the types of predicted value is not always obvious, although there is greater standard error associated with the values forecast on the basis of a new data sample (for example, Neter et al., 1990; Pedhazur, 1997).

With the linear modelling process of prediction so defined, the four linear modelling processes become even more recursive. For example, when selecting a GLM, usually the aim is to provide a best fit to the data with the least number of predictor variables (for example, McCullagh and Nelder, 1989). However, the model checking process that assesses best fit employs estimates of parameters (and estimates of error), so the processes of parameter estimation and prediction must be executed within the process of model checking.

The misconception that this description of general linear modelling refers only to regression analysis is fostered by the effort invested in the model selection process with correlational data obtained from non-experimental studies. Usually in non-experimental studies, many variables are recorded and the aim is to identify the GLM which best predicts the dependent variable. In principle, the only sure way to select the best GLM is to examine every possible combination of predictors. As it takes relatively few potential predictors to create an extremely large number of possible GLM selections, a number of predictor variable selection procedures, such as all-possible-regressions, forward stepping, backward stepping and ridge regression (Neter et al., 1990) have been developed to reduce the number of GLMs that need to be considered. After model selection, parameters must be estimated for each GLM and then model checking engaged. Again, due to the nature of non-experimental data, model checking is likely to detect more problems, which will require remedial measures. Finally, the nature of the issues addressed by non-experimental research make it much more likely that the GLMs selected will be used to forecast new values.

In contrast, a seemingly concise analysis of experimental data occurs. However, consideration reveals identical GLM processes underlying a typical analysis of experimental data. For experimental data, the GLM selected is an expression of the experimental design. Moreover, most experiments are designed so that the independent variables translate into independent (that is, uncorrelated) predictors, so avoiding multi-colinearity problems. The model checking process continues by assessing the predictive utility of the GLM components representing the experimental effects. Each significance test of an experimental effect requires an estimate of that experimental effect and an estimate of a pertinent error term. Therefore, the GLM process of parameter estimation is engaged to determine experimental effects, and as errors represent the mismatch between the predicted and the actual data values, the calculation of error terms also engages the linear modelling process of prediction. Consequently, all four GLM processes are involved in the typical analysis of experimental data. The impression of concise experimental analyses is a consequence of the experimental design acting to simplify the process of GLM selection and only attending to certain model checks.

Andrew Rutherford

Associated Concepts: causal model, econometrics, forecasting, multivariate analysis, path analysis, prediction, regression analysis

Key Readings

Cohen, J., Cohen, P., West, S. G. and Aiken, L. S. (2003) *Applied Multiple Regression/ Correlation Analysis for the Behavioral Sciences,* 3rd edn. Mahwah, NJ: LEA.

McCullagh, P. and Nelder, J. A. (1989) *Generalised Linear Models,* 2nd edn. London: Chapman & Hall.

Neter, J., Wasserman, W. and Kutner, M. H. (1990) *Applied Linear Statistical Models: Regression, Analysis of Variance and Experimental Designs,* 3rd edn. Homewood, IL: Irwin.

Pedhazur, E. J. (1997) *Multiple Regression in Behavioural Research,* 3rd edn. Fort Worth, TX: Harcourt Brace.

Rutherford, A. (2001) *Introducing ANOVA and ANCOVA: A GLM Approach.* London: Sage.

GIS (GEOGRAPHICAL INFORMATION SYSTEMS)

Definition

Generic computer-based facilities comprising hardware and software that process spatial data into digital information concerning, and used to make decisions about, a particular geographical location. Processes include data collection and inputting, the transformation of different types of spatial information, data storage, organization and retrieval, data manipulation and analysis and data presentation in tabular, graphic or map form.

Distinctive Features

The underlying methodology of GIS comes from overlay mapping, which is the process of building data in a series of maps, each representing a specific type or theme of information, which may be, for example, spatial, such as streets or trees, or statistical, such as census data. The maps are then placed over one another so that geographical coordinates align to present a composite picture of a particular geographical location and the interrelated characteristics that pertain to it. However, while mapping has excellent descriptive benefits through pattern generation, the power of GIS lies in two attributes; first, its ability to process and manipulate large volumes of data that would be difficult or impossible using manual techniques (Heywood et al., 1998), and second, its capability for spatial analysis involving complex interrogation of relationships between spatial phenomena (Demers, 2000; Schuurman, 2004). Indeed, as Schuurman (2004) points out, GIS can generate information or knowledge by the visualization of both clear and precise and imprecise data thus allowing room for intuition in analysis and thereby uniting the science and social process.

Although GIS has its roots in geography, having developed from cartography, it is now ubiquitous across a range of disciplines and pervades many aspects of modern life from business to medicine, archaeology to policing. Bernhardsen (2002) notes that its major benefit is its ability to link information from widely scattered sources, such as data obtained from maps, space satellite images, photographic and video information taken from low flying aircraft, statistical data and even data electronically transmitted via the Internet and other electronic sources. Questions that may be posed of GIS include 'the particulars of a given location, the distribution of selected phenomena, the changes that have occurred since a previous analysis, the impact of a specific event, or the relationships and systematic patterns of a region' (Bernhardsen, 2002: 225).

Evaluation

It is important to remember that GIS can only ever represent a simplified view of the piece of world that is its subject matter and a particular application will generally only reflect the specific purposes or research motives of its users. Definitions for GIS analysis of spatial phenomena can, for example, vary according to the socio-political agenda of those commissioning or carrying out the research (Schuurman, 2004). Furthermore, as with any technology, what comes out of the system is only as good as what is put in and therefore the quality and accuracy of data used is paramount. While the power of

GIS lies in its capability to represent spatial and object relationships visually in ways that allow patterns to be interpreted, the outcome is usually to establish cause and effect and this can be particularly problematic where cause and effect may be subject to the influence of phenomena that have not featured in the data gathering process.

It is also important to note that while GIS is valuable in its capacity to generate visualizations of spatial relationships in a way that allows users to interpret patterns, this should not obviate the contribution of other methodologies, such as local knowledge, in discerning patterns when used in conjunction with visual mapping (Schuurman, 2004). Depending on its application, GIS is best seen therefore as a useful complementary tool alongside other forms of empirical research.

Graham Steventon

Associated Concepts: causation, demography, disaster research, nomothetic

Key Readings

Bernhardsen, T. (2002) *Geographic Information Systems: An Introduction*, 3rd edn. New York: Wiley.

Demers, M. N. (2000) *Fundamentals of Geographic Information Systems*, 2nd edn. New York: Wiley.

Heywood, I., Cornelius, S. and Carver, S. (1998) *An Introduction to Geographical Information Systems*. Harlow: Pearson.

Schuurman, N. (2004) *GIS A Short Introduction*. Malden, MA: Blackwell.

GOOD PRACTICE STUDIES

Definition

Studies of good (or 'best') practice aim to identify examples of successful activities and operations in organizations that can be adopted by others to improve their performance.

Distinctive Features

Studies of good practice are a form of policy research, which is characterized by the pursuit of knowledge in order to facilitate action (Hakim, 2000). Research to identify good practice can range from highly systematic reviews of the effectiveness of particular procedures, for example in health services through well-documented case study materials, and audit and inspection reports, to ad hoc examples provided by the organizations themselves. The identification of good practice may form part of a wider strategy of performance improvement such as benchmarking (for example the Best Practice Benchmarking recommended to companies in England by the Department of Trade and Industry).

A key feature of studies of good practice is a particular emphasis on the need for effective dissemination. A study among local policy makers in the United Kingdom (Wolman and Page, 2000) found that nearly all those surveyed stressed the value and importance of learning from the experience of others. But it was also acknowledged that generally there was not a great deal done to ensure that such information was obtained and used.

Even in those areas where there is a tradition of rigorous scientific research, it is naïve to assume that when research information is made available it is somehow accessed by practitioners, appraised and then applied in practice. There is a need to understand the barriers to the adoption of new practices and the necessity to develop strategies to bring about changes in behaviour.

More and more, those responsible for disseminating good practice are devoting considerable resources and energy to developing more effective ways of ensuring that the findings of such work reach the target audience, and are acted upon. The dissemination process is often IT-based.

Evaluation

Because there is such a wide variability in the type of research that generates evidence of good practice, it is not possible to take a single view on the value of such studies. There has, in the past few years, been a substantial interest in evidence-based policy, that is, drawing on the findings of good quality research to inform the development of public policy (Davies et al., 2000). In the UK organizations such as the National Health Service Centre for Reviews and Dissemination, and the Evidence for Policy and Practice Information and Co-ordinating Centre (EPPI Centre), by carrying out systematic reviews of the quality of the research involved, provide reassurance that the practice that is being disseminated is well founded.

Similarly, case studies of good practice are often produced as one of the outputs of well-designed evaluation studies, which aim to assess the extent to which a policy or programme achieves its objectives. Or, they will be documented in an inspection or audit process, whereby they are assessed in terms of agreed criteria that define the required attributes. In such circumstances, the case studies should provide reliable examples of the desired practice.

In other instances, where the method of study is not so rigorous, it will not be possible to be as sure that the recommended practice is indeed all that it is claimed to be. It may be that the activity is of value, or can provide pointers to effective action, but the basis for the recommendation may not be very secure.

This points us to a further cautionary note. Even if the recommended practice is well founded it may not necessarily be applicable in all circumstances. Extraneous factors (for example, substantial differences in the range of problems clients present to a social services agency) may mean that the organization adopting the recommended practice will not achieve the same results as that which provides the exemplar.

Note

The above material does not represent the views of the Department of Education and Skills, UK.

Vince Keddie

Associated Concepts: applied research, auditing, case study method, cost–benefit analysis, evaluation research, messy research, policy-related research, process mapping

Key Readings

Davies, H. T., Nutley, S. M. and Smith, P. C. (eds) (2000) *What Works?* Evidence-based Policy and Practice in Public Services. Bristol: The Policy Press.

Hakim, C. (2000) *Research Design*. London: Routledge.

Wolman, H. and Page, E. C. (2000) *Learning from the Experience of Others: Policy Transfer among Local Regeneration Partnerships*. York: Joseph Rowntree Foundation.

GROUNDED THEORY

Definition

Grounded theory is an approach to research that was developed in response to concerns over the predominance of quantitative methods in social sciences and the tendency for research to be undertaken to test existing grand theories. Glaser and Strauss (1967: p. vii) perceived that there was an 'embarrassing gap between theory and empirical research'. They proposed instead an inductive process in which theory is built and modified from the data collected.

Distinctive Features

The interaction between data analysis, theory building and sampling is central to the development of grounded theory. As soon as sufficient data has been collected to begin analysis, it is used to generate categories. Glaser and Strauss discuss the constant comparative method, whereby sections of the data are continually compared with each other to allow categories to emerge and for relationships between these categories to become apparent.

Concrete categories are then modified into more abstract concepts. Theory building involves arranging these concepts into a logical scheme, which can be modified as further data are collected. The researcher is always ready to add new concepts as they emerge from the data. Data continue to be collected in relation to a category until it is 'saturated', that is, new data coming in are not contributing anything new to the analysis.

The method by which cases are selected for analysis is referred to as theoretical sampling. The aim is not to achieve a representative sample: cases are chosen as it becomes clear that they can contribute to theory generation. Negative case analysis is an important element of the sampling strategy: cases that do not fit the emerging theory should be examined in order that the theory can be modified appropriately. The process of searching for falsifying evidence, and modifying theory until no further disconfirming evidence can be found, is referred to as analytic induction.

The type of theory generated by this process tends to be middle range, that is, somewhere between grand theory and a working hypothesis. Existing theory is not discounted when using a grounded theory approach, but is considered after data analysis rather than before. When data analysis is complete, the researcher examines a number of existing theories to establish which fits best with the grounded theory that has been generated. The existing literature on the subject – particularly unpublished documents – may become part of the analysis, rather than predetermining the nature of the research.

Evaluation

As it is often difficult to theorize beyond the immediate phenomena being studied, there is a danger that an approach that is described as grounded theory will simply become a form of data analysis, with no real theoretical content. It is important, therefore, that data are used to guide theorizing but not to place limits on it.

Grounded theory is sometimes assumed to mean that the researcher approaches the topic without any preconceived conceptual framework and that the framework is formed entirely by the data. In reality, such an approach seems impossible – to choose to research a topic at all, a researcher must have some prior knowledge and/or preconceived ideas about it. A more realistic approach is to acknowledge that a researcher's perspective can shape their inquiry without this perspective simply being applied to the data.

Jamie Harding

Associated Concepts: analytic induction, constant comparative method, induction, methodology, theoretical sampling

Key Readings

Glaser, B. G. and Strauss, A. L. (1967) *The Discovery of Grounded Theory: Strategies for Qualitative Research*. New York: Aldine de Gruyter.

Pidgeon, N. (1996) 'Grounded theory: theoretical background', in J. T. E. Richardson (ed.), *Handbook of Qualitative Research Methods*. Leicester: British Psychological Society.

Pidgeon, N. and Henwood, K. (1996) 'Grounded theory: practical implications', in J. T. E. Richardson (ed.), *Handbook of Qualitative Research Methods*. Leicester: British Psychological Society.

H

HERMENEUTICS

Definition

The study of how we understand the communications, actions and products of other human beings – especially those of past times or other cultures. But it also implies a particular set of views about what such understanding involves, one that stresses the role of inner life experience, culture and/or imagination on the part of the interpreter – as against attempts to found the historical and social sciences on a method that begins from, or tests hypotheses against, description of the external features and/or behaviour of human beings.

Distinctive Features

Originally this term referred to the interpretation of ancient texts, especially of obscure or ambiguous passages in these. Under the influence of the Renaissance, and the revolution in historiography which it stimulated, there was recognition that in order to understand primary historical texts it is necessary to take account of the distinctiveness of the cultures in which they were produced. This emphasis on cultural discontinuity, on the dangers of misinterpreting others by viewing them as if they were members of one's own community, came to be central to much thinking about the nature of historical and social inquiry in the nineteenth century, especially in Germany. It was argued that social phenomena could not be approached in the same way that natural scientists were

assumed to explain physical phenomena: by describing their external characteristics and seeking to identify empirical regularities in their behaviour. Rather, it was argued, what people say and do can only be understood 'from the inside' – against the background of how those people think and feel about the world in which they live. Indeed, it was sometimes suggested that this provides a deeper kind of knowledge than that available to natural scientists.

Dilthey is the most important nineteenth-century theorist of 'understanding' or *Verstehen*. He believed there was a need for a philosophical psychology, or hermeneutics, which would ground the methodology of the social and historical sciences; and he set out to provide it. His earliest formulations portrayed *Verstehen* as a psychological process whereby historians project themselves imaginatively into the lives of people in the past, 're-creating' their experience, so as to capture the meanings embodied in texts and artefacts. His later account portrayed it as cultural interpretation, rather than as a subjective process. It involves locating what is to be understood in terms of objective cultural meanings that constitute the context in which it occurs. Part of Dilthey's concern here was to recognize historical diversity while yet resisting epistemological relativism. And his ideas have had considerable influence within the social sciences, notably through Max Weber's *verstehende* sociology.

In the twentieth century there was an important shift in orientation by some of those writing about hermeneutics, especially

H.-G. Gadamer. He rejected the idea that the past could ever be understood 'as it was', in the way that Dilthey and others assumed. He insisted that what is unknown can never be simply grasped or reproduced, since any interpretation necessarily draws on the particular socio-historical resources available to the interpreter. There is no way in which we can escape reliance on these, because without them there could be no understanding at all.

Where Dilthey saw *Verstehen* as a method that is essential to the scientific character of social research, Gadamer treated it instead as a fundamental aspect of human-being-in-the-world. And, from this point of view, it does not differ from lay forms of understanding; nor does it have the procedural, fixed character of a 'method'.

For advocates of this 'philosophical hermeneutics', interpretation is always necessarily a matter of dialogue. What is involved is the interpreter beginning from assumptions that are a product of his or her own socio-cultural location, while at the same time opening these up to challenge in the course of interpretation. Moreover, for Gadamer, the purpose is not simply to provide knowledge of other cultures but rather to advance our understanding of issues that are of universal concern, whether to do with ethics, politics, or philosophy.

The hermeneutic tradition carries implications both for what sorts of knowledge can be produced by social researchers and for what they ought to aim at. It raises questions about any attempt to understand human behaviour in causal terms, at least as modelled on causality in the physical realm, and thereby about experimental method as the methodological ideal. It emphasizes the importance of openness in seeking to understand other people's beliefs and actions, and therefore distrusts those approaches that employ highly structured elicitation devices, whether questionnaires or systematic observation schedules.

Evaluation

Hermeneutics has been subjected to considerable criticism. Positivists have argued that, at best, *Verstehen* can only supply hypotheses for testing, since it does not involve any rigorous form of validation. Subsequently, some versions of structuralism and post-structuralism have questioned the very possibility of understanding. Indeed, for some there is an obligation to challenge any claim that understanding has been or could be achieved: to celebrate or at least highlight the endless deferral of meaning or the incommensurability of cultural forms.

Martyn Hammersley

Associated Concepts: causality, covering-law model of explanation, cultural research, epistemology, historical analysis, methodology, positivism, reflexivity, *Verstehen*

Key Readings

Caputo, J. D. (1987) *Radical Hermeneutics: Repetition, Deconstruction and the Hermeneutic Project*. Bloomington, IN: Indiana University Press.

Dostal, R. J. (ed.) (2002) *The Cambridge Companion to Gadamer*. Cambridge: Cambridge University Press.

Makkreel, R. A. (1975) *Dilthey: Philosopher of the Human Studies*. Princeton, NJ: Princeton University Press.

Palmer, R. E. (1969) *Hermeneutics*. Evanston, IL: Northwestern University Press.

Truzzi, M. (1974) *Verstehen: Subjective Understanding in the Social Sciences*. Reading, MA: Addison–Wesley.

Weinsheimer, J. (1985) *Gadamer's Hermeneutics: a Reading of 'Truth and Method'*. New Haven, CT: Yale University Press.

HISTORICAL ANALYSIS

Definition

A method that seeks to make sense of the past through the disciplined and systematic analysis of the 'traces' it leaves behind. Such traces may be of many different kinds, ranging from everyday ephemera, artefacts and visual images, to old buildings, archaeological sites or entire landscapes. The most widely used historical traces, however, are written documents, whether of public or private origin.

Distinctive Features

Historical analysis is commonly used in social research as an introductory strategy for establishing a context or background against which a substantive contemporary study may be set. A stronger conception of historical analysis sees it as a pervasive and necessary technique in its own right, without which no account of phenomena in the present may be properly understood. In this more substantial form, historical analysis is often combined with other methods to engage social research questions.

History has the power to challenge dominant assumptions because it records, if in much less detail, the activities of the overlooked and the marginalized as well as elites. For this reason, historical analysis has proved particularly valuable to those researching gender, 'race' and other oppressed groups, and for those interested in developing alternative models of social change. The charting and assessment of currents of continuity, as well as change, is a major concern for the historical method, alongside other key conceptualizations such as chronology, periodization, causation, context and influence. Historical research may be oriented towards thematic or comparative questions and is also often concerned with some of the same debates about the relationship between structure and agency which have characterized the social sciences. Crucially, however, historical analysis has generally defined itself in terms of its essentially diachronic concerns and its complex narrative form, thereby distinguishing itself from the generalizing ambitions of social theory.

The validity of historical data depends on the key requirement that such data must have been produced within the particular time period that is being studied. They must, in other words, be contemporaneous with that period and continue to 'belong' to it, rather than to the present. Where data that purport to represent a particular time period do not themselves come from that time, then the consequence is likely to be anachronistic rather than accurate historical analysis. The requirement for historical accuracy demands that historical sources should be 'found' by researchers rather than 'produced' by them (in the way, for example, of data derived from interviews, social surveys or observation). Claims for the reliability of historical sources depend on the fact that they are preserved in open archives as unmodified traces and are available to multiple successive readings which are therefore themselves open to confirmation or challenge.

Evaluation

The emphasis on contemporary sources points to more general problems upon which all those undertaking historical analysis will need to take a position. These derive from the temporal divide between the past (the site comprising the object of study) and the present (the site occupied by the researcher). To what degree can it be possible to understand life in the past from the perspective of the present? To the extent that all individuals (including social researchers) are shaped by the social and intellectual contexts of their own time, can researchers divest themselves of the limiting biases and preconceptions of the present in order to engage the past openly? If such limitations cannot be overcome, does this mean that historical analysis must rest upon myth, prejudice and misrepresentation?

Historical researchers are divided in their answers, which in each case offer different conceptualizations of the relation between the past and the present. One group argues that the influence of the present may be nullified by trained historians who possess the analytical skills effectively to reconstruct the past. Such scholars adhere to the principle of scientific historicism which requires that researchers immerse themselves in all of the relevant historical data available to them, labouring day after day in archives and record offices. In so doing, they seek to release the true record of the past which is perceived as immanent in the sources. By consulting all such data exhaustively, the claim is that the researcher will be able to transcend the constraints of the present and to know the past 'as it really was'.

A second group holds to the same ambition for achieving historical truth as the first. In this case, however, there is a stronger recognition of the temporal distance between past and present, between object and subject. It is not difficult, for example, to show that the events of the same historical period may be quite differently represented in the analyses of historical researchers from different generations. For this approach, therefore, the present and the past can never be finally reconciled. In consequence, the results of historical analysis are seen to have their truth claims about the past inescapably qualified by the exercise of interpretation on the part of the researcher in the present. The act of interpretation itself is therefore raised to a cardinal position in historical epistemology.

A third, more recent group, drawing upon the assertions of postmodernism and poststructuralism, radically reverses the epistemological flow between past and present in arguing that 'all history is the history of the present'. Here, because it is claimed that there can be no certain truths about a past which has vanished, historical analysis may be transfigured into an entirely discursive or rhetorical exercise. This approach sees little point in the painstaking archival 'fact-grubbing' of traditional historicism and turns instead to constructing expansive analyses based upon very small numbers of isolated, contradictory or obscure historical traces. Such apparently cavalier use of sources is deprecated by more traditional historical practitioners, evoking their earlier critiques of social science history as little more than 'raiding the past'.

Philip Gardner

Associated Concepts: anti-racism research, critical research, diary, discourse analysis, document analysis, epistemology, feminist research, life history interviewing, oral history, phenomenology, postmodernism, validity

Key Readings

Tosh, J. (2000) *The Pursuit of History*, 3rd edn. London: Longman. pp. 55–70.
Tuchman, G. (1998) 'Historical social science: methodologies, methods and meanings', in Norman K. Denzin and Yvonna S. Lincoln (eds), *Strategies of Qualitative Inquiry*. London: Sage. pp. 225–60.

HUNTING

(SNOOPING AND FISHING)

Definition

A form of statistical analysis that involves searching through a data set to identify relationships between variables which are worthy of further investigation.

Distinctive Features

Selvin and Stuart (1966) provide a classification of strategies of survey data analysis which has been influential in guiding social researchers. The classification highlights different types of interchange between research hypotheses and data analysis. 'Snooping' is the process of using a set of data to test a predesignated set of hypotheses. 'Fishing' is the process of dredging data, usually using computer software such as SPSS, in order to decide which variables to include in a causal model on the grounds that each accounts for a worthwhile proportion of the variance in a dependent variable. These contrast with 'hunting' which is a much more flexible strategy aimed at generating hypotheses from the data which can be subsequently tested.

Evaluation

Such a data-dredging strategy can be a useful source of research hypotheses about the relationship between variables, especially as the full data set can be utilized and unexpected relationships may be indicated. However, statistically, it is unwise to test an hypothesis on the same data that generated it. Hypotheses generated by one set of data should be tested for significance on another set. What is more, it should be recognized that where two or more variables are found to be statistically related it does not necessarily indicate that they are theoretically related. Data dredging, hypothesis formulation and testing should be accompanied by meaningful theorizing.

Victor Jupp

Associated Concepts: causal model, correlation, hypothesis, hypothetico-deductive model, multivariate analysis, SPSS, variable analysis

Key Readings

Byrne, D. (2002) *Interpreting Quantitative Data*. London: Sage.

Field, A. (2000) *Discovering Statistics Using SPSS for Windows*. London: Sage.

Selvin, H. C. and Stuart, A. (1966) 'Data dredging procedures in survey analysis', *The American Statistician*, 20: 20–3.

HYPOTHESIS

Definition

An untested assertion about the relationship between two or more variables. The validity of such an assertion is assessed by examining the extent to which it is, or is not supported by data generated by empirical inquiry.

Distinctive Features

Hypothesis formation and testing are closely associated with the quantitative approach in social research and with the viewpoint that abstract concepts can be operationalized – or indicated – by measurable variables. There is a further assumption that social science should proceed by seeking to establish evidence of relationships between variables. This is sometimes referred to as variable analysis.

There can be variations in the specificity and breadth of an hypothesis. Specificity relates to the nature of the relationship between variables which is being hypothesized; breadth relates to the coverage which is being hypothesized. With regard to specificity, an hypothesis may simply assert that a relationship is one of symmetrical covariance; that is, changes in the values of one variable are associated with changes in the values of another, without making any suggestion as to causal influence or causal direction. The assertion that there is a relationship between crime levels and unemployment levels is an example of such an hypothesis. Being more specific, one may postulate the nature of the relationship in terms of values of the variables. A statement which hypothesizes that there is a positive relationship between the variables is suggesting that high levels of crime are associated with high levels of unemployment; and conversely hypothesizing about a negative relationship suggests low values on one variable as being associated with low values on the other. An inverse relationship infers that high values on one are associated with low values on another.

Some hypotheses go further by specifying the *extent* to which changes in one variable are associated with changes in another (whether positive, negative or inverse). Further, where the assertion is that the changes in one variable, say crime levels, are *produced* by changes in another variable, say unemployment levels, the hypothesis is suggesting an asymmetrical, causal relationship. In such cases changes in one variable (the dependent variable) are said to be dependent on another variable (the independent or causal variable).

The breadth of an hypothesis, of whatever level of specificity, is dependent upon whether the investigator is asserting that the relationship between variables holds for particular groups of people, particular contexts, for a particular society or cross-culturally.

Two broad strategies of hypothesis testing can be identified. Verification involves looking for data that support the hypothesis whereas falsification – which involves looking for data that refute the hypothesis – is viewed as a much more stringent test.

The specific process of hypothesis testing usually involves testing the *null* hypothesis that there is no relationship between the specified variables. A statistical test is carried out to seek to refute this null hypothesis. If this is not achieved then it is said that we have evidence to support the *alternative* hypothesis. This is the research hypothesis that is under consideration, namely that there is a relationship as hypothesized by the researcher.

There are risks in the testing of hypotheses. A researcher can make two types of errors. First, the researcher can accept an hypothesis as being correct when it is actually false. Second, the researcher can reject an hypothesis when in fact it should be accepted. The former is known as a Type 1 error and the latter is known as a Type 2 error.

Hypotheses about the relationship between two variables, say unemployment levels and crime levels, represent simplifications of the social world. Many more variables are likely to influence crime levels, or indeed any dependent variable. It is for this reason that more sophisticated procedures have been developed to examine a series of interlocking hypotheses at one and the same time. This is what is known as causal modelling and involves statistical techniques which come under the general heading of multivariate analysis.

Evaluation

Although typically associated with the hypothetico-deductive model and with quantitative research it should not be assumed that hypotheses are irrelevant in qualitative inquiry. Much qualitative research is concerned with producing descriptions of social interactions and social contexts and also moving to a higher theoretical level of generalizing about these. Such generalizations are grounded in observations collected in specific contexts but often seek to suggest that, for example, similar forms of social action are likely to be found amongst other groups and in other contexts. In this sense, they represent a form of hypothesis but not in terms of a statement of relationships between variables. What is more, hypothesis 'testing' in qualitative research is a continuous process, involving the search for cases or contexts that do not square with the assertions being made, rather than a once-and-for-all event. This process of analytical induction implies that generalizations are modified until no further disconfirming evidence can be found. This is known as the point of theoretical saturation and is the point at which the validity of the generalization is at its greatest.

Victor Jupp

Associated Concepts: analytic induction, causal model, falsification, grounded theory, hypothetico-deductive model, indicator, multivariate analysis, Type 1/Type 2 errors, variable analysis

Key Readings

Bryman, A. (2001) *Social Research Methods*. Oxford: Oxford University Press.

Moser, C. A. and Kalton, G. (1971) *Survey Methods in Social Investigations*. London: Heinemann.

Pawson, R. (1989) *A Measure for Measures: A Manifesto for Empirical Sociology*. London: Routledge.

HYPOTHETICO-DEDUCTIVE MODEL

Definition

A general model of science (Popper, 1934, 1959; Hempel, 1970) in which science is stated as involving the formulation of hypotheses and theories from which particular occurrences can be deduced and thus also predicted and explained. As a model of scientific discovery and explanation the hypothetico-deductive method is advanced as an alternative to Baconian 'inductive method' (Bacon 1561–1626) in which the simple accumulation of instances gives rise to generalizations. The model is based on the idea that, rather than the accumulation of facts, hypotheses are essential to science as the basis of proposed generalizations and their empirical testing (cf. 'falsification').

Distinctive Features

In terms of the model, hypotheses and theories are advanced and generalizations and predictions made on the basis of deductions from these, with: (1) successful prediction being taken as a test of the adequacy or plausibility of the hypothesis and theory, and (2) explanation being seen as achieved (at least provisionally) once successful predictions have been made.

At its fullest extent, proponents of the hypothetico-deductive model also advance the view that, ideally, scientific knowledge should be formulated as a network of deductively interrelated propositions and theories. At its fullest extent, the hypothetico-account portrays scientific theories as involving logically (and mathematically) interrelated theoretical statements, bridging principles or correspondence rules that link theories to observations, which include empirical laws and, ideally, sense datum statements.

Evaluation

An emphasis on the importance of the advancing and the testing of empirical hypotheses means that the hypothetico-deductive method is often identical to the 'covering-law model of explanation' and related to 'falsificationism'. In so far as the hypothetico-deductive model also implies that it constitutes *the* method of science, it meets similar objections to those arising in connection with these approaches. For rounded discussions of the combined model within particular social sciences, including its roots in 'positivism' and 'mathematical logic', see Blaug (1980) and Halfpenny (1982).

While the hypothetico-deductive approach to theory and testing, and the construction of systematic formal theories, has sometimes been advocated as a way forward for the social sciences (for example, in sociology, Zetterberg's formalization of Durkheim's *Division of Labour,* 1893), it has more often been strongly opposed (for example, by those who advocate grounded theory). However, 'ideal types' (for example, 'rational action', 'perfect competition') as heuristic aids to explanation or as parts of formal theories have the merit of allowing exploration of the more complex factors involved in empirical 'departures' from these 'idealized' forms.

A further general criticism is that adherence to the hypothetico-deductive model and its emphasis on the formal features of explanation has distracted attention from the concrete practices and complex historical processes of science and the way in which theories and broader 'scientific paradigms' emerge, prosper and are ultimately replaced (as especially discussed by Thomas Kuhn (1970) in his seminal volume *The Structure of Scientific Revolutions*). As Blaug (1980: 9) sees it, it is precisely the aim of the hypothetico-deductive or covering-law model 'to tell it like it should be' and not to 'tell it like it is'. It is this prescriptive, normative function of the covering-law model of explanation that critics find so objectionable. The most general criticism is that there is so much more going on in physical, let alone social science, that is not captured or adequately considered by the hypothetico-deductive model.

More generally, it is apparent that no single model of scientific explanation can be said to enjoy universal support. Originally, logical positivists – in association with the 'verification principle' – sought an absolute grounding for empirical laws in a universal data language and logic but failed in this objective. It is also a problem that generalizations that appear to qualify as 'covering laws' under the D–N schema sometimes seem to lack explanatory power or causal force (causality is anyway a disputed concept for positivists). There are also problems with alternative general accounts of science such as Bhaskar's 'scientific realism' for the grounding (and the links with observations) of its statements concerning the existence and action of underlying powers and mechanisms can be indeterminate (for example, the Marxian theory that social classes exist and determine social forms), since choosing between theories avowedly depends on judgements of the overall plausibility, fertility and elegance of theories.

David Jary

Associated Concepts: analytical induction, causality, covering-law model of explanation, falsification, grounded theory, hypothesis, ideal type, positivism

Key Readings

Blaug, M. (1980) *The Methodology of Economics or How Economists Explain.* Cambridge: Cambridge University Press.

Halfpenny, P. (1982) *Positivism and Sociology: Explaining Social Life.* London: Allen & Unwin.

Hempel, C. (1965) *Aspects of Scientific Explanation.* New York: Free Press.

Kuhn, T. (1970) *The Structure of Scientific Revolutions*, 2nd, enlarged edn. Chicago: University of Chicago Press.

Popper, K. (1934, English trans.; 1959) *The Logic of Scientific Discovery.* London: Hutchinson.

Zetterberg, H. (1961) *On Theory and Verification in Sociology*, Totawa, NJ: Bedminster Press.

IDEAL TYPE

Definition

A conceptual description of any social phenomenon (for example, mental disorder, crime, religion, bureaucracy) that helps researchers understand the subject matter as it exists in its abstract or pure form. The foundations of ideal-type analysis in sociology were adopted from the work of the eminent scholar Max Weber who originally borrowed the practice from economics. Weber's aim was to employ ideal-type descriptions in order to investigate social differences. For example, he explored different *types* of religion by contrasting the *ideal* description of a 'Protestant' with that of the ideal 'Jew', 'Hindu' and Buddhist'.

Distinctive Features

There continues to exist considerable confusion within the social sciences regarding the nature and purpose of ideal-type constructions and their relationship to the real world.

First, while an ideal type is created from observations made in the real world, nothing in reality precisely fits that ideal-type construction. For example, even though existing research evidence may be used to generate an ideal-type description of the causes of crime (for example, biological, psychological, sociological, political), this framework only exists as an abstract, exaggerated 'typical' model to help us explain the behaviour of criminals; it is unlikely that individuals found

in violation of the criminal law will actually conform to all of these attributes.

Secondly, an ideal type is an analytical tool and not an ethical ideal. In other words, there are no value judgements attached to the elements used to describe a particular phenomenon. It is not a moral statement about what *ought to be* the defining features of a particular subject, simply a description of what has been *observed to be* in existence in the real world. Nor should it be viewed as presenting the 'average' type of a particular social phenomenon.

Thirdly, any ideal-type formations must be 'objectively possible' in the sense that although they will not be found to exactly replicate reality, they are at the very least required to approximate what is going on around us. Moreover, they must also satisfy the condition of being 'subjectively adequate' in the sense that the elements defined as being ideal must be understandable in terms of the subjective views of the individual. For example, establishing an ideal-type conceptualization of the causes of crime in terms of demonological explanations (demons, witchcraft, spirits) would probably not satisfy these conditions, as it would have no objective or subjective reality in terms of the popular discourses and experiences found within late-modern Western societies.

Finally, confusion also exists over whether or not these ideal-type models can be used as the basis for research. Weber was not clear on this point, as on the one hand he claimed that ideal-type concepts were not models to be tested, but served a more specific purpose – as heuristic descriptions which help sharpen the classification and comparison of social events across time and place – while on the other hand he often implicitly used them himself during his studies (Rogers, 1969).

Evaluation

Several researchers have successfully demonstrated that there is a great deal to be gained from recognizing the close relationship between ideal types and real world situations. In particular, the present author (Colombo, 1997; Colombo et al., 2003) has managed to:

(1) formulate from existing theoretical knowledge several ideal-type representations of a particular social issue, namely the treatment, management and care of mentally disordered offenders;

(2) employ these ideal-type 'models of mental disorder' as a baseline in order to evaluate current professional practice; and

(3) use the findings in order to redefine or 'improve' the original ideal type models (medical, social, cognitive-behavioural, psychotherapeutic), and integrate them as the basis for training programmes on inter-professional practice.

It is important to note, however, that some sociologists would argue that employing ideal types in this way, that is, to generate a 'meaningful understanding' of specific issues, is inappropriate and that they should only be used in the development of general concepts and theories (Winch, 1958).

Anthony Colombo

Associated Concepts: covering-law model of explanation, deviant case analysis, hypothetico-deductive model, sensitizing concepts, *Verstehen*

Key Readings

Colombo, A. (1997) *Understanding Mentally Disordered Offenders.* Aldershot: Ashgate Press.

Colombo, A., Bendelow, G., Fulford, B. and Williams, S. (2003) 'Evaluating the influence of implicit models of mental disorder on processes of shared decision making within community-based multidisciplinary teams', *International Journal of Social Science and Medicine,* 56: 1557–70.

Freund, J. (1969) *The Sociology of Max Weber.* New York: Vintage Books.

Rogers, R. E. (1969) *Max Weber's Ideal Type Theory.* New York: Philosophical Library.

Winch, P. (1958) *The Idea of Social Science.* London: Routledge.

IDIOGRAPHIC

Definition

An approach or style within social research that focuses on specific elements, individuals, events, entities and situations, documents and works of culture or of art and concentrates on what is particular to these. This differs from research that highlights regularities and repeatable elements of form or behaviour as part of larger processes or patterns concerned with general laws and theories. The latter approach is known as nomothetic.

Distinctive Features

Idiographic (with an 'i') should not be confused with the term ideographic (with an 'e') – which refers to images of graphic symbols that represent things and ideas. Idiographic research is usually explained as distinct from nomothetic research. The idiographic/nomothetic opposition forms a significant distinction within social research. 'Idio' derives from Greek and is concerned with the individual, and 'nomos' refers to 'law' in the sense of order and consistency. Whereas idiographic refers to specific, idiosyncratic cases, the particular circumstances that give rise to them and the occurrence of unique and non-recurrent aspects, nomothetic approaches, on the other hand, emphasize that the social world cannot be characterized as a set of random occurrences, but as repeatable entities that give rise to patterns, predictions and rules. For example, an idiographic research project centred on a strike or labour dispute might investigate the specific nature of the dispute, the local circumstances that gave rise to it, and the groups, individuals, issues, demands and actions involved in creating, conducting and concluding the conflict. On the other hand, a nomothetic approach will place the dispute as part of a series of repeatable occurrences of disputes between employers and workers that show persistent patterns within wider historical trends and symptomatic features of the social and economic relations of production. Interpretivist and qualitative traditions of social inquiry are more readily identified with idiographic research; nomothetic research is identified with quantitative approaches associated with the natural sciences.

Evaluation

Idiographic research typically provides information and data of value to an understanding of the specific case in question. This is only valid for the investigated case and cannot be used to describe the set from which it is drawn. It offers little or no insight into social patterns and regularities. Nomothetic research, because of the nature of its inquiry, requires multiple cases in order to show patterns of repeatable elements but is incapable of dealing with the specificity of any individual case.

The difference between the two research approaches can be viewed in two ways. In what is often referred to as the 'hard' version, the idiographic and the nomothetic are deemed incompatible. For example, adherents of idiographic research might emphasize the primacy of specificity of the element of analysis and insist that generalizations built on two or more cases are impossible. However, the 'soft' version of the idiographic/nomothetic divide recognizes that the two approaches are different ways of coming at social reality, using different research methods, but that the two might be usefully used in conjunction (Wallerstein, 1987). This is akin to mixed-method research and triangulation.

Chris Wharton

Associated Concepts: autoethnography, covering-law model, ethnography, micro-ethnography, nomothetic, qualitative research, quantitative research, thick description, validity of generalization

Key Readings

Crotty, M. (1998) *The Foundations of Social Research*. London: Sage.
Wallerstein, I. (1987) 'World systems analysis', in A. Giddens and J. Turner (eds), *Social Theory Today*. Cambridge: Polity Press.
Wallerstein, I. (1997) 'Social science and the quest for just society', *American Journal of Sociology*, 102 (5): 309–24.

IMPRESSION MANAGEMENT

Definition

The conscious management of self-presentation, image and role in order to gain research access, maintain research relationships and facilitate the general progress of social research.

Distinctive Features

Impression management is a key feature of social research. Creating a good impression can aid research relationships and the collection of data. Alternatively, leaving a poor or bad impression can hinder all stages of the research process, for example, hindering access to settings, people or data, making research relationships difficult to forge or sustain and jeopardizing the establishment of rapport and trust.

Social researchers usually pay particular attention to their self-presentation, or the management of their 'personal front' (Goffman, 1959), during the early stages of research. Creating a positive impression is often vital to the successful negotiation of access, and to the initial establishment of research relationships. The social researcher is tasked with creating a working identity that is acceptable to the setting or to potential informants. This can involve some very practical considerations, including according attention to physical appearance. Dress is one of the ways in which we create an impression of ourselves. Clothing and accessories can be used to fit into a setting, show allegiance with informants, demonstrate deference or the seriousness with which the research is being undertaken. Knowing how to dress (for example to 'dress up' or to 'dress down') is part of the theoretical work of understanding the setting or people being studied, and of knowing what kind of appearance will create the appropriate impression. Other practical considerations might include speech and demeanour, the use of props (there are some settings, for example, when a briefcase may create the wrong impression) and personal habits (such as drinking alcohol).

Impression management is also about creating and maintaining a role over the course of the research. Indeed, the social researcher may adopt a number of different roles, at different times and in relation to different social actors within the research setting (de Laine, 2000). Social researchers may have to respond to different expectations that may be placed on them, and adapt their roles accordingly.

Evaluation

Being sensitive to the research setting is good research practice. However, the active management of the self for the purposes of research might be considered to be unethical. Adopting a completely false persona, entering into non-genuine relationships or making promises you have no intention of honouring raises difficult questions about deception, exploitation and trust.

Self-disclosure can also be an issue for social researchers keen to create a good impression. How far should the researcher go in sharing their lives and experiences with research participants in order to establish rapport and 'fit in'? Self-disclosure may facilitate stronger and more genuine research relationships. However, it does not necessarily

address the issue of power within social research. It also does not guarantee reciprocal research relationships.

Adopting different roles within research settings can be conceptualized in terms of the performance of self. Goffman has argued that all social actors are tasked with the performance of self in everyday social life. The task for social researchers is to be reflexive about this process.

Amanda Coffey

Associated Concepts: access, covert research, fieldwork, gatekeeper, reflexivity

Key Readings

Coffey, A. (1999) *The Ethnographic Self: Fieldwork and the Representation of Identity.* London: Sage.

de Laine, M. (2000) *Fieldwork, Participation and Practice: Ethics and Dilemmas in Qualitative Research.* Thousand Oaks, CA: Sage.

Goffman, E. (1959) *The Presentation of Self in Everyday Life.* Garden City, NY: Anchor.

Kondo, D. (1990) *Crafting Selves: Power, Gender and Discourses of Identity in a Japanese Workplace.* Chicago: University of Chicago Press.

INDICATOR

Definition

A measurable quantity which 'stands in' or substitutes, in some sense, for something less readily measurable.

Distinctive Features

There are three related ways in which this term is used. First, some people would use 'indicator' for any situation where a chain of logic and evidence is needed to reason from the measurements taken to the extent of the criterion. In this sense thermometer readings would be *indicators* of temperature, because what is actually measured is the height of, say, mercury in a tube; inferring temperature from this requires knowledge of physics.

A less inclusive use of the term would encompass those 'measures' where there is a high 'face validity' connection between the measure and the underlying criterion and/or successful effort has been put into demonstrating the measuring instrument's validity. An example would be intelligence testing. Here the underlying concept, the criterion, involves problem-solving ability and mental agility in real-life settings, and most of the measuring instruments are of the 'paper-and-pencil' variety. However, the test items are often themselves puzzles to be solved quickly, and a wide range of studies have demonstrated that the measuring instruments do largely behave as an accurate indicator of intelligence ought to behave. Another example might be indicators of social class, based crudely upon current job (or recent job, or usual job, or head of household's job), which by no means mirrors precisely the complexities of the underlying concept.

A third use, the most common, would be for criterion concepts which we are unable to measure directly but with which some other measurement correlates sufficiently highly to be a useful predictor of them. Examples would be various measures of affluence and material deprivation. It is often not possible to obtain reliable answers to questions about income. In British studies of health and deprivation it has been found that car ownership provides a reasonable proxy; it is not a *measure* of wealth – it is perfectly possible for poor people to own cars – but there is a sufficient correlation with income for it to be a reasonably valid *indicator* of income. Extent of overcrowding – ratio of number of people in household to number of rooms in house – has been used as another indicator. Another occasionally used in cross-national comparisons is extent of literacy, given that there is a tendency for those nations where literacy rates are high to be the wealthier ones. All of these have demonstrable problems. Car ownership, for example, correlates well with income, but only in urban areas; the nature of rural life is different. Overcrowding does not work as a measure of affluence in any area with a high proportion of social housing, because those who allocated the housing make sure that overcrowding does not take place.

Evaluation

One problem with this approach, despite its conceptual clarity, is that it is very much a reflection of a positivistic worldview. It takes for granted, as unproblematic, the underlying nature of what is being measured; the problems are measurement problems. This becomes a less attractive way of conceptualizing the research if one conceives of the indicator and the criterion concept as aspects of the same thing – not correlated, but in some sense formally identical or jointly produced – or if the nature of the criterion might be specific to individuals or settings in ways that do not show an overall regularity, or if the nature of what is being measured is in itself problematic. In measuring material deprivation, for example, one might take income as a measure of poverty or use correlated indicators such as car ownership or density of occupation. However, some might argue that to ascertain whether people are materially *deprived*, as opposed to just *poor*, may require talking to individuals and/or observing their living conditions and life chances in idiographic rather than nomothetic ways.

Roger Sapsford

Associated Concepts: composite measurement, measurement, performance indicators, positivism, projective technique, reliability, scaling, validity of measurement

Key Reading

Sapsford, R. and Jupp, V. (1996) *Data Collection and Analysis*. London: Sage.

INDUCTION

Definition

A form of reasoning from statements about observed cases to statements about other, unobserved, cases or – more usually – to a general claim about most or all cases of the same kind. It is contrasted with deduction (or the hypothetico-deductive model), which is reasoning from a general premise (for example, 'all humans die'), plus a statement about some particular case ('Socrates is human'), to a further conclusion about that case ('Socrates is mortal'). The most important distinction between these two forms of reasoning is that induction is ampliative: the conclusion is not already contained in the meaning of the premises; whereas deduction can tell us no more than what is logically implied by the premises.

Distinctive Features

Some commentators regard 'induction' as central to most forms of inquiry, while others deny that it is a valid form of reasoning. Within philosophy, for much of the second half of the last millennium, a crude contrast can be drawn between those approaches which took deductive logic – or mathematical proof – as the model for scientific reasoning, and those – from Bacon to Mill – which treated induction as the core of scientific method. Early twentieth-century philosophy of science, initially dominated by logical positivism, witnessed a shift from inductivism toward the hypothetico-deductive method. This change in position was motivated by what came to be referred to as the problem of induction: the failure of attempts to provide a logical account of induction equivalent to that available for deduction, one which showed how induction must be pursued if the conclusions reached are to be absolutely certain in validity, and *why* they would be certain.

The most influential twentieth-century opponent of induction was Karl Popper, who waged a war against inductivist accounts of science throughout his long career. For him,

all forms of rational inquiry involve a sharp distinction between generating and testing hypotheses. While inductive inference might play a role in the former, he insisted that it played no role in the latter. Moreover, hypotheses produced by induction were no more likely to be true than those produced in other ways, for example through dreams. However, by no means all twentieth-century philosophers were persuaded by this critique.

A number of approaches within social science have adopted an inductive orientation, in one sense or another. Forms of 'data dredging' in quantitative analysis are one example. In the context of qualitative research, there is the 'analytic induction' developed by Znaniecki and Lindesmith (see Hammersley, 1989) and Glaser and Strauss's 'grounded theorizing' (see Dey, 1999). The latter authors argued that theory 'grounded' in – in other words, developed out of – close empirical study of the social world is more likely to be true than that which is produced by armchair theorists. They criticize the tendency of much empirical research at the time they were writing for 'verificationism', for setting out to test hypotheses derived from speculative theory. Another form of qualitative research which adopts an inductive orientation is conversation analysis (see Hutchby and Wooffitt, 1998: 94–5).

Evaluation

Several kinds of induction can be distinguished:

(1) *Enumerative induction*. This involves generalization from a sample whose features have been studied to a larger, finite population of cases many of which have not been studied. This form of inference serves as a substitute for complete enumeration. Within the social sciences, enumerative induction is fundamental to social survey research.

(2) *Hypothetical induction (also sometimes called 'abduction', 'retroduction', or 'inference to the best explanation')*. Here, inference is from what is observed to what is taken to be the most likely explanation for what has been seen, where this explanation involves a general theoretical principle (usually

other cases.

(3) *Probative induction.* This involves reasoning from evidence collected for the purpose of testing a hypothesis or theory to a conclusion about its validity.

(For a useful discussion of different kinds of induction, see Rescher, 1978.)

It should be clear from the above discussion that whether induction is a valid form of reasoning depends on what sense is given to the term. It seems clear that there is no such thing as logical – that is, demonstrative – induction from knowledge of particulars to knowledge about universals. However, there are various forms of ampliative reasoning that are legitimate in principle, though whether any *particular* inference is likely to be true is of course a matter of judgement on the basis of the evidence available. These forms of reasoning include all three types of induction identified above.

It is also important to stress that these forms of induction serve different functions within the process of inquiry; they are not competitors or substitutes. Part of the problem with arguments about induction, especially criticisms of it, is that the term is often treated as if it referred to a single form of reasoning, demonstrative in character, which constitutes the whole of the research process. And, as Hume made clear, it is not difficult to show that no such logic of inquiry is available: to infer that the sun will rise tomorrow solely from the fact that it rose this morning is of doubtful validity. However, combining the fact that the sun rose this morning with knowledge of the laws of planetary motion, the inference to what will happen tomorrow is much stronger – though, of course, neither those laws nor anything else *guarantees* that the sun will 'rise' tomorrow.

Martyn Hammersley

Associated Concepts: analytic induction, conversation analysis, grounded theory, hunting (snooping and fishing), hypothetico-deductive model, inferential statistics, validity of generalization

Key Readings

Dey, I. (1999) *Grounding Grounded Theory.* San Diego, CA: Academic Press.

Hammersley, M. (1989) *The Dilemma of Qualitative Method.* London: Routledge & Kegan Paul.

Hutchby, I. and Wooffitt, R. (1998) *Conversation Analysis: Principles, Practices and Applications.* Cambridge: Polity Press.

Rescher, N. (1978) *Peirce's Philosophy of Science.* South Bend, IN: University of Notre Dame Press.

INFERENTIAL STATISTICS

Definition

Statistics from which inferences are made about situations or social groupings that have not been observed directly; for example, making inferences about a population based on a sample drawn from that population. In contrast to descriptive statistics, inferential statistics are used to make generalizations derived from estimates based on probability. It is therefore important that the sample on which inferences about a population are based is drawn randomly from that population.

Distinctive Features

Statistics can be either descriptive or inferential. Descriptive statistics simply state what has been observed. Inferential statistics make inferences based on those observations. Rowntree, along with other writers, places much emphasis on that aspect of inferential statistics which involves 'generalizing from a sample to make estimates and inferences about a wider population' (Rowntree, 1981: 19). However, Gayle places them in a wider theoretical context by saying that 'Inferential statistics allow us to make some statistical generalizations about an aspect of the social world' (Gayle, 2000: 385). Inferential statistics enable hypotheses to be tested and generalizations to be made. These can include (i) determining whether a sample came from a particular population, (ii) whether differences observed between groups are likely to be real differences, or are more likely to have occurred by chance, and (iii) whether a relationship between two or more variables is significant. Inferential statistics also enable us to make predictions about what is likely to happen on the basis of what has been observed. Statistics such as chi-square, Student's *t* and Pearson's product moment correlation coefficient are all inferential.

Thus, a descriptive statistic may tell us that 'the mean age of a group of students who answered a questionnaire was 19.7 years'. As long as the students who answered the questionnaire were a random sample of students at their institution, it may then be said that the mean age of students at Institution X is 19.7 years, within a margin of error – an inference. The qualification 'within a margin of error' is important, because error is always liable to occur. In this instance calculations are made to determine the standard error of the mean that enable us to say that there is a 95 per cent probability that the mean age of students at Institution X is, let us say, between 19.5 and 19.9 years. These are the confidence intervals of the mean. So inferences are made on the basis of clear rules and procedures about how they may be deduced.

Inferential statistics enable us to test hypotheses about population parameters. If descriptive statistics based on a sample tell us that, during a particular period, Court A sent 12 per cent of the convicted offenders appearing before it to prison, whereas Court B sent 18 per cent of similar offenders to prison, these proportions can be compared so as to tell us whether this difference could have occurred by chance, or we can be reasonably certain that Court B is more 'punitive' than Court A. Of course, the similarity of the offenders is crucial in drawing any conclusions: if the offenders at Court B have in general committed more serious offences this may explain the difference. So, in addition to testing whether the difference is real or may have occurred by chance, we also need to test for the similarity or difference of the two groups of offenders on other theoretically important variables.

Evaluation

The results of surveys are based on a sample drawn from a population. While the result given by a random sample produces a reasonable estimate of what the population is like, it seldom produces exactly the same result as if the entire population had been surveyed, and different samples drawn from the same population are likely to give slightly different results. For example, if there is a school with 1000 pupils, and if one had enough resources to interview every pupil (the population in this instance), you might find that the mean age of all the pupils in the school is 15 years. If, however, you only have enough time and money to interview 100 pupils, drawn at random, then the mean age of the sample might be 14.5 years. If someone else were to draw another random sample of 100 pupils, their sample might have a mean age of 15.5 years. These variations are known as sampling errors. The larger a sample is (that is, the closer it gets to encompassing the whole population) the closer the result is likely to be to the actual population figure.

Assuming, as is usually the case, that the figure for the population (the mean age in the example above) is not known, and all one has is the sample result, then an inference is made about the mean age of the population based on the sample result, but one knows that it is unlikely to be exactly the same as the figure for the population. So the population figure is going to be an estimate. This estimate is based on probability. Probability theory is therefore the basis for inferential statistics, and an awareness of the role played by probability is important.

Iain Crow

Associated Concepts: chi-square test, correlation, descriptive statistics, error, induction, prediction, probability (random) sample, validity of generalization

Key Readings

Gayle, V. (2000) 'Inferential statistics', in D. Burton (ed.), *Research Training for Social Scientists*. London: Sage. pp. 385–413.

Kranzler, G. and Moursund, J. (1995) 'Statistics for the terrified', is *Introduction to Inferential Statistics*. Englewood Cliffs, NJ: Prentice Hall. ch. 7.

Rowntree, D. (1981) *Statistics without Tears*. London: Penguin.

INFORMED CONSENT

Definition

An ethical principle implying a responsibility on the part of the social researcher to strive to ensure that those involved as participants in research not only agree and consent to participating in the research of their own free choice, without being pressurized or influenced, but that they are fully informed about what it is they are consenting to.

Distinctive Features

Most professional and academic organizations have codes of conduct or codes of ethics to offer guidance to promote good practice and high ethical standards in research. The principle of informed consent ensures researchers conduct themselves with honesty and integrity and with consideration and respect for the research subjects. This can be achieved by establishing guidelines, following good practice, consultation and communication. Under such codes, informed consent is one of the main responsibilities that researchers have towards their research subjects, whose rights should be respected. This particular responsibility implies that researchers should base research, so far as possible, on the freely given informed consent of those studied. Research participants should be made aware of their right to say no, decline or refuse permission and to participate. They should be able to exercise this right whenever and for whatever reason they wish. Moreover, whilst the researched may agree to participate generally they should nevertheless also feel free and be free to exercise their powers of veto during the research process and reject the use of specific data gathering devices such as tape recorders and video cameras.

For consent to be fully informed it is incumbent upon the researcher to explain as fully as possible, and in terms meaningful to participants, the questions of what, who, why and how. That is, what the research is about, who is undertaking and financing it, why it is being undertaken, how it is to be promoted and how any research findings are to be disseminated. None of these aspects of the research design are clear cut or straightforward. *Who* for example are the participants in the research? It is one of the responsibilities of the researcher to determine who informed consent must be obtained from. If access to research is gained through a 'gatekeeper' for instance, informed consent should be sought directly from the research participants to whom access is required. This may mean adhering to the principle of informed consent at several different levels of access. Special care in this respect must also be taken where research participants are vulnerable by virtue of factors such as age, social status, or powerlessness, or are ill or infirm or where proxies may need to be used in order to gather data.

Informed consent places the onus on the researcher to decide what is meant by anonymity and confidentiality whilst research participants should be informed about and understand how far they will be afforded anonymity and confidentiality. The researcher's responsibility extends to a careful consideration about making promises or unrealistic guarantees that might later be difficult, impossible or tempting not to keep.

Evaluation

Whilst informed consent ought to be integral to the research design this can prove difficult to adhere to in practice during the conduct of social research. Informed consent might be seen as an ideal-typical principle to which all social research should aspire. In reality, it may be impossible to achieve consent that is fully informed and in practice informed consent is never likely to be fully attained.

The practice of social research is often a process or activity that involves continuous decision making. As the research progresses it often creates a range of ethical choices and dilemmas. In some research contexts informed consent may need revisiting as the research develops and evolves. The aims and objectives of a research question may be clearly stated at the outset and empirical or experimental fieldwork will be conducted according to an original research design. Informed consent might be sought at an early stage but research is often dynamic and developmental and consequently the nature and use of the material obtained from the research is likely to alter. It may be necessary for the obtaining of informed consent to be regarded, not as a one-off event at the outset, but as a process, subject to renegotiation or reminder, especially during the course of research over prolonged periods of time. Informed consent is an ethical principle that may demand continuous dialogue and communication if participants are to fully understand what the research is about, who is doing and financing it, why it is being done and how it will be used.

Whilst the principle might be generally adhered to, at any stage of the research it is questionable how far consent can ever be informed, especially where research cuts across cultural and linguistic divides. Similarly, it is questionable how far participants can ever fully understand what it is to which they are committing themselves and what use will be made of the research of which they are a part.

Finally, covert methods of social research do not adhere to the principle of informed consent in any respect. This raises particular ethical issues. Where informed consent of those studied has not been obtained prior to

or during the research, it might nevertheless still be obtained afterwards.

Pamela Davies

Associated Concepts: access, confidentiality, ethics, experiment, fieldwork, gatekeeper, participant observation, politics and social research

Key Readings

Barnes, J. A. (1979) *Who Should Know What?* Harmondsworth: Penguin.

Bryman, A. (2001) *Social Research Methods.* Oxford: Oxford University Press.

Bulmer, M. (ed.) (1982) *Social Research Ethics.* London: Macmillan.

Bulmer, M. (2001) 'The ethics of social research', in N. Gilbert (ed.), *Researching Social Life.* London: Sage. pp. 45–57.

Homan, R. (1991) *The Ethics of Social Research.* London: Pearson Education.

Humphreys, J. (1970) *The Tea Room Trade: Impersonal Sex in Public Places.* Chicago: Aldine.

Punch, M. (1994) 'Politics and ethics in qualitative research', in N. K. Denzin and Y. S. Lincoln (eds), *Handbook of Qualitative Research.* London: Sage. pp. 83–97.

INTELLECTUAL CRAFTSMANSHIP

Definition

A way of working, associated with the American sociologist C. Wright Mills, which encompasses a distinctive methodological approach, in terms of the way research questions should be conceptualized, but also includes practical strategies regarding keeping research files and presenting findings and conclusions.

Distinctive Features

'On Intellectual Craftsmanship' is the title of the appendix to a highly influential book, *The*

Sociological Imagination, published in the late 1950s by C. Wright Mills (who died prematurely but who left an important legacy in the social sciences). His writings were very firmly in the critical tradition.

Intellectual craftsmanship is a way of unlocking the sociological imagination, which is characterized by seeking to locate and explain personal troubles in terms of public issues. For example, the personal and private experiences of unemployment need to be understood in terms of structural changes in the economy which displace people's jobs; the pain of marital separation needs to be explained in terms of the pressures on the family system in modern industrial society. In this way, the sociological imagination examines how individual biographies are shaped by social structure and how that structure changes over time. For Mills social science should concern itself with the relationships between individual biographies, social structure and history, and research questions should be framed in these terms.

Intellectual craftsmanship is the means of posing and addressing such questions and has a number of features. First, it involves keeping a file or journal of research ideas and questions. These are continuously under review and revision rather than in the form of a once-and-for-all research proposal (which Mills believed was likely to be a form of window dressing aimed at attracting funding). The sociological imagination, he argued, is released by constantly revisiting and reorganizing the file, by subdividing existing plans and by throwing together what, on the surface, appear to be unrelated facts and ideas. It is *not* released by adopting official or institutional definitions of what is problematic and then perhaps engaging in applied, policy-related contract research. (However, asking why certain matters receive the official seal of being 'problematic' at any given time, and with what consequence would be an important question for the file.)

A second key feature of the intellectual endeavour is reflexivity, that is, developing the contents of the file by systematically reflecting how life experiences shed light on personal problems and public issues: for Mills there should be a continuous interchange between personal experience and scholarship. This is a much wider interpretation of reflexivity than is used by those who simply refer to it in terms of reflecting on the process of fieldwork. He also advocates a number of other reflective devices such as thinking about opposites or extremes from the phenomena under investigation; deliberately inverting the sense of proportion by imagining something as bigger or smaller than it really is; looking at phenomena from a different disciplinary viewpoint, for example that of a psychologist or historian; and imagining instances of the phenomena under consideration in different contexts. All such devices are employed to stimulate the sociological imagination.

A third feature of scholarship relates to the presentation of findings and conclusions drawn from them. This is what Mills describes as 'literary craftsmanship'. Such craftsmanship involves paying attention to the interplay between reflexivity in the development of a research file (the 'context of discovery') and writing in the publication of books and articles (the 'context of presentation'). The former involves thinking clearly and presenting ideas to oneself so that one can eventually write clearly and intelligibly in order to present ideas to a wider audience.

Evaluation

There is much to admire and respect in the writings of C. Wright Mills. He stood steadfastly against theorizing for its own sake and against empirical inquiry for its own sake. In doing so he left a legacy that emphasized the necessity for a close interchange between theory, method and personal and public problems. He was also against those who were so locked in the jargon of theory or the jargon of empirical inquiry that they could not present ideas, findings and conclusions in an intelligible manner.

Perhaps what has not stood the test of time is his use of the term intellectual crafts*man*ship, which for some would seem inappropriate.

However, a critical thinker such as Mills, writing from the distant 1950s, would not deliberately intend this to be sexist language.

Victor Jupp

Associated Concepts: critical research, policy-related research, politics and social research reflexivity, writing research

Key Reading

Mills, C. Wright (1959) *The Sociological Imagination*. Harmondsworth: Penguin (especially the appendix 'On Intellectual Craftsmanship').

INTERNET RESEARCH

Definition

Use of the Internet to conduct primary research, as in recruiting participants, administering materials and collecting data, or secondary research, as in accessing online sources (such as library databases and online journals) which report the results of primary research.

Distinctive Features

Secondary research conducted via the Internet creates possibilities for accessing a particularly large and diverse body of information. Resources relevant to social research include electronic journals (for example, in the UK, Sociological Research Online: www.socreson line.org.uk), bibliographic databases (for example, Bath Information and Data Services [BIDS]), library catalogues, websites containing lists of subject-relevant links, online newspapers (for example, www.guardian.co.uk), subject-based discussion groups, and electronic texts available from individuals' or institutional web pages (for example, bibliographies, lecture notes, unpublished manuscripts). Some of these resources can be accessed free of charge (for example, online newspapers), others require a subscription fee (for example, most online journals). Carrying out secondary research on the Internet requires choosing appropriate tools, for example, search engines, or the resources mentioned above, and using these to locate relevant material. The credibility of the information accessed must then be assessed, before compiling a bibliography or literature review.

Using the Internet to conduct primary research is appealing due to the mass connectivity of millions of individuals worldwide which the Internet affords. The size and diversity of this population is likely to continue to expand (Mann and Stewart, 2000), thus increasing the possibilities for Internet-mediated primary research. The most common approach to date is survey research. Experiments, observational studies, interviews and focus groups, and analysis of linguistic archives have also been conducted. The stages involved in Internet primary research are much the same as in traditional (non-Internet) modes. Extensive piloting during the design phase is especially important in Internet research due to the novelty of the procedures being used. Recruiting participants can be done by posting requests to newsgroups or individual mail accounts, or by placing a study advertisement on the World Wide Web. A number of websites dedicated to listing currently active online studies exist (for example, Psychological Research on the Net: psych.hanover.edu/research/exponnet.html) and can be a useful place to advertise a study (though the possible bias in the type of participants accessed via such sites must be carefully considered). Administering study materials and procedures, and collecting data, can be done via a range of Internet technologies, for example email, FTP (File Transfer Protocol), HTML (HyperText Mark-up Language, which allows interactive forms to be placed on a web page), and Internet chat systems (further discussion of the tools available is provided in Hewson et al., 2003).

A third sense of the term Internet research refers to the study of the Internet itself (for further discussion see Jones, 1999). In the context of social research, this can involve studying online communities and social structures, as well as examining the effects of the Internet on people's lives, behaviour and experience. Research questions that have emerged include: What are the characteristics of Internet users? Is 'Internet addiction' a real phenomenon? Do people interact differently online (compared with offline)? How has the Internet impacted upon the experiences of marginalized or oppressed groups? What is the nature and extent of Internet crime?

Evaluation

Secondary research using the Internet can be both time-saving and allow access to more information than in traditional (for example, library-based) modes. However, it is crucial to assess the relevance, quality, and reliability of sources located. A number of strategies have been outlined to assess the quality of information accessed via the Internet. These include checking author details and affiliation, checking the date of publication and checking whether other sources have been accurately represented (Hewson et al., 2003).

Advantages of primary Internet research include cost- and time-effectiveness, access to a large and diverse participant pool, automaticity of features such as response completeness checking, and availability of data in a format ready for statistical analysis. These features could help enhance data validity, and facilitate cross-cultural research, access to special populations, and projects with limited time and funding. It has also been suggested that the greater levels of interactivity possible while maintaining complete anonymity, for example in an online interview, may help reduce bias due to biosocial attributes of the experimenter or participant (Hewson et al., 2003). Unobtrusive observational research is also made accessible due to the availability of, for example, archives of online discussion groups. Issues of concern in Internet primary research include sample bias, reduced levels of researcher control and difficulty implementing ethical procedures such as obtaining informed consent or ensuring confidentiality. However, a number of studies to date have shown Internet data to be valid, by comparing

Internet and traditional implementations of a study for example (see the chapters in Reips and Bosnjak, 2001). A possible barrier in Internet research is the level of technical expertise required of the researcher, especially when more sophisticated implementations are required. However, a number of tools exist (for example, SurveyWiz: psych. fullerton.edu/mbirnbaum/programs/survey-wiz.htm), designed to aid development of Internet studies with minimal levels of technical expertise. While Internet-mediated primary research is still in its infancy, some encouraging results have been obtained to date. Further implementation and testing of Internet research procedures is needed to clarify the future scope and usefulness of the Internet as a tool for gathering primary data.

Claire Hewson

Associated Concepts: access, confidentiality, data archives, ethics, focus group, informed consent, literature review, media analysis, primary research, secondary analysis

Key Readings

Hewson, C., Yule, P., Laurent, D. and Vogel, C. (2003) *Internet Research Methods: A Practical Guide for the Social and Behavioural Sciences*. London: Sage.

Jones, S. G. (ed.) (1999) *Doing Internet Research: Critical Issues and Methods for Examining the Net*. London: Sage.

Mann, C. and Stewart, F. (2000) *Internet Communication and Qualitative Research*. London: Sage.

Reips, U.-D. and Bosnjak, M. (eds) (2001) *Dimensions of Internet Science*. Pabst Science Publishers: Lengerich, Germany.

INTERPRETIVE REPERTOIRES

Definition

A concept developed to aid the discourse analysis of talk and texts and most commonly used by social psychologists and other discourse researchers to summarize relatively global patterns in people's sense making – particularly around controversial issues and matters of public opinion. Interpretive repertoires operate at a broad semantically based level. They are recognizable routines of connected arguments, explanations, evaluations and descriptions which often depend on familiar anecdotes, illustrations, tropes or clichés. Interpretive repertoires are the building blocks through which people develop accounts and versions of significant events in social interaction and through which they perform identities and social life.

Distinctive Features

The term 'interpretive repertoires' was first developed in 1985 by two sociologists of science, Nigel Gilbert and Michael Mulkay, to describe patterns in the discourse of the scientists they were studying. Gilbert and Mulkay noted that scientists had two contradictory and inconsistent but very regular and familiar ways of describing their scientific activity – an empiricist repertoire (a formal objectivist account of scientific discovery and progress) and a contingent repertoire (which stressed the informal social factors in scientific work such as people's networks and ambitions). Each repertoire constructed a different social world, populated that world with different kinds of characters (heroes and villains) and constructed different teleological histories and causal stories for the same events. These repertoires, separately and in combination, were used to powerful rhetorical effect in different contexts.

This notion was taken up and further elaborated by Jonathan Potter and Margaret Wetherell (1987; see also Wetherell and Potter, 1992; 1998) in their attempt to develop forms of discourse analysis for social psychology (see Edley, 2001, for an extended discussion of the history and use of the term with examples). Whereas the social psychology of beliefs, attitudes and public opinion had worked on the premise that people held consistent, stable and enduring attitudes, Potter and Wetherell noted the pervasive variability, flexibility and

inconsistency of everyday discourse on controversial topics such as race and racism. People's discourse is better described as a patchwork (Billig, 1991) of inconsistent motifs. Much everyday discourse is organized around dilemmas and involves arguing and puzzling over these (Billig et al., 1988). Arguments around meritocracy, for example ('the best person should get the job') are intertwined with equal opportunities discourse ('those disadvantaged in the job market should be positively supported'). Reference to the practical considerations (such as not being 'able to turn the clock backwards'), for instance, give way to arguments of principle ('social justice applies whatever the context'). The concept of interpretive repertoire is an attempt to identify and summarize the regular elements in this shifting mosaic. Interpretive repertoires are 'what everyone knows'. Indeed, the collectively shared social consensus behind an inter-pretive repertoire is often so established and familiar that only a fragment of the argumentative chain needs to be formulated in talk to provide an adequate basis for the participants to jointly recognize and sometimes resist and challenge the version of the world that is developing.

Evaluation

The term interpretive repertoire can be contrasted with Foucault's much wider ranging notion of 'discourses'. Both terms are concerned with the configurations of intelligibility, with global forms of semantic order and with ways in which discourse is constitutive, constructing realities and truths. Interpretive repertoires, however, are more fragmentary, less 'tectonic' (see the debate between Parker, 1990 and Potter et al., 1990) and more concerned with the performative aspects of everyday talk. The use of the word repertoire is apposite and a key notion here is the idea of an interpretive repertoire as like a choreographed dance. People have available a set of familiar cultural resources which they can use to make sense, but these resources are highly flexible, they need to be done anew in each new discursive context, they are a set of steps which can be put together creatively in new routines.

There are some clear parallels and overlaps with Bakhtin's notions of reported voice and genre and with the emphasis in that tradition on the ways in which words move across contexts from voice to voice. In recent years, the concept has been used to signal a more critical form of discourse analysis in social psychology. In contrast to conversation analysis, for instance, this work on interpretive repertoires has sought to make connections between patterns in talk and the broader social context, and the ways in which locally realized argumentative threads implicate discursive history (Wetherell, 1998).

Margaret Wetherell

Associated Concepts: constructionism, conversation analysis, deconstruction, discursive psychology, epistemology, ontology, realism, relativism

Key Readings

Billig, M. (1991) *Ideology and Opinions: Studies in Rhetorical Psychology*. London: Sage.

Billig, M., Condor, S., Edwards, D., Gane, M., Middleton, D. and Radley, A. (1988) *Ideological Dilemmas: A Social Psychology of Everyday Thinking*. London: Sage.

Edley, N. (2001) 'Analysing masculinity: interpretive repertoires, ideological dilemmas and subject positions', in M. Wetherell, S. Taylor and S. J. Yates (eds), *Discourse as Data: A Guide for Analysis*. London: Sage. pp. 189–228.

Gilbert, G. N. and Mulkay, M. (1985) *Opening Pandora's Box: A Sociological Analysis of Scientist's Discourse*. Cambridge: Cambridge University Press.

Parker, I. (1990) 'Discourse: definitions and contradictions', *Philosophical Psychology*, 3: 189–204.

Potter, J. and Wetherell, M. (1987) *Discourse and Social Psychology*. London: Sage.

Potter, J., Wetherell, M., Gill, R. and Edwards, D. (1990) 'Discourse: noun, verb or social practice?', *Philosophical Psychology*, 3: 205–17.

Wetherell, M. (1998) 'Positioning and interpretive repertoires: conversation analysis and post-structuralism in dialogue', *Discourse and Society*, 9: 387–412.

Wetherell, M. and Potter, J. (1992) *Mapping the Language of Racism: Discourse and the Legitimisation of Exploitation*. London and New York: Harvester Wheatsheaf and Columbia University Press.

Wetherell, M. and Potter, J. (1998) 'Discourse analysis and the identification of interpretive repertoires', in C. Antaki (ed.), *Analysing Everyday Explanation*. London: Sage.

INTER-SUBJECTIVE UNDERSTANDING

Definition

Understanding means having a sense of, grasping, or comprehending the meaning of something such as a text or human action. An understanding is inter-subjective when it is accessible to two or more minds (subjectivities).

Distinctive Features

The notion occupies a prominent place in social scientific research in three wide-ranging ways. First, inter-subjective understanding is generally accepted as the basis for the objectivity of judgements and claims made in research. Many social researchers accept a fallibilist epistemology – that is, they hold that there is no absolutely secure foundation for knowledge; hence all claims to know are always in principle uncertain and corrigible. Fallibilists hold that because knowledge claims never literally mirror or represent an independently given reality, objectivity cannot inhere in the results of inquiry (that is, in the claim itself). A knowledge claim cannot be objective by virtue of the fact that it expresses the way things 'really are' because we can never know that for certain. Rather, judging whether a given knowledge claim is objective is a matter of appraising the conduct or procedure of inquiry. Such a process appeals to inter-subjectively shared standards of scientific behaviour (that is, seeking out evidence to disprove one's claim, detaching sufficiently from one's own preferred perspectives so they might be submitted to scrutiny, and so forth) as well as rules of evidence and reason that are accessible to public scrutiny and inter-subjective criticism (Fay, 1996).

Second, a somewhat different notion of inter-subjective understanding is a central tenet of interpretive social theory. Owing, in part, to the influence of phenomenology, especially the work of Alfred Schutz (1899–1956), interpretivists of various schools of thought (ethnomethodology, hermeneutics, social constructionism) hold that the lifeworld – the everyday world of objects, practices and people in which we find ourselves – is inter-subjectively (that is, socially) constituted. This kind of inter-subjectivity is not regarded as a contingent aspect of human existence but rather a fundamental, essential (ontological) dimension of what it means to be human. Inter-subjective meanings and norms expressed in languages and practices are ways in which we experience ourselves and the actions and utterances of others. These meanings are not the property of individual minds *per se* but the common property of society and constitute the social matrix in which individual actors find themselves. A significant consequence that follows from this view is that the activities of knowing and understanding are not a private affair of mind but rather are located in the sphere of social activity (practice, engagement, or relations with others and the artefacts of one's world), discourse and dialogue.

A third significant use of the term follows from the foregoing insight. In social research concerned with the relationship of mind and culture (for example, socio-cultural psychology, activity theory, practice theory), attention is focused on the processes by which people come to know the thoughts, intentions, beliefs and mental states of others and how they adjust accordingly (Bruner, 1990; Chaiklin and Lave, 1996; Wertsch, 1991). These kinds of inquiries argue that inter-personal (that is, computational, private, individualistic, information-processing) models are inadequate for grasping what it means to understand or to know, and they focus instead on intra-personal models in which knowing and understanding are hermeneutic, social, transactional and inter-subjective accomplishments.

Evaluation

Three distinct but related kinds of debates frame the issue of what inter-subjective understanding is and how it happens. The first addresses the question of whether understanding human beings is methodologically different than understanding the physical world; in other words, whether there is something unique or special about inter-subjective understanding (or *Verstehen*) as opposed to causal explanation (or *Erklären*). A second set of debates centres on how inter-subjective understanding happens; how to provide a psychologically realistic account of the capacity to interpret, predict and explain the thoughts and actions of others. In this controversy, some scholars hold that understanding others is principally a matter of empathy, of putting ourselves in their shoes, so to speak (simulation model). Other scholars hold that understanding requires an interpretive reconstruction of the basic beliefs, assumptions and practices of the other (hermeneutic model). Still others hold that understanding and predicting the behaviour of others unfolds very similarly to the way a natural scientist explains and predicts the occurrence of any event.

A third debate surrounds the claim that inter-subjective understanding is the basis for objectivity. The principal issues here are what constitutes the putatively agreed upon, inter-subjectively shared understandings of scientific method; just who is included in and excluded from the 'community' of scientific inquirers that relies on such understandings; and, are concepts of reason, rationality and evidence transcendent or culturally mediated.

Thomas A. Schwandt

Associated Concepts: causality, constructionism, epistemology, ethnomethodology, falsification, hermeneutics, methodology, ontology, phenomenology, realism, *Verstehen*

Key Readings

Bruner, J. (1990) *Acts of Meaning.* Cambridge, MA: Harvard University Press.

Chaiklan, S. and Lave, J. (eds) (1996) *Understanding Practice: Perspectives on Activity and Context.* Cambridge: Cambridge University Press.

Fay, B. (1996) *Contemporary Philosophy of Social Science.* Oxford: Blackwell.

Kögler, H. H. and Steuber, K. R. (eds) (2000) *Empathy and Agency: The Problem of Understanding in the Human Sciences.* Boulder, CO: Westview.

Schutz, A. (1967) *Collected Papers I: The Problem of Social Reality* (ed. M. Natanson). The Hague: Martinus Nijhoff.

Wertsch, J. V. (1991) *Voices of the Mind: A Sociocultural Approach to Mediated Action.* Cambridge, MA: Harvard University Press.

INTERVIEW

Definition

A method of data collection, information or opinion gathering that specifically involves asking a series of questions. Typically, an interview represents a meeting or dialogue between people where personal and social interaction occur. However, developments in computer and information technology have resulted in other formats, for example, Internet interviews.

Distinctive Features

Interviews are typically associated with both quantitative and qualitative social research and are often used alongside other methods. Although interviews can be generally defined and have some commonality of meaning, they can vary enormously in terms of the context or setting in which they are carried out, the purpose they serve as well as how they are structured and conducted. This gives rise to many different types of interview.

Most commonly, interviews are conducted on a face-to-face basis and they can take a variety of forms. They can range from informal, unstructured, naturalistic, in-depth discussions through to very structured formats with answers offered from a prescribed list in a questionnaire or standardized interview schedule. Questions asked as part of attitude scaling are typical of the latter. Thus at one extreme interviews can be conducted as purposeful conversations, as in ethnographic interviews (Burgess, 1984) and at the other extreme they involve little interaction between the researcher and the researched. An example of the latter is Computer Assisted Personal Interviewing (CAPI), where interviewees enter responses into a lap-top computer by 'self-keying'. Since 1994 this mode of interviewing has been used in the British Crime Survey (BCS) for more sensitive topics within the interview and many large-scale surveys now use this form of interview.

In some contexts and for some purposes interviews may be conducted by telephone or by way of electronic communication such as email or fax. Interviews of this nature are popular for reasons of cost-effectiveness and for the speed of data collection. Telephone interviews are routinely used for the conduct of opinion polls by market researchers.

Evaluation

The advantages of interviews are that they enable the interviewer to follow up and probe responses, motives and feelings and their potential added value is that the recording of nonverbal communications, facial expressions and gestures, for example, can enrich the qualitative aspects of the data.

The alternative types of interview are associated with separate and distinct advantages and disadvantages. Unstructured interviews where the respondent talks freely around a topic can produce rich grounded data but can be very time-consuming to analyse and the potential for bias on behalf of the interviewer might be increased. The more guided or focused the interview, generally speaking, the less time-consuming and less problematic is the analysis. This is due to the more standardized nature of the responses. However, in opting for the latter form of interview there is generally an increased likelihood that the researcher might not be asking the most significant questions or unduly structuring responses.

Whilst interviews are often associated with qualitative research, they are not always adopted as the principle research method despite their potential usefulness, on practical grounds. Some research subjects may fall within categories often classified as 'hard to reach groups', for example, the homeless or those in prison. People belonging to different social groups might also require particular or different interview techniques and skills that might deter the use of this method. Thus the appropriate use of interviews is often compromised. In reality interviews might not be feasible or where interviews are part of the research design the precise nature of the interview might be determined by striking a balance between what is practical and feasible and that which represents the ideal. There is often therefore a balance or trade-off between the ideal form that the interview might take and issues related to feasibility.

Pamela Davies

Associated Concepts: CASIC, elite interviewing, ethnographic interviewing, life history interviewing, narrative interviewing

Key Readings

Burgess, R. G. (1984) *In the Field: An Introduction to Field Research.* London: Allen & Unwin.

Keats, D. M. (2000) *Interviewing: A Practical Guide for Students and Professionals.* Milton Keynes: Open University Press.

McCracken, G. (1988) *The Long Interview.* Beverly Hills, CA: Sage.

Mason, J. (1997) *Qualitative Researching.* London: Sage.

L

LIFE HISTORY INTERVIEWING

Definition

An approach that uses a form of individual interview directed to documenting the respondent's life, or an aspect of it that has developed over the life course.

Distinctive Features

Plummer (2001) notes three main types of 'life stories': the naturalistic (stories of a life told in a given culture, unshaped by research intervention); the researched (specifically gathered for research purposes); and the reflexive–recursive (life stories constructed in self-consciousness, being the product of postmodernity's 'crisis of representation').

The method is long-established in social history, anthropology, sociology and psychology, and has also become associated with feminist research (Devault, 1990). It is demanding on respondents and researchers, as it seeks to go into depth and recovers experiences across long periods. It can also uncover strong emotions. The interviews are normally time-intensive, sometimes taking several all-day sessions. Other than topical breadth and extensive duration, characteristics are shared with other semi- and nonstandardized styles of interview (Atkinson, 1998). There tends to be a stronger emphasis on non-directiveness than is usual in semistandardized interviewing, with researchers adopting the posture of the good listener, seeking interviewees' own interpretations of their experience.

The Biographical Interpretive Method (BIM) is a sub-type that emerged from techniques developed to conduct interviews with survivors of Nazi oppression. BIM has a therapeutic element and orientation to handling sensitive topics, exemplified by Hollway and Jefferson's (1997) research exploring fear of crime, where BIM was used to elicit stories non-directively in pursuit of subjects' gestalt (see Wengraf, 2001).

A contrasting application is when detailed and extensive data are needed, like case histories or behavioural records, to enable statistically based analysis. While still intensive, the style is more structured. Freedman, Thornton and Camburn (1988) offer a 'life history calendar' method for such applications. Bertaux and Kohli (1984) suggest a distinction between interpretive and 'scientific' approaches to life histories. The former focuses on meaning in individual lives, and the latter seeks accurate descriptions of life trajectories to uncover processes shaping patterns of social relations.

Cavan's (1929) pioneering contribution emphasized the 'genetic' dimension of life histories, enabling researchers to see how attitudes and behaviour were formed. She noted lack of consensus on analysing life history interviews, an enduring concern. Faraday and Plummer (1979) commend as particularly applicable to life history data an exploratory 'AHFA (Ad Hoc Fumbling Around) approach' which is used to generate concepts.

Bertaux (1995) takes a different tack, using life history data to derive 'social genealogies' to research social mobility where long-term generational effects are important. The unit of observation is not the individual but a set of life trajectories in kinship groups. Bertaux contrasts social genealogies and the more limited information derivable from statistical surveys. Frank's (1979) phenomenological approach disbars such systematic applications. For Frank, the life history is a text resulting from a collaboration involving the consciousness of researcher as well as subject. We always approach life histories with the core question of how this person compares to ourselves.

Ferrarotti (1983) offers an intermediate approach, where life history is 'history from below', a corrective to the elite versions dominating historical texts. The method connects individual biography with structural characteristics of historical situations. Although traditional biographic methods prefer supposedly 'objective' secondary materials, Ferrarotti argues that the 'explosive subjectivity' of primary data should be prioritized. Like Bertaux, he suggests that every individual act is the totalization of a social system, but commends a 'biography of primary groups' because such groups are not reducible to networks of socioeconomic interactions.

Evaluation

Plummer (2001) details ethical issues relating to the method. As he noted in Faraday and Plummer (1979), there is concern about exploiting rapport for research purposes. For example, an empathetic life history interview may confirm the respondent in a deviant identity.

Much commented on is the idea that life history enables interviewing interviewees to 'speak through' published accounts to their own community. For Blackman (1992), the issues here are construction of the self through narrative and the cross-cultural dialogue of narrator and interviewer.

Bowes, Dar and Sim (1997) maintain that the three main criticisms of the method are disguised strengths. Bias is the other side of the coin of reflexivity, where researchers

must acknowledge the situated character of their interpretive work. While life history accounts are cultural constructions, awareness of this stimulates analytic depth. As to the relationship between life history and wider social forces, accounts based on more 'objective' data downplay the role of social actors' agency in favour of structural forces, to which life history data is a corrective. There cannot be a 'pure' life history. Any life history is a cultural construction. The point is to weigh the data with this in mind (Yow, 1994).

Nigel G. Fielding

Associated Concepts: critical ethnography, diary, ethics, ethnographic interviewing, feminist research, historical analysis, idiographic, interview, narrative interviewing, oral history

Key Readings

Atkinson, R. (1998) *The Life Story Interview*. London: Sage.

Bertaux, D. (1995) 'Social genealogies commented on and compared', *Current Sociology*, 43 (2–3): 69–88.

Bertaux, D. and Kohli, M. (1984) 'The life story approach', *Annual Review of Sociology*, 10: 215–37.

Blackman, M. B. (1992) 'The afterlife of life history', *Journal of Narrative and Life History*, 2 (1): 1–9.

Bowes, A., Dar, N. and Sim, D. (1997) 'Life histories in housing research', *Quality & Quantity*, 31 (2): 109–25.

Cavan, R. (1929) 'Interviewing for life history material', *American Journal of Sociology*, 15: 100–15.

Devault, M. (1990) 'Talking and listening from women's standpoint', *Social Problems*, 37 (1): 96–116.

Faraday, A. and Plummer, K. (1979) 'Doing life histories', *Sociological Review*, 27 (4): 773–98.

Ferrarotti, F. (1983) 'Biography and the social sciences', *Social Research*, 50 (1): 57–80.

Frank, G. (1979) 'Finding the common denominator: a phenomenological critique of life history method', *Ethos*, 7 (1): 68–94.

Freedman, D., Thornton, A. and Camburn, D. (1988) 'The life history calendar: a technique for collecting retrospective data', *Sociological Methodology*, 18: 37–68.

Hollway, W. and Jefferson, T. (1997) 'Eliciting narrative through the in-depth interview', *Qualitative Inquiry*, 3 (1): 53–70.

Plummer, K. (2001) 'The call of life stories in ethnographic research', in P. Atkinson, A. Coffey, S. Delamont, J. Lofland and L. Lofland (eds), *Handbook of Ethnography*. London: Sage. pp. 395–406.

Wengraf, T. (2001) *Qualitative Research Interviewing*. London: Sage.

Yow, V. (1994) *Recording Oral History*. London: Sage.

LIKERT SCALE

Definition

A Likert scale is a summated rating scale used for measuring attitudes. The method was developed by Rensis Likert in 1932.

Distinctive Features

The first stage in creating a Likert scale is the production of a series of statements expressing a favourable or an unfavourable attitude towards the concept of interest. For example, if the research is concerned with attitudes towards the police a typical statement might be 'Police officers are not biased in carrying out their duties'. One way of obtaining statements for scale construction is to use statements from interview transcripts, where the topic in question has been addressed. It is also possible to obtain statements from local experts, to use open-ended questions in surveys, to look at magazines and newspapers covering popular culture, or scour the relevant literature for appropriate comments that can be made into statements from more academic sources. Statements should be as clear as possible. These statements are then administered to a sample of an appropriate population, as a part of the test construction. Once the scale has been checked for internal consistency and reliability it can be applied to the research population.

A Likert scales employs a graded response to each of the statements, and these are usually five in number: Strongly Agree (SA), Agree (A), Undecided (U), Disagree (D) and Strongly Disagree (SD). Each statement is then scored according to the meaning of the statement. Where the statement is in favour of the attitude in question, the scores will be 5(SA), 4(A), 3(U), 2(D) and 1(SD); where it is against the attitude in question, the scores for each question will be 5(SD), 4(D), 3(U), 2(A), 1(SA).

Evaluation

Likert attitudinal scales are a useful technique, since it is possible to make a research tool that is very attractive to participants, and they can therefore become much more likely to be completed, improving response rates and generalization reliability.

As with all scales, the Likert scale potentially suffers from the problems of *acquiescence* (respondents acquiescing to that which they believe they should) and *social desirability* (portraying themselves in what they believe is a desirable light).

A good Likert scale is founded on the following: piloting the original statements on a large sample of participants representative of the intended population; reversing the appropriate items on scoring; conducting a reliability analysis; adding more items if the reliability analysis removes too much, and begin piloting again; checking validity to ensure that the scale is measuring the intended construct.

Jeanette Garwood

Associated Concepts: composite measurement, indicator, scaling, semantic differential scale, summated rating scale, Thurstone scale

Key Readings

Anastasi, A. (1988) *Psychological Testing*, 6th edn. New York: Macmillan.

Guilford, J. P. (1956) *Psychometric Methods*. New York: McGraw–Hill.

Kline, P. (1993) *The Handbook of Psychological Testing*. London: Routledge.

Robson, C. (2002) *Real World Research*, 2nd edn. Oxford: Blackwell.

LITERATURE REVIEW

Definition

'A critical summary and assessment of the range of existing materials dealing with knowledge and understanding in a given field … Its purpose is to locate the research project, to form its context or background, and to provide insights into previous work' (Blaxter et al., 1996: 110).

Distinctive Features

Kumar (1996) argues that one of the essential initial responsibilities of the researcher is to locate and review the existing literature that pertains to the research topic. For all social researchers, 'information search and information management skills are the fundamental building blocks of all research projects' (Burton, 2000: 137). The literature review therefore involves a detailed search through a range of resources such as books, journals, the Internet and electronic journals, abstracts and microfiche. Kumar argues that a literature review has three functions. First, the literature review clarifies and focuses the research question. It helps the researcher understand the subject area more fully and identify the different theoretical approaches that have previously been applied. The literature review therefore enables the researcher to conceptualize the research question and point to gaps in existing social research into the chosen area of study. Second, the literature review may improve the researcher's methodology. By reviewing the existing literature the researcher can observe how other investigators have studied the chosen social phenomena, and how valid these methodologies were. By reading previous studies, the researcher may be influenced as to which is the most effective methodological tool to employ. Third, at a more immediate level, undertaking a literature review will widen the researcher's knowledge of the chosen area of research and grant a greater command of the research area and relevant issues. Such a command of the existing knowledge will therefore reinforce the validity and findings and 'convince the reader of the legitimacy of your assertions by providing sufficient logical and empirical support along the way' (Rudestam et al., 2001: 57–8).

Carrying out a literature review is a distinct skill in which the student must marshal material in a manner that is effective and manageable; the literature review is a selective process. The wealth of existing academic material is vast, and must therefore be broken down into only the information relevant to the specific study. Such an approach has its roots within C. Wright Mills's *The Sociological Imagination* (1959). As Mills states, the 'craft' of social thinking and social research requires the researcher to compile a file in which to 'develop self-reflective habits' and 'build up the habit of writing' (1959: 197). The contents of this file, argues Mills, include 'ideas, personal notes, excerpts from books, bibliographical items, (1959: 198). This is effectively a guide to the creation of a literature review. As Mills advises, as the sociological file grows, the researcher must take detailed notes and keep accurate bibliographical information. This is the foundation of a successful literature review.

The primary steps in undertaking a successful literature search are to formulate relevant search terms, or themes that may be used within electronic search engines or printed sources of information (Burton, 2000). For instance, if investigating the impact and status of postmodernist thought, relevant search terms might include postmodernism, post-structuralism, ontology, anti-foundationalism, post-Fordism, hyperreality, globabalization, modernism, late capitalism, or discourses; or the names of specific theorists such as Baudrillard, Lyotard, Jameson and Foucault. Within such a search, certain articles and books will be central to a study and will be read thoroughly, but no researcher can, or should attempt to read *all* of the potentially relevant material. Burton (2000) suggests that effective search techniques of selected literature should include surveying journal abstracts, the indexes of books, introductory paragraphs, concluding paragraphs, graphs, tables, diagrams and photographs, or section or paragraph headings. These will enable the researcher to move quickly through a range of literature examples. Additionally, as the process continues, researchers will develop the ability to scan articles or book chapters and take out the relevant data. In addition to the taking of detailed notes from some sources of information, the use of photocopying (copyright issues permitting) also enables rapid consultation with numerous examples of potentially relevant literature. As the review progresses, and as Mills notes, some information will not be valid to the chosen area of study, therefore the ability to quickly assess the validity of a book, article, chapter or graph is essential. The number of literature examples will of course be dependent upon the nature of the topic. If researching postmodernism, or crime, then there will be a wealth of material uncovered. However, some research topics may yield very few existing examples within the literature. If a literature review is properly carried out and few sources are unearthed, this may well underscore the originality of the research.

Evaluation

Failure to undertake a literature review prior to carrying out social research may have serious repercussions as the research progresses because the literature review serves to establish the originality of a chosen research project/thesis. The literature review may support the research questions raised by the researcher, and assist in establishing a valid, workable research framework. The literature review can enable the researcher to identify gaps in existing knowledge and whether the chosen research project has already been undertaken. A comprehensive literature review will also ensure that the research project is suitably up-to-date. If no adequate literature review is undertaken, this may mean that on completion the researcher discovers that he or she has simply repeated existing research and has therefore not contributed anything of significance to the academic community.

Lee Barron

Associated Concepts: exploratory research, intellectual craftsmanship, Internet research, research design, writing research

Key Readings

Blaxter, L. Hughes, C. and Tight, M. (1996) *How to Research*. Milton Keynes: Open University Press.

Burton, D. (2000) 'Using literature to support research', in D. Burton (ed.), *Research Training for Social Scientists: A Handbook for Postgraduate Researchers*. London: Sage.

Hart, C. (1998) *Doing a Literature Review*. London: Sage.

Kumar, R. (1996) *Research Methodology: A Step-by-Step Guide for Beginners*. London: Sage.

Mills, C. Wright. (1959) *The Sociological Imagination*. Harmondsworth: Penguin.

Rudestam, Kjell, Newton, E. and Rae, R. (2001) *Surviving Your Dissertation: A Comprehensive Guide to Content and Process*, 2nd edn. London: Sage.

LOG-LINEAR ANALYSIS

Definition

A form of multivariate analysis used to examine relationships between categorical variables with a view to modelling these relationships.

Distinctive Features

Log-linear analysis involves the construction of a multivariate contingency table in which all the variables are treated as independent variables. The dependent variable is treated as the number of cases found in each cell in the table. Analysis proceeds by examining the degree of fit between the predicted or expected frequencies in cells and the actual frequencies. The closer the fit the better the explanatory power of the theoretical model which has been proposed. This is because the model can accurately predict the values found in the cells in the multivariate contingency table.

One variant is logit analysis, which facilitates an examination of relationships between two or more categorical independent variables and a dichotomous dependent variable and to predict values of the dependent variable from these independent variables.

Evaluation

Log-linear analysis is similar to the chi-square test of independence between two variables which also examines the degree of fit between predicted cell frequencies and observed cell frequencies. However, log-linear analysis is much more advanced because it can deal with complete patterns of relationships and interactions between several variables simultaneously.

Victor Jupp

Associated Concepts: causal model, chi-square test, discriminant function analysis, general linear modelling, multivariate analysis, path analysis

Key Readings

Byrne, D. (2002) *Interpreting Quantitative Data*. London: Sage.
Sapsford, R. and Jupp, V. (1996) *Data Collection and Analysis*. London: Sage.
Wright, D. B. (2002) *First Steps in Statistics*. London: Sage.

LONGITUDINAL STUDY

Definition

Any social or developmental research involving collection of data from the same individuals (or groups) across time. Observing change in these individuals gives a better basis for causal inference than a cross-sectional study, because of the temporal sequencing involved. In this sense the longitudinal study (without manipulation of the sample) is a form of 'quasi-experimental design'.

Distinctive Features

Longitudinal studies can range from repeated measures of a treatment group and a control group measured at two time points in an experimental design, to a large-scale long-term birth cohort study, involving follow-ups of the same sample of individuals from birth through to adult life. The distinctive feature of such work is *prospective* data collection, that is to say, information is collected about individual sample members to assess current behaviours, feelings and circumstances; though retrospective information covering the period between 'sweeps' (also called 'waves') may also be collected. Intervals between sweeps can range from daily contact with sample members to periods of several years.

Such longitudinal data support analysis concerned with predicting likely outcomes from earlier circumstances and experiences and contribute to explaining outcomes in terms of situations earlier in life. Both approaches enable models to be estimated in which statistical controls can be placed on potential biases due to 'confounding' variables and to 'selection effects'. (Thus, in concluding that a given experience such as higher education leads to a given outcome, we need to be sure that people who had the experience can be equated in terms of past circumstances of experiences to those who have not had the experience.) Causal inference is further strengthened by the use of repeated measurements of key variables so that relationships can be 'conditioned' on baseline measures.

The major problem with prospective longitudinal studies is attrition, that is to say exit from the study of sample members brought about by such factors as mobility, death, changing name through marriage, or refusal. However, one advantage of the longitudinal study is that in principle the distributions of key variables in the original sample can be restored by differential weighting of the sample in later sweeps. The related problem is missing data, occurring at question level, which can seriously reduce the size of the data set for analysis across different sweeps. Statistical methods of imputation are often used to estimate missing values in these instances, but none is able fully to address the possible biases brought about by this form of sample loss.

The other problematic feature of longitudinal studies concerns measurement, including its reliability and validity. Random measurement error can have escalating effects in longitudinal analysis, with the possibility of drawing wrong inferences from estimated relationships between variables. Validity issues arise particularly in connection with memory loss of past events occurring in the intervals between sweeps and 'fading relevance'. The design of surveys early on in the series reflects scientific concerns prevailing at the time and is unlikely to anticipate the concerns that may take over later.

Methods of dealing with these problems include maintenance of contact with cohort members between surveys, tracing operations through national databases to locate their current whereabouts, and expert advice on variable coverage to ensure the long-term value of the data collected in the study.

Evaluation

Despite their flaws, longitudinal studies on a large scale and from a representative sample of the population are a powerful tool in social and developmental science. They may be seen at one level as comprising a sample of life histories offering enormous potential at individual and aggregate level for identifying and modelling sequences of cause and effect relationships in people's lives. For them to be effective, however, an infrastructure is needed to support their continuation, and especially the maintenance of contact with study members between surveys. In large and complex examples, data also need to be formatted and documented in such a way as to supply easy access for users. The major large-scale national longitudinal studies are typically deposited in data archives under such conditions. The huge investment of resources that has to go into a longitudinal study to ensure its continuation means such studies are still relatively rare in social science.

John Bynner

Associated Concepts: attrition, causal model, causality, cohort study, cross-sectional survey, panel study, prospective study, retrospective study

Key Readings

Alwin, D. F. 'Taking time seriously: studying social change, social structure and human lives', in P. Moen, G. M. Elder and K. Lüscher (eds), *Linking Lives and Contexts: Perspectives on the Human Ecology of Development*. Washington, DC: American Psychological Association.

Giele, J. Z. and Elder, G. H. (1998) *Methods of Life Course Research*. London: Sage.

Magnusson, D. and Bergman, L. (1990) *Data Quality in Longitudinal Research*. Cambridge: Cambridge University Press.

Magnusson, D., Bergmann, L., Rüdinger, G. and Törestad, B. (1994) *Problems and Methods in Longitudinal Research*. Cambridge: Cambridge University Press.

M

MARKETING RESEARCH

Definition

The systematic collection, analysis and dissemination of information about the external environment, consumers and customers to enable organizations to keep in touch with the people who use their products or services and to make informed decisions about their short-and longer-term objectives.

Distinctive features

Marketing research is a form of applied research with a practical purpose. It is a 'pervasive activity' (Churchill, 1999) that can take many forms. It is used in the public sector and nonprofit organizations as well as in business. Its main purpose is to help managers to make better decisions that have an impact across the organization, not just in marketing. The particular focus of marketing research is on consumption and human and organizational behaviour and it draws freely from academic disciplines in the social sciences, statistics, sociology, psychology and social anthropology.

The information collected through marketing research links the consuming public to managers, who use it to identify marketing opportunities; to warn of problems; to evaluate marketing activities; and to monitor the performance in the market place of their own and other organizations. Marketing research is sometimes distinguished from market research, though the terms are also used interchangeably. In the past market research has tended to refer to research into the characteristics of a single market, while marketing research is directed at finding out about the full range of an organization's activities in that market. These would normally include analysing trends, marketing planning and evaluation, as well as problem solving.

Marketing research that supports the planning function of an organization aims to collect and analyse data on consumer trends and customers, on market size and on the channels of distribution in order to support key management decisions. Problem-solving studies in marketing research will generally focus on one or more aspects of the marketing of the product or service and whether it needs changing, in order to meet the organization's objectives. It might involve a study of pricing, for example the impact of a change in prices on sales or on competitors. Other problem-solving studies might focus on the design, use or packaging of the product, or the effectiveness or otherwise of its distribution channels. Studies of the reactions of consumers to advertising campaigns or of the efficacy of particular promotions are also common.

Three research designs are commonly distinguished for marketing research (Malhotra and Birks, 2003). These are exploratory, descriptive and causal research designs. Exploratory research designs enable the development of theories that may be tested later in bigger studies or over a longer time period. An exploratory study might, for example, be looking for possible reasons why sales appear to have peaked in a particular area and then declined, or why a re-launched service has not yet reached its predicted level of customer awareness. A series of focus groups, some depth interviews and the analysis of secondary data might be sufficient to explore the issues and suggest possible avenues for further research. Alternatively, they may be sufficient in themselves to answer a research question.

Descriptive research designs tend to be quantitative and typically use surveys or observations to profile consumers, collect data on the price and availability of products in store, or to monitor customers' exposure to a promotional campaign. Causal research designs are used when the organization commissioning the marketing research wants to identify the trigger for a change in sales or in customer behaviour. Causal studies therefore investigate the relationship between two or more variables. They try, for example, to measure the effectiveness of an advertising campaign in changing consumer behaviour, or the impact of a price change. Since the aim of the study is to determine the cause of something, such studies are carried out in a relatively controlled environment that enables the researcher to manipulate one of the variables. The main research method used in these studies is the experiment.

Evaluation

Most organizations carry out some kinds of marketing research but the key issue in many of them is how to capture and to use this information effectively. Sales records, customer complaints, returned goods, personnel records and accounts data can all provide valuable secondary data for marketing research studies, if it is made available in the right form. Business decisions can be very risky and the goal of good marketing research is to supply accurate information to help reduce this risk and to improve the quality of decision making. The use of information technology is at last enabling marketing research to be continuously updated and made available to managers on their computers,

rather than in the past where too often it was buried in voluminous printed reports.

A large international marketing research industry has grown up, dominated by some very big companies. The size of some of the firms in the marketing research industry deters many potential clients for fear of the costs involved, and the belief that they will be sold dull, packaged solutions to marketing problems, which may not be what the client needs (McGivern, 2003). The sheer scale of the industry means that there is something of a divide between the academic approach to marketing research, with its stress on developing theory, and the practitioners, with their stress on client-oriented solutions.

While marketing research may be very good at analysing trends that have already happened, it is not necessarily a good predictor of the future, which is really what businesses want to know about. As a result, marketing research studies can help people in organizations to make more informed decisions but it can never substitute for the making of careful judgements about the risks of action or inaction. Many products and services have been launched successfully by ignoring the results of early marketing research.

Teresa Smallbone

Associated Concepts: applied research, auditing, causal model, experiment, exploratory research, forecasting, modelling, organizational research, secondary analysis, social survey

Key Readings

Churchill, G. A. (1999) *Marketing Research Methodological Foundation*, 7th edn. Fort Worth, TX: The Dryden Press.

Malhotra, N. K. and Birks, D. F. (2003) *Marketing Research: An Applied Approach*, 2nd European edn. Harlow: Financial Times/Prentice Hall.

McGivern, Y. (2003) *The Practice of Market and Social Research: An Introduction*. Harlow: Financial Times/Prentice Hall.

MEASUREMENT

Definition

Any process by which a value is assigned to the level or state of some quality of an object of study. This value is given numerical form, and measurement therefore involves the expression of information in quantities rather than by verbal statement.

Distinctive Features

A famous (though contested) dictum by Lord Kelvin, carved on the exterior of the Social Science Building at the University of Chicago, maintains that 'when you cannot measure ... your knowledge is ... meagre ... and ... unsatisfactory'. Measurement is a most powerful means of reducing qualitative data to a more condensed form for manipulation, processing and analysis. Measurement is the basic process that makes quantitative social research possible.

Four levels of measurement are usually distinguished. First, *nominal* measurement, which involves using numbers to represent categories, and permit more efficient summarization of the data. An example would be: Woman = 1; Man = 2. Second, *ordinal* measurement, which in addition to having numbers represent categories, also permits the ranking of the categories in terms of the possession of some quality. An example would be the scale in attitude research: Strongly agree/Agree/Neither agree nor disagree/Disagree/Strongly disagree. Third, *interval* measurement shares the characteristics of ordinal measurement, and in addition, the property of a unit (or scale) by which differences in magnitude can be expressed precisely. Examples would be: a temperature scale in physics; number of years spent in full-time education. Fourth, *ratio* measurement shares the characteristics of interval measurement, plus the property that the scale has a true zero. Examples would be: a temperature scale starting from absolute zero (−273 degrees centigrade); an income scale can also be treated as a ratio scale.

Nominal and ordinal measurement are non-metric; interval and ratio measurement are metric. Most sociological measurement is non-metric, using numbers essentially as convenient ways of summarizing data where the differences between observations are qualitative rather than expressed in metric terms. The level of measurement is of criticial importance for the use of different statistics in social research. Different statistical tests and techniques make different assumptions about the properties of the data being analysed. Parametric statistics assume that the data are metric; to use such statistics on non-metric statistics is incorrect. Non-parametric statistics may be used with scores that are not exact in any sense, but are nominal or ordinal. Data for most social variables (for example, religion, occupation, social class) are non-metric. Hence non-parametric statistics are of particular importance in sociological research.

Evaluation

The strengths of sociological measurement are displayed in the achievements of quantitative studies in fields such as social mobility, social stratification, status attainment, voting behaviour and medical sociology. The feasibility of measurement has been the subject of enduring controversy. Critics ask the fundamental question, 'If social action is subjectively meaningful, how can it be reduced to quantities?' In defence, proponents of quantitative research maintain that the measurement of objective characteristics is relatively straightforward, while the measurement of subjective states (for example, using scales of attitudes) is feasible and produces reliable results.

Martin Bulmer

Associated Concepts: coding, composite measurement, parametric tests, qualitative research, quantitative research, reliability, scaling, validity of measurement

Key Readings

Duncan, O. D. (1984) *Notes on Social Measurement: Historical and Critical*. New York: Russell Sage Foundation.

Lieberson, S. (1985) *Making It Count: The Improvement of Social Theory and Research*. Berkeley, CA: University of California Press.

MEDIA ANALYSIS

Definition

The examination, interpretation and critique of both the material content of the channels of media of communication and the structure, composition and operations of corporations that either own or control those media. Media, in this sense, refers to what used to be called the mass media, the means of communication of information to large numbers of people – television, radio and newspapers. It now encompasses multimedia, the electronic networks of communication made available by the Internet.

Distinctive Features

Media considered worthy of investigation are typically those that have the potential for disseminating influential ideas, whether in the form of information, entertainment, or rhetoric (designed to persuade, or influence). These include: purveyors of words, such as books, newspapers (and analogous print media) and radio; those concerned with the combination of words and images, especially television, film and advertising; and, to a lesser extent, conduits of images, including visual art forms.

Traditionally, the systematic study of media was based on the premise that there were three components to communication: producers, receivers and, between them, the linking medium. Telegraphy was the exemplar, literally as well as metaphorically. An apparatus for transmitting electrically messages or signals over distance, it used wires supported by poles. Messages were sent via an electrical connection and were decoded in much the same way as they were discharged.

While he was not the first writer to expose this approach as naïve, Marshall McLuhan was its singlemost influential critic. His *Understanding Media*, published in 1964, commanded almost biblical reverence. Written shortly after a decade that had witnessed the astonishingly rapid rise of television, McLuhan's thesis became known through its central maxim 'the medium is the message'.

Television's influence was due almost wholly to its direct style of presentation; the actual content of the programmes was irrelevant. It seems an elementary observation now, though, in the early 1960s it was iconoclastic. Any medium, because it is an instrument, modifies our understanding of the world and, by implication, our experience of it. We make sense of material in different ways, depending on whether we read newspapers, listen to the radio, surf the Web or watch television.

McLuhan's stress on the significance of the medium itself, the context in which it is sent and, importantly, the manner in which it is received, effectively diverted analysts' attention away from the sheer content of media and towards the particular relationships human subjects had with the various media. While content analysis of, for example, newspapers proceeded inductively, accumulating large banks of data that built into a picture of how media portray information about the world, they did not present conceptual analyses capable of informing critical evaluation.

Similar criticisms were raised about the school of thought originating in the research of Paul Lazarsfeld and Robert Merton in the 1940s (most clearly summarized in 1948). Our reliance on mass media of communication was surrendering us to a form of passivity, argued Lazarsfeld and Merton. Their research concluded that the mass media had a 'narcotizing' effect on us, 'transforming the energies of men from active participation into passive knowledge'.

While the critical sting in the tail was salutary, the theoretical model on which it was based was found faulty. Like recipients of narcotics, consumers of print and auditory media were considered helpless recipients rather than active contributors. New and, occasionally hysterical, evaluations and prognostications about its impact accompanied television's growth period in the 1950s. Research showed its effects were manifold.

Neil Postman's *Amusing Ourselves to Death* (New York, Viking Penguin, 1985) argued that the arrival of television constituted the beginning of a new age in humanity. The break with previous forms of mass communication heralded a different type of relationship. Humans engaged differently when staring at a screen than when reading a script or listening to sounds. Enclosed in Postman's analysis was a warning about the functions of television, or more specifically function – there was only one: amusement. Television's public service utility was strictly of secondary importance. The title of Postman's book served notice.

Critics not only of Postman but of the whole doomwatch tradition insisted that media analyses had laboured with a flawed conception of the subject as having their critical abilities blunted and their powers of reasoning diminished by exposure to television. Viewers merely succumbed to the overbearing power of the media, so that they became mere absorbers of messages rather than creators of them.

With the rise of cultural studies during the 1980s, media analysts sought to restore some faculties to the human subject. Consistent with the intellectual turn of the period, media analysis focused on how media are read by subjects. In other words, rather than explore the content, the channel and the impact, analysis centred on how a subject interprets, decodes and, generally, makes sense of the media. In *Television Culture,* John Fiske's interest lay not in the messages of the media themselves, but in how subjects produce meanings from them. The content of the media is rendered text – it is comprehensible. But, the ways in which we comprehend is what concerned Fiske and like-minded writers.

Contemporary media analysis encompasses many features of earlier work, much of it concerned with the quantitative exposition of biases in media reportage. Textual analyses concentrate on the exploration of how we read media. Perhaps the most neglected area of media analysis is one of the most important. The media's close associations with commerce have led to corporate realignments that have massively affected the content of media, the manner in which it is packaged to cater for global audiences and the influence it has on political regimes.

Ellis Cashmore

Associated Concepts: content analysis, cultural research, document analysis, netnography, textual analysis, videography, visual methods

Key Readings

Barker, C. (1999) *Television, Globalization and Cultural Identities*. Milton Keynes: Open University Press.

Fiske, J. (1987) *Television Culture.* London: Routledge.

Giles, D. C. (2002) *Media Psychology.* Hillsdale, NJ: Lawrence Erlbaum.

Lazarsfeld, P. and Merton, R. (1948) 'Mass communication, popular taste, and organized social action', in L. Bryson (ed.), *The Communication of Ideas.* New York: Free Press.

Miller, T. (ed.) (2002) *Television Studies London.* London: British Film Institute.

MESSY RESEARCH

Definition

Research that does not follow the tidy pattern generally recommended and which aims to evaluate an intervention programme as a whole, as opposed to a specific focused social intervention. Such research is sometimes also called *complex evaluation.*

Distinctive Features

A 'tidy' design for an evaluation project would be one that demonstrated with as little ambiguity as possible that a given social intervention did or did not have the desired effect. Typical of this kind of design is the field experiment or quasi-experimental analysis – making an intervention in one area or group and not another (with the participants allocated randomly to treatment or control group, in the case of the field experiment) and comparing the outcomes. Even here it would probably be desirable to use a range of methods, to assess experiential side effects as well as its gross effect on output statistics, but in principle it is possible to 'design out' sources of error or control for them in analysis.

Increasingly, however, researchers have to employ a mix of methods in a comparatively unfocused way when carrying out evaluations. This can be for a number of reasons. First, the programme itself may be complex and heterogeneous – funded social intervention now often involves a 'basket' of projects which bear only a loose thematic relationship to each other. Second, while it is possible to assess the outputs and even the impact of particular projects, their contribution to the overall programme 'theme' or 'rhetoric' may be less easy to establish. Third, the audience for funded evaluations is generally heterogeneous, with each fraction of it interested in a different kind of outcome and convinced by a different kind of evidence. Finally, social interventions often occur in areas that are targeted by a range of providers; some cities may be in receipt of government, charitable or other funds for many more than one intervention project. It is therefore not at all easy – often not possible at all – to separate the effects of one programme from those of another.

For example, the present author recently carried out an evaluation of a 'rehousing' programme targeted in the first instance at vulnerable young people discharged from the armed services before they had finished their training (generally, having failed it) and before they became eligible for the full military resettlement packages; there had been evidence that that such people were disproportionately represented among the homeless and rough sleepers. For practical reasons the programme ran as a housing service for *all* discharged people who were not rehoused straightforwardly by the armed forces. This gave a range of aims for the research, necessitating the use of different kinds of data collection. For example, statistical monitoring of the clients was the first step – who they were (and specifically, whether they fell into the original target group) and whether they were found accommodation. In the process we were able to note (1) that a number of clients referred themselves inappropriately (the agency dealt only with *single* personnel) but that these were consistently referred on to a more appropriate agency, (2) that some solutions were regarded by the agency and the client as at best temporary but that these files remained open and work continued, and (3) that where time was short before discharge the solution was less likely to be an immediately satisfactory one.

Another obvious strand to the research was to monitor the establishment and development of the agency, to report back to the funders on how their money was being spent, to identify possible areas for improvement and possibly to establish lessons for other similar projects.

Whether the 'solutions' were successful was another strand. The method adopted, in view of resources being limited, was to follow up each case by telephone interview, to see whether the arranged accommodation had been taken up and whether it was regarded as satisfactory in the long or short term. We were able to gain further information from the agency's records, because part of their mission was to follow up on placements which they regarded as at best a temporary solution and to remain available to discharged clients who needed further advice or help some time after discharge.

Client satisfaction was another obvious issue – with the service before discharge, with the accommodation provided and with the outcome of any further approaches to the agency after discharge. This was tackled by face-to-face interviews with a sample of people awaiting discharge and telephone interviews, over a period, with discharged people. We also issued a brief 'satisfaction questionnaire' in an attempt to increase the numerical base for judgement of satisfaction, but the response rate was too low for this to be useful.

We also interviewed the staff of the agency (because an agency cannot be counted an unqualified success if its staff are not satisfied with it), key 'players' among the referring agencies and a small sample of local authority departments which would otherwise have been housing these people. The interviews gave insight into how the work of the agency fitted into the forces' discharge processes and how it helped outside departments to fulfil statutory requirements.

Our interviews with housing and social services departments, and the 'literature', enabled us to make very rough estimates of what the cost of discharging these people homeless might have been, which gave us a basis on which to talk about value for money and the wider concept of 'best value' (which takes into account human as well as financial costs).

Evaluation

Messy research does not provide a clear-cut assessment of the outcome of one intervention as, say, in a field experiment or quasi-experiment. However, as the above example illustrates, it does permit more complex evaluation. By applying a wide range of methods, some well designed and some more 'scrappy' and opportunistic, it was possible to produce information useful for all the different players involved.

Roger Sapsford

Associated Concepts: applied research, evaluation research, field experiment, methodological pluralism, mixed-methods research, policy-related research, quasi-experiment

Key Readings

Jupp, V., Davies, P. and Francis, P. (eds) (2000) *Doing Criminological Research.* London: Sage (especially chapters by Nick Tilley and Iain Crow).
Thomas, A., Chataway, J. and Wuyts, M. (eds) (1998) *Finding Out Fast: Investigative Skills for Policy and Development.* London: Sage.

META-ANALYSIS

Definition

The synthesizing of existing research studies related to a specific research hypothesis. Here the findings from the studies become the inputs to, and cases of the analysis, rather than the resultant output. That is to say, they become the data upon which the study is going to be based. Meta-analysis has been a major method of investigation in the area of health care but the principles can be utilized in any area of research. The methodology can utilize both quantitative and qualitative studies.

Distinctive Features

Glasziou et al. (2001) give an overview of how to undertake a systematic review. They note the following discrete steps: first, question formulation; second, finding studies; third, appraisal and selection of studies; fourth, summary and synthesis of relevant studies; and finally, determining the applicability of results with regard to question formulation.

It is important to ask the right question. Perhaps this is more important in meta-analysis than in the more conventional forms of research. This is because the question one asks has implications for knowing which studies to include in the analysis, the accuracy of the analysis and the confidence in and validity of the conclusions. This takes on greater importance when the study has an element of forecasting or prediction.

Finding the studies involves a search for relevant literature and sources of data. In recent years this has become less daunting with the evolution of the World Wide Web, online catalogues (OPACs), online databases and CD-ROMs.

Appraisal and selection of studies may not seem like a daunting task but the reality is somewhat different. It is necessary to decide which studies are going to be included and, more importantly, why one is included and another is not. Clearly this relates directly with the research question or hypothesis under consideration. The inclusion of articles must be based upon some systematic rules, which need to be derived. Quality and bias are key issues in this area, as both have a direct effect on the validity of the subsequent meta-analysis.

The summary and synthesis of relevant studies tends to be based upon a quantitative approach, however, a qualitative methodology can yield important results. Combined tests use a range of procedures (from simple counts to summation tests based upon significance levels and/or weighted tests) to establish the statistical significance of combining the various studies. Such tests do not look at the strength of the relationship and therefore it is prudent to use the combined test in conjunction with measures of the size of the effect of combining studies.

With regard to determining the applicability of results questions need to be asked as to the validity of the synthesis, the degree of confidence in the results, generalizability, and prediction and forecasting.

Evaluation

Four main criticisms can be levelled at meta-analysis. These relate, first, to the comparison of studies. It can be argued that it is impossible to compare studies since one is not comparing like with like. Very few studies employ exactly identical methodologies and measuring systems. Therefore any comparison is not logical or valid, and little confidence (if any) can be placed in the resultant discussions.

A second issue relates to the quality of studies included. The results and discussions can be further downgraded as a result of including poor-quality studies alongside high-quality studies. To a certain extent this may be nullified by choosing the correct filter rules to apply when thinking which studies to include and which to exclude.

Thirdly, it is argued that the results that tend to get published are those that have statistically significant findings. Non-significant results are not given such prominence but perhaps should be included in any meta-analysis. It may be argued that the goal of social research is equally met when a relationship is found not to exist. Such findings still add to our knowledge. The potential for bias resulting from such omission can be reduced by looking at articles that have not been published. Due care and attention must be exercised at this point to ensure that any such study is not inherently flawed in some way and that this was the reason for non-publication.

Finally, regarding independency of results, it is not unusual to see multiple results used from the same piece of research. This may make the results of the meta-analysis appear more valid and generalizable than they actually are.

Paul E. Pye

Associated Concepts: applied research, evaluation research, good practice studies, methodological pluralism, mixed-methods research, policy-related research, validity

Key Readings

Edgger, M., Davey Smith, G. and Altman, D. G. (eds) (2001) *Systematic Reviews in Health Care: Meta-analysis in Context,* 2nd edn. London: BMJ Books.

Glass, G. V., McGaw, B. and Lee Smith, M. (1981) *Meta-analysis in social research.* Beverly Hills, CA: Sage.

Glasziou, P., Irwig, L., Bain, C. and Colditz, G. (2001) *Systematic Reviews in Health Care: A Practical Guide.* Cambridge: Cambridge University Press.

Hedges, L. V. and Olkin, I. (1985) *Statistical Methods for Meta-Analysis.* New York: Academic Press.

METHODOLOGICAL PLURALISM

Definition

An approach that advocates flexibility in the selection of social research methods, based on the principle of choosing the most suitable methods for the nature of the problem being researched. More generally, methodological pluralism calls on the researcher to be tolerant of other people's preferred methods even when they differ from one's own.

Distinctive Features

From time to time, disagreements among social scientists about which are the 'best' social research methods become more vocal and indeed, confrontational. An example of this is the competition between older, ethnographic research styles associated with sociologists at the University of Chicago, and the (then newer) work based on social surveys being promoted by Harvard and Columbia after World War II. In the UK a conflict between quantitative methods and several newer forms of qualitative research took place during the 1970s. These disputes are usually marked by antagonistic criticisms of published work, lengthy expositions in defence of particular methods, and even personal abuse.

Methodological pluralism, promoted by Bell and Newby (1977), rejected the idea that one type of methods was automatically better than another. They argued that it was healthy for sociology to contain a number of different theoretical perspectives, and that while each perspective tended to imply a given method of research, each new research project should be tackled on the basis of its own particular features. The research methods selected for the project should be the ones that best fitted the characteristics of the phenomena being studied.

For example, studies of the national rates at which something was occurring, or projects dealing with simpler concepts that could be relatively easily measured, were better suited to social surveys, pre-coded questionnaires and other quantitative methods. On the other hand, when more detail was required, or phenomena were complex, subtle, or unclear, this was more suited to research by observation, less structured interviews, ethnographic description and other qualitative styles. Not every researcher would use every style of research during their careers, nor should they be proficient in all research methods. The plurality would be achieved in the total research output of the discipline as a whole (Bell and Roberts, 1984).

Evaluation

Despite the common sense of methodological pluralism, more sociologists pay lip-service to it than actively adopt it as a philosophy. The main reason is that during their education and early careers, each researcher acquires a set of personal preferences for one type of social science over others. This is not just a question of technical skills, but rather an interest in certain topics and a philosophical view of the social world and how it can be analysed.

There are genuine differences between schools of research, from those seeking to involve and empower the people being researched, through to those that regard 'respondents' merely as sources of information, and from those that see the social world as intricately interconnected and difficult to 'know', to those that concentrate on the generality of patterned associations between small sets of 'variables'. While not always consciously returning to the complex social theories that underlie their positions, researchers read mainly a sub-set of the literature written by like-minded colleagues, defining research problems in specific ways, and therefore carry out their research using a narrow repertoire of methods.

In some cases, this results only in a rather focused approach, without much concern for other approaches. In others, the intellectual context of the research is strongly associated with a particular method: the context defines what is worth researching, how it should be researched and what order of interpretations can be made. In its more extreme form this results in ritualized denunciation of alternatives often becoming a part of publication. Where some researchers adhere to a 'standpoint' position, their intention is an explicitly ideological one which goes beyond just making new discoveries, to the promotion of the interests of one particular group. Challenging other researchers' methods is one way of undermining the position of rival interest groups (Payne and Payne, 2004: 89–93, 152–7).

Such out-of-hand dismissal because of the type of methods a study has used is a different matter from legitimately debating the competency of its research basis, when that is part of a general evaluation. However, it would be wrong to portray academic life as consisting solely of calm, rational, philosophical debate. Academics also compete for resources (research funding, access to journals, tenured posts, career promotion) in just as determined a way as do people in other walks of life. Attacking the type of research methods used by rivals is one weapon in the struggle between individuals, and institutions, for supremacy.

Not surprisingly, methodological pluralism's failure to recognize these processes has meant that its call for toleration has largely gone unheeded. For example, in the UK the sociology that has been published in recent years has depended heavily on a narrow range of qualitative methods. A recent study of journal papers found only a minority using quantitative methods: only 2.6 per cent 'involved bivariate analysis and were written by sociologists at British universities, and only 8 (3.5%) involved multivariate techniques … This can hardly be described as methodological pluralism' (Payne et al., 2004: 160).

Geoff Payne

Associated Concepts: critical research, epistemology, methodology, mixed-methods research, positivism, qualitative research, quantitative research, relativism

Key Readings

Bell, C. and Newby, H. (1977) *Doing Sociological Research*. London: Allen & Unwin.
Bell, C. and Roberts, H. (eds) (1984) *Social Researching*. London: Routledge & Kegan Paul.
Payne, G. and Payne, J. (2004) *Key Concepts in Social Research*. London: Sage.
Payne, G., Dingwall, R., Payne, J. and Carter, M. (1981) *Sociology and Social Research*. London: Routledge & Kegan Paul.
Payne, G., Williams, M. and Chamberlain, S. (2004) 'Methodological pluralism in British sociology', *Sociology*, 38 (1): 153–63.

METHODOLOGY

Definition

The philosophical stance or worldview that underlies and informs a style of research.

Distinctive Features

Methodology is the philosophy of methods. It encompasses, first, an epistemology – the 'rules of truth' for warranting the validity of conclusions – and secondly, an ontology – establishing the 'objects' about which questions may validly be asked and conclusions may be drawn.

In virtually all research (but see below) the epistemology is 'rules of science' – conclusions based on arguments cast in terms of information that has been collected 'transparently' by known, and in principle, testable and reproducible means. The ontologies of research, however, reflect the wordview or 'map' with which the researcher engages.

One position, commonly labelled 'positivistic', takes for granted the nature of the real world and reserves all its doubts for the nature of the evidence about it; problems within positivism are problems of measurement – how to measure the real world most accurately – rather than about its ontology.

In social and developmental psychology this position is well illustrated by the nature/nurture debate, where the 'objects' are behaviours or character traits or attitudes – reductionist aspects of persons – and the physiological or 'personal history' elements which give rise to them. The question is whether you were *born* this kind of person, or made this way by *socialization* or *learning*, or made this way by the pressure of the immediate *environment*. Explanations in terms of *reasons* or *preferences* are ruled out as ill formed – the question becomes why you are the sort of person who has these reasons or preferences, and whether it is because of biology, socialization/learning or the environment. What was radical about the behaviourist revolution of the middle of the last century was its success in exiling one class of objects from valid use in this context – the class of hypothesized structures or processes 'in the head'.

The equivalent in the earlier history of sociology was focus on 'social facts' by structural functionalists. Though many of the social facts – suicide rates, crime statistics – are now discredited as measures of anything useful, this kind of explanation in terms of collective differences between areas or segments of a social nexus and the underlying institutional/structural mechanism which produces them is still a common form of argument in sociology. It was reinforced by the emphasis in the more economistic kind of Marxist analysis on relations of production and economic/structural power and by the analysis of patriarchy, male power processes and family institutions produced by many feminists. The 'objects' of positivistic sociology tend therefore to be 'facts' about societies or social groups and factual descriptions of social institutions and processes.

Interactionist sociology, a reaction against structural functionalism, came into social research as 'ethnography' or 'grounded theory' and made a fundamental impact on its methodology. While the same emphasis is placed on a fundamentally scientific epistemology – arguments based on transparent evidence – the ontology changed to accommodate a worldview in terms of meanings and understandings rather than 'objective' factors. Ethnographic research is concerned with what addiction means to those involved with it rather than the number of addicts and with the social processes undergone when close to death rather than with the number of deaths and their causes. This position found a second natural home in social psychology and psychotherapy, in the humanistic concern with how individuals experience their world and how their understanding of their social world determines its nature for them. It has also been influential in feminist research on gender and family relations and in research on other disadvantage and prejudice experienced by other interactionally defined groups such as disabled people or minority ethnic groups.

'Qualitative' research of this kind has developed into a third methodological position, generally characterized as 'critical' or 'discursive' or, more recently, 'postmodern'. Here the ontology still centres around meanings, but meaning is differently defined and understood – as something historically constructed within cultures rather than negotiated between individuals (though taken up, used and perhaps modified by individuals and groups for their own particular purposes). Even in psychology this has meant a move away from individual understanding to the materials, available to us in our (multiple) social worlds, out of which current understanding is to be put together.

Evaluation

It has been taken for granted, above, that the epistemological component is the same in all methodologies. All are concerned with establishing 'truth' on the basis of transparent evidence, and all would test and reject propositions that were frequently contradicted by the evidence. If it follows from a given theoretical line that such and such should be possible to the individual, for example, and individuals most often prove to be unable to do it, then we would question the soundness of the theoretical line.

However, this line of logic fails when confronted with *emancipatory* theory – theory that aims to *change* things. Here what would be being tested would not be that individuals *do* do such and such, but that they *could* do it if they tried, at least some of the time. This claim is not logically refuted by cases where the effect is not achieved, even if this appears to be the invariant outcome; it remains logically possible that the next individual *will* succeed. This is a problem for the social sciences because a great deal of research and theory is directed at changing things – improving individuals' capacity for dealing with their lives, undoing power inequalities, at least making people *aware* of ways in which their world is currently being shaped by factors that are outside their control while they remain unaware of them.

Roger Sapsford

Associated Concepts: causality, critical research, emancipatory research, ethnography, inter-subjective understanding, ontology, positivism, postmodernism, *Verstehen*

Key Readings

Hammersley, M. (ed.) (1993) *Social Research: Philosophy, Politics and Practice*. London: Sage (See articles in Part I: 'Philosophy').
Plantinga, A. (1993) *Warrant: The Current Debate*. Oxford: Oxford University Press.
Willig, C. (2001) *Introducing Qualitative Research in Psychology: Adventures in Theory and Method*. Milton Keynes: Open University Press.

MICROETHNOGRAPHY

Definition

Research that attends to big social issues through careful examination of 'small' communicative behaviours. Analysts study the audible and visible details of human interaction and activity, as these occur naturally within specific contexts or institutions; micro-

analysis may be coupled with ethnographic methods such as informant interviews and participant observations, all in an effort to better understand social organizations, practices and problems.

Distinctive Features

Multimedia technology has been an impetus for microethnographic research because it facilitates close analysis of vocal and visible behaviour. This approach emerged in the 1960s and 1970s, when scholars, concerned about social inequality within public schools, used a new technology, called videotape, to record and analyse people's 'micro-behaviours' within particular classrooms. Researchers focused on the social interaction, rather than the individual. They showed how social realities and problems are formed and maintained turn by turn and moment to moment, through forms of talk and nonverbal behaviours that are the building blocks of microcultures. Today, digital and computer technologies support close analysis of video data. For example, Goodwin (1994) conducted a frame-by-frame analysis of the courtroom activity that led to an acquittal of the LA policemen who beat Rodney King. The study showed how defence attorneys organized the jury's perception of the videotaped beating so that King, rather than the policemen, was seen as the aggressor. Similarly, the author used computers to analyse the talk and spatial manoeuvres of police interrogators who had a reputation for getting confessions from suspects later found to be innocent.

Contemporary microethnographic research represents a convergence of competencies from various disciplines, including anthropology, psychology and sociology. Careful studies of visible (or nonverbal) behaviour have been influenced by context analysis, a method pioneered by psychologist Albert Scheflen, who closely examined people's use of space (relative location, distance, orientation and posture) within social situations. Context analysis has been further developed by Adam Kendon, who attends to the sequential unfolding of human interaction through time and space. Examinations of talk have been heavily influenced by conversation analysis, a rigorously empirical method for studying the interactive structures and the social forms that talk embodies. Microethnographic studies regularly include conversation analytic arguments and analysis, but talk is not privileged at the expense of other symbol systems and communicative resources that warrant close examination.

From a microethnographic perspective, vocal and visible behaviours are best understood through their relationship to each other and their social-material surround. This view contrasts with traditional social scientific research that has artificially separated verbal and nonverbal messages, regarding them as independent rather than co-occurring and interrelated phenomena. When people gesture with their hands, they usually talk to someone at the same time, coordinating their visible and vocal behaviours to be understood altogether. People occupy and move within three-dimensional spaces that include physical objects and structures, and movements may be largely recognized and understood through their relationship to the material world within reach. Also, communication is a process of interaction among participants who co-author each other's vocal and visible messages and meanings. Furthermore, talk and visible behaviours may be embedded within extended processes or activities such that any particular behaviour is understood through its relationship to the whole activity.

Although microethnographic research takes various forms, depending on the preferences of the analyst and the nature of the project, the method typically involves the following steps (see LeBaron, 2004):

(1) *Select a research site.* A site is a location within time and space where people associate and communicate to constitute something recognizably their own. Basic communication research, that is, discovering and documenting features of the interaction order – could be conducted almost anywhere because there is 'order at all points' of social life. Patterns of interaction found within a courtroom might as easily be found in a boardroom or a beauty salon. However, site selection is usually guided by a research agenda. A concern for social stratification within public schools might guide a researcher to a classroom where children have a variety of socio-economic backgrounds. Whether sites are selected for basic research or to pursue a particular research agenda, communicative phenomena are examined as inherently embedded within the local scene.

(2) *Collect naturally occurring data.* Communication is considered to be 'naturally occurring' if it would have occurred whether or not it was observed or recorded by the researcher. Participant observations, field notes and audio or video recordings of everyday interaction are considered premium data for microethnographic work, but videotape has become a mainstay because it helps analysts avoid an artificial separation of verbal and nonverbal channels, and it captures subtle details of interaction that analysts can review and others can verify.

(3) *Observe data carefully and repeatedly.* Careful and repeated observation is the gristmill for empirical verification. A videotaped moment may 'jump out' as obviously noteworthy, but it requires repeated observation to be fully explicated and understood. Through repeated observation, moments may become a focus of analysis as the features and patterns of interaction are noticed and appreciated. Throughout this inductive process, analysts' eyes are unavoidably informed by research agendas and literatures. Induction gives way to abduction as researchers look for specific kinds of phenomena related to their emerging claims and conclusions. In the end, research claims must agree with what can be observed in the videotaped data.

(4) *Digitize and transcribe key moments of interaction.* When computers are used for repeated observation, analysts can get

different 'views' of an analytic object. Digital video can be manipulated temporally (for example, slowed down) and spatially (for example, zoomed in); different interactional moments are easily juxtaposed on the computer screen for comparison. New technology cannot replace the eyes and ears of a well-trained analyst, but it can support smart and rigorous research. Transcription reduces interaction to a two-dimensional page, which highlights (precisely) structural aspects of talk and its coordination with nonverbal behaviours.

(5) *Describe and report research findings.* Microethnographic studies describe the details of visible and vocal behaviours that subjects performed for each other and thereby made available for analysis. Claims may appear on the same printed page as transcripts (featuring vocal behaviours) and frame grabs (showing nonverbal behaviour) taken from videotaped data. Empirically grounded claims may be supplemented by ethnographic insights and evidence from participant observations, field notes, interviews and so forth. Although generalizability is not the *sine qua non* of microethnographic work, researchers assume and argue that site-specific findings have relevance beyond, and that particular patterns of behaviour resonate with larger social orders.

Curt Le Baron

Associated Concepts: conversation analysis, ethnography, ethnomethodology, induction, transcription, videography

Key Readings

Jones, S. and LeBaron, C. (2002) 'Research on the relationship between verbal and non-verbal communication: emerging integrations', *Journal of Communication*, 52 (3): 499–521.
LeBaron, C. and Streeck, J. (1997) 'Space, surveillance, and interactional framing of participants' experience during a police interrogation', *Human Studies*, 20: 1–25.
LeBaron, C. and Streeck, J. (2000) 'Gesture, knowledge, and the world', in D. McNeill (ed.), *Language and Gesture*. Cambridge: Cambridge University Press.
LeBaron, C. (2004) 'Considering the social and material surround: toward microethnographic understandings of nonverbal communication', in V. Manusov (ed.), *The Sourcebook of Nonverbal Measures: Going Beyond Words*. Mahwah, NJ: Erlbaum.
Streeck, J. (1983) *Social Order in Child Communication. A Study in Microethnography*. Amsterdam: Benjamins.

MIXED METHODS RESEARCH

Definition

The combined use of both quantitative and qualitative methodologies within the same study in order to address a single research question.

Distinctive Features

Mixed-methods research draws upon both quantitative and qualitative methodological approaches to answer a particular research question. For example, a researcher may start by conducting semi-structured interviews and then use the results from this phase to formulate specific closed-ended survey questions. This is an illustration of what has been termed *sequential* mixed-methods research (Cresswell, 2003), whereby qualitative data collection and analysis is undertaken first, followed by quantitative data collection and analysis (or vice versa). Alternative strategies within mixed-methods research have been identified. Cresswell (2003) refers to *concurrent* and *transformational* strategies. Concurrent techniques involve data collection using both quantitative and qualitative approaches simultaneously, for example, administering a questionnaire which contains both closed-ended and open-ended questions.

Transformational techniques make use of an overriding theoretical perspective (for example, participatory research) to guide the entire study design and to drive the choice of methods used.

Within the three general mixed-methods research strategies outlined above, a number of different approaches can be taken. One question concerns whether both approaches are to be given equal weight, or one approach given priority, and this will depend on the individual researcher's goals and orientation as well as the nature of the research question. Another choice concerns the stage, or stages, at which integration of the two approaches will occur. In relation to this latter issue, Tashakkori and Teddlie (1998) have defined mixed methods research as that which combines quantitative and qualitative *methodologies* in a specific aspect of a study (for example, data analysis) and contrast this with mixed-*model* research which combines both approaches at all stages in the research process (for example, conceptualization, data analysis, interpretation).

Two concepts closely associated with mixed-methods research are *triangulation* and *pragmatism*. Triangulation refers to a research strategy that involves approaching a research question from two or more angles in order to converge and cross-validate findings from a number of sources (for example, different data sources). A researcher may converge self-report data derived from interviews with observational data. In combining both quantitative and qualitative approaches mixed-methods research embodies the notion of triangulation.

Pragmatism is the term given to a particular *paradigm* (or 'worldview') which has been identified as providing a rationale for mixed-methods research. Pragmatism rejects the traditional conception that the paradigms underlying quantitative and qualitative approaches (positivism and constructivism, respectively) are essentially incompatible and in conflict. Instead, pragmatists argue that both quantitative and qualitative approaches have their own distinctive strengths and weaknesses and can be usefully combined to compliment one another. Essentially pragmatism advocates using whatever 'works best' in any particular research context, and thus opens the way for mixed-methods approaches. Pragmatism is a form of methodological pluralism.

Evaluation

As with any approach, mixed-method research embodies a number of advantages and disadvantages. Among the advantages is the potential for gaining a fuller, richer and more complete understanding of a research question by combining both quantitative and qualitative perspectives. This potential is one of the key elements emphasized by pragmatists. Secondly, the results from using one approach, strategy or method may help to guide and inform another approach or method, as in the case where the results of a semi-structured interview provide a useful basis for devising more specific questions for a structured survey. A potential disadvantage of mixed-methods approaches, however, is the often lengthy data collection and analysis phases required (especially in sequential designs) leading to heavy demands on both time and funding resources. A further possible disadvantage is the demand placed on the researcher to be expert in the use of both quantitative and qualitative approaches. Thirdly, the validity of mixed-methods research has been called into question in debates over the extent to which the underlying paradigms and methods of quantitative and qualitative research can be seen as compatible. There have been advocates for both the 'compatibility' and the 'incompatibility' theses. While these theoretical debates are ongoing, a number of researchers across a range of disciplines in the social and behavioural sciences are utilizing and further refining mixed-methods approaches.

Claire Hewson

Associated Concepts: messy research, methodological pluralism, paradigm, qualitative research, quantitative research, triangulation, validity

Key Readings

Cresswell, J. W. (2003) *Research Design: Qualitative, Quantitative and Mixed Methods Approaches*. London: Sage.

Greene, J. C., Caracelli, V. J. and Graham, W. F. (1989) 'Toward a conceptual framework for mixed-method evaluation designs', *Educational Evaluation and Policy Analysis*, 11 (3): 255–74.

Tashakkori, A. and Teddlie, C. (1998) *Mixed Methodology: Combining Qualitative and Quantitative Approaches*. London: Sage.

Tashakkori, A. and Teddlie, C. (2003) *Handbook of Mixed Methods in the Social and Behavioural Sciences*. London: Sage.

MODELLING

Definition

The process of organizing knowledge about a given system. The resulting model represents a goal-directed simplification of the system under study, which is achieved by abstraction and aggregation.

Distinctive Features

In the first step the boundary that separates the system from its environment, its relevant components and their interrelations is identified. This 'system identification' is followed by the phase of model building, a term which is sometimes used synonymously to modelling but emphasizes more strongly the result of the modelling process, that is, the model. Modelling is not constrained to the construction of formal models. However, in the context of this definition, we will focus on models that describe dynamic systems in a formal language and can be executed by computer simulation, that is, dynamic simulation models. To develop a dynamic simulation model, existing knowledge about the system and its underlying dynamics and available data are evaluated to determine the component's variables and their value ranges,

to estimate parameters and to define the behaviour pattern.

Modelling formalisms subsume approaches that support the description of continuous, discrete and hybrid systems. A *continuous* system is one in which state variables change continuously over time (Cellier, 1991). Continuous systems are described by differential equations. Time base and state are represented by real-valued variables. Graphical representations, for example block diagrams or systems dynamics diagrams, facilitate the development of models.

In a *discrete* system only a finite number of state changes occur during a finite time span (Banks et al., 2001). Discrete systems can be divided into those with a discrete and those with a continuous time base. In the former case the system develops step-wise. Examples of formalisms that support the modelling of discrete time systems are cellular automata, Petri Nets and difference equation systems. Formalisms for discrete event systems are based on a continuous representation of the time base where state changes, that is, events, can occur at any time. Examples for this type of formalisms are DEVS, timed Petri Nets and queuing models. The state of discrete systems can be described by arbitrarily scaled variables. Thus, discrete event models typically combine continuous and discrete, that is, quantitative and qualitative variables, whereas formalisms for continuous system modelling are restricted to quantitative variables.

Hybrid systems combine continuous and discrete behaviour (Zeigler et al., 2000). Many continuous modelling formalisms allow the integration of events, for example to model the switching from one continuous behaviour to the next. Also discrete event formalisms like state charts can easily be extended to capture continuous aspects of a system's behaviour.

Models may be further classified as being deterministic or stochastic. Models that contain no random variables are classified as being deterministic. Given a set of inputs the simulation run will result in a unique set of outputs. A stochastic simulation model has one or more random variables as inputs. The resulting random outputs are estimates for the true characteristics of the modelled system (Banks et al., 2001).

Another important distinction is whether systems are described on macro, micro or on multiple levels of organization (Gilbert and Troitzsch, 2000). Macro models define one entity of interest. All variables and dynamics are attributed to it. Micro models comprise multiple entities with individual states, but with homogeneous state space and behaviour pattern. Since many phenomena cannot be explained with reference to one organizational level only, in multilevel models interdependencies between systems and subsystems and different subsystems can be explicitly modelled and different abstraction levels can be combined. Both the network and hierarchical structure of systems are taken into account. Depending on the supported flexibility of interaction and behaviour pattern of modelled entities, individual-based, object-oriented and agent-oriented approaches are distinguished in multi-level modelling.

Evaluation

Modelling is a central activity in all scientific and engineering endeavours. While scientists in sociology and ecology are primarily interested in a better *understanding* of systems and their dynamics, the purpose of model building in engineering is *designing* better systems. The application areas, the objectives of the modelling are diverse, as are the modelling formalisms. As 'the limits of my language means the limits of my world' (Ludwig Wittgenstein, Tractatus 5.6), it is very important to be aware about the many modelling formalisms available and to deliberately choose among them.

Simulation models are not constructed for a system *per se*, but for a system and an experiment. Thus, a model of a system might be valid for one experiment and invalid for another. Bernard Zeigler introduced the concept of experimental frame, which establishes

the set of experiments for which a model is validated. This information should be kept with the model, because each simulation model is always related to the pair: system and experiment. As models are influenced by the modeller's background and his/her perception as well, this pair could easily be extended to an *n*-tuple.

Adelinde Uhrmacher

Associated Concepts: causal model, econometrics, experiment, simulation methods, validity

Key Readings

Banks, J., Carson, J. S., Nelson, B. L. and Nicol, D. M. (2001) *Discrete Event System Simulation*. New York: Prentice Hall.
Cellier, F. E. (1991) *Continuous System Modeling*. New York: Springer.
Gilbert, N. and Troitzsch, K. G. (2000) *Simulation for the Social Scientist*. Milton Keynes: Open University Press.
Zeigler, B. P., Praehofer, H. and Kim, T. K. (2000) *Theory of Modeling and Simulation*. New York: Academic Press.

MULTIPLE INDICATORS

Definition

Observable variables used to measure or represent some theoretical construct that is not directly observable. If an individual score on a construct is inferred from more than one single datum point, the measurement is referred to as being based on multiple indicators.

Distinctive Features

Some variables of interest to social scientists (for example, demographics like gender or age) can be measured satisfactorily by obtaining data on a single indicator. However, virtually all social research also involves the investigation of theoretical concepts for which there is no simple one-to-one correspondence to an item from the domain of observables. Nevertheless, it is not an uncommon practice to employ single indicators to measure complex underlying constructs.

Such practice may have serious negative consequences for the quality of measurement, however. Shortcomings of single indicators take on two different forms, known as *deficiency* and *contamination*, respectively. Single indicators are typically deficient in that they do not represent the domain of interest comprehensively, and they are contaminated by variables, which actually do not belong to that domain. For instance, if the construct of 'job performance as a salesperson' is measured by the single item 'volume of sales per year', that measure would be deficient because many relevant aspects of job performance are missing. At the same time, the measure will be contaminated because sales volume does not only depend on the salesperson's behaviour but also on external conditions, which lie outside his or her responsibility. As a consequence, the indicator will be both relatively unreliable (that is, lack stability in repeated measurement and show weak relationships to other indicators of the same construct) and invalid (weakly related to the entire underlying construct domain). Moreover, single indicators do not permit empirical assessment of the internal structure of the construct domain, one important facet of construct validity.

All of these flaws can be partially overcome by employing multiple indicators instead of just one: a more representative (less deficient) sample of the construct's observable manifestations can be obtained, contaminations by irrelevant outside variables (measurement errors) tend to cancel each other out in aggregates, and structural analyses through procedures like psychometric item analysis or factor analysis become applicable. Thus, the use of multiple indicators is one key to sound measurement.

Evaluation

The impact of increasing the number of indicators on reliability and validity can be substantial. For example, Jaccard (1974) has shown that correlations between a personality scale and a behavioural criterion rise from an average of about 0.20 to 0.60 when multiple instead of single acts are used as dependent variables; Rushton et al. (1983) demonstrated largely the same effect across a wide range of fields of social research. However, researchers have to consider a trade-off between measurement quality and cost-effectiveness in practical applications. The functional relationship between number of indicators and measurement quality is asymptotically increasing in the typical case whereas that between number of indicators and cost-effectiveness is typically linearly decreasing. Thus, there is usually a point when adding new indicators no longer 'pays off'. Furthermore, positive effects of increasing the number of indicators can only be expected under the assumption that the new indicators have comparable individual properties as the ones already applied.

Bernd Marcus

Associated Concepts: composite measurement, indicator, measurement, performance indicator, social indicators, reliability, validity of measurement

Key Readings

Jaccard, J. J. (1974) 'Predicting social behaviour from personality traits', *Journal of Research in Personality*, 7 (4): 358–67.

Nunnally, J. C. and Bernstein, I. H. (1994) *Psychometric Theory*, 3rd edn. New York: McGraw–Hill.

Rushton, J. P., Brainerd, C. J. and Pressley, M. (1983) 'Behavioural development and construct validity: the principal of aggregation', *Psychological Bulletin*, 94 (1): 18–38.

MULTIVARIATE ANALYSIS

Definition

The set of statistical methods employed in the interpretation of data when more than one variable property is measured for each case in the sample or population of interest. The methods explore covariation among variables – how the variables vary together – either in order to establish relationships among variables or to allocate cases to categories.

Distinctive Features

Multivariate methods require the construction of a case-variable matrix in which the rows of the matrix contain all measurements (or recorded missing data) for each case and the columns contain all measurements for each variate aspect of those cases. Common statistical packages (MINITAB, SPSS) lay out the data spreadsheet in this way. Methods fall into two kinds. The first, and better known, describe the relationships among variables through the construction of models. Most are examples of the general linear model, in which the relationships between variables are assumed to be proportionate in that changes in one or more variables produce changes in one or more other variables which can be described by a linear equation or set of simultaneous linear equations. Typically the form of the relationship is expressed by a coefficient which describes how one or more dependent variables change consequent on changes in one or more independent variables (regression coefficient or analogues) and the strength of the relationship is expressed through a coefficient which describes how much of the variation in one or more dependent variables is known when the variation in one or more independent variables is known (correlation coefficient or analogues).

Usually, consideration of multivariate modelling begins with methods applicable to variables measured at the continuous level but multivariate modelling includes procedures that relate categorical variables to each other (the analysis of multi-dimensional tables through log-linear and related procedures), categorical variables to continuous variables (multiple analysis of variance) and analyses of covariation among variables at all levels of measurement (logistic regression). The objective of modelling is to establish a description of the mechanism which generates the observed pattern of covariation. This is fundamental for variable-based causal reasoning and consequent prediction.

The other set of methods focuses on the cases rather than the variables and uses variate information to allocate cases to pre-existing categories (discriminant analysis) or to construct a system of categories from scratch and allocate cases to those categories (cluster analysis). A generic term for such procedures is 'numerical taxonomy' – the use of quantitative information in sorting things 'into kinds'.

Evaluation

The use of multivariate methods of any kind depends on the degree to which measurements produce a description of reality – the issue of operationalization. There are two aspects to this. The first is whether our 'variables' correspond to anything at all in reality or whether they are just our constructs with no real existence – the problem of reification. The second is whether we measured in such a way that our measurements do describe the real variation – the problem of validity. The only way to resolve these problems is careful attention to measurement as a social process concerned with the quantitative description of reality.

Statistical modelling, which employs linear techniques, faces the problem that social change is generally nonlinear in form. In other words, things do not change proportionately but rather what interests us is changes of a kind which cannot be investigated through linear modelling. Numerical taxonomy procedures do not face this problem and are important exploratory procedures in social investigation.

David Byrne

Associated Concepts: analysis of variance (ANOVA), causal model, cluster analysis, correlation, covariance, discriminant func-tion analysis, general linear modelling, log-linear analysis, prediction, regression, SPSS, validity of measurement, variable analysis

Key Readings

Byrne, D. S. (2002) *Interpreting Quantitative Data*. London: Sage.

Everitt, B. (1993) *Cluster Analysis*. London: Arnold.

Stevens, J. (1996) *Applied Multivariate Statistics for the Social Sciences*. Mahwah, NJ: Lawrence Erlbaum Associates.

NARRATIVE ANALYSIS

Definition

In the human sciences the term refers to a family of approaches to diverse kinds of texts, which have in common a storied form. As nations and governments construct preferred narratives about history, so do social movements, organizations, scientists and other professionals, ethnic/racial groups, and individuals in stories of experience. What makes such diverse texts 'narrative' is sequence and consequence: events are selected, organized, connected and evaluated as meaningful for a particular audience. Storytelling interprets the world and experience in it. Narratives are storied ways of knowing and communicating. The focus here is on oral narratives of personal experience.

Distinctive Features

Research interest in narrative emerged from several contemporary movements: the 'narrative turn' in the human sciences away from positivist modes of inquiry and the master narratives of theory, for example Marxism; the 'memoir boom' in literature and popular culture; identity politics in US, European and transnational movements, such as emancipation efforts of women, gays and lesbians, and other marginalized groups; and the burgeoning therapeutic culture – exploration of personal life in therapies of various kinds.

Among investigators there is considerable variation in definitions of personal narrative, often linked to discipline. In social history and anthropology, narrative can refer to an entire life story, woven from the threads of interviews, observation and documents. In socio-linguistics and other fields, the concept of narrative is restricted, referring to brief, topically specific stories organized around characters, setting and plot. In another tradition (common in psychology and sociology), personal narrative encompasses long sections of talk – extended accounts of lives in context that develop over the course of single or multiple interviews.

Investigators' definitions of narrative lead to different methods of analysis, but all require them to construct texts for further analysis, that is, select and organize documents, compose field notes and/or choose sections of interview transcripts for close inspection. Narratives do not speak for themselves or have unanalysed merit; they require interpretation when used as data in social research. Numerous typologies of methods of narrative analysis exist. The one sketched here is a heuristic effort to describe a range of contemporary approaches particularly suited to oral narratives of personal experience. The typology is not intended to be hierarchical or evaluative. Also, in practice, different approaches can be combined; they are not mutually exclusive and, as with all typologies, boundaries are fuzzy.

Thematic analysis Emphasis is on the content of a text, 'what' is said more than 'how' it is said, the 'told' rather than the 'telling'. A philosophy of language (albeit unacknowledged) underpins the approach: language is a direct and unambiguous route to meaning. As grounded theorists do, investigators collect many stories and inductively create conceptual groupings from the data. A typology of narratives (for example, narratives about experiencing illness) organized by theme is the typical representational strategy, with case studies or vignettes providing illustration.

The thematic approach is useful for theorizing across a number of cases – finding common thematic elements across research participants and the events they report. A typology can be constructed to elaborate a developing theory. Because interest lies in the content of speech, analysts interpret what is said by focusing on the meaning that any competent user of the language would find in a story. Language is viewed as a resource, not a topic of investigation. But does the approach mimic objectivist modes of inquiry, suggesting themes are unmediated by the investigator's theoretical perspective interests and mode of questioning? The contexts of an utterance – in the interview, in wider institutional and cultural discourses – are not usually studied. When many narratives are grouped into a similar thematic category, readers must assume that everyone in the group means the same thing by what they say. What happens to ambiguities, 'deviant' responses that do not fit easily into a typology, the unspoken?

Structural analysis   Emphasis shifts to the telling, to the *way* a story is told. Although thematic content does not slip away, focus is equally on form – how a teller by selecting particular narrative devices makes a story persuasive. Unlike the thematic approach, language is treated seriously – an object for close investigation – over and beyond its referential content.

Arguably the first method of narrative analysis, developed by William Labov and colleagues more than thirty years ago, this structural approach analyses the *function* of a clause in the overall narrative – the communicative work it accomplishes. Labov (1982) later modified the approach to examine first person accounts of violence – brief, topically centered and temporally ordered stories – but he retains the basic components of a narrative's structure: the abstract (summary and/or point of the story); orientation (to time, place, characters and situation); complicating action (the event sequence, or plot, usually with a crisis and turning point); evaluation (where the narrator steps back from the action to comment on meaning and communicate emotion – the 'soul' of the narrative); resolution (the outcome of the plot); and a coda (ending the story and bringing action back to the present). Not all stories contain all elements, and they can occur in varying sequences. Labov's microanalysis convincingly shows how violent actions (in bars, on the street, etc.) are the outcome of speech acts gone awry. From a small corpus of narratives and prior work of Goffman, he develops a theory of the rules of requests, which explains violent eruptions in various settings experienced by a diverse group of narrators.

Because structural approaches require examination of syntactic and prosodic features of talk, they are not suitable for large numbers, but can be very useful for detailed case studies and comparison of several narrative accounts. Microanalysis of a few cases can build theories that relate language and meaning in ways that are missed when transparency is assumed, as in thematic analysis. Investigators must decide, depending on the focus of a project, how much transcription detail is necessary. There is the danger that interview excerpts can become unreadable for those unfamiliar with socio-linguistics, compromising communication across disciplinary boundaries. Like the thematic approach, strict application of the structural approach can de-contextualize narratives by ignoring historical, interactional and institutional factors. Research settings and relationships constrain what can be narrated and shape the way a particular story develops.

Interactional analysis   Here the emphasis is on the dialogic process between teller and listener. Narratives of experience are occasioned in particular settings, such as medical, social service and court situations, where storyteller and questioner jointly participate in conversation. In interactional analysis, attention to thematic content and narrative structure are not abandoned, but interest shifts to storytelling as a process of co-construction, where teller and listener create meaning collaboratively. Stories of personal experience, organized around the life-world of the teller, may be inserted into question-and-answer exchanges. The approach requires transcripts that include all participants in the conversation, and is strengthened when paralinguistic features of interaction are included as well.

Some research questions require interactional analysis. Jack Clark and Elliot Mishler (1992) sought to distinguish the features that differentiated 'attentive' medical interviews from others. By analysing pauses, interruptions, topic chaining and other aspects of conversation, they show how medical interviews can (and cannot) result in patient narratives that provide knowledge for accurate diagnosis and treatment.

An interactional approach is useful for studies of relationships between speakers in diverse field settings (courts of law, classrooms, social service organizations, psychotherapy offices and the research interview itself). Like structural approaches, studies of interaction typically represent speech in all its complexity, not simply as a vehicle for content. As in conversational analysis, transcripts may be difficult for the uninitiated. Pauses, disfluencies and other aspects of talk are typically included, but what cannot be represented in a transcript (unlike a videotape) is the unspoken. What happens to gesture, gaze and other displays that are enacted and embodied?

Performative analysis Extending the interactional approach, interest goes beyond the spoken word and, as the stage metaphor implies, storytelling is seen as performance – by a 'self' with a past – who involves, persuades and (perhaps) moves an audience through language and gesture, 'doing' rather than telling alone. Variation exists in the performative approach, ranging from dramaturgic

to narrative as praxis – a form of social action. Consequently narrative researchers may analyse different features: actors allowed on stage in an oral narrative (for example, characters and their positionings in a story, including narrator/protagonist); settings (the conditions of performance, and setting of the story performed); the enactment of dialogue between characters (reported speech); and audience response (the listener(s) who interprets the drama as it unfolds, and the interpreter in later reading(s)). Performative analysis is emergent in narrative studies (although the dramaturgic view originated with Goffman), and researchers are experimenting with it, for example, in studies of identities – vested presentations of 'self' (Riessman, 2003).

Kristin Langellier and Eric Peterson (2003) provide a compelling theory and many empirical examples, ranging from detailed analyses of family (group) storytelling, and an illness narrative told by a breast cancer survivor. The authors analyse the positioning of storyteller, audience and characters in each performance. They show how storytelling is a communicative practice that is embodied, situated and material, discursive and open to legitimation and critique.

The performative view is appropriate for studies of communication practices, and for detailed studies of identity construction – how narrators want to be known, and precisely how they involve the audience in 'doing' their identities. The approach invites study of how audiences are implicated in the art of narrative performance. Integrating the visual (through filming and photography) with the spoken narrative represents an innovative contemporary turn.

Evaluation

Analysis of narrative is no longer the province of literary study alone; it has penetrated all the human sciences, and the practising professions. There are several systematic methods for data analysis, and each has its critics. None of the approaches is appropriate for studies of large numbers of nameless and faceless subjects. Some modes of analysis are slow and painstaking, requiring attention to subtlety: nuances of speech, the organization of a response, relations between researcher and subject, social and historical contexts – cultural narratives that make 'personal' stories possible. In a recent reflexive turn, scholars in autoethnography and other traditions are producing their own narratives, relating their biographies to research materials (Riessman, 2002).

Narratives do not mirror, they refract the past. Imagination and strategic interests influence how storytellers choose to connect events and make them meaningful for others. Narratives are useful in research precisely because storytellers interpret the past rather than reproduce it as it was. The 'truths' of narrative accounts are not in their faithful representations of a past world, but in the shifting connections they forge among past, present and future. They offer storytellers a way to re-imagine lives (as narratives do for nations, organizations, ethnic/racial and other groups forming collective identities). Building on C. Wright Mills's narrative analysis can forge connections between personal biography and social structure – the personal and the political.

Catherine Kohler Riessman

Associated Concepts: autoethnography, content analysis, conversation analysis, discourse analysis, ethnographic interviewing, grounded theory, intellectual craftsmanship, interpretive repertoires, microethnography, narrative interviewing, textual analysis, transcription, videography

Key Readings

Clark, J. A. and Mishler, E. G. (1992) 'Attending to patients' stories: reframing the clinical task', *Sociology of Health and Illness*, 14: 344–70.
Cortazzi, M. (2001) 'Narrative analysis in ethnography', in P. Atkinson, A. Coffey, S. Delamont, J. Lofland and L. Lofland (eds), *Handbook of Ethnography*. London: Sage.
Labov, W. (1982) 'Speech actions and reactions in personal narrative', in D. Tannen (ed.), *Analyzing Discourse: Text and Talk*. Washington, DC: Georgetown University Press. pp. 219–47.
Langellier, K. M. and Peterson, E. E. (2003) *Performing Narrative: The Communicative Practice of Storytelling*. Philadelphia, PA: Temple University Press.
Riessman, C. K. (2002) 'Doing justice: positioning the interpreter in narrative work', in W. Patterson (ed.), *Strategic Narrative: New Perspectives on the Power of Personal and Cultural Storytelling*. Lanham, MA and Oxford: Lexington Books. pp. 195–216.
Riessman, C. K. (2003) 'Performing identities in illness narrative: masculinity and multiple sclerosis', *Qualitative Research*, 3 (1).

NARRATIVE INTERVIEWING

Definition

A form of interviewing that involves the generation of detailed 'stories' of experience, not generalized descriptions. Narratives come in many forms, ranging from tightly bounded ones that recount specific past events (with clear beginnings, middles and ends), to narratives that traverse temporal and geographical space – biographical accounts that cover entire lives or careers.

Distinctive Features

The idea of narrative interviewing represents a major shift in perspective in the human sciences about the research interview itself. The question and answer (stimulus/response) model gives way to viewing the interview as a discursive accomplishment. Participants engage in an evolving conversation; narrator and listener/questioner, collaboratively, produce and make meaning of events and experiences that the narrator reports (Mishler, 1986). The 'facilitating' interviewer and the vessel-like 'respondent' are replaced by two active participants, who jointly produce meaning (Gubrium and Holstein, 2002). Narrative interviewing has more in common with contemporary ethnography than with mainstream social science interviewing practice that relies on discrete open-ended and/or fixed-response questions.

When the interview is viewed as a conversation – a discourse between speakers – rules of everyday conversation apply: turn-taking, relevancy, entrance and exit talk to transition into, and return from, a story world. One story can lead to another; as narrator and questioner/listener negotiate spaces for these extended turns, it helps to explore associations and meanings that might connect several stories. If we want to learn about experience in all its complexity, details count: specific incidents, not general evaluations of experience. Narrative accounts require longer turns at talk than are typical in 'natural' conversation, certainly in mainstream research practice.

Opening up the research interview to extended narration by a research participant requires investigators to give up some control. Although we have particular experiential paths we want to cover, narrative interviewing means following participants down their trails. Genuine 'discoveries' about a phenomenon can come from power-sharing in interviews.

Narratives can emerge at the most unexpected times, even in answer to fixed-response (Yes/No) questions (Riessman, 2002). But certain kinds of open-ended questions are more likely than others to provide narrative opportunities. Compare 'When did X happen?', which requests a discrete piece of information, with 'Tell me what happened ... and then what happened?', which asks for an extended account of some past time. Some investigators, after introductions, invite a participant to 'tell your story' – how an illness began, for example. But experience always exceeds its description and narrativization; events may be fleetingly summarized and given little significance. Only with further questioning can participants recall the details, turning points and other shifts in cognition, emotion and action.

Evaluation

In general, less structure in interview schedules gives greater control to research participants – interviewee and interviewer alike – to jointly construct narratives using available cultural forms. Not all parents tell stories to children on a routine basis and not all cultures are orally based (in some groups, of course, stories are the primary way to communicate about the past). Storytelling as a way of knowing and telling is differentially invoked by participants in research interviews. Not all narratives are 'stories' in the strict (socio-linguistic) sense of the term.

Sometimes it is next to impossible for a participant to narrate experience in spoken language alone. Wendy Luttrell (2003), working as an ethnographer in a classroom for pregnant teenagers, mostly African Americans, expected 'stories' from each girl about key events: learning of pregnancy, telling mothers and boyfriends, making the decision to keep the baby, and other moments. She confronted silence instead, only to discover a world of narrative as she encouraged the girls' artistic productions and role plays. When she asked them to discuss their art work, they performed narratives about the key moments for each other – group storytelling. It is a limitation for investigators to rely only on the texts constructed from individual interviews – 'holy transcripts'. Innovations among contemporary scholars include combining observation, sustained relationships and conversations over time with participants, even visual data with narrative interviewing (for example, video taping of participants' environments, photographs they take and their responses to photographs of others).

In sum, narrative interviewing is not a set of 'techniques' nor is it necessarily 'natural'. If creatively used, it offers a way in some research situations for us to forge dialogic relationships, and greater communicative equality in social research.

Catherine Kohler Riessman

Associated Concepts: discourse analysis, elite interviewing, ethnographic interviewing, exploitative research, idiographic, interview, narrative analysis, videography

Key Readings

Gubrium, J. F. and Holstein, J. A. (2002) 'From the individual interview to the interview society', in J. F. Gubrium and J. A. Holdstein (eds), *Handbook of Interview Research: Context and Method*. Thousand Oaks, CA: Sage.

Luttrell, W. (2003) *Pregnant Bodies, Fertile Minds: Gender, Race, and the Schooling of Pregnant Teens*. New York: Routledge.

Mishler, E. G. (1986) *Research Interviewing: Context and Narrative*. Cambridge, MA: Harvard University Press.

Riessman, C. K. (2002) 'Positioning gender identity in narratives of infertility: South Indian women's lives in context', in M. C. Inhorn and F. van Balen (eds), *Infertility Around the Globe: New Thinking on Childlessness, Gender, and Reproductive Technologies*. Berkeley, CA: University of California Press.

NATURALISTIC DATA

Definition

The form of records of human activities that are neither *elicited by* nor *affected by* the actions of social researchers.

Distinctive Features

For much of the twentieth century social scientists worked predominantly with materials that involved self-reports (social surveys, interviews, questionnaires) or measures of the effects of experimental manipulations.

Early critics of this work argued for more use of unobtrusive measures (Webb et al. [1966] 1999) and systematic observation (Barker, 1968). Yet in practice the unobtrusive measures proposed mainly took the form of traces of gross behaviour (worn flooring identifies popular museum exhibits; contents of human garbage identifies consumption habits) with relatively little in the way of theory to deal with the more complex records noted (diaries, newspapers). The observation research proposed by Barker involved grossly defined behaviours and, in these pre-video days, typically involved some kind of tick-box time sampling of occurrences. These researchers were hampered by shortcomings in theory, transcription, analysis and technology.

The analysis of records of people interacting was stimulated most fundamentally by Harvey Sacks and the tradition of conversation analysis which he and colleagues Gail Jefferson and Emanuel Schegloff developed (Sacks, 1992). This work started to exploit developments in recording technology (at first audio, more recently video).

Advantages commonly offered for working with naturalistic data include the following:

(1) It does not flood the research setting with the researcher's own categories (embedded in questions, probes, stimuli, vignettes and so on).

(2) It does not put people in the position of disinterested experts on their own and others' practices, thoughts and so on, encouraging them to provide normatively appropriate descriptions (as many interview and questionnaire studies do).

(3) It does not leave the researcher to make a range of more or less problematic inferences from the data collection arena to the topic. Claims about counselling, say, are not dependent on what counsellors or clients *say* about counselling.

(4) It opens up a wide variety of novel issues and concerns that are outside the prior expectations embodied in questionnaires, experimental formats, interview questions and so on.

(5) It is a rich record of people living their lives, pursuing goals, managing institutional tasks and so on. (Modified from Potter, 2002)

In addition to these reasons for working with naturalistic data, researchers have stressed its role in validating claims. The readers and referees of an article can access transcripts of the material and, increasingly, Web-based audio and video records. As Sacks put it, the goal is to develop analysis where 'the reader has as much information as the author, and can reproduce the analysis' (1992, vol. I: 27).

Ethnographers in anthropology and sociology have often worked with materials collected from participant or non-participant observation. Although these involve making records of people living their lives largely uninfluenced by social scientists, in practice the actual data are typically field notes of some kind. Such field notes will involve a range of summarizing and categorizing practices that may pre-impose a range of understandings on what is going on as well as making it particularly hard to recover the original organization of the interaction.

The *goal* of generating naturalistic material is easily distinguished from the goals of hypothetico-deductive research using experiments, surveys and so on. In practice, of course, there are likely to be a variety of sources of 'reactivity' as participants have filled in ethics permission forms, may be aware of the recording, may have some idea of research questions and so on (Speer, 2002). Moreover, the process of transcription is embedded in a theoretical and analytic tradition that emphasizes some phenomena (for example, overlap between speakers) and downplays others (for example, regional accent). So although the data may not be 'got up' by the researcher, it is unwise to treat it as something independent of the research enterprise. The term natura*listic* (rather than natural) marks a caution about the status of such data (Potter, 2002). Nevertheless, every effort should be made to eliminate or manage these problems.

Despite the strong contrast to be made by work using interviews, experiments and other forms of data elicitation, it is possible to study research practices as forms of natural interaction in their own right. That is, rather than using a survey to discover something about a sample of people, the interaction involved in administering that survey (including the situated identities of those involved, the practices of questioning and answering, the construction of social science categories such as 'opinions' and so on) can be taken as a topic. In effect, the research interaction has been naturalized (see Maynard et al., 2002), with

two rather different kinds of social science research going on simultaneously.

Evaluation

The significance of naturalistic data is controversial because it is bound up with broader theoretical issues about the conduct of social science. For some it undoubtedly pulls the researcher away from social scientists' traditional grand questions and deflects them onto a concern with the trivial details of interaction. Sacks disparages an approach that assumes 'that you could tell right off whether something was important [and thus should] start by looking at what kings did, or to look at votes, or revolutions' (1992, vol. I: 28). He proposed instead the possibility that we might be able to 'read the world out of the phone conversation as well as we can read it out of anything else we're doing' (1992, vol. II: 548).

In recent years, the successes of conversation analytic studies of institutional interaction (for example, Clayman and Heritage, 2002), of discursive psychological studies of mind in action (for example, Edwards, 1997), and video-based ethnography (Goodwin and Goodwin, 1997) have moved the debate on. The virtues of using naturalistic material have been demonstrated and the onus is increasingly on researchers to justify using other kinds of data. Moreover, researchers are just starting to exploit the enormous fluidity in working with audio and video that digital technology combined with cheap powerful computing power has made available.

Jonathan Potter

Associated Concepts: conversation analysis, discursive psychology, participant observation, transcription, unobtrusive measures, validity of measurement, videography

Key Readings

Barker, R. G. (1968) *Ecological Psychology: Concepts and Methods for Studying the Environment of Human Behaviour*. Stanford, CA: Stanford University Press.

Clayman, S. E. and Heritage, J. (2002) *The News Interview: Journalists and Public Figures on the Air*. Cambridge: Cambridge University Press.

Edwards, D. (1997) *Discourse and Cognition*. London: Sage.

Goodwin, C. and Goodwin, M. H. (1997) 'Contested vision: the discursive constitution of Rodney King', in B-L. Gunnarsson, P. Linell and B. Nordberg (eds), *The Construction of Professional Discourse*. London: Longman. pp. 292–316.

Maynard, D. W., Houtkoop-Steenstra, H., Schaeffer, N. C. and van der Zouwen, J. (eds), *Standardization and Tacit Knowledge: Interaction and Practice in the Survey Interview*. New York: Wiley.

Potter, J. (2002) 'Two kinds of natural', *Discourse Studies*, 4: 539–42.

Sacks, H. (1992) *Lectures on Conversation*, Vols I and II (ed. G. Jefferson). Oxford: Blackwell.

Speer, S. (2002) '"Natural" and "contrived" data: a sustainable distinction?', *Discourse Studies*, 4: 511–25.

Webb, E. J., Campbell, D. T., Shwartz, R. D. and Sechrest, L. (1996/1999) *Unobtrusive Measures*, 2nd edn. London: Sage.

NETNOGRAPHY

Definition

Ethnography conducted on the Internet; a qualitative, interpretive research methodology that adapts the traditional, in-person ethnographic research techniques of anthropology to the study of the online cultures and communities formed through computer-mediated communications (CMC).

Distinctive Features

Ethnography refers to in-person participative-observational fieldwork among particular social groups, and also to the representations based on such studies. In the past decade, the mass adoption of networked personal computing gave rise to new cultural formations. These new formations, in their novel online context, required the development of new research methodologies.

At least four aspects of online, computer-mediated or virtual, interaction and community formation are distinct from their in-person, real life (RL), or face-to-face (F2F) counterparts. First is the textual, nonphysical, and social-cue-impoverished context of the online environment. Second is an unprecedented new level of access to the heretofore unobservable behaviours of particular interacting peoples. Third, while traditional interactions are ephemeral as they occur, online social interactions are often automatically saved and archived, creating permanent records. Finally, the social nature of the new medium is unclear as to whether it is a private or public space, or some unique hybrid. Ethnography adapts common participant observation ethnographic procedures – such as making cultural entrée, gathering and analysing data, ensuring trustworthy interpretation, conducting member checks and conducting ethical research – to these computer-mediated contingencies (see Kozinets, 2002 for a detailed explication).

Given the wide range of choices of online communal form, including boards, rings, lists and dungeons (see Kozinets, 1999), researchers should spend time matching their research questions and interests to appropriate online fora, using the novel resources of online search engines such as Yahoo! and Google groups, before initiating entrée. Before initiating contact as a participant, or beginning formal data collection, the distinctive characteristics of the online communities should be familiar to the netnographer.

In a netnography, data take two forms: data that the researcher directly copies from the computer-mediated communications of online community members, and data that the researcher inscribes. Reflective field notes, in which ethnographers record their observations, are a time-tested and recommended method. However, distinct from traditional ethnography, rigorous netnographies have been conducted using only observation and download, without the researcher writing a single field note.

193

As with grounded theory, data collection should continue as long as new insights on important topical areas are still being generated. For purposes of precision, some netnographers may wish to closely track the amount of text collected and read, and the number of distinct participants. Software solutions expedite coding, content analysis, data linking, data display and theory-building functions. Contextualizing online data is necessary to its analysis, and often proves to be challenging in the social-cues-impoverished online context of netnography. Because netnography is based primarily upon the observation of textual discourse, ensuring trustworthy interpretations requires a different approach than the balancing of discourse and observed behaviour that occurs during in-person ethnography. Although the online landscape mediates social representation and renders problematic the issue of informant identity, netnography seems perfectly amenable to treating behaviour or the social act as the ultimate unit of analysis, rather than the individual person.

Research ethics may be one of the most important differences between traditional ethnography and netnography. Ethical concerns over netnography turn on contentious and still largely unsettled concerns about whether online forums are to be considered a private or a public site, and about what constitutes informed consent in cyberspace (see Paccagnella, 1997). In a major departure from traditional methods, netnography uses cultural information that is not given specifically, and in confidence, to the researcher. The consumers who originally created the data do not necessarily intend or welcome their use in research representations.

Ethical procedures that involve full disclosure of the researcher's presence, affiliations and intentions, and extensive member checking, are recommended. Gaining feedback on research from community members is facilitated by the online medium. In addition, researchers should ensure the confidentiality and anonymity of informants. To show additional concern for ethics, researchers might contact specific community members to obtain their permission to directly quote specific postings, or idiosyncratic stories, in the research.

Evaluation

Compared to surveys, experiments, focus groups and personal interviews, netnography is a far less obtrusive method. It is conducted using observations in a context that is not fabricated by the researcher. Netnography also is less costly and timelier than focus groups and personal interviews. It is a naturalistic and unobtrusive technique – a nearly unprecedented combination.

The limitations of netnography draw from its more narrow focus on online communities, its inability to offer the full and rich detail of lived human experience, the need for researcher interpretive skill, and the lack of informant identifiers present in the online context that leads to difficulty generalizing results to groups outside the online community sample. Researchers wishing to generalize the findings of a netnography of a particular online group to other groups must therefore apply careful evaluations of similarity and consider employing multiple methods for triangulation. Netnography is still a relatively new method, and awaits further development and refinement at the hands of a new generation of Internet-savvy ethnographic researchers.

Robert V. Kozinets

Associated Concepts: access, confidentiality, covert research, ethics, ethnographic interviewing, ethnography, impression management, informed consent, Internet research, participant observation, unobtrusive measures

Key Readings

Kozinets, R. V. (1998) 'On Netnography: initial reflections on consumer research investigations of cyberculture', in J. Alba and W. Hutchinson (eds), *Advances in Consumer Research*, Volume 25. Provo, UT: Association for Consumer Research. pp. 366–71.
Kozinets, R. V. (1999) 'E-tribalized marketing: the strategic implications of virtual communities of consumption', *European Management Journal*, 17 (3): 252–64.

Kozinets, R. V. (2002) 'The field behind the screen: using Netnography for marketing research in online communities', *Journal of Marketing Research*, 39 (February): 61–72.

Paccagnella, L. (1997) 'Getting the seats of your pants dirty: strategies for ethnographic research on virtual communities', *Journal of Computer-Mediated Communications*, 3 (June). Available online at http://ww.ascusc.org/jcmc/

NETWORK ANALYSIS

Definition

Analysis of any pattern of relations between individuals, groups, institutions or any other social collectivities.

Distinctive Features

Network analysis has its roots in social anthropology, for example, in examining kinship networks and also trading networks (for example, Malinowski's study of exchange relations amongst Trobriand Islanders). It has subsequently been used in social psychology to examine interpersonal relations in small groups. An example is Moreno's development of sociometry in which he introduced the idea of a social network as a diagram – a sociogram – in which points, representing people, were connected by lines, representing social relationships. Sociometry can be used to study group formation and group dynamics, for example, the formation of cliques and the flow of information. It has also contributed to the study of economic, political, criminal and familial networks within communities. An example of network analysis in relation to kinship is Elizabeth Bott's study of kinship networks in terms of the degree of their connectedness but without any element of measurement of such connectedness. A further development of network analysis involved the application of sophisticated mathematical techniques, based on graph theory, and using computer software, to develop various measures of density, strength, connectedness and also to examine structure in terms of cliques, blocks and the flow of information in terms of 'sources' (initiators of information flows) and 'sinks' (receivers of information).

Evaluation

Network analysis is predominantly a form of analysis rather than a way of theorizing. There are different levels of analysis, from exploratory visual mapping to mathematical modelling. Its strength lies in the different ways in which it can be applied. For example, it can be used at different levels and with different units of analysis (individuals, small groups, communities) and in different subject areas. It can be quantitative or qualitative and it can be used as a business tool or in interventionist and policy-related ways, for example, in mapping AIDS and other sexually transmitted diseases. When used in the latter way it is akin to snowball sampling.

Victor Jupp

Associated Concepts: community study method, snowball sampling, sociometry

Key Readings

Bott, E. (1957) *Family and Social Network.* London: Tavistock.

Mitchell, J. C. (ed.) (1969) *Social Networks in Urban Situations.* Manchester: Manchester University Press.

Moreno, J. L. (1953) *Who Shall Survive?* New York: Beacon.

Scott, J. P. (1991) *Social Network Analysis: A Handbook.* London: Sage.

NOMOTHETIC

Definition

Research into regularities and patterns in social behaviour and in social arrangements. This is in contrast to idiographic research, which is concerned with the detailed examination of specific instances, cases or contexts.

Distinctive Features

Typically, nomothetic inquiry is part of a wider endeavour of the search for universal explanations or covering laws. In the 'hard' sense such explanations or laws are deemed to be causal and deterministic, involving universal conditional statements such as 'if *a* occurs then *b*'. In a 'softer' sense they can take the form of probabilistic statements such as 'if *a* occurs then there is a probability that *b* will follow'.

In its search for broad patterns and regularities nomothetic inquiry usually involves large-scale, macro research. Also, it is usually – but not always – quantitative research. This is in contrast with idiographic inquiry which is typically qualitative and concerned with the detailed analysis of specific cases, for example life histories, documents, events, institutions. Whereas the idiographic stands for the viewpoint that such specific cases can only be understood and explained in their particular context and time period, the nomothetic stands for the search for patterns and regularities which are common to all such cases. It would, for example, look for consistencies in the management structure of organizations, from different sectors, which are undergoing rapid technological change. Further, it would aim to reach explanations, even laws, which 'cover' these consistencies.

Evaluation

The idiographic–nomothetic divide is often presented as starkly as quantitative–qualitative, micro–macro, thick description–thin description, on the grounds that they represent contrasting and incompatible epistemological and ontological positions. There is, however, a 'softer', more pragmatic and less adversarial strand in social research. This is one that recognizes both the objective and subjective aspects of social life and the need to understand the specific as well as search for

under-structural and historical patterns. This strand is likely to favour forms of triangulation, mixed or even messy research methods.

Victor Jupp

Associated Concepts: causal model, covering-law model of explanation, epistemology, idiographic, messy research, mixed-methods research, qualitative research, quantitative research, thick description, triangulation

Key Readings

Crotty, M. (1998) *The Foundations of Social Research*. London: Sage.
Wallerstein, I. (1987) 'World systems analysis', in A. Giddens and J. Turner (eds), *Social Theory Today*. Cambridge: Polity Press.

NON-PROBABILITY (NON-RANDOM) SAMPLING

Definition

Forms of sampling that do not adhere to probability methods. Probability methods choose samples using random selection and every member of the population has an equal chance of selection. Some types of non-random sampling still aim to achieve a degree of representativeness without using random methods. Several different techniques are associated with this approach, for example accidental or convenience sampling; snowball sampling; volunteer sampling; quota sampling, and theoretical sampling.

Distinctive Features

Convenience samples are also known as accidental or opportunity samples. The problem with all of these types of samples is that there is no evidence that they are representative of the populations to which the researchers wish to generalize. This approach is often used when the researcher must make use of available respondents or where no sampling frame exists. A good example is provided by my own experience of conducting evaluative research designed to explore the efficacy of community treatment programmes for sex offenders. Here an accidental sample of those men sentenced to treatment was used by necessity (Davidson, 2001). TV, radio station, newspaper and magazine polls and question-naires are also an example of this type of sampling, where respondents may be asked to 'phone in' or fill in a questionnaire.

Quota sampling is very popular with market researchers, first because instant opinions might be needed and probability sampling would take too much time, and sec-ondly because it is less costly than probabil-ity sampling. A typical example is the market researcher who stands in the high street, and selects certain types of shoppers, often by age and gender. A quota number is set for each of the categories of people required for the study. The problem with this method is that bias can enter the process because the inter-viewer has an element of choice in how to select people to fill the quota. Snowballing, which is akin to a chain-letter, is used when it is difficult to find a sample in any other way (there is no accessible sampling frame for the population from which the sample is to be taken), and it is often used with difficult to access groups. Here the researcher finds one respondent, who in turn introduces another, and so on. This technique might be used in research on deviant lifestyles, illegal drug users or any population with unknown characteristics. Theoretical sampling seeks to select respondents who will enhance the theoretical development of the research. Such sampling aims to identify cases which may challenge emergent concepts. Finally, as the term indicates, volunteer sampling relies on individuals or groups of individuals volun-teering to be the subjects of research.

Evaluation

Non-probability sampling has been criti-cized for its lack of representativeness and generalizability. In quota sampling, for example, the people who are interviewed are those who are on the streets and available at the time of fieldwork, and those who agree to form a volunteer sample might be those who have a particular interest in the topic or hold especially strong views about it. They are a self-selected sample and there is no way of knowing whether their views are representative.

Whilst it cannot be denied that such sam-pling techniques may not produce a represen-tative response, some of the most influential and interesting qualitative research has never-theless been conducted on this basis.

Julia Davidson

Associated Concepts: marketing research, opportunity sampling, probability (random) sampling, purposive sampling, quota sam-pling, sampling, validity of generalization

Key Readings

Bryman, A. (2001) *Social Research Methods.* Oxford: Oxford University Press.

Davidson, J. (2001) The Context and Practice of Community Treatment Programmes for Child Sexual Abusers. PhD thesis unpublished.

Kumar, R. (1999) *Research Methodology: A Step by Step Guide for Beginners.* London: Sage.

May, T. (1997) *Social Research: Issues, Methods and Process.* Milton Keynes: Open University Press.

NUD*IST

Definition

One of the pioneer software packages for qualitative analysis. Designed to assist researchers in handling Non-numerical Unstructured Data by Indexing, Searching and Theorizing, it supports rapid coding and code-based access for small or large bodies of qualitative data in academic, governmental and other settings.

Distinctive Features

NUD*IST provides symmetrical handling of data documents and ideas, with emphasis on rapid access for interpretation, coding and searching. Experience with users led to development of a sister product for smaller projects with more detailed analysis, NVivo.

Distinctive features of the NUD*IST line of software have been:

- Themes or categories that emerge in qualitative analysis and may be used in coding are presented as items (nodes) that can be managed and explored in index systems as the understanding grows.
- Symmetrical explorers show documents and nodes. Selecting an item sets coding or searching processes to apply to that data item.
- Coding of passages of text can be done interactively, selecting text on the screen, or by typing in the unit number to be coded.
- Viewing and reviewing coded data live, the researcher has immediate access to context and the ability to *code on* as interpretation of the coded material suggests finer categories.
- Browsing the text of a document or all the text coded at a node moves the user between linked windows on the textual data.
- Records of the interpretative processes are in annotations and memos; document text, coded.
- Ability to edit coded data without invalidating coding.
- Storing of information about cases, documents, respondents, sites etc. as coding, accessible to all search processes.
- Exploring patterns of coding and text via a logically complete and linked set of search tools.
- Iterative exploration, using the results of any search saved as coding, so another question can be asked.

- Automation of clerical tasks by command files to handle large or repetitive processes.
- Import and export of information or coding from and to statistical research packages.

Evaluation

Whilst QDA software grew more sophisticated, NUD*IST was developed as a responsive, stripped-down toolkit for rapid handling of even very large data sets. Data imported or pasted to NUD*IST appears in plain text, and is automatically formatted to a unit specified by the researcher (line, sentence or paragraph). These constraints mean NUD*IST can handle small or large quantities of data flexibly. Facilities for automating coding and data handling support many types of qualitative–quantitative linking, and handling of data that would not traditionally be called qualitative, such as the open-ended answers to surveys.

Projects can be moved from NUD*IST for more subtle analysis to its QSR stable-mate, NVivo, where data can be handled in rich text, with character-level coding, linking, subtle ways of filtering and refining searches and modelling. Team or multi-site projects can be merged with an accompanying package for combining multiple projects, comparison between projects or combining work of multiple researchers.

Lyn Richards

Associated Concepts: CAQDAS, coding, The Ethnograph, QSR NVivo, qualitative research

Key Readings

Richards, L. (2002) *Using N6 in Qualitative Research*. Melbourne: QSR International.
Richards, T. (2002) 'An intellectual history of NUD*IST and NVivo', *International Journal of Social Research Methodology*, 5 (3): 199–214.

OFFICIAL STATISTICS

Definitions

Two definitions may be offered:

(1) Measurements produced by local or national states or international bodies which describe the general social condition with particular reference to change, to monitor the activities of state and related bodies, and indicate relative performance of providers of collective services.

(2) A system of collecting statistical data, gathering, storing and generalizing collected data; and announcing, providing and disseminating the results of statistical surveys as the official statistical data.

Distinctive Features

Strictly speaking 'official statistics' is an oxymoron because the literal meaning of statistics is measurements made by the state describing state and society. The original charter of the UK's Royal Statistical Society stated that its purpose was:

> to collect, arrange, digest and publish facts, illustrating the condition and prospects of society in its material, social, and moral relations; these facts being for the most part arranged in tabular forms and in accordance with the principles of numerical method.

Such measurements by states, together with accounts of the state's own activities in quantitative form, were the original official statistics. Desrosières (1998) notes that between 1835 and 1935 governments in Europe and the United States universally established official statistical departments and engaged in systematic measurement of social conditions. Simultaneously the accountancy and related monitoring activities of governments generated quantitative information describing the operations of governments themselves. The extension of the range of government activities into both the economy and civil society generated an ever-increasing number of data streams. State macro-economic management reinforced this tendency and the development of international bodies – the UN and its agencies, the European Union and other global regional blocks – generated new international data sets. Many data sets were intended for the original purpose of statistics – to enable comparisons among states (including local states) on a quantitative basis.

There are two general sources of official statistics. The first is from the monitoring processes of administration through bureaucratic data collection. Schools return data on pupil numbers, exam successes and related matters. These data are used to construct a set of data series, including league tables. The other is from outreach investigative activities such as the UK decennial census but there are a series of other investigations, both into general social conditions and into specific areas of interest such as health. In either case, users of the data sets, whether inspecting published tables or working with raw secondary data sets, must pay particularly careful attention to the operationalization of the variables measured.

In the 1960s there was a general effort to move official statistics beyond being mere description towards becoming a systematic and organized model of social processes at every level. This was the 'social indicators' movement. At the simplest level a social indicator is simply a measure of something considered to be socially significant as an index of some wider social process or context – which can change. So the UK's most accessible general official statistical publication is *Social Trends* in which a set of data series describe changes through time. However, the social indicators movement sought to move beyond description of isolated and distinctive trends towards the construction of a social information system on the lines of the economic information system, which, using economic official statistics, underpins predictive models of the economic system. This project has not been successful but there has been a considerable development of evaluative indicators as tools for assessing the success of particular policies or projects. There has also been a development of overall indicators – for example of deprivation at a ward level in the UK or the United Nations Development Programme's Human Development Index for nation-states. The purpose of such indices is comparison on a single measure which incorporates multiple dimensions within that measure.

A recent and very significant extension of this has been the publication of data series describing the outputs of a range of public sector institutions. The most important of these in England and Wales are state schools and a wide range of performance data which are widely disseminated. Data of this kind have a novel purpose. Official statistics traditionally have been seen as sources of information for the state itself, at whatever level, and as part of the information base that can inform an active and collectively minded citizenry. Now institutional level data are published to inform individual consumption choices, for example about choice of school for a child, and directed not at a socially conscious citizenry but at an aggregate of individual consumers. This has meant that overall performance data, for example on hospital waiting lists, have become an important political issue to an unprecedented degree.

Evaluation

Statistics are always social constructs and this is the origin of two related but ultimately different sets of criticisms of official statistics. The first, which we might call radical statistics, is that being products of the state, official statistics represent the positions of powerful groups in society which have an undue influence on the ways in which measurements are both defined and constructed. In other words, official statistics investigate things which state agencies and powerful interests want investigated *and* the actual measures are distorted by political interests and pressures. The issue of the integrity of official statistics has been taken up in the UK through the appointment of a Statistics Commission and is central to the UN Fundamental Principles of Official Statistics adopted in 1994 which focus particularly on official statistics as part of the public information of a democratic society. This was the content of the mission statement of UK official statistics in the 1960s and 1970s, although the Rayner reforms of the 1980s (see Levitas and Guy, 1996) shifted the focus towards the state's own requirements and the commercial provision of information on a market basis. Now there is more emphasis on social statistics as sources of information for the consumers of public services. The other set of criticisms of official statistics is the general rejection of quantified social measurement as reification rather than in any way being a real version of how society works. This leads to a general dismissal of any social measurement including official statistics whereas the radical statistics position argues instead with the nature of the process and the role of interest and power in that process.

The central point to recognize is that official statistics are constructs, not crude facts which are given. However, the reasonable position adopted by most social scientists is that they are made out of something, not nothing, and that provided we pay careful attention to the ways in which they are made, and in particular the processes of operationalization, they can be of very considerable value to us.

David Byrne

Associated Concepts: auditing, comparative method, critical research, data, descriptive statistics, econometrics, forecasting, performance indicator, primary research, secondary analysis, social indicators

Key Readings

Byrne, D. S. (2002) *Interpreting Quantitative Data*. London: Sage.

Desrosières, A. (1998) *The Politics of Large Numbers*. Cambridge, MA: Harvard University Press.

Levitas, R. and Guy, W. (1996) *Interpreting Official Statistics*. London: Routledge.

ONE-SHOT DESIGN

Definition

A study design where a single group of individuals (or other interesting unit of analysis) is selected for observation over a single, limited time period, usually because they have experienced some factor taken as important in shaping some outcome. It is akin to one-off cross-sectional design.

Distinctive Features

An example of one such design might be a one-off survey of unemployed people in a specific local area to assess their health status and the impact of unemployment on health. Thus there is no attempt to approximate to the classical experiment. There is no comparison group of employed people, there is no attempt to study changes over time and the sample

selected may not be truly random. One-shot case study designs are favoured on grounds such as the proximity of the research site to the research team. The choice may also be made when the current state of the knowledge base justifies a preliminary exploratory case study prior to a more fully developed theoretically informed design to test a developed set of theoretical arguments, which may require a longitudinal dimension.

Evaluation

The findings from one-shot case study designs need to be treated with care. A one-shot case study of the unemployed in London might find that 65 per cent were in poor health and conclude that unemployment had a negative effect on health status. Such a conclusion would not be warranted however for a number of reasons. First, it is assumed that the 65 per cent level of poor health revealed is a consequence of the factor used to select the subject group. If older workers or those working in high health risk industries were more likely to be made unemployed these factors would 'explain' the 65 per cent finding. Second, the conclusion assumes that the 65 per cent figure is indeed 'high' when similar levels might be found in a study of the employed. Third, it assumes that the time order of the variables is that implied in the causal inference, namely, that unemployment is the cause of health and not vice versa. Fourth, it neglects to seek out other relevant events such as the impact of unemployment on family relationships: unemployment may have little effect on the health status of those whose domestic relationships remain intact. Fifth, asking the unemployed about their health status may also lead them to overstate health problems.

One-shot case studies may redress these inherent design limitations by the use of sophisticated statistical manipulations of the data such as multivariate modelling. In the above example, there could be a test to link the length of unemployment to the quality of health controlling for the other known and measured factors. However, the results of such analysis could not be taken as valid for subjects outside the group chosen or outside the locality of the chosen group.

Aidan Kelly

Associated Concepts: causality, cohort study, covariance, cross-sectional survey, longitudinal study, multivariate analysis, panel study, prospective study, quasi-experiment, research design, sampling, social survey

Key Readings

Campbell, D. T. and Stanley, J. C. (1966) *Experimental and Quasi-Experimental Designs for Research*. Chicago: Rand McNally.
Marsh, C. (1982) *The Survey Method: The Contributions of Surveys to Sociological Analysis*. London: Allen & Unwin.
Sapsford, R. and Jupp, V. (1996) *Data Collection and Analysis*. London: Sage.
de Vaus, D. (2001) *Research Design in Social Research*. London: Sage.

ONTOLOGY

Definition

A concept concerned with the existence of, and relationship between different aspects of society, such as social actors, cultural norms and social structures.

Distinctive Features

Commentators on the process of social research generally concede that any instance of social inquiry is based upon the dual fundamental principles of epistemology and ontology. Epistemology deals with the issue of knowledge, and specifically, who can be a 'knower'. For example, within feminist research, Sandra Harding (1987) argues that women have been systematically excluded as 'knowers' from 'masculine' sociology and therefore must establish a feminist 'standpoint', and legitimate female epistemological

knowledge. However, ontological issues are concerned with questions pertaining to the kinds of things that exist within society. Again using feminist thought as an example, ontological issues concern the idea of 'being', and would stress the existence of patriarchal social relations and the negative implications these have for women. The issue of ontology within social thought is a longstanding one, traceable, at least, to the philosophy of Aristotle. Within social research, however, whilst epistemological issues concern the question of what is or should be regarded as acceptable knowledge in a discipline such as sociology or philosophy, ontological issues are concerned with the nature of social bodies or entities.

Research traditions are similarly underpinned by a distinctive epistemological and ontological nature. For instance, the ontological principles underpinning examples of quantitative research are typically held to belong to that branch of social thought collectively dubbed the 'objectivist perspective' such as positivism, within which, the ontological nature of society is based upon the view that society is a separate entity, existing quite distinctly from the social actors that comprise a given society. Alternatively, the ontological outlook of qualitative research examines the relationships between social actors and society drawing from interpretative sociology (for example, symbolic interactionism, phenomenology or ethnomethodology). The ontological assumptions of sociologists studying the social world from this perspective are guided by the desire to investigate the differing ways in which social actors are constantly interpreting the social world from their own particular perspective. The ontological basis for qualitative, interpretative sociologists is one in which social reality is seen 'as a constantly shifting emergent property of individual creation' (Bryman, 1988: 20).

Evaluation

The relationship between ontological questions and interpretative sociology is particularly insightful within the qualitative research tradition. Within qualitative types of research there is the conspicuous acknowledgement that social reality is not a fixed set of phenomena. This is intrinsic to the concept of ontology, because, as Fay (1987) argues, the way in which social research is carried out is intimately connected to the ways in which social researchers actually observe the world. Social researchers are guided by whatever knowledge perspective they adhere to and this informs the concepts they subsequently develop. Therefore, feminist researchers will see the world in ways that seek to uncover and understand the existence and effects of patriarchy. Alternatively, critical social researchers will seek to identify the relationship between social actors and social institutions in relation to power and class with a view as to how such systems can be revealed and overcome. However, if the beliefs of researchers change over time, then so will the ontological (and epistemological) questions such researchers ask. Fay (1987) cites the example of scientific knowledge, and the ways in which past explanations for concepts such as 'nature' have changed radically as new forms of thinking have displaced older models. This is analogous to Thomas Kuhn's notion of the 'paradigm', those systems of knowledge that can, and do give way to more sophisticated paradigms, which then transform the form and manner in which ontological and epistemological questions are asked.

However, there are examples of research that actually takes the issue of ontology as the central research question rather than epistemological concerns, such as McHale's *Postmodernist Fiction* (1987). Based upon the textual analysis of novels, McHale argues that the primary concern of postmodernist fiction is the raising of questions of an ontological nature rather than epistemological questions. Returning to the definitions in which epistemology equates with 'knowing', and ontology describes 'being', modernist fiction is characterized by epistemological issues, raising questions such as: 'What is there to be known?' 'Who knows it?' Postmodernist fiction is very different. Postmodernist fiction foregrounds questions such as: 'Which world is this?'

'What happens when different kinds of world are placed in confrontation, or when boundaries between worlds are violated?' (McHale, 1987: 10). Whereas the 'typical' modernist, epistemological genre is detective fiction, McHale argues that the primary ontological genre is science fiction, because this genre habitually stages 'close encounters' between different worlds, placing them in confrontation (alien invasions, time/dimension travel, the discovery of lost worlds). On a wider social scale, theorists such as David Harvey, within *The Condition of Postmodernity* (1989), argue that the ontological nature of postmodernist fiction may indeed reflect distinct 'postmodernist' trends apparent within 'post-Fordist' Western societies, and describe the ontological condition of the 'postmodern subject'.

Lee Barron

Associated Concepts: critical research, epistemology, feminist research, phenomenology, postmodernism, qualitative research, quantitative research, realism

Key Readings

Bryman, A. (1988) *Quantity and Quality in Social Research.* London: Routledge.
Fay, B. (1987) *Critical Social Science.* Cambridge: Polity Press.
Harding, S. (ed.) (1987) *Feminism and Methodology.* Milton Keynes: Open University Press.
McHale, B. (1987) *Postmodernist Fiction.* New York: Methuen.

OPERATIONAL RESEARCH
MANAGEMENT

Definition

The scientific-based approach used traditionally by businesses (although recent studies using operational research management techniques may be found in health, education and other public sectors) to improve their decision-making process regarding the allocation of scare resources. The decision-making process is based upon the scientific school of thought and consequently studies tend to be quantitative in nature, and involve the analysis of probability and risk.

Distinctive Features

The overall aim of operational research management (ORM) is to provide a sound rational basis for decision making. ORM recognizes, and is based upon the economic fact, that resources are limited, yet wants are unlimited. Given this situation, businesses are never in the position where they can undertake all of their would-be future plans or investments. In other words, some form of choice has to be made. ORM is the mechanism for making that choice. In addition, ORM makes the process more transparent, such that business can provide detailed analysis why one particular course of action has been favoured above all others.

Traditionally ORM is thought of as only being used by large businesses, corporations or governments. However, the principles involved with ORM can be applied to very simple and also to very complex business decisions. Clearly there are links between ORM and the discipline of economics. However, utilizing ORM in differing situations will lead to other disciplines being incorporated into the decision-making process. For example, utilizing ORM techniques in the building of a new space station will bring together engineers, space experts, nuclear scientists, physicists, to mention only a few.

The history of ORM can be traced back many hundreds of years. Elements of ORM can be found in the military campaigns of Napoleon. It is within this military tradition that we find ORM techniques being developed in World War I, and in particular during World War II. The logistics of large-scale troop and machine movements meant that generals had to be aware of making a bad decision. Lack of ammunition and support does not win battles. After World War II, ORM was further developed by the military

along with other decision-making procedures such as cost-benefit analysis. Large businesses developed in the 1960s, in part due to the expansion in world trade. These businesses had to make decisions regarding products, new markets and investment in new plants and machinery, and they consequently adopted ORM techniques.

The methodology of ORM is one of completing a series of steps, these being:

- Identifying the nature of the problem.
- Formulating the nature of the problem in relation to the various techniques available.
- Building the model from the available data.
- Deriving a solution or solutions.
- Evaluating the solution(s).
- Implementing the chosen solution.

This methodology is deemed to be the classical approach to ORM. There are many variations on it, but the general pattern covers the steps above. The techniques available in ORM are wide ranging, and large steps in the development in ORM techniques have been taken with the introduction of the desktop computer. The most commonly used techniques include: linear programming, critical path analysis, statistical modelling and multivariate analysis, simulation and forecasting.

Evaluation

Clearly the ORM specialist has decisions to make as to which of the above techniques should be utilized along with the validity of the solution generated. From the techniques available an ORM specialist has to have considerable knowledge of the area under consideration in order to generate a feasible solution.

Paul E. Pye

Associated Concepts: applied research, auditing, decision-making research, econometrics, forecasting, modelling, organizational research, performance indicator, prediction, simulation methods

Key Readings

French, S., Hartley, R., Thomas, L. C. and White, D. J. (1986) *Operational Research Techniques*. London: Edward Arnold.
Hillier, F. (2000) *Introduction to Operational Research*. New York: McGraw–Hill.
Taha, H. A. (2002) *Operations Research: An Introduction*. New York: Prentice Hall.

OPERATIONALIZATION

Definition

The process of devising ways of measuring theoretical concepts.

Distinctive Features

Theoretical concepts are tools for organizing knowledge. They are not, however, directly observable and measurable. What researchers do is devise rules for recognizing instances or indicators of such concepts. For example, the theoretical concept 'social class' is typically operationalized and measured by asking subjects questions about their occupation. There are established rules for assigning occupations to social class categories. Such rules are sometimes referred to as correspondence rules because they link theoretical concepts to observable instances which correspond to them. Where a number of measures or indicators are combined in the operationalization of a concept it is common to refer to composite measurement or multiple indicators.

Evaluation

There are issues regarding operationalization linked to ontological and epistemological debates about the nature of social reality and whether it can be measured. However, in social research literature most of the discussion is cast in terms of levels of measurement (nominal, ordinal, interval or ratio), what items to include in a scale (such as a Likert or semantic differential scale) and the practicalities of assessing reliability and validity of indirect measures of concepts.

Victor Jupp

Associated Concepts: composite measurement, measurement, multiple indicators, reliability, scaling, validity of measurement

Key Readings

Blalock, H. M. Jnr (1968) 'The measurement problem: a gap between the language of theory and research', in H. M. Blalock Jnr and A. B. Blalock (eds), *Methodology in Social Research*. New York: McGraw–Hill. pp. 5–27.
Moser, C. A. and Kalton, G. (1971) *Survey Methods in Social Investigation*. London: Heinemann.
Smith, H. W. (1975) *Strategies of Social Research*. Englewood Cliffs, NJ: Prentice Hall.

OPPORTUNITY SAMPLING

Definition

A sampling tool to identify and gain access to data sources. Opportunity sampling uses the knowledge and attributes of the researcher to identify a sample, for example, using a researcher's local knowledge of an area on which to base a study or using a researcher's past experiences to contact participants or gatekeepers.

Distinctive Features

Opportunity sampling is often grouped together with incidental types of sampling such as convenience sampling, volunteer sampling and purposeful sampling. Opportunity sampling is often viewed as the weakest form of sample selection. It is also regarded by some as being less demanding on researchers, in terms of resources or expertise, than other methods of sampling.

Opportunity sampling is often employed by social researchers studying covert or hard-to-access groups of people, objects or events. These groups are often vulnerable, hidden, fluid or uncooperative. The traditional formula used to identify a sample may not apply in these circumstances. Often groups such as these are not collectively identified in society by any agency and so no sampling frame exists. In such cases opportunity sampling may be the only viable technique from which to create a sample. For example, Goode used her own knowledge of the drug agencies in the West Midlands of the UK to identify a suitable area to base her study of drug-using mothers (Goode, 2000).

In some instances it may be appropriate to combine opportunity sampling with probability sampling techniques. For example, a researcher aiming to study drug sellers in nightclubs may use her own knowledge or experience to identify a particular town or city where this activity takes place. She may then use a random or systematic sample to choose which nightclubs to investigate.

Evaluation

For research that investigates 'invisible' issues in the social world, opportunity sampling has some advantages. First, and possibly most importantly, it can allow researchers access to groups that would remain hidden if they had relied on conventional sampling techniques. Secondly, it allows the researcher to define who and where to study. In qualitative research that aims to understand and describe social issues this can be useful as non-responses are then limited and only relevant data are recorded. In such cases this can be cost- and time-efficient. Thirdly, it releases researchers from relying on structural institutions in society to identify samples and allows them to engage with the social world proactively.

However, this sampling technique also has disadvantages. Although some would argue that all social research is inherently subjective and based on the politics and values of researchers and institutions, the positivist perspective maintains that social research and the methods it employs should strive to be value-free and objective. From this positivist perspective opportunity sampling is weak on external validity as it is impossible to generalize from the data it produces because it is not representative of the social world in general.

Some may see it as an 'easy' way to collect data, but it is important that the researcher be aware of its limitations and appropriateness for the aims of the study. Therefore, the sampling technique employed must tally with the epistemological starting point of the research. The researcher must clearly make the reader aware of the sampling techniques used so that the limitations and validity of the research conclusions are fully understood.

Angela Brady

Associated Concepts: covert research, probability (random) sampling, purposive sampling, sampling, snowball sampling, validity of generalization

Key Readings

Goode, S. (2000) 'Researching a hard-to-access and vulnerable population: some considerations on researching drug and alcohol-using mothers', *Sociological Research Online*, 5 (1).
Mason, J. (2002) 'Sampling and selection in qualitative research', in *Qualitative Researching*, 2nd edn. London: Sage. ch. II
Shipman, M. (1997) *The Limitations of Social Research*, 4th edn. New York: Longman.

ORAL HISTORY

Definition

A method that seeks to open novel routes for understanding the past, the relation of past to present and the lives of others through time, by listening to the voices of individuals talking extensively about the events and experiences through which they have lived. The characteristic form through which oral history data are gathered is the in-depth interview.

Distinctive Features

The expansion of oral history as an important technique for modern social research dates from the 1960s. The initial impetus and impact of this movement was symbolic as well as substantive. Not only did it open up sources of data of rare quality – revealing in content, rich in detail, intimate in character, evocative in tone – which were extremely difficult to locate through more traditional documentary methods, it also promised to shift the locus of conventional historical inquiry to a more democratic and inclusive plane. Early exercises in oral history were often marked by the impulse to rescue or recover the accumulated experiences of marginalized or forgotten groups, those for whom the surviving documentary record was largely silent. More recently, the scope of the approach has widened to generate new insights into professional or establishment groups which were themselves originally marginalized by the initial trajectory of the new method. At the same time, oral history has undergone significant advances in methodological sophistication. Particularly important have been new concerns for understanding the importance of social or collective memory, identity, myth and the self, together with the means by which life narratives are constructed. In these respects, oral history research – in which the spoken word is privileged – has worked towards the refinement of its conceptual repertoire. It has also contributed to a constructive critique of conventional approaches for the analysis of documentary sources – the written word – the majority of which are marked by their radically different character as inscribed and crafted texts directed towards unseen audiences.

In its nature, the reach of oral history is demarcated by the span of human memory, and this is one of the reasons why many projects involve disproportionate numbers of elderly respondents. In practice, oral history is also defined by the capacity of audio and video recording technologies, the increasing sophistication of which continues to enhance the practical viability of oral history interview and also to facilitate the more effective archiving and dissemination of oral history data. Some researchers use the term 'oral history' as synonymous with 'life history' and, in their central methodological characteristics, the two are very close. Both utilize in-depth unstructured or semi-structured interview formats; both recognize interview data as a production of dialogue in which the interviewer is himself or herself an integral part; both respect the intense ethical and personal implications of the interview relationship; both acknowledge the requirement for strong conventions governing the ownership and end use of data; both recognize the challenges raised by attempts to engage with conventional criteria for sampling, reliability and generalizability concerns; above all, both approaches are predicated upon the centrality of the individual life as the most powerful lens through which may be revealed the complex social contexts within which lives are lived. Whilst the concerns of life history originate in illuminating the course of individual lives, however, oral history projects often start with a substantive historical question, for which oral history interview presents itself as the most appropriate method.

Evaluation

One of the major epistemological difficulties for oral history has been its necessary reliance upon memory – a faculty not infrequently invested as 'the enemy of history'. To the extent that memory may be shown to be factually inaccurate, the reliability of oral history data are open to challenge. However, it can be argued that the mixing of factual and fictive elements in oral history narratives itself constitutes an important insight into the ways in which memory operates. In this respect the notion of narrated stories which may be '"right" if untrue' indicates an important area in which oral historians need to do more theoretical work. Further advances may also accrue from oral history research designs in which relevant documentary ('factual') sources are systematically employed alongside, or even within, the elaboration of respondents' testimonies (which is akin to the notion of triangulation). This may further help to promote the reconciliation of the spoken with the written word for explaining and understanding the past. In particular, it may help to break down a common association of the document as concerned principally with 'hard' explanation and 'truth', and oral testimony principally with 'soft' understanding and 'authenticity'.

A further problem relates to the accessibility of oral history data for third-party researchers. The historical document in an archive has a pristine and public quality in that it can be consulted by a succession of researchers who each share the same initial status in approaching it. This is not so in the case for oral history data, where the two original participants are necessarily privileged in their access to the full range of ostensive reference within which the interview took place. The interview transcript is the documentary device by which the interview data are opened to other researchers, but such documents – 'speech masquerading as text' – are often difficult to make full sense of because of the absence of ostensive reference. Whilst some have experimented with augmented transcription protocols in the manner utilized by conversation analysts, such documents are often difficult to read. The freeing of oral history data from the bonds that unavoidably join them to their original producers remains an important issue in achieving the wider utilization of data that are often incomparable in their originality, depth and impact.

Philip Gardner

Associated Concepts: conversation analysis, document analysis, ethnographic interviewing, historical analysis, life history interviewing, naturalistic data, qualitative data archives, transcription, triangulation

Key Readings

Dunaway, D. K. and Baum, W. K. (eds) (1996) *Oral History: An Interdisciplinary Anthology*, 2nd edn. Walnut Creek, CA: AltaMira Press.
Perks, R. and Thomson, A. (1998) *The Oral History Reader*. London: Routledge.

ORGANIZATIONAL RESEARCH

Definition

The systematic collection, analysis and interpretation of data with the clear purpose of finding things out about an organization or organizations. This can include analysing, reviewing, explaining, understanding, evaluating or describing some aspect or aspects of an organization or organizations to answer a question or number of questions.

Distinctive Features

Organizations are created by groups in society in order to achieve specific purposes or meet specific needs through planned and coordinated activities. Given an almost infinite variety of possible purposes and differing needs, it is not surprising that organizations differ in nature and type as well as their structure, management and the way they function. Despite this, there are a number of components that are common: human or people resources, other non-human resources, purpose, structure and planning and coordinating of activities. It is from these components and their interactions that the subject matter of organizational research is drawn.

Organizational research has a number of features, other than its subject matter, that make it distinctive. These relate to the setting in which the research is conducted and the way in which researchers can draw upon knowledge developed across a range of social science disciplines.

Many writers (for example, Bulmer, 1988; Saunders et al., 2003) have highlighted that organizations, as research settings, possess a number of distinctive but interrelated features.

First, in order to undertake research within an organization, physical access must be negotiated and gained through an organizational gatekeeper. An organization may not be prepared to engage in such additional and voluntary activities because of the time and resources involved. The research may be perceived to be of little value, it may be felt that the research topic is too sensitive, or there may be doubts about the researcher's credibility and competence.

Secondly, after physical access has been gained, the researcher needs to gain access to the data that she or he needs the intended participants to provide. In granting such access the organization's gatekeeper may restrict the pool of participants or the data to which the researcher is allowed access. Subsequently research participants within the organization may also restrict cognitive access. Such restrictions can be minimized by the researcher establishing and maintaining her or his credibility with those individuals who can provide the data. Consequently, whilst an organization has power both initially to grant or refuse access and subsequently to restrict or withdraw it at any time, individual data providers also have power to prevent access.

Thirdly, although an organization may have granted a researcher access there may be preconditions. For example, in exchange for access, the organization may insist upon a particular research method being used or their right to veto the reporting of sensitive or unfavourable findings. Alternatively, it may request anonymity in the research report. The researcher may also face ethical dilemmas, such as a request by the organization to name participants who have been promised anonymity, or to present data in such a way that it breaks confidentiality. Such requests must be resisted.

Finally, organizational research is often transdisciplinary, that is, it draws upon knowledge from a range of social science disciplines such as business and management, geography, psychology and sociology. It has been argued that combining knowledge from a range of disciplines allows such research to gain new insights that could not be obtained through all of these disciplines separately (Tranfield and Starkey, 1998).

Evaluation

Organizational research is undertaken within different philosophical approaches using a wide variety of research strategies and data collection techniques. Data can be collected and analysed both cross-sectionally and longitudinally. Levels of analysis might include the individual, work teams, departments and divisions, or comparative studies between organizations. The balance of power between the researcher and the organization means that where choices of data collection strategies and techniques have not been specified clearly or agreed, the researcher's independence may be compromised. Consequently there needs to be prior agreement between the researcher and the organization regarding the precise data collection strategies and techniques that will be used as well as regarding associated issues of confidentiality and anonymity. However, given the power relationship between the researcher and the organization, organizational research is likely to be what is feasible and practicable rather than what is theoretically desirable.

In recent years the purpose of organizational research has been subject to some debate, particularly within disciplines such as business and management. Two interrelated aspects of this debate that have received considerable attention are a requirement that such research should complete a virtuous circle between theory and practice (Tranfield and Starkey, 1998) and the need for the research to surmount a double hurdle of being both theoretically and methodologically rigorous and of practical relevance (Hodgkinson et al., 2001). This implies that organizational research should enable the development of new ideas and relate them to practice thereby allowing research on practice to inform theory that could, in turn, inform future practice. Building upon this, it could be argued that organizational research should engage with both theory and practice and, perhaps, have an applied focus. However, it must be remembered that opinions differ regarding whether the practical implications of research findings for organizations must also be considered. Research undertaken purely to understand the processes of organizations and their outcomes is also organizational research. Like all social research, it should be theoretically and methodologically rigorous.

Mark N. K. Saunders

Associated Concepts: access, applied research, confidentiality, decision-making research, ethics, gatekeeper, informed consent, operational research management

Key Readings

Bulmer, M. (1988) 'Some reflections on research in organisations', in A. Bryman (ed.), *Doing Research in Organizations*. London: Routledge.

Hodgkinson, G. P., Herriot, P. and Anderson, N. (2001) 'Re-aligning the stakeholders in management research: lessons from industrial, work and organizational psychology', *British Journal of Management*, 12, Special Edition, pp. 41–8.

Saunders, M. N. K., Lewis, P. and Thornhill, A. (2003) *Research Methods for Business Students*. Harlow: Financial Times Prentice Hall.

Tranfield, D. and Starkey, K. (1998) 'The nature, social organization and promotion of management research: towards policy', *British Journal of Management*, 9: 341–53.

PANEL STUDY

Definition

In some social science literature a panel study comprises any form of longitudinal inquiry, of which the longitudinal cohort study is a special case. More generally, the panel study refers not to a single cohort followed up through time, but the monitoring over time of a cross-section of a population, that is to say, multiple cohorts of different ages. This usually involves replacement of panel members as they leave the study through no longer meeting age criteria or movement or refusal. Examples include household panel studies, audience research panels and product testing panels.

Distinctive Features

Cross-sectional sample surveys provide descriptive estimates of the parameters of a particular population. In repeated cross-sectional surveys, such estimates provide a means of gauging the extent to which society is changing – 'net effects'. Panel studies extend the monitoring over time to the individual sample members, enabling the investigation of the interactions of societal change with personal characteristics in affecting individual lives – 'gross effects'. They are therefore powerful tools for gaining understanding of social processes and for policy evaluation.

One branch of panel studies uses the household rather than individual members as the sampling unit, though all members may become included in the survey when they reach a specified age. As households are followed up over time, their composition is likely to change as people join or leave the household. In some cases there are 'following rules' to pursue panel members into the new households they are entering, which means that at the individual level the panel continually expands in size.

A major attraction of panel studies is the facility they offer to investigate relatively short-term social processes. Thus in the typical household panel study, surveys are carried out every year or at the most two years, which enables fine-grained analysis of household dynamics to be undertaken. We can assess the extent to which people are moving in and out of poverty both at an individual and a household level, and how that is being affected by other experiences in their lives, including the national policy framework. By way of example, a whole set of panel studies concerned with income dynamics has been set up in different countries, starting in 1965 with the US Panel Study of Income Dynamics (PSID) conducted by the University of Michigan Institute of Social Research.

Panel studies suffer from the problems common to all longitudinal surveys of attrition of respondents – owing to non-response, movement and refusal – and missing data at the variable level. In so far as the panel differs in its characteristics at any given time from that of the population at large then weighting can be introduced to reflect the population more precisely. Statistical imputation procedures are typically used to estimate population values.

To minimize respondent burden and thereby reduce data loss, measurement of some variables is rotated through the study at more extended intervals rather than repeated in all surveys. 'Panel maintenance' procedures involving communications with panel members between surveys and 'refusal conversion' to encourage drop-outs to rejoin the study are also in common use.

Evaluation

Panel studies are effective instruments for studying social dynamics under a number of headings, including family, income, housing, education, relationships and so on. Short-term changes are well assessed by the studies, which are not subject to the memory effects that can bedevil longer-term cohort inquiries. However, the major weakness of panel studies is the limited numbers of members in any one cohort. Thus for effective analysis of the impact of social change in specific cohorts born at different times we need to take age ranges from the population that can be as wide as ten years or more. This limits analysis capability in relation to the identification and follow-up of special population cohorts such as people with disabilities, for example, though the way the panel study is designed can compensate for this to a certain extent, for example, by 'over-sampling' households containing such individuals. Another attraction of the panel study is that its continual renewal through members joining the panel does, in principle, gives it a representativeness of the current population, which the cohort study cannot claim.

John Bynner

Associated Concepts: attrition, cohort study, cross-sectional survey, longitudinal study, one-shot design, quasi-experiment, time series design

Key Readings

Blossfeld, H-P. and Rohwere, G. (2002) *Techniques of Event History Modelling.* London: Lawrence Erlbaum.

Dale, A. and Davies, R. B. (1994) *Analysing Social and Political Change.* London: Sage.
Magnusson, D., Bergmann, L., Rüdinger, G. and Törestad, B. (1998) *Problems and Methods in Longitudinal Research.* Cambridge: Cambridge University Press.
Rose, D. (ed.) (1998) *Researching Social Change: Household Panel Studies: Methods and Substance.* London: UCL Press.
Scarborough, E. and Tanenbaum, E. (1998) *Research Strategies in the Social Sciences.* Oxford: Oxford University Press.

PARADIGM

Definition

A 'cluster of beliefs and dictates which for scientists in a particular discipline influence what should be studied, how research should be done, how results should be interpreted, and so on' (Bryman, 1988: 4).

Distinctive Features

The term is chiefly associated with Thomas Kuhn and his research concerning the history of science, discussed in the book *The Structure of Scientific Revolutions* (1962/1996). Kuhn's argument is that researchers who share a commitment to a particular paradigm are committed to the same rules and standards for scientific practice. His approach has been influential within the social sciences within which two broad research paradigms are often identified – the quantitative and the qualitative. Each paradigm rests upon distinctive foundations and applies a specific approach to researching the social world. For instance, quantitative research is a research strategy that emphasizes measurement in the collection and analysis of data. The quantitative approach is underpinned by a distinctive epistemological and ontological nature. The epistemological basis for quantitative research is typically, but not exclusively, characterized as positivist. Positivism advocates the application of the methods of the natural sciences to the study of social reality. Positivism is usually associated with the sociologists Auguste Comte and Emile Durkheim. The general principles of the positivist paradigm are that only phenomena, and therefore knowledge, confirmed by the senses can genuinely be warranted as knowledge; that the function of theory models is to generate hypotheses that can be tested and that will allow explanations of law to be considered. One would cite Comte's 'Law of the Three Stages' and Durkheim's social explanation as to the causes of suicide as examples of this principle. Ultimately, according to the positivist school, the scientific study of society must be undertaken in a manner that is value-free that is predicated upon an objective study of the social world. The positivist approach rests upon an epistemological foundation, which emphasizes the principles of measurement, causality, generalization and replication. These theoretical underpinnings therefore presume a certain category of research methods, which are conducive to an objective, positivistic approach such as surveys, questionnaires, structured interviews, experiments, quasi-experiments and official statistics, and content analysis of documents.

The second dominant research paradigm is qualitative research. The qualitative research strategy differs markedly from the quantitative approach and is underpinned by very different epistemological and ontological foundations. Qualitative research is concerned with subjective social issues and has its roots in the phenomenology of Edmund Husserl and Alfred Schutz; the understanding of social action, or *Verstehen* approach of Max Weber; and symbolic interactionism as formulated by G. H. Mead and Herbert Blumer. Such approaches emphasize the need to understand society as social actors perceive and interpret it, and interpretations of social phenomena can vary markedly according to the standpoint of the social actor. In light of such an epistemological grounding, qualitative researchers do not typically seek objective appraisal of social phenomena, therefore the arsenal of research methods utilized differs from the quantitative tradition and includes participant observation, unstructured/semi-structured interviews, focus groups, case studies and secondary analysis of diaries, letters, autobiographies, newspapers, photographs and documentaries.

Evaluation

Social researchers who identify themselves as affiliates to either the quantitative or qualitative approaches strictly adhere to the appropriate research methods that reflect the theoretical traditions that underscore them. However, this does not mean that such positions are permanently fixed, nor that one *must* utilize the seemingly appropriate methods. Within scientific research, paradigms do indeed shift as new discoveries are made; but more vitally in relation to social research, combining elements of the quantitative and qualitative paradigms may enhance the validity of research findings. Because different methods can reinforce and complement each other, the theoretical value of a study can be enhanced by combining methods. This is called 'triangulation' and sometimes mixed methodology.

Lee Barron

Associated Concepts: causality, covering law model, critical research, epistemology, ethnography, hypothesis, hypothetico-deductive model, inter-subjective understanding, mixed-methods research, ontology, positivism, qualitative research, quantitative research, triangulation

Key Readings

Barnes, B. (1982) *T. S. Kuhn and Social Science*. Basingstoke: Macmillan.
Bryman, A. (1988) *Quantity and Quality in Social Research*. London: Allen & Unwin.
Bryman, A. (2001) *Social Research Methods*. Oxford: Oxford University Press.
Hughes, J. A. (1976) *Sociological Analysis: Methods of Discovery*. Middlesex: Nelson.
Kuhn, S. (1962/1996) *The Structure of Scientific Revolutions*, 3rd edn. Chicago: University of Chicago Press.

PARAMETRIC TESTS

Definition

Tests of statistical significance which are based on certain assumptions about the shape of the distribution of population scores, for example that it is normally distributed (or bell-shaped). In statistical analysis, parametric significance tests are only valid if such assumptions are met. If they are not, non-parametric tests can be used.

Distinctive Features

A parameter is a measure of an entire population, such as the mean height of every man in London. In statistical analysis, one practically never has measurements from a whole population and has to infer the characteristics of the population from a sample of that population. The sample measure, such as the mean height of 500 randomly selected London men, is a statistic. Parameters are real entities, statistics are estimates.

In many statistical analyses, the researcher draws inferences about the parameters of the population from the sample statistics. This requires making assumptions about the shape of the distribution of the population's scores. Techniques that do not make these assumptions are called non-parametric (or distribution-free) techniques.

The assumptions required by the parametric tests, such as the t-test or the F test, are: (1) observations are drawn from normally distributed populations; (2) the populations have the same variance; (3) interval scale measurement has been used. It is usually clear if interval measurement has not been used: the data is in the form of ranks or frequency counts. To test whether the data is normally distributed, one can examine a plot of the distribution and its skewness and kurtosis. Tests such as Levene's can be used to see whether sets of data have equal variances. The t-test and F test are robust, and can be used if the first two assumptions are not valid so long as there is the same number of cases in the groups being compared.

Non-parametric tests use either rank (ordinal) data or frequencies. If they are applied to sets of interval data, the data have to be reduced to rank or nominal form before the test is carried out.

There are non-parametric equivalents for the common parametric tests which compare the scores of two or more groups to see whether the differences between them are statistically significant and for tests that determine whether there is a relationship between two or more sets of scores.

Evaluation

Non-parametric tests can be used with skewed data. They are not influenced by outliers, which are extreme scores that can affect parametric tests because they increase the variance of the data set. Non-parametric tests are less sensitive than the parametric equivalents, and do not permit one to test the significance of interactions between independent variables.

Jeremy J. Foster

Associated Concepts: chi-squared test, descriptive statistics, inferential statistics, measurement

Key Reading

Howell, D. C. (2002) *Statistical Methods for Psychology*, 5th edn. Pacific Grove, CA: Duxbury.

PARTICIPANT OBSERVATION

Definition

A qualitative method of social investigation, whereby the researcher participates in the everyday life of a social setting, and records their experiences and observations.

Distinctive Features

Participant observation is part of the repertoire of qualitative methods. It is most often associated with ethnography and also with the theoretical framework of symbolic inter-actionism. It is a method widely used within social and cultural anthropology, as well as within allied social science disciplines such as sociology and education. Participant obser-vation is often used in conjunction with qual-itative interviewing.

The 'field' refers to the setting within which the participant observation is under-taken. The extent to which the researcher or 'fieldworker' fully participates in the field may depend upon the nature of the setting, the quality of the research relationships that are formed and the opportunities for partici-pation. Participation and observation can be conceptualized as being at either end of a continuum of research positions. Sometimes it is not possible or desirable to become a full participant. This may be due to demographic factors such as age or gender, or to factors such as the particular activities or skills under observation. (While a social researcher may be able to be present in a hospital oper-ating theatre it is highly unlikely that they will be able to participate fully in the surgical procedure, unless they happen to have advanced medical training). Sometimes full participation may be an essential element of the fieldwork for example in the case of covert research. However, all participant observation relies upon some degree of active engagement with the setting on the part of the researcher. Hence there is an assumption that social scientific understandings of social worlds can be enhanced by observing, expe-riencing and talking to others in the field.

The main method for recording observa-tions is through field notes. These are notes that are preferably taken in situ, and then expanded upon after the fieldwork encounter. However, sometimes it may be difficult to take notes during participant observation, and in these circumstances field notes are con-structed retrospectively. Participant observa-tion, therefore, relies upon the memory work of the researcher. This can be aided by photo-graphic, documentary or audio materials, or by artefacts collected in the field. Field notes give detailed descriptive accounts of everyday

social worlds. They can also be used to record the personal feelings and experiences of the researcher. It is usual practice for the partici-pant observer to keep a fieldwork diary as part of the research process.

Access is a particular issue for participant observation. While public settings may not require any formal access negotiations, there are still issues of managing the researcher role within the field. In private settings, as well as gaining formal permission, there may well be an extensive period of negotiation needed for the participant observer to be accepted into the field. This may entail paying particular attention to the management of the fieldwork identity and the adoption of roles within the field. Participant observation usually involves a prolonged period of fieldwork and can lead to long-term relationships.

Evaluation

Participant observation is a long-established method of social inquiry, and can provide rich accounts of social life and social worlds. There has been a recurrent concern about the posi-tion of the researcher within the field, and the ways in which this may alter the social reali-ties under investigation. Does the researcher change the setting by being there? The researchers should certainly be reflexive about their presence within the setting, but in gen-eral it is difficult to sustain the argument that the hospital ward, school classroom, factory production line or swimming pool would really be different if the researchers were not present. Specific encounters may not or will not have occurred but the general processes, with which participant observation is primar-ily concerned, will have continued without, as well as with, the researcher's presence.

It is possible for researchers engaged in par-ticipant observation to become full members of the setting they are studying. This can lead to a blurring of the boundary between research and the self, or between personal and professional life. This can be considered as disadvantageous to the research, as overfamiliarity may make it difficult to assume or resume the role of observer. The setting may become so familiar that it is difficult to get any analytical purchase on it. Of course, some researchers choose to undertake participant observation in settings with which they are already familiar (for example a teacher-researcher observing a classroom). Indeed there can be advantages to having some understanding of the processes, language and everyday activities of the setting, prior to undertaking participant observation. The key issue is that researchers engaged in participant observation should always be reflective about their positioning within the setting and how that is challenged or changed over the course of the research, as well as recognizing the experiences, knowledges and assumptions they bring to the field.

There are also ethical issues associated with participant observation. It is a method that has been used for covert research. Sometimes this may be purposive (for example, in a setting where it is assumed that research access may be denied) or it may be unavoidable (for example, in a public setting where there are no obvious permissions to be sought). Covert participant observation raises particular concerns over the informed consent of research participants and the ways in which any data generated can or should be used. Overt participant observation is not without its own ethical dilemmas: for example, the conscious forging of relationships in the field and the extent to which these are, or can be genuine; or participating in or observing activities that are personally difficult – on moral, political or legal grounds.

Amanda Coffey

Associated Concepts: access, covert research, ethics, ethnography, fieldwork, gatekeeper, ideographic, impression management, naturalistic data, qualitative research, reflexivity, research bargain, validity of measurement

Key Readings

Bailey, C. A. (1998) *A Guide to Field Research*. Thousand Oaks, CA: Pine Forge.

Emerson, R. M., Fretz, R. I. and Shaw, L. L. (2001) 'Participant observation and field-notes', in P. Atkinson, A. Coffey, S. Delamont, J. Lofland and L. Lofland (eds), *Handbook of Ethnography*. London: Sage. pp. 352–68.
Hammersley, M. and Atkinson, P. (1995) *Ethnography: Principles in Practice*. London: Sage.
Lofland, J. and Lofland, L. (1995) *Analyzing Social Settings: A Guide to Qualitative Observation and Analysis*, 3rd edn. Belmont, CA: Wadsworth.

PARTICIPATORY ACTION RESEARCH

Definition

One of the categories into which action research can be divided. Participatory action research (PAR) consists in an approach that includes both understanding a situation (creating knowledge) as well as changing or acting upon that situation – using participatory methods, that is, challenging the dichotomy between researchers and researched.

Distinctive Features

Participatory action research has emerged as a response to conventional, elitist research which assumes that people are not capable of doing research, which consequently seldom benefits directly those who are its object. Within PAR people themselves are researchers and the knowledge generated during the research process is used to create action or improvements that benefit them directly. The role of the outsider professional or researcher is not that of an expert but a mere facilitator of the research/action process.

PAR has three major distinctive elements: people, power and praxis. It is people-centred as it is informed by, and responds to, the needs of the people, usually oppressed or disenfranchised people. PAR is about power, since projects aim to promote empowerment of the research participants. This type of research challenges the power relation between researcher and 'objects', since the action researcher is a peer of other research participants. Finally, it is about praxis, since participatory action research recognizes the inseparability of theory and practice (Sohng, 1995).

The key methodological feature of participatory research is dialogue. Ideally, dialogue within action or participatory research is empowering by bringing 'isolated people together around common problems and needs' (Sohng, 1995: 6). Thus, participatory research methods vary greatly from the more conventional research techniques such as interviewing, which gives primacy to the researcher and implies a one-way flow of information.

Participatory methods have been developed to challenge and counteract '*the intellectual colonialism of western social research into the third world development process*' (Sohng, 1995: 3). The aim of this approach is to involve disenfranchised people in the research processes that will enable them to find solutions in their daily struggle for survival. Thus, participatory research is research as collective action in the struggle over power and resources, where knowledge is identified as power (Sohng, 1995: 3).

PAR has its roots in the work of Paulo Freire (1972), whose educational work emphasizes dialogue, informed action, educational activity based on the lived experiences of the participants, community enhancement and 'consciencialization' – a process by which individuals deeply analyse their own realities.

However, the term 'action research' was first used by social psychologist Kurt Lewin (1946). Lewin attempted to improve relations in industrial situations and minimize hostility between different racial groups in the United States of the 1940s. He described action research as a spiral of steps, each one comprising the stages of planning, acting, observing and reflecting. This 'action research spiral' is Lewin's main legacy to action researchers. Although many models and diagrams have been developed, all action research processes are cyclical rather than linear.

Evaluation

Participatory action research may be abused, when researchers use its good reputation as a methodology while simultaneously they actually maintain conventional relations with the project participants, using them as mere puppets. Moreover, empowered communities have started to question the need for PAR projects' facilitators. The critique being put forward is that PAR does not go far enough and that the communities themselves are able to develop their own theory and research bases.

Ana Lopes

Associated Concepts: action research, applied research, disability research, disaster research, emancipatory research, politics and social research, practitioner research, research bargain

Key Readings

Freire, P. (1972) *Pedagogy of the Oppressed.* Harmondsworth: Penguin.

Kemmis, S. and McTaggart, R. (1990) *The Action Research Planner.* Geelong: Deakin University Press.

Lewin, K. (1946) 'Action research and minority problems', *Journal of Social Issues,* 2 (4): 34–6.

Sohng, S. S. L. (1995) Participatory Research and Community Organizing. A working paper presented at The New Social Movement and Community Organizing Conference, University of Washington, Seattle, WA, 1–3 November 1995. http://www.interweb-tech.com/nsmnet/docs/references_sohng.htm

PATH ANALYSIS

Definition

A variant of multivariate regression analysis in which causal relations between several variables are represented by a path or flow diagram and path coefficients provide estimates of the strength of relationship between two variables when all the other variables are held constant.

Distinctive Features

Path analysis allows a researcher to examine the causal effects of several variables simultaneously. In this way, it is used to examine the degree of 'fit' between the model and the data. Path coefficients provide estimates of the strength of the relationships between pairs of variables within the model when all the other variables are held constant. The coefficients are standardized regression scores and are expressed as z-scores. Residual values measure the amount of variation in the dependent variable, which cannot be explained by the combination of independent variables.

The causal model can be portrayed visually by a path or flow diagram, which shows the 'paths' along which causal influences are said to flow. Lines between variables indicate relationships and arrowheads indicate causal direction. Path coefficients are stipulated on each line or 'path'. Sometimes the strength of relationship is also represented visually by the thickness of a line.

The nature of path analysis in relation to ordinary multiple regression is that it is possible to portray direct and indirect pathways from independent variables to a dependent variable and also to calculate the direct and indirect effect of an independent variable on the dependent variable whilst other effects are held constant.

Evaluation

As with other forms of causal modelling, path analysis has the advantage of being able to examine the effects of several variables simultaneously. This allows such models to represent the complexity of the social world in a way that is not possible with crosstabular or three-way analysis. However, path analysis requires that certain assumptions are made. Some are the assumptions of multiple regression such as linearity of variables. Over

and above these it is assumed that the model is recursive, which means that the causal flow is in one direction. In other words, causal direction is assumed to be asymmetrical. Further, path analysis does not by itself give evidence of causal direction. This must be provided by the researcher. Also, more fundamentally, there is an in-built assumption that social phenomena can be explained in terms of causality. This is an assumption that is challenged by researchers who come from different methodological positions.

Victor Jupp

Associated Concepts: causality, causal model, correlation, econometrics, general linear modelling, multivariate analyses, regression analysis, SPSS

Key Readings

Black, T. R. (2001) *Understanding Social Science Research*, 2nd edn. London: Sage.

Byrne, D. (2002) *Interpreting Quantitative Data*. London: Sage.

Sapsford, R. and Jupp, V. (1996) *Data Collection and Analysis*. London: Sage.

Wright, D. B. (2002) *First Steps in Statistics*. London: Sage.

PERFORMANCE INDICATOR

Definition

An indirect (or 'proxy') measure that is used when it is not possible to derive a direct measure of the activity concerned. An example is the use of performance indicators (PIs) of hospital waiting times, numbers of complaints and length of referral lists as indicators of the overall quality of service provided by hospitals.

Distinctive Features

The introduction of PIs in North America and Europe coincided with the development of scientific management (or 'Taylorism'), which required the application of efficiency measures and cost–benefit analysis (Van den Berghe, 1997). The growth of the use of PIs in areas such as the provision of education, health and policing from the late 1970s onwards resulted from the increasing application of managerial approaches in public service provision (Pollitt, 1993).

There has been a major growth in the use of PIs as a means of assessing the performance of public bodies. In the United Kingdom for example there are requirements on local authorities, the National Health Service, Social Services departments and central government departments to agree performance targets and to publish performance indicators.

PIs are often used as part of a more comprehensive performance information system which can be used to measure progress toward targets, meet the requirements of public accountability, compare the activities of a number of organizations, or promote performance improvement (Audit Commission, 2000).

It is common practice to distinguish PIs that measure aspects of *economy, efficiency, effectiveness* and *quality* (HM Treasury, 1992). *Economy* refers to the extent to which costs of inputs are minimized. An example performance indicator would be the costs of administration as a percentage of total costs. *Efficiency* refers to the ratio between inputs and outputs. An example performance indicator would be, in relation to the work of the Employment Service, the average cost involved in placing an unemployed person in a job. *Effectiveness* identifies the extent to which a particular outcome achieves the original objective of the programme. Taking another Employment Service illustration, an example performance indicator would be the numbers (or proportions) of people leaving the unemployment register. *Quality* indicators relate to the usefulness or value of a service (they are sometimes seen as an element of effectiveness). A performance indicator from local government would be the percentage of citizens satisfied with the overall service provided by their local authority.

Evaluation

While PIs are a useful contribution to the assessment of how an organization meets its declared objectives, their limitations have to be acknowledged. PIs do not explain *why* differences exist between organizations, but they do raise issues that need to be addressed – they act as a 'can opener'. For example, the average cost per pupil will not, on its own, mean that one school is more efficient than another, for there may be many reasons why costs vary. But we need to consider *why* the differences exist.

Economy, efficiency and effectiveness do not always 'march together' (Pollitt, 1993: 59). The achievement of greater economy, for example, may have negative impacts on effectiveness and efficiency. This may encourage the focus on certain indicators rather than others, in order to minimize such discrepancies. Another possible distorting influence is the pressure to opt for PIs for aspects that are easy to measure. Linked to this is another possibility that the bodies required to produce the PIs may, for administrative reasons, seek to limit the number of measures they have to generate. A consequence of such restrictions or distortions may be the emergence of what could be termed 'perverse incentives'. For example, a school may attempt to restrict entry and encourage poor achievers to leave in order to improve its relative position in a table of performance based on examination results.

It is generally recognized that PIs must be used in a wider performance management arrangement, which will also include, for example, direct performance measures, inspections and audits, and research and evaluation studies. Some would argue (Ranson and Stewart, 1994) that the possibility of achieving an adequate performance measurement system for public sector activities is fundamentally limited because of such factors as the inherent complexity of performance, the fact that market 'forces' do not apply in many instances, and that final judgements on outcomes have to be the subject of political debate.

Note

The above material does not represent the views of the Department of Education and Skills, UK.

Vince Keddie

Associated Concepts: auditing, evaluation research, good practice studies, indicator, meta-analysis, policy-related research, social indicators

Key Readings

Audit Commission (2000) *On Target: The Practice of Performance Indicators.* London: The Audit Commission for Local Authorities and the National Health Service in England and Wales.
HM Treasury (1992) *Executive Agencies: A Guide to Setting Targets and Measuring Performance.* London: HMSO.
Pollitt, C. (1993) *Managerialism and the Public Services.* Oxford: Blackwell.
Ranson, S. and Stewart, J. (1994) *Management for the Public Domain: Enabling the Learning Society.* London: Macmillan.
Van den Berghe, W. (1997) *Indicators in Perspective: The Use of Quality Indicators in Vocational Education and Training.* Thessaloniki, CEDEFOP – European Centre for the Development of Vocational Training.

PHENOMENOLOGY

Definition

A school of philosophy developed in the first quarter of the twentieth century by Edmund Husserl (1859–1938). It has been influential in sociology, particularly in the writings of Alfred Schutz (1962). An associated school of psychology has been vigorously developed by a small group of enthusiasts, without attaining widespread influence, though, on its more philosophical side, it has been advanced by Maurice Merleau-Ponty (1962).

Distinctive Features

For Franz Brentano the study of the domain of conscious awareness was the basic field for a scientific psychology. All human experience was characterized by *intentionality*. According to Brentano ([1874] 1973), 'Every mental phenomenon is characterized by what the scholastics in the Middle Ages called the intentional (and also mental) inexistence of an object, and what we could also, although in not entirely unambiguous terms, call the reference to a content, a direction upon an object'. Thoughts, perceptions and so on have this direction whether or not there really exists such an object as that to which the experience points.

After a brief but promising career as a mathematician, including serving as assistant to the great Weierstrass in Berlin, Husserl turned to philosophy as a student in Vienna with Brentano. He seems to have accepted the general outlines of Brentano's point of view while at the same time being dissatisfied with his teacher's account of the relation between act and object. Consciousness is directed. It is *as if of* an object, whatever the status of that object might be. Surely the task of the philosopher/psychologist is to get to the bottom of what that 'as if of' relation might be.

Kant had emphasized the role of concepts in the genesis of objects perceived, shaping an inchoate flux of sensation into a determinate perception. Husserl too realized that somehow the mind brings it about that there are objects without creating them. How can we explore what it is that is implicit in the structure of conscious experience that this should be possible? Sometimes it seems as if Husserl is necessarily locked within his own subjectivity, as he turns his attention exclusively to his own experience. Yet, he insists that he is not denying that a real world exists. His project is only to identify the marks in our experience that express that basic presupposition. Persons, in their fullness as conscious beings, each with a unique point of view on the world, are as much givens as are material things. Again, he bypasses the traditional problem of 'other minds' by insisting that his project is only to extract and make 'visible' the defining characteristics of our experience *as if of* people and things. However, given his insistence on the root character of the domain of conscious experience it is not easy to see how Husserl can consistently take such a stand. Acknowledging the natural attitude to experience as of an independent world, and combining that with the revelations of the transcendental attitude leads to a conception of the *life world*, the world that human beings as centres of consciousness actually inhabit.

The directedness of acts of consciousness towards objects is a cluster of structural properties of experience. This he calls the *noema*. Noematic structures are generic, and take specific form in particular thoughts and perceptions as *noesis*. Since noesis is particular, it is a process in time, while the noema is timeless. Like many another philosopher breaking free from the rigidity of Kant's twelve a priori categories, Husserl makes a point of emphasizing the possibility that many different noemata are compatible with any particular flux of sensations.

How can this line of analysis be made to fit with Husserl's insistence on the existential fullness of the experience of things and people? Noema can be thought of as clusters of anticipations of further experience. Suppose a hundred years ago someone saw the moon as a sphere. The noema would have included the anticipated experience of the curvature of its hidden side.

The third element in the fullness of experience is *hyle*, derived from the Greek word for 'matter'. Not every logically possible noema is compatible with the conditions of experience. The flux of sensations is limited.

Here then are the three 'elements' that are involved in the fullness of all experience as if of the world and its inhabitants,

whatever their nature. However, we still lack a method by which these 'constituents' of mental acts could be brought to light. In our everyday lives we just carry on in the 'life world' performing our ordinary tasks, and never pausing to ask ourselves about the noemata that make our experiences *as if of* vegetables, guests and furniture. From the point of view of the sources of a psychology, this step is the most important of all Husserl's innovations.

Research into the constitution of experience consists in performing two kinds of *reductions*. An *eidetic* reduction is achieved as we turn our attention to the generic characteristics or essences of whatever it is the experience points to. The *transcendental* reduction or *epoché* is accomplished by turning our attention to the noemata, noeses and hyle that are the structures of a certain act of consciousness. We 'bracket' what we have hitherto taken for granted, that there is a person in the other armchair. Setting aside that taken-for-granted aspect of experience *as if of* brings the relevant structures of consciousness to light. The method as a whole consists in the phenomenological reduction in which the transcendental and eidetic reductions are applied successively.

Husserl himself achieved his greatest success with this research method in studying the role of time in consciousness. There is a back and forth between fulfilled and unfilled expectations and retrospective and prospective aspects of my conscious experience of any current state of affairs.

Evaluation

Phenomenology has been very much more influential on the continent of Europe than in the English-speaking world. It has played a major role in the development of ideas of the social construction of reality (Berger and Luckmann, 1967). It was brought to North America by Alfred Schutz in his influential studies (Schutz, 1962). The influence of Husserlian 'reductions' can also be seen in the techniques of ethnomethodology through which the taken-for-granted world is made strange (Garfinkel, 1967).

Rom Harré

Associated Concepts: discursive psychology, epistemology, ethnomethodology, hermeneutics, methodology, ontology, positioning theory, realism, relativism

Key Readings

Bell, D. (1990) *Husserl: The Arguments of the Philosophers.* London: Routledge.

Berger, P. L. and Luckmann, T. (1967) *The Social Construction of Reality.* London: Penguin Books.

Brentano, F. ([1874] 1973) *Psychology from an Empirical Standpoint* (trans. A. C. Rancurrello, D. B. Terrell and L. L. McAlister). London: Routledge & Kegan Paul.

Garfinkel, H. (1967) *Studies in Ethnomethodology.* Englewood Cliffs, NJ: Prentice Hall.

Gurwitsch, A. (1966) *Studies in Phenomenology and Psychology.* Evanston, IL: Northwestern University Press.

Husserl, E. (1964) *The Idea of Phenomenology* (trans. W. P. Alston and G. Nakhmikian). The Hague: Nijhoff.

Husserl, E. (1965) *Phenomenology and the Crisis of Philosophy* (trans. Q. Lauer). New York: Harper and Row.

Husserl, E. (1987) *The Phenomenology of Internal Time Consciousness.* Ann Arbor, MI: University of Michigan Press.

Merleau-Ponty, M. (1962) *The Phenomenology of Perception* (trans. C. Smith). London: Routledge & Kegan Paul.

Schutz, A. (1962) *The Phenomenology of the Social World* (trans. G. Walsh and F. Lehnert). Evanston, IL: Northwestern University Press.

PHOTOGRAPHY

Definition

The analysis and production of photographs as part of social science research. This might focus on the context in which photographs are produced, their visual content, their tangible material qualities and the context in which they are interpreted and made meaningful.

Distinctive Features

Social researchers analyse photographs 'found' during their research and also produce their own photographs during the research process. The use of photography might include the analysis of historical photographs from public or private collections, the analysis of contemporary personal, published or exhibited photographs, the production of photographs during research as a visual record, or in collaboration with informants as a way of learning about their lives, the study of processes of production and consumption of photographs, and the use of photographs to represent the findings of one's work.

Photographs can be analysed for both the visual information they provide and the meanings that are attached to them. The visual content of photographs can provide information not revealed through verbal interviews or noted through observation. For example, who was at a particular event, or in what order did people stand in a procession? Thus photographs (whether they belong to an informant's own collection, are published, or were taken by the researcher) can serve as visual records and information sources. Nevertheless, social researchers do not usually simply study the visual content of a photograph in isolation. Instead they might contextualize it by examining the social relationships and cultural conventions that were involved in its production and the subjectivities by which it is interpreted. For instance, studies of people's existing photographic collections often reveal the ideal configurations of relationships and experiences that exist in their cultures. A good example of this is the study of family photography (see, for example, Chalfen, 1987). Often family photographs represent the 'ideal' family, rather than the experienced relationships between family members. Therefore it is often more interesting not only to use photographic content as an information source, but to examine how and why photographs were taken and how they are later used. In addition, social researchers are interested in how people interpret photographs. One method that addresses this is 'photo-elicitation' by asking informants to comment on photographs in interviews they are often inspired to provide knowledge and information that would not have emerged from verbal questioning (Harper, 2002).

In addition to analysing photographic content and the narratives it both inspires and is embedded in, social researchers are concerned with the material properties of photographs. As material objects, photographs are inscribed with additional cultural meanings and social uses. For example, researchers might focus on a photograph's smell or texture, the writing on its back, how it is framed, hung on a wall, or pasted in an album. All these additional material and sensory features of photographs contribute to the meanings they have for people and their significance for researchers.

As well as studying other people's photographs, social scientists take their own photographs or ask their informants to take photographs for them during fieldwork. A researcher's own photographs represent her or his own subjective view of the research context. However, the method of 'directed photography' (see Banks, 2001), whereby informants tell researchers what to photograph, allows researchers to understand what is important to *them*. Alternatively, informants can be given cameras and briefed to document a particular aspect of their experience visually. By later discussing the photographs with the informant the researcher can combine visual and verbal methods to learn more about how the informant experiences her or his world.

Finally, researchers increasingly use photographs to represent the findings of their work. This is still largely confined to illustrations in books. However, specialist journals such as *Visual Studies* include photo-essays and some researchers produce exhibitions and photographic books based on their research (see, for example, Kratz, 2002).

Digital photography has impacted on the use of photography in research. First, the new technologies invite innovations in fieldwork uses of photography, for example enabling researchers to show informants photographs in their camera screen. Second, online exchange and exhibition has changed the way we can represent and share our photographic work with others (both viewers of our academic work and informants whom we might invite to comment on the photographs by email as part of a photo-elicitation study). However, generally social science uses of digital images employ new media to enhance the existing methods established for printed photographs rather than signifying a radical change of approach.

Evaluation

Photography in some form or other is part of almost all cultures and societies. We use photographs as part of our everyday communication and our extraordinary celebrations. As such it is appropriate that the production and analysis of photographs form part of qualitative research.

However, social researchers' uses of photography should be theoretically informed. It is now generally accepted that notions of photographic realism are not appropriate for understanding photography in social research. Instead photographs are seen as representations that are inevitably subjective. Therefore it is necessary for researchers to be aware of their own intentions as both photographers and analysts of images, and those of the people they photograph, and to analyse how these subjectivities intersect to produce photographic meanings. Similarly, it is not sufficient simply to analyse the visual content of an image, without locating it within the social, cultural and personal contexts that give it meaning and accounting for its materiality.

Photography has a key role to play in social research. However, to avoid naïve realist approaches that have sometimes characterized its use in the past, it is necessary to attend to the points made above.

Sarah Pink

Associated Concepts: cultural research, ethnographic interview, ethnography, historical analysis, life history interviewing, naturalistic data, oral history, qualitative research, triangulation, unobtrusive measures, visual methods

Key Readings

Banks, M. (2001) *Visual Methods in Social Research*. London: Sage.
Chalfen, R. (1987) *Snapshot Versions of Life*. Bowling Green State University: Popular Press.
Edwards, E. (1992) *Anthropology and Photography*. New Haven, CT: Yale University Press.
Harper, D. (2002) 'Talking about pictures: a case for photo-elicitation', *Visual Studies*, 17 (1): 13–26.
Kratz, C. (2002) *The Ones that Are Wanted*. Berkeley, CA: University of California Press.
Pink, S. (2001) *Doing Visual Ethnography: Images, Media and Representation in Research*. London: Sage.

POLICY-RELATED RESEARCH

Definition

Research which the various stakeholders in the decision-making process make use of in the formulation, implementation or evaluation of policy. The research may not always have been meant to be of use in policy making, but when it is so designed (or commissioned) we can speak of policy-related research.

Distinctive Features

There has been debate about the features, if any, that distinguish policy-related research from other kinds of research. Hakim (2000), for example, argues that policy research differs from theoretical research in three major respects. First, whereas theoretical research is mainly interested in explanations of social phenomena and the construction of models and theories, policy-related research is primarily concerned with finding answers to problems which can then be turned into action or policy. Secondly, the audience for theoretical research tends to be other scholars working in the same discipline. The language of theoretical research, therefore, is specialized as it is only meant to be understood by members of a particular academic community. Policy-related research, in contrast, intends to reach a wider audience, including decision makers and anyone with an interest in the issue being researched. As such, the technical jargon of academic disciplines is replaced by more easily understood forms of expression. Thirdly, Hakim argues that whereas theoretical research is geared towards reporting any statistical association between variables, policy research is more interested in the size and strength of relationships. As she puts it: 'results [in policy research] must report large and strong effects rather than small but statistically significant effects' (Hakim, 2000: 7).

Bechhofer and Paterson (2000), however, disagree with Hakim's distinction between theoretical and policy research. They argue that it forces too rigid a separation between the two. In practice, policy researchers do address theoretical issues and are interested in causal explanations even though these matters are not of primary concern in the short-term exigencies of policy making. Theoretical researchers, for their part, can have an important role in the policy process. When decision makers engage in major reviews of policy areas it is sometimes necessary to undertake exercises that map out or model the salient variables, factors and processes, often in an abstract or conceptual way. Such exercises can usefully draw on the work of theoretical researchers.

Evaluation

A great deal has been written about how research *can* relate to policy; much less about how it *does*. In the former category, rational or knowledge-driven models see research contributing information that will directly help policy makers choose between alternative courses of action. Critics see this as a misrepresentation of the policy process: decisions, it is argued, are rarely made through the rational analysis of options against predetermined goals. Instead, policies are politically negotiated compromises, and problems are typically dealt with in a piecemeal or incremental fashion (Lindblom, 1980). According to this view, research can contribute to policy making in a variety of ways, and should be seen as one of many influences. Carol Weiss, who has made a significant contribution to discussion about the uses of research (Weiss, 1979, 1992), reminds us that researchers are one of many participants in the policy process, including politicians, advisers, civil servants and journalists. Any of these actors can use research – often selectively – to suit their own purposes, for example to bolster their own case or denigrate that of their opponents. The suggestion here is that research is mainly used indirectly and that evidence of the direct impact of research is limited.

Several explanations have been put forward to account for the relatively low uptake of social science research as compared with, say, medical research. In some accounts the focus is on research and researchers: either social science research is not usable because it does not have the precision associated with medical science, or social scientists are not inclined to be 'useful' and prefer to keep their distance from policy makers (Payne and Cross, 1991). Other accounts emphasize how difficult it is for research to permeate the policy process. This may be something to do with the nature of policies themselves, that is, they are the product of a political process and as such represent a compromise of what it is possible to do rather than what is the rational or 'best' thing to do (Leicester, 1999). Policy makers, too, may be less than accommodating to the results of research. The economist John Maynard Keynes, for example, is often quoted as saying that there is nothing a government hates more than to be well informed.

This could not be said of the New Labour administration elected to power in the UK in 1997. In a departure from what was seen as ideologically driven policy making in the 1980s and early 1990s, Prime Minister Blair and his colleagues committed themselves to *evidence-based policy*, epitomized by the slogan 'what matters is what works' (Davies, et al., 2000). As a result, there have been vigorous attempts since then to commission more policy-relevant research, and also to ensure that new policy initiatives are rigorously piloted and evaluated before being fully implemented.

John Newton

Associated Concepts: action research, applied research, critical research, emancipatory research, evaluation research, politics and social research

Key Readings

Bechhofer, F. and Paterson, L. (2000) *Principles of Research Design in the Social Sciences*. London: Routledge.

Davies, H., Nutley, S. and Smith, P. (eds) (2000) *What Works? Evidence Based Policy and Practice in Public Services*. Bristol: Policy Press.

Hakim, C. (2000) *Research Design: Successful Research Designs for Social and Economic Research*, 2nd edn. London: Routledge.

Leicester, G. (1999) 'The seven enemies of evidence-based policy', *Public Money and Management*, 19 (1): 5-7.

Lindblom, C. (1980) *The Policy Making Process*. Englewood Cliffs, NJ: Prentice Hall.

Payne, G. and Cross, M. (1991) *Sociology in Action: Applications and Opportunities for the 1990s*. London: Macmillan.

Weiss, C. (1979) 'The many meanings of research utilization', *Public Administration Review*, 39 (5): 426-31.

Weiss, C. (1992) *Organizations for Policy Analysis: Helping Government Think*. Newbury Park, CA: Sage.

POLITICS AND SOCIAL RESEARCH

Definition

A narrow definition states that politics is the pursuit or exercise of state power. Broader definitions portray politics as the exercise of any kind of power; or as action relying on value commitments or furthering particular interests. Some conceptions of social research, whether as serving public policy making or as the work of intellectuals committed to a particular political party or cause, make it political in the narrow sense. In the broader sense, most researchers would acknowledge, or insist, that their work is political (and it is difficult to see how it could not be in some senses).

Distinctive Features

The relationship between social research and politics is complex. This is because each of these terms can refer to a range of activities, and because the relationships among these can take a variety of forms. Furthermore, the issue involves judgements about how things are, how they can be, and how they ought to be.

What comes under the heading of 'research' varies in ways that have implications for the relationship to politics. Some research is commissioned by and/or designed to serve government departments, interest groups, commercial organizations or political parties. More broadly, many researchers see themselves as public intellectuals whose task is to facilitate democratic discussion of social problems. However, much social research has a more distant relationship to state policy, being concerned with myriad features of human life – micro as well as macro, historical as well as contemporary.

If we turn to the *relationship* between politics and social research, this has a number of aspects about which contrasting views can be taken:

(1) *The immediate goal of research.* Some argue that the only goal should be the production of knowledge. Others believe that research should be directed towards achieving other goals: social improvement or social change of some kind, causing a shift in public policy or professional practice, the emancipation of the oppressed or the pursuit of social justice.

(2) *The sponsorship of research, including its funding, and the implications for problem setting and research design.* There are those who insist that there should be a close, and interactive, relationship between researchers and those who sponsor their research or are likely to use it in policy making and practice. Others argue that it is essential for researchers to remain independent of both sponsors and users in how they carry out and report their work.

(3) *The effects on inquiry of the prior attitudes, assumptions and commitments, etc. of the researcher.* Some declare that researchers cannot but be biased, in the sense that they cannot avoid having prior attitudes, assumptions and commitments which will shape how they do their research. Others, while recognizing the danger of political bias, insist that researchers can and should seek to minimize this.

(4) *The social relationships between researchers and researched.* There are those who require that researchers include the people they are studying as partners in decision making about how the inquiry is to be pursued, on the grounds that to do research 'on' people reproduces an unequal society. At the other extreme are those who insist that the people studied must not be allowed to control the research, that the maximum possible power must be exercised by the researcher in order to extract the information required (notably in studying dominant social groups).

(5) *The implications and consequences of research findings for policy and practice.* Some believe that unless research has a progressive impact on human social life it is worthless, and that researchers are responsible for achieving this. Others argue that, while researchers must

endeavour to produce knowledge that is relevant to matters of human concern, there is no obligation or distinctive right on their part to draw policy conclusions from their findings or to work for the implementation of these.

Over the past several decades, broader interpretations of 'politics' have become more influential. There has also been a shift away from seeing research as an activity in its own right, towards emphasizing the contribution it can, and should, make to political activity, in both broad and narrow terms. As a result, research has increasingly been regarded as properly having practical or political goals, in addition to (and sometimes instead of) any commitment to producing knowledge. For some, this requires a greater role in the research process for sponsors, likely users and/or the people studied. Along with this, claims to value neutrality or objectivity have come to be dismissed by many as ideological, as simply serving the interests of researchers (see Hammersley, 2000).

These arguments are sometimes used as a basis for insisting that all research should be explicit about the political agenda it is serving; in other words that researchers must make clear 'whose side they are on' or what they are working for. However, a few commentators have recognized that if some political goals are to be served effectively then researchers must be covert about their political intentions, not least because otherwise they would be cut off from funds or from important sources of information. For this reason, claims to objectivity or value neutrality may not be abandoned even by those who see their research as serving political goals, but used instead as a conscious ideological strategy (Back and Solomos, 1993).

Evaluation

Given the complexity of the issue, important distinctions need to be recognized. Inquiry may inevitably be political in some senses – for instance, in that all researchers have political attitudes – but need not be political in others – for example in the sense of pursuing

any immediate goal other than the production of knowledge (see Hammersley, 1995: ch. 6). Furthermore, it is important to recognize that researchers may take on their role or may carry out a particular piece of research because they hope that this will contribute to achieving political goals, without conducting inquiry *in such a way* as to serve those goals.

Of course, the relationship between politics and social research is not determined solely by the views, or even by the actions, of researchers. It is also shaped by the environment in which they operate, and in particular the pressures they come under. These can arise from commercial organizations and political pressure groups as well as from governments. Some funders place restrictions on the publication of findings, or they may cancel funding where the research seems likely to produce what they regard as bad news (see Crossen, 1994; Norris, 1995; Pettigrew, 1994). There are even external pressures towards the adoption of some research methods rather than others. And published research may be subjected to public critique where it is deemed to have undesirable implications. Political efforts to 'manage' knowledge in this and other ways are likely to have an increasing impact on the pursuit of social inquiry in the future.

Martyn Hammersley

Associated Concepts: applied research, bias, critical research, emancipatory research, participatory research methods, policy-related research, sensitive research, standpoint research

Key Readings

Back, L. and Solomos, J. (1993) 'Doing research, writing politics: the dilemmas of political intervention in research in racism', *Economy and Society*, 22 (2): 178–99.

Crossen, C. (1994) *Tainted Truth: The Manipulation of Fact in America*. New York: Simon and Schuster.

Hammersley, M. (1995) *The Politics of Social Research*. London: Sage.

Hammersley, M. (2000) *Taking Sides in Social Research: Essays on Partisanship and Bias*. London: Routledge.

Norris, N. (1995) 'Contracts, control and evaluation', *Journal of Education Policy*, 10 (3): 271–85.

Pettigrew, M. (1994) 'Coming to terms with research: the contract business', in D. Halpin and B. Troyna (eds), *Researching Education Policy*. London: Falmer.

POSITIONING THEORY

Definition

Positioning theory involves the need to attend to local moral orders and the viewpoint that the local distribution of rights and duties to determine different kinds of acts determines the way episodes unfold.

Distinctive Features

The shift from a cause/effect paradigm to a rule/meaning pattern for identifying and explaining psychological phenomena has led to the development of new models of psychological processes, particularly those based on an analogy between cognition and 'conversation'. Standard methodologies like the 'questionnaire method' have been reinterpreted as revealing rules of discourse. At the same time attention has shifted to the interpersonal nature of psychological phenomena, both in mature forms and in development (Vygostky, [1929] 1962).

The inspiration for the development of positioning theory as an analytical scheme to deal with complex patterns of discursive acts, be they in words or making use of some other medium, came partly from longstanding dissatisfaction with the essentially static conception of the psychological bases of social interactions. This conception had taken root in the 1950s and 1960s tied in with the concept of role. The alternative preferred by positioning theorists is to regard social episodes as displaying story lines, as if they were the living-out of narrative conventions. For example, an apparently mundane episode might be conceived and lived by one of the participants as the undertaking of a heroic quest. Analysis of the expressive conventions displayed in that actor's performance reveals the story line being lived out. Many social episodes are carried through wholly by discursive means, by things said; the *story* of a conflict may be almost all there is. Only occasionally is blood let, are bombs thrown and houses stoned. Many conflicts are sustained by the adoption by the hostile parties of conflicting story lines, in the light of which incompatible and irresolvable contradictions in meanings have become entrenched.

The other major influence that has nourished positioning theory has come from feminist studies. The psychology of interactions between women and men seems to involve presuppositions about the rights each sex allows the other as to the kinds of social acts that a man or a woman *can* be understood to perform. Deborah Tannen's (1990) study of how men and women interpret what each says in conversation highlighted persisting tendencies of mutual misunderstanding. Positioning theory offers a way of getting at the underlying presumptions that sustain such misunderstandings and the conflicts that stem from them. It seems that what people are taken to mean by what they say and do is partly a matter of what the various people involved in a social episode believe that persons of this or that category are entitled to say and do. Such entitlements are called 'positions'. Children, for instance, are usually not accorded the same speaking rights as adults. They are positioned as recipients of disciplinary admonitions rather than as sources of them.

Social psychology seemed to stand in need of a new approach that combined attention to the small-scale and very rapid dynamics of social interactions with insights into the presumptions about rights and duties that were invoked, explicitly or implicitly, by the actors. Everyone does not have equal access to the local repertoire of meaningful actions. Some members of a group are more advantageously positioned than others. Some categories of persons are accorded rights and duties distinct from those of others in the same episode.

In many cases, people are satisfied with their rights. In other cases, the distribution of rights and duties can be challenged (Davies and Harré, 1999). Revealing the subtle patterns of the distributions of rights to speak and act in certain ways can open up the possibility of their transformation. At the same time, analysis of patterns of meaningful actions in terms of story lines can bring to light previously unnoticed presumptions about what is going on in an episode.

The phenomena to be identified and classified in social interactions, hostile or friendly, are the repertoire of meanings available to the actors. How are activities of the 'meaning-making' and 'episode-forwarding' kinds distributed among participants?

To find the right level of analysis, one must be careful to maintain a distinction between intended actions and the *various* acts that can be performed by carrying out those intentions. Two actions that come under the same material description – say, shaking hands with someone – may serve for the performance of different acts in differently developing episodes. One may be a greeting and another may be a way of offering congratulations. Positioning theory is concerned exclusively with analysis at the level of acts; that is, of the meanings of actions. It is only rarely necessary to take account of the vehicles by which acts are performed.

The basic principle of analysis is that positions, as open sets of rights and duties, speech and other act categories and story lines are mutually determinative. Fixing one vertex of the positioning triangle fixes the other two. Successfully challenging any vertex redefines both of the others.

Evaluation

Positioning analysis can be applied to episodes of different scales – from individual persons face to face, to rival scientific teams, up to nation-states – whenever there is an issue of the distribution of rights and duties among the participants. What people do is drawn from what they believe they may do, which is itself drawn from what they believe they can do. Positioning analysis allows the social psychologist to examine the relations between 'does', 'may do' and 'can do' in specific social and cultural circumstances.

Rom Harré

Associated Concepts: constructionism, conversation analysis, discourse analysis, discursive psychology, epistemology, interpretive repertoires, phenomenology, realism, relativism

Key Readings

Davies, B. and Harré, R. (1999) 'Positioning and personhood', in R. Harré and L. van Langenhove (eds), *Positioning Theory*. Oxford: Blackwell. pp. 32–52.
Tannen, D. (1990) *You Just Don't Understand.* New York: William Morrow.
Vygtosky, L. S. ([1929] 1962) *Thought and Language* (trans. E. Hanfmann and G. Vakar). Cambridge, MA: MIT Press.

POSITIVISM

Definition

One of two methodological approaches recognized by many textbooks on social research, the other being: interpretivism. Positivism is said to be the methodological underpinning of survey research and experimental approaches, though in describing it thus there is a conflation between scientific approaches to social research in general and the particular position of positivism.

Distinctive Features

There have been several versions of positivism, and though all favour a scientific approach to investigation they are not synonymous with science and indeed in the natural sciences positivism disappeared as an important methodological position many decades ago (Philips, 1987). Nevertheless, it was via the positivist movement that social science became science and was the form in which scientific method entered the study of the social world. There are three main forms of positivism that have been historically important to social science, though arguably none is present to any great extent today.

(1) *Comtean.* The term positivism was coined by Auguste Comte (1798–1857), along with the term 'sociology'. His use of the word positivism implied that this was a positive philosophy and little to do with later positivist philosophy of science influenced by empiricism. He did, however, advocate the development of sociology as a science, but in the context of a shift in societal belief systems from theological, to metaphysical and finally scientific. This was his Law of the Three Stages. Comte's positivism has had little influence on social research and is only of historical importance in sociology.

(2) *Durkheimian.* Emile Durkheim's (1858–1917) influence was altogether greater and he was one of the pioneers of the numeric analysis of large data sets in his comparative international study of suicide (Durkheim, 1952). In recent years the positivistic aspects of Durkheim's work have been less accentuated and indeed his emphasis on 'social facts' as knowable objects places him closer to realism than positivism. Nevertheless, he equally stressed the importance of scientific detachment and value freedom in sociological research, an approach shared by the later logical positivists. However, unlike the latter, Durkheim was a methodological holist arguing that social facts (for example, rules, laws, practices) could not be reduced to explanations at an individual level.

(3) *Logical positivism.* This is also known as logical empiricism. Logical positivism was enormously influential on US social science in the period of its great expansion in the 1930s. Though it had its critics, such as R. S. Lynd and C. Wright Mills, positivism continued to dominate social science research up until the 1960s in the United States and was the principle methodological approach in most other countries where social research was undertaken. Indeed, it has left a lasting legacy, in the United States, in the form of a strong quantitative tradition. The term 'logical' was not much used in social science and the different historical strands of positivism became conflated, particularly by its critics.

Positivist social science was criticized for ignoring the importance of individual subjectivity and the role of consciousness in shaping the social world, though the vigorous criticism of positivism from the 1960s needs to be seen in the context of an anti-science sentiment and a growth in the popularity of interpretivist methods in studies of the social world. Unlike the natural sciences, social science has proposed few alternative scientific methodologies to positivism, the main exception being the realist programme (see, for example, Pawson, 1989; Byrne, 2002).

Evaluation

The complex history of positivism and its conflation with science generally have rendered any simple definition difficult. However, the Table compares some key characteristics of science with some key characteristics of positivism. Positivists would align themselves with the characteristics of both columns, whereas methodologists committed to scientific method in social science need only align themselves with the items in the first column.

Some writers, for example Philips (1987), have argued that positivism is dead. It is certainly true that few social scientists would

Key characteristics of science and positivism

Scientific method	Positivism
Explanatory	Prioritizes observation
Predictive	Verificatory (procedures should show whether a statement
Evidence-based	is true of false)
Seeks truth	Value-free (moral values have no part in science)
Objective	Operationalist (scientists can only deal in those things
Logical	which are measurable)
Parsimonious	
Numerative	

Source: Williams, 2003

now claim to be positivists and the more radical representations of the characteristics in the second column are now rare. What lives on, particularly in survey research, is more properly referred to as an empiricist tradition, which in its various forms may draw on some or none of the latter characteristics, but would certainly identify with the characteristics in the first column.

Malcolm Williams

Associated Concepts: empiricism, experiment, methodology, ontology, phenomenology, postmodernism, realism, relativism, social survey, subjectivity

Key Readings

Byrne, D. (2002) *Interpreting Quantitative Data*. London: Sage.
Durkheim, E. (1952) *Suicide*. London: Routledge & Kegan Paul.
Pawson, R. (1989) *A Measure for Measures: A Manifesto for Empirical Sociology*. London: Routledge.
Philips, D. (1987) *Philosophy, Science and Social Inquiry: Contemporary Methodological Controversies in Social Science and Related Applied Fields of Research*. Oxford: Pergamon.
Williams, M. (2003) *Making Sense of Social Research*. London: Sage.

POSTMODERNISM

Definition

Any 'ism', is more difficult to summarize as a single movement or concept than any other. Indeed, its anti-foundationalist character would be quite at odds with such a summary or classification. The best that can be done is to provide some clarification of what is meant by the term 'postmodern' and how it impacts upon social research.

Distinctive Features

A plethora of labels exist to describe both a condition and a movement and some of the thinkers described as postmodernist reject the appellation. Some will argue that there is a distinction between post-structuralism and postmodernism whilst others see no important distinctions, or at least see each as having common intellectual roots in post positivism and the advocacy of 'the abandonment of the entire intellectual culture of modernity' (Delanty, 1997: 95). Though the roots of postmodernism are complex intellectually and historically there are some commonalities of emphasis. First, on the centrality of language in the production of the individual and the social, and second, the claim that there has been a shift in the nature of society from modernist, homogeneous and production-led to postmodernist heterogeneous and knowledge-led. The linguistic turn, particularly in the work of Jacques Derrida, is as much associated with post-structuralism as postmodernism, but provides the basis of a 'method', in the form of deconstruction, for postmodernism. Derrida emphasized the importance of language and focused on the role of discourse. Yet unlike the structuralists, he made no separation between 'things' and the language that describes them: instead, he maintains difference is produced through the difference in significance speakers attach to words (Williams and May, 1996: 166). The social and cultural world can be read like a text, but importantly no one reading can be privileged and all readings are equally valid, only the emphasis changes, according to the reading. Meaning is never fixed, nor readily apparent. Though Derrida denies being a postmodernist, the relativization of knowledge, particularly scientific knowledge, as partial and local has been a key feature of postmodernism since.

The writings of Jean François Lyotard and Jean Baudrillard strongly emphasize such linguistic anti-foundationalism, but also give prominence to social context – what Lyotard termed 'the postmodern condition' in society (Lyotard, 1979/1984). Lyotard's view was that the myths of truth in science and liberation through science and scientific rationality had become undermined since the early 1960s. What are termed 'meta-narratives' (in social science these might include Marxism and functionalism for example), attempt to explain the social world through transcultural and transhistorical truths. These, he maintains, obfuscate and are ultimately to be seen as simply discourses (albeit historically powerful at the time), 'texts' that can be differently interpreted.

In the social sciences the denial of scientific rationality as a basis for social investigation shifts the emphasis of the study of the social from the scientific to the cultural. Methodological objectives and values, originally derived from natural science 'discourse', such as explanation, generalization, validity and reliability, have no useful meaning within the anti-foundationalist rhetoric of postmodernism. The implications for social research are profound. Those who have described their research as 'postmodern' have placed emphasis on the textual characteristics of data and their interpretation. Thus investigations have used interpretive methods, but have denied any claim to epistemological privilege as a result of research. Whilst non-postmodern interpretivists might aim to clarify meaning or produce valid representations of the people studied, this is not the case in a postmodern approach. Some postmodern anthropologists have attempted to avoid producing any representations at all, for (it is claimed) 'the point of discourse is not how to make a better representation, but how to avoid representation' (Tyler, 1986: 128), the argument being that any representation amounts to a privileging of one reading of a text over another, when all are equally valid.

Paradoxically, postmodernists often advocate the abandonment of political meta-narratives but politicize the social research process through the use of deconstruction 'to examine the presuppositions that are buried in the texts produced in the course of everyday activities' (Williams and May, 1996: 169). It is held that the task of social research is the deconstruction of texts to expose values and interests embedded in them. In doing so they must avoid themselves producing new hegemonies of knowledge.

Evaluation

Whilst postmodernism was taken seriously in theoretical writings in social 'science', its impact on research has been minimal, possibly because the activity of *research* is inevitably imbued with notions of the search for explanation and representation. The problem of postmodernist research was well summed up by Todd Jones when he said 'Postmodern social scientists, I fear, successfully avoid giving biased hegemonic views about the people they study at a cost of not giving us much information at all' (1998: 58) and 'I believe that spending a great deal of time and money studying a people in order *not* to represent what they are like is a grave waste of resources' (ibid). Even if one accepts the correctness of postmodernism's epistemological relativist stance, this does beg the question of whether there is then any point to doing research. Furthermore, its moral relativism would seem to forbid any political or policy project and thus any research that would provide data to support such projects.

Though the popularity of postmodern approaches is in decline, in social science it may leave some useful legacies. The emphasis on language, though not new, did at least remind social scientists of its importance in the creation and maintenance of social order and the multiple layers of meaning in language (or 'texts' generally) which can produce variable and unintended consequences in individual thought and action. Secondly, the emphasis on the heterogeneity of social and cultural forms has led to a sensitivity toward their complexity. At least one writer (Paul Cilliers) has taken the relationship between postmodernism and complexity in the literal sense of the mathematical complexity of systems, whereby 'the interaction between the system and its environment, are [sic] of such a nature that the system as a whole cannot be fully understood simply by analysing its components'. Complex relationships are nonlinear, they are not fixed, 'but shift and change, often as a result of self organisation.' (Cilliers, 1998: x–ix).

Cilliers's work is perhaps representative of the view that whilst we can accept many of the arguments about a societal shift from the modern to the postmodern, it does not follow that we should abandon the goals of explanation or representation. Though it may well mean that we will need to develop new tools of investigation, or use our existing tools in quite different ways (Byrne, 2002).

Malcolm Williams

Associated Concepts: cultural research, deconstruction, discourse analysis, empiricism, ontology, positivism, realism, relativism, reliability, validity

Key Readings

Byrne, D. (2002) *Interpreting Quantitative Data*. London: Sage.

Cilliers, P. (1998) *Complexity and Post-modernism: Understanding Complex Systems*. London: Routledge.

Delanty, G. (1997) *Social Science: Beyond Constructivism and Realism*. Milton Keynes: Open University Press.

Jones, T. (1998) 'Interpretive social science and the "native's" point of view', *Philosophy of the Social Sciences*, 28 (1): 32–68.

Lyotard, J. (1979/1984) *The Postmodern Condition: A Report on Knowledge*. Minneapolis: Minnesota University Press.

Tyler, S. (1986) 'Post modern ethnography: from document of the occult to occult document', in J. Clifford and G. Marcus (eds), *Writing Culture: The Poetics and Politics of Ethnography*. A School of American Research Advanced Seminar. Berkeley, CA: University of California Press.

Williams, M. and May, T. (1996) *Introduction to Philosophy of Social Research*. London: Routledge.

PRACTITIONER RESEARCH

Definition

Research concerned with issues and problems that arise in professional practice. It is conducted by practitioners and aims to bring about change, or influence policy in the practice arena. Practitioner research provides a framework for formulating practice knowledge and allows such knowledge to be disseminated to other professionals.

Distinctive Features

The development of practitioner research has a number of roots. The establishment of action research, which itself takes a number of forms, is significant, as too is the development of reflective practice. It is essentially an expression of the politics of researching professional practice, which reverberate through the control of research, setting of research agendas and professional training. Through practitioner research, practitioners become researchers into their own practice and engage in a continuing process of professional development.

Some common concerns investigated by researcher/practitioners include: deficiencies in services or resources, conflict between professional values and agency requirements, and the improvement of practice. Practitioner research provides a framework for formulating practice knowledge and allows such knowledge to be disseminated to other professionals. Many of the skills and competencies associated with practice are transferable to the conduct of research. Practitioners are trained to engage with clients in a respectful and meaningful way, and to encourage clients to express themselves. They collect information and develop understandings that are then disseminated to those concerned. Such activities are also central to the conduct of research.

A traditional, linear view of professional development is that theory informs practice, an idea that has led to the separation of practice and research both physically and intellectually. In recent years, this has been challenged by the notion of reflective practice, which has been encompassed within and propagated through widespread developments in professional training. Reflective practice is the capacity to think, talk or write about a piece of practice with the intention to review or 're-search' a piece of practice for new meanings or perspectives on the situation. Practitioner reflexivity is just as central to the conduct of research as it is to practice. Indeed, Schön suggests that practice and research are inextricably linked through the process of reflection. When someone reflects-in-action he or she becomes a researcher in the practice context (Schön, 1983). Adopting a reflective approach to research allows the practitioner to question the power relations of research. Such an approach can affirm the importance of experiential and interconnected ways of knowing the world and favours more emancipatory and participatory research practices (Fook, 1996).

Practitioner research is grounded in the everyday world of practice and can reflect the voices of stakeholders in that context. To be of value, research does not have to be large-scale or 'scientific'. Methods such as case study and life history are familiar territory for practitioners and have the potential to be more emancipatory than those methods that do not give participants a voice. Formalizing practitioner knowledge through research enhances professional credibility and strengthens the influence of practice knowledge in the policy-making arena. In addition, the products of this kind of research are more accessible to practitioners because they are written by and for practitioners.

Evaluation

The participatory and emancipatory paradigms represent an overarching framework for informing the conduct and evaluating the products of practitioner research. All research has the potential to exploit and oppress participants if attention is not paid to the power imbalances between researchers and researched.

Whilst practitioner knowledge is regarded as an asset in the conduct of practitioner research, it can also be seen as a source of bias that could invalidate it. The researcher practitioner role is potentially confusing for all those involved in the process. For example, research participants may find it difficult to distinguish between the professional-as-researcher and the professional-as-practitioner and may be puzzled by a professional's unwillingness to take up a practice issue during a research interview. Similarly, a practitioner may find it difficult to distinguish between questions that are meant to be about collecting data, and those that are aimed at promoting change. Practitioner researchers may feel uneasy about using practice knowledge and insight in their analysis of data, while respondents may well divulge information to a practitioner researcher, on the basis of a close, professional relationship, that they may not have given to a 'researcher'. Practitioner researchers need to examine their research practice in order to identify whose interests and concerns are being served. While it is recognized that practitioner research should be designed to give a say to all participants and can involve practitioners trying to see issues from the viewpoints of clients (Reed and Proctor, 1995), such a participatory approach is at the discretion of the professional, who is already in a position of power with clients.

Maureen Gillman and John Swain

Associated Concepts: action research, applied research, disability research, emancipatory research, good practice studies, participatory action research, policy-related research, politics and social research, reflexivity

Key Readings

Fook, J. (ed.) (1996) *The Reflective Researcher*. London: Allen & Unwin.
Fuller, R. and Petch, A. (1995) *Practitioner Research: The Reflexive Social Worker*. Milton Keynes: Open University Press.
Reed, J. and Proctor, S. (eds) (1995) *Practitioner Research in Health Care*. London: Chapman & Hall.
Schön, D. (1983) *The Reflective Practitioner*. New York: Basic Books.

PREDICTION

Definition

A statement about what will be observed before the actual event, a foretelling of some future happening. We are all in the business of making predictions about something: tomorrow's weather, this week's lottery numbers, the outcome of sporting events, the likelihood of a terrorist attack.

Distinctive Features

The ability to make accurate predictions about the phenomena under consideration is usually considered as the ultimate way to test the explanatory power of a scientific theory.

In order to understand why social scientists attempt to make predictions, it is important to recognize from the outset that science assumes the world to be made up of a series of cause-and-effect relationships. For example, if Mr Smith jumped out of an aeroplane at 1,000 feet and realized half-way down that he had inadvertently forgotten his parachute, then we might reasonably conclude, on the basis of what we already know about gravity and solid objects, that the effect of falling such a distance will be to cause our absent-minded friend's demise. However, no matter how often one might come across *true* instances confirming this relationship, there always exists the *chance* that the former will not cause the latter. It's all a matter of *probability*, a way of thinking which states that all cause-and-effect relationships, even the most apparently obvious, must be viewed as a matter of chance which have a higher or lower probability of occurring (usually defined as a percentage score or a value between 0 and 1). After all, there are many 'stranger than fiction' accounts about people who defy the *odds* and survive such horrific events. Scientists, therefore, are currently working with an internal contradiction by first assuming that there are such things as cause-and-effect relationships that need to be determined, but then settling for the empirical reality that such relationships may not always exist.

Thus, the act of making predictions acknowledges the existence of these chance fluctuations, even though it is currently beyond our ability to understand why they occur. Generally, there exist two procedures for making predictive assessments.

(1) the *actuarial* approach: a highly standardized process which involves statistically testing a pre-defined set of factors relevant to a particular situation. For example, an actuarial risk model designed to predict an individual's likelihood of committing a criminal offence will require: (a) precise data about the subject's age, gender, number of youth custody sentences, total number of court appearances, type of offence; (b) an established

(statistically validated) prediction formula, usually employing sophisticated multiple regression techniques, into which the data are entered in order to calculate the subject's risk of committing another offence within a pre-defined time period (say the next two years), and (c) an outcome in the form of a prediction scale result (Copas and Marshall, 1998). This result represents the subject's prediction score which will show that on the basis of all the statistically relevant facts imputed into the formula, there exists an *x* per cent chance that this person will re-offend within the next two years. If the value of *x* were 75 per cent, then we would classify this person as a high risk.

It is important to note, however, that the social scientist is not making a predictive judgement *directly* about this particular person, even though it was this subject's data that was used to make the assessment. All that the scientist can say is that out of a group of 100 people with similar characteristics and histories of offending as this person, 75 will re-offend within the next two years. With prediction measures it is not possible to say whether the individual subject we are currently concerned about constitutes one of the 75 who will re-offend or one of the 25 who will not.

(2) The *clinical* approach: this contrasts with actuarial prediction and represents a highly interactive process between the person making the assessment and the risk subject. The clinical method involves employing in-depth interviewing and observational skills in order to uncover information about the precipitating factors underlying each subject's behaviour. The data relied upon to make predictions differ according to the circumstances of each case. Typically, the data are highly subjective as they are largely dependent upon the beliefs, values and normative judgements held by the person doing the predicting. The knowledge base of this method appears to focus on the predictor's ability to collect data and then employ their own impressions and ideas as a means of generating information about a particular subject. In turn, these impression/ideas are probably formulated as a consequence of their training, previous experience and ability to reason intuitively.

Evaluation

An import issue in the development of prediction methods is whether the future behaviour of an individual can be more accurately measured through the use of either an essentially subjective understanding of the person being assessed based on the clinical approach or an objective evaluation of the subject using pre-defined statistical scales. One solution has been to look at developing combined risk/needs assessment measures that attempt to integrate the respective strengths of both measures (Colombo and Neary, 1998).

Scholars have also noted society's growing preoccupation with employing increasingly sophisticated prediction technologies in order to identify, assess, prevent and manage risk, especially regarding a myriad of risk issues within areas such as crime, medicine, personal lifestyle, leisure pursuits, economics and the environment. According to Adams (1995), risk is now 'big business' and in fact constitutes the 'world's largest industry'. The word 'risk' has several literal origins that translate as 'run into danger' or 'take a chance' and is a highly complex phenomenon with philosophical, social, ethical and political consequences. For example, should we punish criminals on the basis of their past offences or their predicted risk of re-offending in the future?

Anthony Colombo

Associated Concepts: causal model, causation, econometrics, estimation, forecasting, inferential statistics, regression analysis

Key Readings

Adams, J. (1995) *Risk*. London: University of Central London Press.
Beck, U. (1992) *Risk Society*. London: Sage.
Colombo, A. and Neary, M. (1998) 'Square roots and algebra: understanding perceptions of risk/needs assessment measures

in probation practice' *Probation Journal*, 45 (4): 213–19.

Copas, J. and Marshall, P. (1998) 'The offender group reconvictions scale: a statistical reconviction score for use by probation officers', *Journal of Applied Statistics*, 47 (1): 159–71.

Kemshall, H. (2003) *Understanding Risk in Criminal Justice*. Milton Keynes: Open University Press.

PRIMARY RESEARCH

Definition

The generation of new data in order to address a specific research question, using either direct methods such as interviews, or indirect methods such as observation. Data are collected specifically for the study at hand, and have not previously been interpreted by a source other than the researcher.

Distinctive Features

Traditionally, primary research has been categorized into quantitative and qualitative approaches. These approaches can be seen as forming two distinctive clusters of research strategy, where research strategy refers to a 'general orientation to the conduct of social research' (Bryman, 2001: 20). The distinction is not always clear-cut, however, and some studies may share characteristics of both quantitative and qualitative approaches. Characteristics of quantitative approaches are a focus on numerical data and statistical analysis, with emphasis on producing objective, reliable, valid data. Qualitative approaches are characterized by a focus on language (rather than numbers), and an emphasis on participants' interpretations and understandings of their social world. The two strategies are underpinned by different ontological and epistemological assumptions, quantitative approaches being associated with objectivism and positivism, and qualitative approaches with constructionism and interpretivism.

Examples of approaches associated with quantitative research are experiments, structured observation, survey, and statistical analysis of documents and texts. Experiments examine behaviour in a controlled environment, typically a laboratory setting, and strive to determine causal relationships by precisely manipulating variables. Structured observation involves observing behaviour in terms of predefined categories; for example, a researcher may observe the occurrence of different types of activity in a classroom. Surveys may be conducted using methods such as structured interviews or questionnaires, which use predetermined questions to elicit self-report data on attitudes, behaviour and beliefs, in a format amenable to numerical analysis. Analysis of documents and texts in quantitative research (for example, content analysis) places emphasis on precise coding and statistical analysis.

Examples of qualitative approaches include ethnography and participant observation, semi-structured and unstructured interviews, focus groups and analysis of language. Ethnography and participant observation involve the researcher becoming immersed in a group or community and observing language and behaviour in order to gain insight into people's understandings. Semi- and unstructured interviewing emphasizes letting the interviewee guide the nature of the topics and themes covered in the course of an interview, and avoids limiting the discussion to what has been predetermined by the researcher. Focus groups are group interviews, facilitated by the researcher, but with a focus on letting the group guide discussion topics. Analysis of language (for example, conversation analysis, discourse analysis) in qualitative research emphasizes exploring the meanings inherent in language use.

The process of carrying out primary research can be seen as involving a number of stages, including: formulate a research question, select a research design, choose an appropriate method, administer the method to collect data, analyse the data, interpret the results in relation to the original research question. Emphasis on either of these stages can vary depending on the type of research strategy and methods being adopted.

Evaluation

Primary research allows the social researcher to gather data appropriate and tailored to the specific research question to be addressed. However, it can be a time-consuming and costly process, especially in large-scale survey research, for example. The concepts of validity and reliability have been considered fundamental in primary research, the former referring to whether the conclusions drawn from a study are accurate and correct, and the latter whether the results can be replicated (for example, if people obtain vastly different scores every time they take an IQ test, then the test is not reliable). In quantitative research these concepts have been considered crucial, and largely focus around the idea of accuracy of measurement; however, qualitative approaches are less concerned with precise measurement and there has been some debate about the extent to which these concepts are applicable. Some authors have argued that alternative concepts should be applied in judging qualitative research, such as 'credibility' and 'confirmability'.

Historically, social researchers have debated the relative merits of quantitative and qualitative approaches. Criticisms levelled against quantitative approaches include a lack of ecological validity (behaviour in constrained and artificial conditions is not representative of behaviour in the real world), and the failure to recognize that, unlike molecules and atoms, people interpret their social world and therefore the natural science model is inappropriate in social research. Qualitative research has been criticized for being overly subjective and lacking replicability and generalizability. Recently there has been recognition that a mixed-method approach, which combines aspects of both qualitative and quantitative research, may be useful. However, some authors have objected to the multi-method approach, arguing that the underlying philosophies of quantitative and qualitative approaches are fundamentally different and therefore cannot be united (for example, Smith, 1983).

Claire Hewson

Associated Concepts: content analysis, data, ethnography, experiment, focus group, methodological pluralism, mixed-methods research, participant observation, qualitative research, quantitative research, reliability, social survey, validity

Key Readings

Bryman, A. (2001) *Social Research Methods.* Oxford: Oxford University Press.
Robson, C. (2001) *Real World Research: A Resource for Social Scientists and Practitioner-Researchers.* Oxford: Blackwell.
Smith, J. K. (1983) 'Quantitative versus qualitative research: an attempt to clarify the issue', *Educational Research*, 12: 6–13.

PROBABILITY (RANDOM) SAMPLING

Definition

Any method of sampling that uses some form of random selection, that is, one that will ensure that all units in the population have an equal probability or chance of being selected. Random selection is an assumption of probability theory and the ability to draw inferences from samples to populations. Random sampling techniques include: the simple random sample; the stratified random sample; the systematic random sample; and multi-stage cluster samples. Probability sampling is most closely associated with quantitative research, and particularly with survey research.

Distinctive Features

In simple random sampling all units within the sampling frame have an equal chance of being selected. Computer software is often used to generate random numbers. MS Excel, for example, has a random number generator facility. Simple random sampling is not the most statistically efficient method of sampling as there may not be good representation of the subgroups in a population. If, for example, the views of a minority group are to be represented in the research, it may be necessary to weight the sample in order to ensure that a large enough proportion are included. Therefore, stratified random sampling is often used (as simple random sampling does not necessarily mean that the sample selected will be representative of all the units within a given population). Stratification enables the researcher to select specific categories, or strata, for inclusion within the sample. However, stratified random sampling is only feasible when the relevant information on the stratifying criteria is available.

Systematic random sampling is also known as proportionate sampling and uses a fixed sampling interval to determine the sample. Here it is important to ensure that the manner in which the list is constructed does not introduce some form of bias. For example, if a particular family name is very common (in Wales, for example, you may frequently find the name Evans) then people with that name might stand more chance of being included. Care would need to be exercised if this were to lead to over- or under-representation. Multi-stage cluster sampling can be used to avoid the wide dispersal that simple random sampling or systematic random sampling could yield in some forms of research, such as a large, national survey.

For example, at the first stage a random sample of cities might be selected; at the second stage a sample of districts in the chosen cities; at the final stage all individuals in the chosen districts may be interviewed. In this way, fieldwork is concentrated in particular districts, with considerable savings of time and costs.

Evaluation

Sampling decisions are an important part of the research design for both qualitative and quantitative approaches. Random or probability sampling is considered most suited to

quantitative research and is appropriate for making inferences from samples to populations (within calculable levels of probability). It is, however, inappropriate in research where populations are transient or difficult to access, or where a complete list of the population (sampling frame) is not available. In such cases it is not possible to ensure that every unit in the population will have an equal chance of selection.

Julia Davidson

Associated Concepts: cluster sampling, inferential statistics, non-probability (non-random) sampling, opportunity sampling, purposive sampling, quota sampling, sampling, snowball sampling, social survey, volunteer sampling

Key Readings

Bryman, A. (2001) *Social Research Methods.* Oxford: Oxford University Press.

May, T. (2001) *Social Research: Issues, Methods and Process,* 3rd edn. Milton Keynes: Open University Press.

Sapsford, R. and Jupp, V. (eds) (1996) *Data Collection and Analysis.* London: Sage.

Silverman, D. (ed.) (1997) *Qualitative Research: Theory, Method and Practice.* London: Sage.

de Vaus, D. A. (1996) *Surveys in Social Research,* 4th edn. London: UCL Press.

PROCESS MAPPING

Definition

A method of identifying the formal and informal structures and processes within an agency or organization involved in the delivery of a particular function.

Distinctive Features

Process mapping often forms an important feature of research techniques such as evaluative methods, since it is generally

239

implicit to an understanding of the mechanisms underpinning the programme or initiative to be evaluated. It may therefore help to explain the reasons why a particular project has either succeeded or failed to meet its objectives. It may also inform the research process in terms of suggesting the types of data that should be collected through the identification of the critical stages of a project that require measurement. Process mapping may be a pre-requisite to projects where the organizational structure for the delivery of the project is not recorded or is unclear, or where national organizations have devolved responsibilities to regional areas. This is a particular feature of, say, evaluations of police initiatives, where local practices within the forty-three police force areas in England and Wales vary widely. In such circumstances, process mapping provides a full picture of the operational context of a particular research project. Therefore, mapping takes the form of an investigation, which may entail interviews with large numbers of personnel, and can be very labour-intensive.

In agencies where processes vary, mapping can help to explain differences in performance or outcomes, thereby revealing the comparative effectiveness of different organizational structures. In the UK and elsewhere, the growth in multi-agency approaches to a variety of social interventions has increased the need for process mapping, as an operational understanding of a partner's systems and organization may be fundamental to the development of future working practices and for improving effectiveness. For example, criminal justice agencies in the UK are now required to work with a number of other service providers, such as health, education and social services. An understanding of how systems operate to allow this interaction in practice may be a fundamental component of evaluating their effectiveness in terms of reducing crime and reforming offenders.

Evaluation

Process mapping can perform a very important function in its own right since it can provide research funders with an enhanced understanding of the operation of its own and partner agencies in practice. It may also shed light on organizational failings that have impeded the delivery of a project. Process mapping may also be essential to the dissemination of good practice, since replication can be ineffective in organizations with differing processes. However, the exposure of varying local practices may in itself compromise the overall research process, since it suggests that, in terms of outputs and outcomes, one is not comparing like with like.

Whilst, in some circumstances, variations in project outcomes may be partially attributable to the alternative processes between organizations, this should not be overstated. Discrepancies in findings may be attributable to variables other than processes, such as the response that a particular initiative generates or the context in which it operates, and accordingly process mapping should be used as part of a wider evaluation of a project.

Helen Poole

Associated Concepts: applied research, cost–benefit analysis, evaluation research, good practice studies, organizational research, policy-related research

Key Readings

Laycock, G. (2002) 'Methodological issues in working with policy advisers and practitioners', in N. Tilley (ed.), *Analysis for Crime Prevention*. Cullompton, Devon: Willan.

Pawson, R. and Tilley, N. (1997) 'An introduction to scientific realist evaluation', in E. Chelimsky and W. R. Shadish (eds), *Evaluation for the Twenty-First Century*. Thousand Oaks, CA: Sage. pp. 405–18.

PROGRESSIVE FOCUSING

Definition

A term used in discussions of ethnography, and sometimes of qualitative research generally. It represents the process of inquiry as involving a gradual clarification, and sometimes transformation, of the research problem; and perhaps also a re-formulation of the initial research questions into hypotheses that can be tested against data from the field.

Distinctive Features

The need for progressive focusing reflects the fact that ethnography is governed by an 'inductive' or 'discovery' orientation, rather than by a conception of inquiry which requires specific hypotheses to be set up for testing at the start of the process. From this point of view, inquiry is as much about discovering the right questions to ask as about testing hypotheses. This orientation is captured in Glaser and Strauss's notion of grounded theorizing, which they specifically oppose to 'verificationism', emphasizing the value of developing theoretical ideas through the analysis of data (Glaser and Strauss, 1967).

Underlying the concept of progressive focusing is an emphasis on the fact that any formulation of initial research problems or questions involves presuppositions – about relevant social phenomena and how they can be known – and that these might turn out to be false. Such a concern arises, in part, from an emphasis on the way in which human actions are culturally diverse, so that understanding them requires learning the relevant culture. However, the danger of setting out on false premises is recognized even in the context of natural scientific research, where cultural variation is not an issue.

Evaluation

The concept of inquiry underlying progressive focusing has been questioned from at least two directions. Some argue that the emphasis it gives to the *exploration* of ideas and of data means that insufficient time is allowed for the testing of hypotheses. A result of this is that ethnographers may engage simply in pattern-making or storytelling, without the necessary degree of attention to whether the patterns or stories are sound representations of the phenomena being investigated. While there is some truth in this argument, it assumes that the unit of inquiry is the single investigation, rather than a programme of studies addressing a particular issue. Within such a programme, different studies could have varying emphases across the spectrum from exploration to hypothesis-testing.

A very different criticism of the idea of progressive focusing challenges the assumption that social inquiry can produce accounts that represent social phenomena, insisting that creating illuminating or entertaining stories is its only possible goal. Alternatively, there are those who would question whether 'focus' is required in research, the proposal being that researchers should produce writerly, rather than readerly, texts: that is to say, texts that are open-ended or only loosely organized in internal structure, thereby encouraging the reader to create his or her own creative understanding from the materials provided. The model here is those forms of art and literature that subvert conventional ways of seeing, or forms of knowledge. In the context of research, such ideas challenge – indeed, some would say that they completely undermine – the very concept of inquiry itself.

Martyn Hammersley

Associated Concepts: ethnography, grounded theory, hypothetico-deductive model, induction, research problems, sensitizing concepts, theoretical sampling

Key Readings

Glaser, B. G. and Strauss, A. (1967) *The Discovery of Grounded Theory*. Chicago: Aldine.

Hammersley, M. and Atkinson, P. (1995) *Ethnography: Principles in Practice*, 2nd edn. London: Routledge.

PROJECTIVE TECHNIQUE

Definition

Any technique in which the respondent is given some task to complete that it is assumed will tell the researcher something about the respondent. The technique is regarded as a projection of the respondent's perceptions and attitudes.

Distinctive Features

Projective techniques vary in the degree of their structure: for example, attitude scales whereby an individual's score is used to make inferences about that person's attitude towards a particular topic tend to be highly structured in their format and in the response options available. Whilst this assists data analysis and facilitates comparison between subjects there are potential problems: for example, that an inappropriate structure is imposed or indeed that there is too much structure. Also, there is the risk of acquiescence effects (where a respondent acquiesces with what he or she believes the researcher wants) and social desirability effects (where a respondent attempts to portray him/herself in a desirable light). For such reasons, less structured techniques that permit free-flow responses are sometimes used. Such techniques can vary in their degree of ambiguity, with the most ambiguous stimuli used to explore an individual's inner states or feelings (sometimes in clinical or therapeutic context). They include abstract paintings, cartoons, single words and Rorschach inkblots. The sentence completion test, in which a respondent is given a number of sentence beginnings to complete, is less structured.

Unobtrusive or trace measures and also garbology can be viewed as forms of projective techniques in so far as they may tell the researcher something about individuals. For example, how a person dresses, what music he or she listens to or what a person eats can be used to make inferences about that person.

Evaluation

The use of a projective technique in research can be very stimulating and creative. However, the main problem is one of making valid and reliable inferences from a person's responses to stimuli, or traces which are left

behind, to that person's values, attitudes, perceptions or inner feelings. The risks, especially with unstructured methods, are that inferences are dependent on the interpretations on the part of the researcher of a respondent's responses and traces and that different researchers would make different inferences.

Victor Jupp

Associated Concepts: indicator, scaling, trace measures, unobtrusive measures, validity

Key Readings

Moser, C. A. and Kalton, G. (1971) *Survey Methods in Social Investigation.* London: Heinemann.
Oppenheim, A. N. (1966) *Questionnaire Design and Attitude Measurement.* London: Heinemann.

PROSPECTIVE STUDY

Definition

A study that follows cases forward in time, measuring attributes at multiple time points. Change is measured by examining differences between each time point or study wave. Unlike experimental designs, prospective designs do not include randomized control groups or experimental interventions.

Distinctive Features

Social researchers employ four main types of prospective design. The first is the ongoing single cohort design. This type of study consists of a single cohort that is tracked indefinitely. The cohort may be a birth cohort, as in the UK-based Millennium Cohort Study, an educational cohort (the graduating class of 2000) or a marriage cohort (those marrying in 2000). A second type of prospective study tracks multiple cohorts. Investigators using the multiple cohort data ideally use broad-based representative samples from which they may focus on single cohorts within the sample or construct and track multiple cohorts from the sample. The British Household Panel Survey and the US Panel Study of Income Dynamics are excellent examples of this type of prospective study.

A third type of prospective study is the rotating panel design consisting of a series of staggered, limited-life panels. This design is used in many national labour force surveys where a sample (panel) is interviewed each month for, say, six months and then leaves the study. Each month a new, six-month panel is added to replace one whose six-month involvement ends.

A fourth type of prospective design links data from administrative records and does not require interviewing people at each time point. An example of such a design might focus on the period for which lone mothers receive government income support. Administrative records are kept regarding when recipients of income support begin receiving payments, when they stop, the reason for stopping (obtained job, change of relationship status etc.), whether they return to the payment system and so forth. From these records a data set can be constructed containing information regarding the length of time for which lone mothers typically receive payments, the number of times they move off payments, the reasons for which they leave the payment system and the number of times they return.

Prospective studies can vary in a number of other ways. These include how many waves of data are collected, whether the study has a finite life or is ongoing and how long the gap between waves will be.

Evaluation

The major strength of prospective studies is that they can help establish the time sequence of events and thus establish causal direction more effectively than can either cross-sectional or many retrospective studies. However, their capacity to do this effectively depends on the length of the gap between waves and how much reliance must be placed on recall data to establish the sequence of events within the gap between study waves.

Since prospective designs track the same cases over time they have a major advantage over repeated cross-sectional studies which use the same measures at different points of time but recruit a new sample each time. Tracking the same cases over time allows investigators to identify change at the individual level while repeated cross-sectional studies only allow the identification of change at the aggregate level (Rose, 1995). Finally, prospective designs avoid the problems of the reconstruction of the past that are encountered in retrospective studies. Since information is, ideally, collected about contemporary events, behaviour and attitudes the problems of memory, selective recall and the reconstruction of the past are avoided.

However, prospective studies can encounter important problems. One of the major problems encountered is attrition. Tracking people across time, especially if waves are frequent, can impose a considerable burden on respondents which can cause them to drop out. This in turn can affect the representativeness of the study. Simply keeping track of people can be difficult – especially of the more mobile members of a population. The effort required to track respondents can add considerably to the cost of prospective studies. Representativeness can be undermined in other ways. If a sample is collected to represent a population at a particular point of time and that sample is tracked over time the sample can become unrepresentative if the nature of the wider population changes due to certain types of people leaving and other types joining the population through outward and inward migration.

A prospective study is not appropriate if a quick answer is required. Change must be studied in real time rather than the 'compressed time' that is used in retrospective studies. Depending on the types of changes to be observed this may take many years.

A further difficulty with most prospective designs is that they lack a randomized control group, which means that uncontrolled and unmeasured factors may be responsible for observed changes. While multivariate analysis can control for the influence of measured factors the problem of the influence of unmeasured factors remains.

Studies of change are only as good as are the measures being used at each time point. Unless highly reliable measures are used it can be difficult to distinguish between real change and apparent change due to measurement error. This problem is compounded in studies where there is likely to be developmental change (for example, in studies of children), where measurement instruments need to be adapted between waves to ensure that they are age-appropriate and therefore measure the underlying construct (for example, intelligence) reliably and validly.

David de Vaus

Associated Concepts: attrition, causality, cohort study, cross-sectional survey, experiment, longitudinal study, one-shot design, panel study, representativeness, retrospective study, sampling, survey, validity

Key Readings

Buck, N., Ermisch, J. and Jenkins, S. (1996) *Choosing a Longitudinal Survey Design: The Issues.* Occasional Paper 96-1. London: Institute for Social and Economic Research.

Duncan, G. and Kalton, G. (1987) 'Issues of design and analysis of surveys across time', *International Statistical Review*, 55: 97–117.

Menard, S. (1991) *Longitudinal Research.* Quantitative Applications in the Social Sciences Series, 76. London: Sage.

Rose, D. (1995) 'Household panel studies: an overview', *Innovations*, 8: 7–24. http://iserwww.essex.ac.uk/pubs/occpaps/index.php

de Vaus, D. (2001) *Research Design in Social Research.* London: Sage. chs 7–9.

PURPOSIVE SAMPLING

Definition

A form of non-probability sampling in which decisions concerning the individuals to be included in the sample are taken by the researcher, based upon a variety of criteria which may include specialist knowledge of the research issue, or capacity and willingness to participate in the research.

Distinctive Features

Some types of research design necessitate researchers taking a decision about the individual participants who would be most likely to contribute appropriate data, both in terms of relevance and depth. For example, in life history research, some potential participants may be willing to be interviewed, but may not be able to provide sufficiently rich data. Researchers may have to select a purposive sample based on the participants' oral skills, ability to describe and reflect upon aspects of their lives, and experience of the specific focus of the research.

A case study design is another type of research that often requires a purposive sample. Imagine that a research team wishes to explore the types of academic support provided for students in a single high school. In selecting that school the researchers may need to take a variety of factors into account. They may want a school in which academic support is sufficiently innovative to make the final research report of wide interest in the profession. They will require a school in which the management are supportive of the research, and in that the teachers and students show a willingness to participate. The researchers may want a school that is exceptional in terms of overall academic performance, or that has an average level of attainment. Finally, they may prefer a school that is reasonably accessible for members of the research team. When all relevant factors have been considered, the research team will select the case study school, which will constitute the purposive sample. If it is appropriate, a purposive sample may be combined with a probability sample. Once the high school has been selected, a random sample of teachers and students could be selected from whom to collect data.

Evaluation

The advantage of purposive sampling is that the researcher can identify participants who are likely to provide data that are detailed and relevant to the research question. However, in disseminating the findings, the researcher should make fully transparent the criteria upon which the sampling process was based.

The principal disadvantage of purposive sampling rests on the subjectivity of the researcher's decision making. This is a source of potential bias, and a significant threat to the validity of the research conclusions. These effects may be reduced by trying to ensure that there is an internal consistency between the aims and epistemological basis of the research, and the criteria used for selecting the purposive sample.

Paul Oliver

Associated Concepts: case study method, cluster sampling, good practice studies, life history interviewing, non-probability (non-random) sampling, opportunity sampling, quota sampling, snowball sampling, validity

Key Readings

Krathwohl, D. R. (1998) *Methods of Educational and Social Science Research*, 2nd edn. New York: Longman.

May, T. (2001) *Social Research: Issues, Methods and Process*, 3rd edn. Milton Keynes: Open University Press.

Robson, C. (2002) *Real World Research: A Resource for Social Scientists and Practitioner-Researchers*, 2nd edn. Oxford: Blackwell.

QSR NVivo

Definition

A software package for qualitative researchers. From the developers of the NUD*IST software, NVivo provides a range of tools for handling data, ideas, information and theories built up from observations, interviews, document analysis, literature reviews and other qualitative research processes. Like NUD*IST, NVivo (for 'NUD*IST Alive') supports coding and retrieval of coded material, searching and theorizing, combined with ability to annotate and edit documents. But NVivo is designed for methods requiring more flexible development of rich data in dynamic documents, and more subtle ways of linking data to ideas and showing and reflecting on the results.

Distinctive Features

NVivo pioneered rich text in QDA software, freely edited and coded, and the integrating of coding with many ways of qualitative linking, shaping, searching and modelling. Users can:

(1) create documents or import and freely edit them in a rich text editor and edit them at any time without affecting coding or pointers to other data;

(2) include non-text data (e.g. video clips) by hyperlinks to sound, image or any other files; and call up that data (links appear live in coded text);

(3) manage documents and nodes flexibly in sets that can be filtered and explored;

(4) create nodes to represent ideas and hold coding, and manage these flexibly in an index system;

(5) store attributes of sites, data sources, people, organizations etc. and use these in searching and sorting data. Attributes of documents or nodes are managed as in a spreadsheet; their values can be text, numeric or date/time;

(6) code any characters in the text at new or existing categories, using drag and drop or other rapid methods, whilst viewing coding displays in margin stripes;

(7) ask questions about any occurrences of words in text, or patterns of coding or attributes, and scope the question to exactly the data to be explored; combine such questions to explore data iteratively: results are saved as more coding;

(8) display and explore relationships in live matrices of coding, attributes or text, to investigate patterns, jumping to the text represented by any cell;

(9) show, filter and assay the relationships of data, using tools for seeing patterns, integrated with tools for searching;

(10) draw models of emerging ideas, use layers to show stages in the analysis or different interpretations, and jump to the data represented by any item in the model;

(11) using a separate program, Merge for NVivo, align projects in great detail for thorough comparison of their emerging analyses, and optionally merge them for a wider picture.

Evaluation

The design of NVivo responds to widespread experience with early code and retrieve software and to complaints that such software encouraged students to a linear approach to data gathering, coding and reporting. Whilst many researchers still use it mainly for code-based analysis, it offered many (for some, too many) ways of linking data and ideas and of directing analysis accurately to the pertinent data. In a second revision (2002), the options, particularly for search and filter, were clarified and streamlined. Used in graduate and undergraduate methods teaching, across an expanding range of disciplines, NVivo became the first QDA software to be supported by teaching textbooks.

Lyn Richards

Associated Concepts: Atlas.ti, CAQDAS, The Ethnograph, NUD*IST, qualitative research

Key Readings

Bazeley, P. and Richards, L. (2000) *The NVivo Qualitative Project Book.* London: Sage.

Gibbs, G. (2002) *Qualitative Data Analysis: Explorations with NVivo.* Milton Keynes: Open University Press.

Morse, J. M. and Richards, L. (2002) *Read Me First for a User's Guide to Qualitative Methods.* Thousand Oaks, CA: Sage.

Richards, L. (2002) *Using NVivo2 in Qualitative Research.* Melbourne: QSR International.

QUALITATIVE DATA ARCHIVES

Definition

A data archive is a tool used to preserve data sets that are the products of research. In social research, the majority of archives are used to preserve quantitative data in computer-readable format. A number of qualitative archives have developed as qualitative methods have become more popular and more sophisticated.

Distinctive Features

Qualitative data archives are growing in number around the world. There are two established qualitative archives at the present time, with more in progress. The aim of these archives is to enhance and assist social research by obtaining, sharing and re-using qualitative data.

Archives hold a vast quantity of data collected from various research projects. In most cases the archives also hold details of the methodological approach of the research project in order to contextualize the data set. Usually an archive holds a diverse range of materials, which can include interview transcripts open questionnaires, newspapers, magazines, diaries, letters, audio tapes, video footage, observation schedules and field notes from the researcher.

In some cases, an archive will allow original copies of data (such as hard copies of questionnaires or field notes) to be used by new researchers. More commonly, data are archived by scanning the original material or by transcribing interviews and field notes. A popular method of accessing such qualitative data is to link the archive to the Internet. This allows researchers worldwide access to qualitative data from different cultures and historical periods. Data can be extracted using a search function that identifies the most relevant material to the criteria entered by the user.

Archived qualitative data can be manipulated in many ways. It can be sampled, and in most cases the archive will hold demographic data on the respondents from the original project. Therefore probability sampling techniques such as stratified sampling can be applied to the data in order to extract the most appropriate cases. As the data are usually listed (by some criteria such as respondent number or case number), random and systematic methods of sampling can also be applied by selecting cases from the list. In some instances it may be appropriate to apply non-probability sampling to the archived data. When cases are hard to identify or are few in number then using snowball or opportunity sampling can be useful. Each data set can be used to link to similar data sets as archives usually provide links to similar studies.

An example of one such archive is the Murray Research Centre archive at Radcliffe University in the United States. It holds research data from 1976 onwards and stores some classic longitudinal research projects. The stock consists of video cassettes, audio tapes, transcripts from interviews and case histories. The archive can be searched using the Internet and new researchers can download data sets.

The most advanced qualitative data archive in the world is Qualidata held as part of the UK Data Archive at the University of Essex in the UK. Qualidata has been acquiring data since 1994 and is the only stand-alone data archive of its kind. The archive is fully connected to the Internet and data can be searched, refined and downloaded by researchers.

This archive aims to actively encourage the secondary use of qualitative research data collected during ESRC (Economic and Social Research Council) funded projects. The ESRC stipulate that all projects they fund, which ethically qualify, must submit the data set from the research to Qualidata. This archive is a pioneer in its field. Qualidata organizes international conferences to promote qualitative data sharing and to encourage other countries to set up similar archives. It also gives seminars on how to archive material to social researchers around the world.

Countries currently developing qualitative data archives are: Canada, Czech Republic, Denmark, Finland, France, Germany, Netherlands, Slovenia and Switzerland.

Evaluation

Qualitative data archives are a tool used to share and re-use social research data. Before any social researcher uses material from an archive they must address the ethical issues this creates. Perhaps most importantly, the prospective user must address the context in which the data were collected and assess whether this would tally with the current research project. Another important issue is

the extent to which it is ethical or valid to use a subject's response to a particular question or situation for a different purpose.

The data held by any archive must be evaluated in terms of reliability, validity and authenticity, as any other data would be. The researcher must always address the way the data have been collected, for example whether informed consent was obtained or whether the research was covert. Researchers must consider the suitability of the secondary use of data for the project in hand. Potential users of archived data sets must bear in mind the theoretical approach taken by the original researcher and critically evaluate the original data, and the method in which they were collected, in terms of the perspective of the current research.

Angela Brady

Associated Concepts: data, ethics, Internet research, naturalistic data, opportunity sampling, purposive sampling, qualitative research, sampling, secondary analysis

Key Readings

ESDS website (December 2003) (Online): www.esds.ac.uk/

IASSIST website (December 2003) (Online): http://datalib.library.ualberta.ca/iassist/

ICPSR (December 2003) Guide to Social Science Data Preparation and Archiving. ICPSR website (Online): www.icpsr.umich. edu/access/dpm.html

Ryssevik, J. and Musgrave, S. (2001) 'The social science dream machine: resource discovery, analysis, and delivery on the Web', *Social Science Computing Review*, 19 (2): 163–74.

QUALITATIVE RESEARCH

Definition

Research that investigates aspects of social life which are not amenable to quantitative measurement. Associated with a variety of theoretical perspectives, qualitative research uses a range of methods to focus on the meanings and interpretation of social phenomena and social processes in the particular contexts in which they occur.

Distinctive Features

Qualitative research is not a single set of theoretical principles, a single research strategy or a single method (Silverman, 1993). It developed in the nineteenth and twentieth centuries, across a range of disciplines, on varied and sometimes conflicting philosophical and theoretical bases, including cultural anthropology, interpretive sociologies (such as symbolic interactionism), phenomenology and, more recently, hermeneutics, critical theory, feminism, post-colonial theory, cultural studies, post-structuralism and postmodernism. These diverse approaches inevitably give rise to substantial differences and disagreements about the nature of qualitative research, the role of the researcher, the use of various methods and the analysis of data.

However, qualitative research is often based upon interpretivism, constructivism and inductivism. It is concerned to explore the subjective meanings through which people interpret the world, the different ways in which reality is constructed (through language, images and cultural artifacts) in particular contexts. Social events and phenomena are understood from the perspective of the actors themselves, avoiding the imposition of the researcher's own preconceptions and definitions. There is also often a concern with the exploration of change and flux in social relationships in context and over time.

The methods used in qualitative research, often in combination, are those which are open-ended (to explore participants' interpretations) and which allow the collection of detailed information in a relatively close setting. These methods include depth interviewing, ethnography and participant observation, case studies, life histories, discourse analysis and conversational analysis. It is in the nature of qualitative research, with its emphasis on depth and detail of understanding and interpretation, that it is often small-scale or micro-level.

Evaluation

Qualitative research is sometimes seen as lacking the rigour of quantitative research, producing 'soft' data that is subjective and not easy to replicate, often based on small samples or case studies. There are difficulties in meeting the usual scientific criteria of validity, reliability and representativeness. However, the extent to which these criteria, derived from quantitative research, are applicable to the nature of qualitative research has been a matter of debate (see, for example, Hammersley, 1992; Seale, 1999).

Because it is predicated on traditions that point to the contested nature of social reality and which are critical of the idea of a single objective 'truth' about the world, qualitative research fits well with critical perspectives, such as feminism, which aim to challenge the political assumptions embedded in social institutions and in the research process itself.

Although qualitative and quantitative research have traditionally been seen as opposed, and there are differences in terms of the underlying philosophical approaches, these differences are not always clear-cut (Layder, 1993). For example, qualitative research is increasingly used for theory testing as well as theory generation (Silverman, 1993). Many studies have used a combination of qualitative and quantitative methods. The value of qualitative research in a variety of settings, including market research and applied social research, has increasingly been recognized.

Maggie Sumner

Associated Concepts: constructionism, critical research, discourse analysis, epistemology, ethnography, ethnomethodology, feminist research, inter-subjective understanding, methodological pluralism, naturalistic data, participant observation, phenomenology, quantitative research, *Verstehen*

Key Readings

Denzin, N. K. and Lincoln, Y. S. (eds) (1994) *Handbook of Qualitative Research*. London: Sage.

Hammersley, M. (1992) *What's Wrong With Ethnography*. London: Routledge.

Layder, D. (1993) *New Strategies in Social Research*. Cambridge: Polity Press.

Seale, C. (1999) *The Quality of Qualitative Research*. London: Sage.

Silverman, D. (1993) *Interpreting Qualitative Data*. London: Sage.

QUANTITATIVE RESEARCH

Definition

Research involving the collection of data in numerical form for quantitative analysis. The numerical data can be durations, scores, counts of incidents, ratings, or scales. Quantitative data can be collected in either controlled or naturalistic environments, in laboratories or field studies, from special populations or from samples of the general population. The defining factor is that numbers result from the process, whether the initial data collection produced numerical values, or whether non-numerical values were subsequently converted to numbers as part of the analysis process, as in content analysis.

Distinctive Features

Quantitative research tends to be associated with the realist epistemology, the approach to knowledge that maintains that the real world exists, is directly knowable (although not necessarily at this moment) and that the real world causes our experiences. That is, real things exist, and these can be measured, and have numerical values assigned as an outcome measure, and these values are meaningful. These values can only be meaningful if researchers accept some of the criteria associated with the positivist standpoint.

Gaining numerical materials facilitates the measurement of variables and also allows statistical tests to be undertaken. For example, descriptive statistics can be used to illustrate and summarize findings, detect relationships between variables, as in correlation coefficient values, or inferential statistical analysis can be undertaken to establish the effects of different interventions, as in analysis of variance, analysis of covariance and multivariate analysis of variance (Johnson and Wichern, 1998). Interactions between variables can also be investigated within experimental designs and also as part of the analysis of data from surveys or secondary sources (Pilcher, 1990).

Changes over time can be more easily tracked using quantitative methods, as measures of the same properties can be taken at several points during an intervention. For example, if a community project is intended to engage young people, comparing those inclined towards antisocial behaviour with those who are not, measures of shoplifting, juvenile arrests, nuisance calls to the civil services, such as fire and ambulance, can be used across the time of the intervention in order to establish the efficacy of the project. It would be very difficult to establish actual effects without numerical data.

Evaluation

Quantitative research has certain strengths and weaknesses as a methodology, and is mostly associated with the positivist tradition. Quantitative research produces 'facts' about the world and behaviour, and these are viewed as adding to the sum of human knowledge. That is, the data thus collected tend to be accepted as they stand, and as valid measures of the variables they purport to indicate. Qualitative researchers tend to criticize these methods on the basis that most sources of data are not quite what they appear to be. They do not pay attention to social meanings and the ways in which the world is socially constructed. Also, from the viewpoint of critical researchers, the data are obtained using methods where the person or group under study are given no status, being subject to unequal power relations (Tavris, 1993).

There is a considerable tension between the qualitative and quantitative methodologies, and the researchers who deploy them. It has been suggested that the qualitative methodologies are best used when an area is little known, and so hypotheses cannot be generated for testing by those who support the hypothetico-deductive method. But this viewpoint negates the place of qualitative research as a methodology in its own right. Strong qualitative methodologists suggest that in quantitative research, the positivist view of facts leaves no place for participants as agents, and that many constructs do not exist except in the social world, and so cannot be investigated outside social interaction. Pragmatists suggest that quantitative methods, on the other hand, should be best deployed when more is known, so that hypotheses and research questions can be formulated, and easily tested. Researchers intending to use any methodology need to have very clear ideas about the questions they need to address, and the most appropriate ways of investigating them.

The greatest advantage of quantitative research is the fact that the data obtained via these methods can be subject to considerable statistical analysis, can generalize beyond the sample under investigation, allowing the testing of hypotheses, and the evaluation of the efficacy of interventions in various area of interest, including social policy. In addition, experimentation would have no meaning without quantitative research methods.

Jeanette Garwood

Associated Concepts: correlation, data, descriptive statistics, experiment, hypothetico-deductive model, indicator, inferential statistics, measurement, methodology, positivism, qualitative research, realism, *Verstehen*

Key Readings

Cramer, D. (1994) *Introducing Statistics for the Social Sciences*. London: Routledge.
Johnson, R. A. and Wichern, D. W. (1998) *Applied Multivariate Statistical Analysis*, 4th edn. Englewood Cliffs, NJ: Prentice Hall.

Pilcher, D. M. (1990) *Data Analysis for the Helping Professions: A Practical Guide*. Newbury Park, CA: Sage.
Tavris, C. (1993) 'The mismeasure of woman', *Feminism and Psychology*, 3 (2): 149–68.

QUASI-EXPERIMENT

Definition

An experiment that attempts to test a hypothesis about the effects of an intervention by methods other than those used in a 'true experiment', where the latter is deemed to require random allocation to experimental and control conditions.

Distinctive Features

Quasi-experiments are conducted when true experiments are either impracticable or impossible. They are often used in evaluation research. True experiments supposedly deal at a stroke with alternative explanations for any change brought about by the introduction of an experimental measure. They do so by randomly allocating potential cases to experimental and control conditions. Any variation in change between the sets of cases may be explained by reference to the presence in the one but not the other of the experimental measure. Random allocation ensures that the experimental and control groups are equivalent, maturation will affect both groups equally, events unrelated to the experiment will also affect both groups equally and so on. Selection bias and alternative sources of change in the experimental group are dealt with by the design of the study. However, practical problems for true experiments do arise, for example, where the unit of intervention is too large for sufficient numbers to be allocated to experimental or control conditions, where a policy is being introduced which will affect the whole population, or where it is not possible to contain the measures introduced to the experimental group in ways that prevent them from reaching potential members of control groups. Under these circumstances, something short of a true experiment has to be undertaken *faut de mieux*.

True experiments become especially difficult where communities rather than individuals are the units of analysis. Communities often cannot be insulated from one another, random allocation is often impracticable and finding sufficient experimental sites for statistical analysis is generally prohibitively expensive. In these circumstances quasi-experimental studies are conducted.

Evaluation

Non-equivalent pre- and post-test designs are often used as a next best choice where true experiments cannot be conducted. Here, one or two experimental sites are identified alongside one or two nearby areas, with similar social and physical attributes, to act as controls. One of the key difficulties here is that the comparisons of experimental and control areas assume no significant difference in terms of the responses either would have to the experimental measure. In the absence of tested theory there is no basis for this assumption.

True experiments cannot be generalized beyond the populations from which random assignment has been made, and cannot assure external validity. Results of quasi-experimental studies using non-equivalent groups of the design described here do not even enjoy internal validity. Alternative, theory-based approaches in evaluation research attempt to make good shortfalls in experimental methods and quasi-experimental methods which depend on non-equivalent pre- and post-test designs.

Donald Campbell, the most influential writer on experimental and quasi-experimental designs for the social sciences, recognized that the quasi-experimental tradition resembles the laboratory experiment of the natural sciences more closely than 'true experiments' involving random assignment to treatment (Campbell and Russo, 1999)!

Nick Tilley

Associated Concepts: causality, evaluation research, experiment, field experiment, messy research, validity

Key Readings

Campbell, D. and Russo, M. Jean (1999) *Social Experimentation*. Thousand Oaks, CA: Sage.
Campbell, D. and Stanley, J. (1966) *Experimental and Quasi-Experimental Designs for Research*. Boston, MA: Houghton Mifflin.
Pawson, R. and Tilley, N. (1997) *Realistic Evaluation*. London: Sage.

QUESTIONNAIRE

Definition

A set of carefully designed questions given in exactly the same form to a group of people in order to collect data about some topic(s) in which the researcher is interested.

Distinctive Features

There is often a great deal of confusion in the use and the meaning of the word 'questionnaire'. For instance, some researchers reserve this term exclusively for self-administered or postal questionnaires, while others would include interview schedules (personally administered face-to-face) under the general rubric of 'questionnaire'. Examples of the latter type of questionnaire are market researchers stopping shoppers in the street, or a researcher conducting a study into the retail habits of a particular group. Administered, or postal questionnaires, have many advantages. Even though the researcher should consider postal and printing costs, postal questionnaires tend to be much less expensive than travelling to far away places to conduct interviews. Collected data can be inputted into a computer either automatically by the use of a scanning device or manually by using computer programs such as SPSS. This saves the researcher a great deal of time and, with the advent of new technology, allows the researcher to establish correlations between different variables. In addition, as the researcher has no direct contact with the respondent, the issue of interviewer bias tends not to arise.

On the other hand, many criticisms can be levelled against this type of research method, the largest one being response rate. The intended respondent may regard postal questionnaires as something of a nuisance; therefore, the researcher may find that he or she can only obtain a 25 per cent response rate, which is not unusual in these types of study. Those who do take the time to complete the questionnaire may therefore be unrepresentative of the sample population. A more substantive criticism of questionnaires is that they simply cannot capture the true extent of a social phenomenon. Reality, according to this argument, is much more complex than the few variables that are found in a questionnaire. Interpretative scholars often level this criticism. Finally, it is erroneous to assume that questionnaires are an 'easy' research technique. In order to understand a topic, and therefore be able to create a good questionnaire, the researcher needs to understand the subject matter. Therefore, before designing a questionnaire, the researcher must be fully aware of all of the various debates that surround it.

Evaluation

Questionnaires provide an excellent means of collecting large-scale quantitative data. The closed-question nature of this technique, however, demonstrates that a researcher may need to employ further methods, such as a semi-structured interview, to gain a full understanding of a given issue.

Craig McLean

Associated Concepts: interview, quantitative research, research design, social survey

Key Reading

Oppenheim, A. N. (1992) *Questionnaire Design and Attitude Measurement.* London: Pinter.

QUOTA SAMPLING

Definition

A non-probability method of selecting respondents for surveys. The interviewer begins with a matrix of the target population that is to be represented and potential respondents are selected according to that matrix. Quota sampling is also known as a purposive sample or a non-probability sample, whereby the objective is to select typical, or representative, subjects and the skill and judgement of selectors is deliberately utilized (Abrahamson, 1983).

Distinctive Features

Quota sampling allows the researcher to control variables without having a sampling frame. This method is often used for market research because it does not require a list of potential respondents. The interviewer finds respondents, usually in public areas, who fit into the predetermined categories until the quotas are filled. To that end, quota sampling is a convenient and inexpensive method of research. If the interviewee is unavailable or refuses to participate they can easily be replaced with another potential respondent who meets the same criteria.

Evaluation

Statisticians criticize quota sampling for its methodological weakness. Although the interviewer 'randomly' chooses respondents he or she comes across on the street, quota sampling cannot be considered a genuinely random method of sampling because not every member of the population has an equal chance of survey selection (for example, those who are at work or at home). Therefore, the principles of statistical inference cannot be invoked.

There are a number of factors that can result in research bias. First, interviewers may misjudge a potential respondent's characteristic, such as their age. Secondly, the interviewer runs the risk of subconsciously making a subjective judgement before approaching a potential respondent. As a result, the interviewer may not approach those deemed unfriendly and runs the risk of distorting the findings. This is also known as systematic bias (Abrahamson, 1983). Finally, quota sampling can never be truly representative because certain factors may prevent certain groups of people from being chosen for the research. For example, as noted above, market research conducted during the day may over-represent housewives shopping in the city centre and under-represent office workers.

Despite these limitations, quota sampling continues to be used because there are circumstances when random or stratified random sampling is not possible.

Rachael Beth Moss

Associated Concepts: inferential statistics, non-probability (non-random) sampling, opportunity sampling, probability (random) sampling, purposive sampling, sampling, social survey, volunteer sampling

Key Readings

Abrahamson, M. (1983) *Social Research Methods*. Englewood Cliffs, NJ: Prentice Hall.

Gilbert, N. (2001) *Researching Social Life*, 2nd edn. London: Sage.

Moser, C. A. and Kalton, G. (1971) *Survey Methods in Social Research*. London: Heinemann.

R

RANDOM SAMPLING

See Probability (Random) Sampling

REACTIVITY

See Validity of Measurement

REALISM

Definition

Realism takes a number of forms depending on how 'the real' is understood. All approaches to knowledge that endorse realism accept that a world exists that is in some respect independent of the knowing subject. This real external world may be a purely empirical reality so that what has not yet been observed will at some point appear to us. Alternatively, it may be a reality that is concealed from us in some way beyond appearances and independent of our knowledge of the world. These different ontological assumptions about what really exists have produced corresponding epistemologies – the first associated with empiricism and idealism and the second with critical realism – that are central to social research. Whereas for empiricism real objects can only ever be accessed through sense data and for idealists empirical reality can be understood through a synthesis of sensation and mental constructs, for advocates of critical realism aspects of the real can only be ascertained through rational abstraction. Indeed, the social relations that exist for critical realists, such as 'capitalism', can never be observed in the strict sense (that is, we can only observe individual companies and groups of workers in the context of markets but not capitalism, the bourgeoisie or the proletariat).

Distinctive Features

For empiricists the real world is composed of discrete entities that are not intrinsically complex and which in combination produce the complex empirical patterns we can identify through our sensations, impressions and perceptions. By taking these objects at face value, empiricists are able to identify a limited number of them, observe and measure their frequency and (subject to the screening out of extraneous variables) begin to identify and predict clear relationships between them (for example, between independent variables and dependent variables). This combination of assumptions is often referred to as a closed system. In social research it is important to focus three approaches to knowledge, each with their own distinctive characterization of causality (empiricism, idealism and realism).

Empiricists accept that observed empirical regularities (constant conjunctions of events whereby *if x happens then y will follow*) are necessary *and* sufficient for establishing a causal law. For idealists and realists, this fails to sustain the intelligibility of perception: that sensations, impressions and perceptions are organized and make sense only through their synthesis with prior mental constructs. This rejects the view that characterizes some forms of empiricism (especially positivist versions) that human beings are blank slates or empty vessels passively accepting sensations. For idealists, the phenomenal world of appearances is the product of both our experiences of the object of analysis (which as 'things-in-themselves' or *noumena* are beyond cognitive faculties and thus unknowable) and the a priori conditions within which the mind provides shape to this experiential content. For this reason, an empirical regularity is still necessary for establishing a causal law but it is not sufficient for two reasons: first, it needs to take account of the range of possible empirical factors that may produce the effect in question; second, it needs to make sense in terms of the existing body of knowledge and be relevant to the values evident in the context.

Given that empirical reality is seen by idealists as too complex to fully reconstruct and that there is no unmediated access to the 'real', then this has generated a distinctive tradition in social research that recognizes the limitations of its own theories, concepts and models of that world – that they should be seen as necessary simplifications. For this reason, it is often labelled the 'interpretive' approach. For example, Max Weber developed the technique of ideal types (such as habitual, emotional and rational action) as simplistic exaggerations in order to organize empirical evidence, while phenomenologists such as Alfred Schütz advocated the use of typifications or types to establish closer relations between the second order concepts of the researcher and the first order constructs of everyday life. Not all idealists are so humble; advocates of rational choice theory and game theory tend to be so convinced that rational and instrumental logic is the basis for all human action in all situations they risk imposing their own assumptions on their objects of analysis.

Critical realists, building on idealist assumptions about the intelligibility of experience, challenge the assumption that 'the real' is purely empirical (an assumption characteristic of empiricism and idealism). In so doing,

realists often conflate these two different epistemologies to 'the empirical real'. For realists, such as Roy Bhaskar, one should start by distinguishing between the transitive dimension (rival theories and approaches about the world that imagine what the real is like, transitive objects) and the intransitive dimension (what the world is like regardless of our current state of knowledge). This is tied to the view that objects are intrinsically complex with undiscovered capacities or susceptibilities that are only identified in certain conditions. Indeed, for critical realists experiments are only intelligible if the objects already have an unknown internal structure (such as a capacity to produce certain effects prior to the discovery and consequent knowledge of that real capacity) (Bhaskar, 1978). Their account of causality reflects these assumptions. The structures of these objects can produce certain effects or events but do so when the conditions are right for that structure to generate a causal mechanism. These conditions include the presence of other structures, mechanisms and events. If the conditions are not appropriate then we may not identify an effect in terms *if x then y,* but for a realist this does not mean that the structure does not exist. In terms of establishing a causal law, an empirical regularity is neither necessary nor sufficient (Smith, 1998).

In social research, critical realists argue we have to take into account the ontological or real differences between natural and social objects. Social structures do not exist independently of the activities they govern, they do not exist independently of the agent's conceptions of what they are doing, they are time-space specific and only relatively enduring and they are reproduced, modified or transformed through the activities of agents. In short, we should start with the assumption of an open rather than a closed system. In turn the activities of agents are shaped by the pre-existing social structures they are thrown into and have capacities to do things and susceptibilities to other forces depending on their position in the structures (Bhaskar, 1979; Sayer, 1992, 2000). Social structures are both the medium and the outcome of the activities of agents. These 'real' structures include relationships such as that between tenants and landlords, capitalists and workers or tutors and students (in each case they are mutually defining). If over time and across different contexts the operation of these kinds of structures becomes deeply embedded then they can be seen as institutionalized, making change more difficult compared to the more flexible structured relations, for example, between speakers and listeners in a conversation.

Evaluation

Challenges to critical realism fall into three main camps. The empiricist critique argues that critical realism is a form of objectionable metaphysics constructing imaginary and ideologically inspired visions of the social world as oppressive and exploitative. For critical realists, such responses are conservative attempts to prop-up an unjust society. For realists, explaining and understanding social structures is the first step to identifying how to transform it so that unwanted forms of social determination can be replaced by wanted ones. For this reason, critical realism is an emancipatory approach seeking social change though there are disagreements between critical realists as to whether the problem that needs changing is the social class system, patriarchy or other forms of structured social division such as those based on racism and other forms of cultural difference.

The idealist critique highlights the difficulties caused by the battlelines between critical realism and empirical realism. Critical realists argue that it is possible to accommodate the insights of empiricism and idealism by changing one's assumptions about what is real. At its most strident, realism assumes that empiricism and idealism have the same flaw of a 'flat ontology' (being unable to distinguish between 'sensations, impressions and perceptions' and the 'events and states of affairs' that serve as our objects) and refusing to accept the existence of a deep reality beyond observation. As indicated above, this is not an accurate description of idealist approaches nor of some epistemologies associated with empiricist research such as falsificationism (for example,

Karl Popper's 'objective third world'). Indeed, aspects of 'the real' are present in experience and in the mental constructs we use to make sense of this. Recent attempts to portray idealist theorists as diverse as Max Weber, Alfred Schütz and Niklas Luhmann as embryonic or proto realists merely highlight the problem. More symptomatic of the problems of critical realism is their tendency to draw upon their own cultural values and assumptions in the accounts of the real. Both idealist and discursive approaches to knowledge draw attention (in their different ways) to the way that social context is relevant to the kinds of knowledge produced and how organized knowledge regulates what can and cannot be thought and spoken. As a result of ignoring the complexities of representation and values, critical realism has often reproduced the language of pathologization that stigmatizes certain social groups in much the same way as crude versions of positivism (Smith, 2000).

Mark J. Smith

Associated Concepts: causality, empiricism, epistemology, ontology, relativism

Key Readings

Bhaskar, R. (1978) *A Realist Theory of Science,* 2nd edn. Hemel Hempstead: Harvester Wheatsheaf.

Bhaskar, R. (1979) *The Possibility of Naturalism: A Philosophical Critique of the Contemporary Human Sciences.* Hemel Hempstead: Harvester Wheatsheaf.

Blaikie, N. (1993) *Approaches to Social Enquiry.* Cambridge: Polity Press.

Sayer, A. (1992) *Method in Social Science: A Realist Approach,* 2nd edn. London: Routledge.

Sayer, A. (2000) *Realism and Social Science.* London: Sage.

Smith, M. J. (1998) *Social Science in Question: Towards a Postdisciplinary Framework.* London: Sage.

Smith, M. J. (2000) *Culture: Reinventing the Social Sciences.* Milton Keynes: Open University Press.

REFLEXIVITY

Definition

The process of monitoring and reflecting on all aspects of a research project from the formulation of research ideas through to the publication of findings and, where this occurs, their utilization. Sometimes the product of such monitoring and reflection is a reflexive account which is published as part of the research report.

Distinctive Features

Although important in all areas of social research, reflexivity has an especial role in ethnography, in which the researcher is close to the subjects and to the data. What is more, the whole process of formulating ideas, collecting observations, analysing and reaching conclusions is part of the role of the investigator *vis-à-vis* those who are the objects of inquiry. It is for this reason that ethnographers see reflexivity as part of research in its own right and not as a collection of afterthoughts on how a project has been accomplished.

At one level, a reflective account will be descriptive in terms of providing an account of, for example, how interviews were carried out, what methods of recording data were used and so on. However, at another – much more important – level a reflective account should be evaluative in terms of providing some assessment of the likely validity of the conclusions that have been reached. This might, for example, involve a consideration of whether respondents selected for interview are typical of the group about which conclusions are to be made; whether there is a possibility that responses to questions were the outcome of exaggeration or even downright falsification; and whether the method of recording data resulted in only a partial or even distorted, account of reality. These are what are known as 'threats to validity'. A researcher may not be able to anticipate and rule these out. However, he or she should be aware of them and provide some assessment of their potential effects on the validity of conclusions. At a minimum, the expectation is that the researcher will provide sufficient

detail about the research process – and decisions taken within it – to allow readers to make some judgement by themselves.

On occasions reflexivity involves not just monitoring and assessing validity (to what extent are conclusions credible and plausible?), but also questions of ethics (has anyone been harmed by the research?) and questions of politics (whose side am I on, if any?). Validity, ethics and politics can impact one on another. For example, a decision not to publish interview material collected from corrupt policemen, for fear of exposing them, will not result in a full and valid account of the realities of police sub-cultures. Therefore, reflexivity often involves the researcher in reaching a personal standpoint in relation to trade-offs which often have to be made between validity, politics and ethics.

Evaluation

In assessing the potential threats to validity, reflexivity is concerned with the social production of knowledge. It involves reflecting on the various social roles, interactions and processes which resulted in the kinds of observations and conclusions which emerged. It is possible to consider reflexivity in a sense wider than that of monitoring and assessing the validity of a particular research project. This involves viewing critical reflection as a form of research in its own right, and as part of the school of critical thinking and theorizing in the social sciences in general. A critical research agenda could include a consideration of why particular (say, punitive) law and order discourses take the form that they do and come to be accepted as 'truth' when they do. What is more, it could consider the role of research in the production and dissemination of such 'truths'. This would involve reflecting on the research enterprise as a whole and asking what gets studied, when, by whom, what gets published, and with what effect?

Victor Jupp

Associated Concepts: critical research, disastrous research, ethics, impression management, politics and social research, research bargain, validity

Key Readings

Findlay, L. and Gough, B. (eds) (2003) *Reflexivity: A Practical Guide for Researchers in Health and Social Sciences*. Oxford: Blackwell.

Mason, J. (2002) *Qualitative Researching*. London: Sage.

Steir, F. (ed.) (1991) *Research and Reflexivity*. London: Sage.

REGRESSION ANALYSIS

Definition

A body of statistical techniques in which the form of the relationship between a dependent variable and one or more independent variables is established so that knowledge of the values of the independent variables enables prediction of the value of the dependent variable or likelihood of the occurrence of an event if the dependent variable is categorical.

Distinctive Features

Regression analysis is a method by which quantitative social science seeks to establish how things are caused. The objectives are both scientific description and prediction. If we know the form of the relationship between things we have measured and know to be causal to something else, then we can predict the value of the caused thing. For example, using logistic regression, knowledge of the blood levels of various hormones and of the results of an X-ray in a patient with prostate cancer can be used to predict if the cancer has spread to the patient's lymph nodes.

The relationship between independent and dependent variables is expressed through a regression equation. In the simplest case of the linear relationship between two continuous variables this can be written as:

$$Y = a + bX$$

Here Y is the value of the dependent variable, X of the independent variable, a the value Y has when X is zero, and b the amount Y changes when X changes by one unit. We can extend this simple bivariate relationship to become multivariate by adding in more independent variables thus:

$$Y = a + b^1 X^1 + b^2 X^2 + b^3 X^3 \dots + b^n X^n$$

There is usually a difference between the actual value of Y and the value predicted by the regression equation – the residual. In simple linear regression – linear because changes in Y are proportionate to changes in X – the line fitted minimizes the sum of the square of these residuals – squares because squaring eliminates negative numbers and some residuals will be positive and some negative. The simplest way to see the relationship between variables in the two or three variable case is to generate a scatter plot in two or three dimensions. Standard statistical packages, such as SPSS, fit a line to the plot for the two variable case and the degree of spread of the real values around the line can be inspected. The correlation coefficient is a measure of the degree to which the real values of Y correspond to those predicted by the regression equation.

Logistic regression is a robust technique in which the dependent variable can be categorical or ordinal. The independent variables can be at any level of measurement and at different levels of measurement. Logistic regression can handle nonlinear relationships and gives us an indication of the likelihood of the dependent variable having a particular value.

Evaluation

Traditional regression analysis requires that a series of demanding conditions be met by the data, especially when the data comes from a sample. However, the biggest drawback is that traditional regression procedures assume that the relationships among variables are linear. Linear relationships are not always, indeed perhaps not often, present in the social world. The detection of interaction, of the relationships among variables depending on the specific values of those variables, and changing as those values change, is an indication of nonlinearity. Logistic regression makes fewer assumptions and can cope with nonlinear relationships because it is essentially a predictive tool rather than an analytical method of establishing causal models.

David Byrne

Associated Concepts: causal model, causality, correlation, discriminant function analysis, econometrics, forecasting, general linear model, log-linear analysis, multivariate analysis, prediction

Key Readings

Byrne, D. S. (2002) *Interpreting Quantitative Data*. London: Sage.

Menard, S. (2001) *Applied Logistic Regression Analysis*. London: Sage.

Schroeder, L. D., Sjoquist, D. L. and Stephan, P. E. (1986) *Understanding Regression Analysis*. London: Sage.

RELATIVISM

Definition

There is considerable variety in the uses of the term relativism, but all endorse the view that no single absolute principle or concept is adequate to explain and understand events and states of affairs in all times and places, and that no single criterion holds for attributing value. By challenging the idea that universal statements can be established or that universal entities exist, relativism undermines truth, objectivity and the necessity of foundations. Nevertheless, there are two quite different interpretations of what this means. One case for relativism asserts that no

description can be true, no approach can be privileged and that no assessment of the value of human conduct is valid. Another case merely claims that all descriptions are equally true, all approaches have the same standing and all considerations of value are equally valid (Harré and Krausz, 1996).

Distinctive Features

These two interpretations, which can be described as the strident case and the reasonable case respectively, assume that what is said and acted upon in a particular location should be understood in its own terms and according to the standards of that location. On a note of caution, the strident case for relativism is more often deployed by those who argue against it, such as critical realists. Rather like the label totalitarian, there are few who claim to be strident relativists. Most who favour relativism simply seek to problematize, deconstruct or place in question the certainties and essences that generally serve as starting points for analysis. In this way, the canonized points of reference such as rationality, instrumental or self-interested actions, cognitive processes and various conceptions of agency are seen as topics for research rather than the unquestioned conceptual resources of social scientists.

Sometimes relativism is seen as associated with social constructionism, especially the claim that both 'the natural' and 'the social' (or for that matter 'appearance' and 'reality') are linguistic concepts or discursive constructs. A strident case would claim that all categories and terms are discursively constituted and that 'the real' or 'the deep' do not exist independently of the way we construct them; in short, that they are just convenient fictions for those keen to believe in their existence. The reasonable case for relativism would simply state that since we can only ever consider the existence of 'the real' through a specific discourse and that the way human beings have viewed reality has undergone significant changes then we should not place too much faith in the currently fashionable forms of imagining reality. As Foucault argued, how can we have a history of truth if truth has its own history (see Smith, 1998). Discourses are texts or writing that can be seen as sets of signifying practices and systems of representation in order to constitute a 'reality' to provide the conditions within which subjects experience the world (bearing in mind that the conceptions of knowing subjects and objects of analysis are themselves discursive categories rather than independent of the accepted procedures for knowing about the world).

Relativism is often linked to Thomas Kuhn's account of the scientific revolutions that take place as one paradigm replaces another. In this historical narrative of the sudden shifts between long periods of puzzle-solving normal science (in which Kuhn was in fact much more interested) and the point at which a radically new account of reality came into existence has often been described as akin to a 'Gestalt shift' or religious conversion experience. Each paradigm has its own internalized standards as to what knowledge is legitimate. According to Kuhn, paradigms are incommensurable, that is, it is impossible to use the criteria of one paradigm to judge the adequacy or truthfulness of another. Paradigms are thus mutually exclusive and inhabitants of different paradigms can be said to be living in 'different worlds' (Kuhn, 1970). Cultural relativism raises similar questions. If we use the standards established in one's own culture to make a judgement as to the adequacy of the values and practices of another, then the likely outcome is to infer the superiority of one's own culture and the inferiority of other cultures. By privileging the taken-for-granted assumptions of what is considered to be true, good and beautiful in a specific society, so that these become the measure of value, one falls into the trap of ethnocentrism.

Another kind of relativism was developed by the philosopher Paul Feyerabend, though it must be added that at times in his life he sought to establish a single criterion for comparing incompatible theories and research programmes. In addition, Feyerabend worried that relativism encouraged too great a leniency in assessing the significance of theoretical and empirical tests, weakening the scientific method. Feyerabend's contribution is his description of the accidental, messy and discontinuous character of the history of science and the problems of methodological monism (the idea that one scientific method fits all cases). In its place, he proposes the *principle of proliferation* (the 'anything goes' approach), whereby a range of different theories and research programmes (with different assumptions about the world and appropriate procedures for studying it) co-exist in order to generate new knowledge. Stung by criticisms that this led to an inability to make judgements on events such as the holocaust (Gellner, 1979), he replied that his work, far from being relativist, actually contained a normative project for methodological pluralism. He saw this as a means of defending the freedom of the individual against the homogenization of opinion that characterized modern science. Sociologists of science have similarly demonstrated how epistemologies such as falsificationism are idealized reconstructions that have very little to do with logics-in-use – what scientists actually do.

Relativism has been taken to be relevant in three distinctive areas concerned with kinds of human judgement – epistemology (as with Feyerabend), ethics and aesthetics. The reasonable case for relativism draws our attention to tacit assumptions social researchers hold regarding what is true, good and beautiful as they engage in research. It also alerts us to how easy it is to assert that the greatest benefit for the greatest number can be achieved by using scientific procedures for establishing the maximum benefits at minimum costs. In social research where utilitarian assumptions are embedded there is a constant play between the good and the true. Reasonable relativism can be seen in phenomenological social science which recognizes how knowledge is situated in the plausibility structures that exist in specific social contexts. This means that the researcher should seek to find ways of drawing upon the first order constructs of everyday life in constructing their own second order constructs and reap the benefit of being intelligible to the people being studied – *the postulate of adequacy* (Schütz, 1953).

Evaluation

Critics of relativism argue that without assumptions that provide for absolute or more specifically universal judgement, this undermines the possibility of developing a common language for describing the world, a common theoretical and conceptual systems for analysing and evaluating social relations and a common basis for moral and aesthetic judgements. For defenders of the intellectual heritage of Western civilization, relativism challenges the values and assumptions that have served well for generations. This is often associated with the claim that relativism prevents us from possessing a moral compass, leaving us in a position where it is impossible to make judgements as to the right course of action or the good outcome on crucial matters such as genetic modification or events such as genocide. For critics of existing social relations, such as Marxists, relativism undermines the belief that alternative forms of rationality and morality can be forged to replace the exploitative and oppressive social structures; that relativism destroys the possibility of social change and removes all hope from politics. All such critics level their charges at the strident case for relativism and not the reasonable case. The difficulty of contrasting universal judgement with judgements that are relative to a time and place is that even the statement that 'all forms of knowledge are situated' is still a kind of universal statement.

Mark J. Smith

Associated Concepts: causality, empiricism, epistemology, ontology, realism.

Key Readings

Gellner, E. (1979) *Spectacles and Predicaments*. Cambridge: Cambridge University Press.
Harré, R. and Krausz, M. (1996) *Varieties of Relativism*. Oxford: Blackwell.

Kuhn, T. ([1962] 1970) *The Structure of Scientific Revolutions*, 2nd edn. Chicago: University of Chicago Press.
Schütz, A. (1953) 'Common-sense and scientific interpretation of human action', *Philosophy and Phenomenological Research*, XIV (1): 1–38.
Smith, M. J. (1998) *Social Science in Question: Towards a Postdisciplinary Framework*. London: Sage.

RELIABILITY

Definition

The extent to which a measuring instrument, for example a test to measure intelligence, gives consistent results.

Distinctive Features

There are three broad ways of assessing reliability. First, test–retest reliability involves administering the same test to the same set of respondents but on different occasions. Correlation coefficients are calculated to compare the different data sets. The higher the coefficient the more reliable the measuring instrument. Values of 0.7 are considered good. The problem with test–retest reliability is that individuals may become familiar with items and simply answer on the basis of their memory of what they answered on the previous occasion.

A second type is alternate-form reliability, which involves using differently worded items to measure the same variable. Items are either administered to the same sample at different points in time or to two sub-samples at the same point in time (known as the split halves method). Correlation coefficients are calculated to compare the two data sets and measure reliability. Where the split halves method is used it is important to ensure that the two sub-samples are as similar as possible. Whichever method is used the two tests should measure the same concept despite wording changes.

Third, internal consistency reliability involves using groups of items (as opposed to a single item) to measure different aspects of the same concept. Internal consistency is measured by Cronbach's alpha, which is a measure of how well the different items complement each other in measuring the same concept and form a single scale.

Evaluation

Reliability assessments are essential, especially in scaling, but they are not sufficient in themselves. It is also vital to assess validity of measurement, that is, assessing the extent to which a scale measures what it purports to. A scale that is reliable but measures the wrong thing is not particularly helpful.

Victor Jupp

Associated Concepts: composite measurement, correlation, indicator, measurement, multiple indicators, scaling, social indicators, validity of measurement

Key Readings

Smith, H. W. (1975) *Strategies of Social Research: The Methodological Imagination.* Englewood Cliffs, NJ: Prentice Hall.

Torgeson, W. S. (1958) *Theory and Methods of Scaling.* New York: Wiley.

REPERTORY GRID TECHNIQUE

Definition

A technique that can be used to elicit the personal constructs that, it is argued, individuals use to interpret the social world and to form judgements about appropriate forms of action. For this reason it is known as an elicitation technique.

Distinctive Features

Repertory grids were developed in the 1950s by the American social psychologist George Kelly. His landmark publication was *The Psychology of Personal Constructs*, which appeared in 1955. His work was part of a broad theoretical and research agenda which was, and still is, concerned with the ways in which people make sense of their worlds. In theoretical terms it can be described as constructionist and in methodological terms it tends towards qualitative research strategies. As such, Kelly was against psychological behaviourism, determinism and explanations in terms of causality. Instead, he emphasized the ways in which individuals are creatively engaged in giving meaning to events, situations and other people. They do this via a personal construct system which is not fixed; rather it constantly undergoes 'testing' and modification as new events, situations and people are encountered. Kelly's theoretical ideas included 'constructive alternativism', that is, different individuals may create different and alternative construct systems in relation to the same social situations.

The repertory grid technique was developed to elicit an individual's personal construct system at any given point in time. The grid is assumed to comprise two components: first, *elements* to which individuals relate, for example situations, objects and other individuals; second, *constructs*, which are ways of describing such elements. The personal construct system comprises the array of constructs in relation to elements. Some constructs are peripheral and relatively unimportant whereas others are core, being central to the individual's value system. Each construct is assumed to have opposite poles because Kelly believed that we all make sense of the world by looking for likenesses and differences. So, for example, we might experience and describe situations as more or less 'supportive' or 'threatening'.

The specific application of repertory grids typically involves a process of 'triad elicitation' whereby an individual is asked to consider elements in groups of three drawn from a larger pool. He or she is asked to describe what features (i.e. constructs) make two of these similar to each other and different from the third. For example, an individual may be presented with pen portraits of three occupations (for example, a joiner, a plumber and a company director) in order to elicit constructs relating to social class. Once the first bipolar construct (say, income) has been identified the individual is asked to rate the three occupations on that construct. Then the process of eliciting a second construct proceeds by presenting another triad of occupations. The process continues until the respondent cannot offer any further ways of distinguishing between elements. This can be described as the point of theoretical saturation. Sometimes they are asked to offer new ways of distinguishing elements or offer further constructs, without going through triad elicitation, in order to ensure that theoretical saturation has indeed been reached.

The outcome of the process is a completed grid that describes the individual's personal construct system and comprises a set of interrelated bipolar constructs on which each element is assigned a rating. Computer software packages have been developed to facilitate detailed analyses of patterns between constructs and elements.

Evaluation

The repertory grid is not an 'off the peg' tool, as is usually the case with attitude scales or personality tests. It does have a set of procedures, for example triad elicitation, but it is also a flexible methodology which fits with Kelly's theoretical viewpoint that personal constructs are actively developed and revised.

The repertory grid was originally developed for use with individual clients in a clinical and therapeutic setting and in this sense was an idiographic rather than nomothetic tool. However, Kelly was always of the belief that there could be a sharing of meanings and this has led to the use of repertory grids with a small number of individuals as an exploratory tool and a preliminary to the development of more formal scales that can be administered to much larger samples of people. For example, grids can be a forerunner to the development of semantic differential scales for examining how criminal justice personnel differentiate between ethnic groups and with what consequences.

In short, repertory grid techniques are fruitful and versatile tools of social research which can embrace the micro and the macro, the idiographic and the nomothetic, the qualitative and the quantitative.

Those who are critical of repertory grid and other techniques would argue that constructs are not context-free and also that, although it is claimed that the respondents' own constructs are accessed, the research situation is artificial and they might be putting forward 'official' rather than their own constructs.

Victor Jupp

Associated Concepts: constructionism, exploratory research, idiographic, nomothetic, qualitative research, scaling, summated rating scale

Key Readings

Fransella, F. (1995) *George Kelly.* London: Sage.
Fransella, F. and Bannister, D. (1977) *A Manual for Repertory Grid Technique.* London: Academic Press.
Kelly, G. A. ([1955] 1991) *The Psychology of Personal Constructs,* 2 vols. London: Routledge.

RESEARCH BARGAIN

Definition

The agreement made between a researcher and a research participant such as a gatekeeper or respondent regarding what the participant can expect from the researcher in return for their cooperation with the research.

Distinctive Features

Within social research, research bargains are made throughout the research process between researchers and participants to help ensure cooperation. They include bargains reached with gatekeepers at the start of the research in return for enabling access, as well as those made with respondents to secure their cooperation when collecting data, such as contributing to a focus group, responding to interview questions or completing a questionnaire.

Although the bargain made by a researcher with a gatekeeper is likely to outline the entire research process, it provides the gatekeeper with an opportunity to ensure that, in return for granting access, she or he receives something useful from the research. This may take a variety of forms, including an opportunity to influence the research so that it incorporates issues that she or he believes are pertinent, preferential access to the research findings, and in extreme cases, the right of veto. Whilst ethical considerations and, in particular, issues relating to anonymity and confidentiality normally form part of the research bargain with the gatekeeper, they tend to take on greater prominence in the bargains made with individual respondents. Such respondents usually agree to participate through a belief that the research will not cause them harm and is of value. Although often participants do not expect payment, this does not preclude research bargains containing some form of incentive for the respondent to take part in the research. These include donations to charity, payment or some form of gift.

Evaluation

Increasingly within social research, research bargains are being formalized as part of research governance through the use of agreed research proposals and consent forms. This means that research bargains are less likely to be either implicit or vague than was the case a few years ago.

Research bargains require careful thought as, although research bargains can help in securing research participants' cooperation, they may place restrictions on the researcher. For this reason some researchers argue that, other than for ethical considerations, research bargains need to be treated with caution. Although it is difficult for a researcher to know in advance what issues will arise during the research, it is important to establish the extent to which the proposed research can be amended to agree a research bargain. If the changes required interfere too much with that which is deemed essential for the research, then the researcher may consider it wrong to proceed (Horwood and Moon, 2003).

Mark N. K. Saunders

Associated Concepts: access, confidentiality, ethics, gatekeeper, informed consent, organizational research

Key Readings

Bryman, A. (2001) *Social Research Methods.* Oxford: Oxford University Press.
Horwood, J. and Moon, G. (2003) 'Accessing the research setting: the politics of research and the limits to enquiry', *Area*, 35 (1): 106–9.

RESEARCH DESIGN

Definition

A design or strategy that justifies the logic, structure and the principles of the research methodology and methods and how these relate to the research questions, hypothesis or proposition.

Distinctive Features

There are several reasons for devising a research design. First, an effective research design will demonstrate that the research will produce valid and credible conclusions that flow logically from the evidence generated. Second, it sets out the research strategy for the benefit of the audience, readership, funders, gatekeepers and those researched. Third, the process of devising it not only ensures that the research will be of value in terms of intellectual credibility, external accountability, coherence and rigour, but that it becomes a useful plan or schedule for the researcher.

Specific elements of an effective research design cannot be prescribed and there is no standard format, however some key components are likely to include the following. First, a clear, researchable set of questions or hypothesis. This aspect of the research design is perhaps most fundamental and the question of *what* is to be done will require justification in terms of *why* it is being done and a carefully planned strategy of *how* it will be carried out. Second, the research design will show how the research questions will be aligned to the relevant data sources and research methods, the selection of which should be clearly justified taking account of issues surrounding validity and representative methods of sampling, reliability and generalizability, comparative issues, ethical considerations (consent, anonymity, confidentiality) and practicalities (such as resources, access and skills). Third, in addition to selecting and justifying the data collection methods, specifying the sampling criteria and timing of the research, the research design should identify how data processing will operate and how the analysis will be conducted.

Evaluation

To design an effective research project requires skill. In principle it is straightforward to address the questions of *what* is being researched and to delineate *why* and *how* the research will be effected. In practice, these are often much bigger questions than they might at first appear. For example, fully addressing the fundamental question of *what* the topic is, might include a consideration of ontological and epistemological positions for some researchers. Whilst *how* research is executed is often a complex process involving many decision-making stages where choices are made under different and often difficult conditions and within different and perhaps changing constraints. In reality the research design will often require flexibility. Selecting the best method for any research will usually involve compromise or a delicate balance or blend of intellectual and practical concerns where, for example, precision may be tempered by factors such as feasibility due to cost or other restrictions.

Although many of the hallmarks of an effective research design outlined above apply to both qualitative and quantitative research projects, there has been resistance, in particular from the qualitative research tradition, to the need for a precise research design. Some feel that it is not possible or desirable to have a rigid research design as this militates against the fundamental questions or problems they are researching and against the need for continuous reformulation of research questions and also for the process of exploration.

Pamela Davies

Associated Concepts: exploratory research, gatekeeper, intellectual craftsmanship, literature review, messy research, methodology, reliability, validity

Key Readings

Jupp, V., Davies, P. and Francis, P. (eds) (2000) *Doing Criminological Research*. London: Sage. chs 1 and 2.

Mason, J. (1997) *Qualitative Researching*. London: Sage.

Sapsford, R. and Jupp, V. (eds) (1996) *Data Collection and Analysis*. London: Sage.

RESEARCH PROBLEMS

Definition

A diverse range of pitfalls encountered during the research process. These can include getting started, framing general and specific research questions, and discovering that one's data do not address the research questions that have been set.

Distinctive Features

Perhaps one of the most difficult tasks that students face in large research projects, particularly dissertations, is that of getting started. The student may have already taken the decision to look at a general research area, but then struggle to narrow this down to some manageable size. Hence, one of the main failings of undergraduate dissertations is that the student has been unable to specify precisely the main focus of his or her particular dissertation. Instead of analysing the internal dynamics of the Communist Party of East Germany in 1989, in effect trying to evaluate how this precipitated the fall of the Berlin Wall in that year, a poor dissertation by contrast may study nothing more specific than the demise of euro-Communism in 1989. The former project may be manageable; the latter would, at best, offer a superficial overview of the subject matter.

The process of getting started need not be too daunting, however. Provided that the student tries to be as systematic as possible, honing down a research proposal can be greatly simplified. As Kenneth Punch (2001) argues, research problems may be ameliorated by following an inductive–deductive hierarchy. Following Punch's model, we could begin at the broadest possible degree (the research area) by choosing a very broad research theme. This may be the fall of euro-Communism in 1989, or youth suicide. At this level, any project would be too broad and general. We would then need to narrow down our focus, effectively choosing certain issues to study, whilst ignoring others. This can be achieved by constructing a research topic. Using the latter example, this could be either suicide rates among young groups (a quantitative approach) or youth culture and the meaning of suicide (which would entail a qualitative strategy). Focusing down again, the student would then frame one or several general research questions, for example, what is the relationship between family background and the incidence of youth suicide? Finally, specific research questions are constructed, which may include: what is the relationship between family

income and the incidence of youth suicide? Or, what is the relationship between parental break-up and the incidence of youth suicide? Because the subject matter has been focused down to such a degree, data collection questions will become easier to generate. This is important because the data collection questions are the most specific questions the researcher addresses. At this stage, one could conduct a quantitative study into divorce and suicide rates, or conduct interviews with bereaved parents, although ethical and sensitive interviewing techniques would need to be considered in the latter case.

Punch's framework is elegant because it encourages the student to systematically hone what may be a very abstract idea down into a project that would be manageable. Nevertheless, research problems do not end there. As Jupp (2000) reminds us, the conclusions of research will be credible and plausible only to the extent to which the questions and problems they address are clearly formulated and expressed and followed through in a consistent manner during the inquiry. In effect, this refers to data collected from empirical research not matching the original research questions. Another of the common failings of students writing dissertations is that although they may have collected a wide range of empirical material, they have not been able to link it back to the original objectives of their thesis.

On such occasions, it may be necessary to revise completely, or in part, the original research design. Specifically, if empirical data indicated that rates of parental divorce had no influence on youngsters taking their own life, and that suicide among the young was caused by drug abuse, then the original general and specific research questions would need to reflect this in some way. Tempting as it may be, a researcher should avoid writing a dissertation that concentrates on one particular area, only to completely disregard this area in his or her conclusion. Factors that suddenly appear in the conclusion as being the most important issue in youth suicide, for example, and that have not been discussed elsewhere in the work, tend to weaken the overall argument of the author. Finally, the researcher should be aware that not all interviews may be of equal importance. Some interviewees give responses that are irrelevant to the research on hand. At the time of writing up, the author should always filter out data that are not relevant to the research questions.

Evaluation

Although the student or researcher may be more interested in beginning their research as soon as possible, they should not underestimate the benefits of good research design. Being careful to prioritize and narrow down one's research can ultimately save a great deal of time and effort, and thereby eliminate many research problems. Yet even when one follows a methodical research design, it is often the case that research problems will arise. The author should therefore be aware that he or she may need to alter their research questions, and may have to prune the data that he or she may have collected. In sum, research problems can be tackled by continually revising and updating one's research design.

Craig McLean

Associated Concepts: disastrous research, exploratory research, hypothesis, research design

Key Readings

Jupp, V. (2000) 'Formulating research problems', in V. Jupp, P. Davies and P. Francis (eds), *Doing Criminological Research*. London: Sage. pp. 13–28.
Punch, K. F. (2001) *Developing Effective Research Proposals*. London: Sage.

RETROSPECTIVE STUDY

Definition

A study that involves collecting data about past events. This design is mainly employed to measure and understand change and to include a time dimension to the data that can be used to identify causal factors contributing to any observed change. The capacity of a retrospective study to adequately detect change and ascertain causes depends on how well the investigator can reconstruct the past from the vantage point of the present.

Distinctive Features

The main purpose for collecting retrospective data is that such data provide a means of measuring change for either descriptive or explanatory purposes. Retrospective studies rely on recalling information about the past but vary in the extent to which they rely on such recall. An oral history, for example, is totally reliant on people recalling the past. Other retrospective studies involve collecting information about the past and comparing that with contemporary information collected from the same cases. An example of such a study might be one in which parents are asked to describe their current marital satisfaction, say, five years after having children and then to recall their level of marital satisfaction just before they had children. More often than not, retrospective information is collected as part of a study that collects contemporary data or even as part of the first phase of a longer-term prospective study.

Many studies that are primarily cross-sectional (that is, collect data about the present) contain some retrospective questions to detect individual change. For example, respondents are often asked about parental occupation when they were 14 years old, or to recall how often they attended church when they were 14. These retrospective measures are then compared with contemporary circumstances to construct measures of the individual's social mobility or religious change.

Other studies collect information that enable the study of change at the aggregate level. For example, some surveys ask about relationship histories that can provide insight into aggregate change over time. For example, respondents may be asked to recall when they first married and then if they lived with their partner before they married. This enables the investigator to determine whether the person's first marriage was a direct marriage (no premarital cohabitation) or an indirect marriage (included premarital cohabitation with the partner). By asking these questions of a range of age groups it is possible to identify people who entered marriages directly and indirectly in, say, the early 1970s, the late 1990s or some time in between. Using retrospective data it is possible by collecting data at just one time point to plot changes in marriage patterns.

Retrospective studies can be distinguished from cross-sectional and prospective designs. Prospective studies collect information about the present time and then track cases *forward* in time and collect new, contemporary information at each time point to construct measures of change. In the pure form, a cross-sectional study collects information only about the present and cannot construct measures of change at all.

Evaluation

The main reason advanced for collecting retrospective information is that it provides a quick and efficient way of obtaining measures of change and of constructing life histories and avoids the expense and time of waiting for change to occur. Furthermore, where data about past patterns simply were not collected at the time (for example, levels of premarital cohabitation), there is little alternative to using retrospective data to explore patterns of change.

Collecting information about significant past events can be quite reliable. For example, the date when a person first married, the date when they divorced or the date of birth of children can be reliably collected – especially from women. Major changes in jobs can be collected with a good degree of accuracy. As such, retrospective designs can be quite useful in constructing life histories about particular types of past events.

However, there are serious concerns about the ability of retrospective methods to reliably collect information about subjective states and even about less significant events and more objective information. To use retrospective methods to learn about feelings at some earlier time or to reliably recall past opinions is fraught with dangers. The most obvious problem is that of faulty memory. Faulty memory has two elements. People may simply misremember. For example, to ask a person how much they earned five years ago risks people simply inaccurately recalling their level of income. The other element is that of 'telescoping' and 'reverse telescoping'. What people recall as occurring five years ago may have been just two years ago or may have been seven years ago.

A further difficulty with recalling the past, especially when recalling more subjective states, is the tendency for people to reconstruct the past in the light of present circumstances. For example, retrospective studies of voting behaviour demonstrate that the way people recall their vote overestimates the extent to which people voted for the winning party. A related shortcoming of retrospective studies can be that of selective recall. For example, the recollection of the quality of a marriage after a divorce will often be different from that provided before the divorce. Certain characteristics will be remembered and seen as significant while others will be forgotten or re-interpreted.

Retrospective studies have a valuable role to play in social research. They are best suited to the construction of sequences of significant events and in that respect can provide valuable insights into the sequence of events in individual lives or into historical changes at the aggregate level. However, considerable care should be taken in using retrospective designs for studying subjective states and less memorable events.

David de Vaus

Associated Concepts: causality, cross-sectional surveys, life history interviewing, longitudinal study, panel study, prospective study, sampling, social survey

Key Readings

Dex, S. (1995) 'The reliability of recall data: a literature review', *Bulletin de Methodologie Sociologique*, 49: 58–89.

Freedman, D. S., Thornton, A., Camburn, D., Alwin, D. and Young-de Marco, L. (1988) 'A life history calender: a technique for collecting retrospective data', *Sociological Methodology*, 18: 37–68.

Scott, J. and Alwin, D. (1998) 'Retrospective versus prospective measurement of life histories in longitudinal research', in J. Z. Giele and G. H. Elder (eds), *Methods of Life Course Research: Qualitative and Quantitative Approaches*. Thousand Oaks, CA: Sage. pp. 98–127.

RISK RESEARCH

See Prediction

S

SAMPLING

Definition

Techniques used to select groups from a wider population. This is done because it is not usually possible to include whole populations in research, for example as a result of time or financial constraints. Whom we study and how we choose to study them is linked to the theoretical context of the research and the hypotheses or aims. Sampling theory is therefore based on the assumption that inferences can be made, or conclusions drawn about the population from which the sample is taken. Sampling is an important element in research planning and design.

Distinctive Features

In sampling, the term 'population' has a very specific meaning and refers to the group of people or other unit of analysis which is the focus of the study. The population as defined will depend upon the research aims and theoretical context.

The sampling frame may be defined as the listing of all units in the working population from which the sample will be selected. For example, if we were going to undertake a survey of young people's experiences of bullying, we could decide to define the working population as all young people between the ages of 12 and 15 attending schools in a particular city. The schools would have lists of addresses of registered pupils, although parental permission would be needed before they could be made available. These lists would comprise the sampling frame. A sampling frame can be any listing, for example, members of an organization, addresses (the post office address file) or an electoral register.

The sampling unit is the unit of study. Whilst a unit is often an individual, it could also be groups of people. Advertisements, newspapers or television programmes can also be sampling units, on which content or other forms of textual analysis could be undertaken. The sample may be defined as the segment of the population that is selected for the research.

Random or probability sampling refers to an approach where each element of the population has an equal and known chance of being selected for inclusion in the sample. Non-random or non-probability sampling is an umbrella term that includes all forms of sampling that do not adhere to probability methods.

Evaluation

It is generally accepted that sample representativeness is an important issue in social research. If the views expressed by the sample upon which research findings are based do not reflect the views of the 'population', the validity of the findings might be questioned. This is the issue of generalizability or external validity. Some researchers do argue, however, that this should not necessarily be the aim of sample selection in qualitative research (Silverman, 1997), where the uniqueness of respondents' experiences and the depth of data provided are more important. The following issues are identified as important in the literature on sample design (the caveat regarding qualitative research should be borne in mind).

Sample response rates are important in survey research. Non-response introduces error or bias. Non-response may relate to an entire survey or to particular items (item non-response). Non-response is important because it affects the amount of data collected and the comprehensiveness of the data, in relation to the sample. It can also be a source of bias in the evidence collected, for example when certain types of people may be less likely to respond than others. This is not solely a sampling problem and response rates can be affected by other factors such as the method of data collection. Statistical methods may be used to correct for non-response.

Sample size is an important issue in random sampling, as this approach is based upon mathematical concepts such as probability theory and upon inferential statistics. Some statistical calculations can only be performed on random samples and some require a minimum sample, size. Generally, larger samples provide more accurate findings in quantitative research.

Julia Davidson

Associated Concepts: bias, cluster sampling, inferential statistics, non-probability (non-random) sampling, opportunity sampling, panel study, probability (random) sampling, quota sampling, snowball sampling, social survey

Key Readings

Bryman, A. (2001) *Social Research Methods.* Oxford: Oxford University Press.

May, T. (2001) *Social Research: Issues, Methods and Process,* 3rd edn. Milton Keynes: Open University Press.

Sapsford, R. and Jupp, V. (eds) (1996) *Data Collection and Analysis.* London: Sage.

Silverman, D. (ed.) (1997) *Qualitative Research: Theory, Method and Practice.* London: Sage.

de Vaus, D. A. (1996) *Surveys in Social Research,* 4th edn. London: UCL Press.

SCALING

Definition

Methods used by researchers to quantify human psychological responses to stimuli. Many scaling methods have been developed to capture feelings, judgements, opinions and perceptions of stimuli. From such procedures, one can assess many human attributes, including attitudes, emotions, perceptions and personality. They can also be used to capture human judgements, such as in the evaluation of performance of athletes in Olympic competition or employees in the workplace.

Distinctive Features

Every scaling procedure consists of two components – stimuli and a response method. The stimuli can be actual objects, but typically they are written words or phrases that describe the stimuli or situation. Responses can be spoken or written using a structured procedure. Part of that procedure is the way in which the responses are quantified. Responses are made on a specified dimension, such as evaluation or liking. For example, a researcher might wish to assess how much voters like each candidate running for a particular office in an election. A scaling method could provide a score for each candidate that reflects how much voters like him or her.

Scaling methods were developed to assess human responses at ordinal or ratio levels of measurement. However, although in theory these methods can achieve this goal, it is quite difficult to demonstrate measurement level. Thus, measurement level with scaling methods is debatable, as many researchers feel only ordinal measurement is achieved. Nevertheless, these methods are widely used in human assessment.

One of the simplest methods is *paired comparisons.* With this method stimuli are presented in pairs, and a response dimension is defined. People are asked to indicate which stimulus in each pair is higher or lower on the dimension of interest. For example, they can be asked to indicate which of two candidates they like best. Mathematical procedures can be used to translate the pattern of responses into scores for the stimuli. The paired comparison method is one of the easiest for people to use, but unless there are very few stimuli the number of comparisons is too large for most applications.

The *rank order method* is a good alternative to paired comparisons when there are many stimuli. With this method respondents are asked to place the stimuli in order along the defined dimension. For example, respondents might list candidates in order from least to most liked. Mathematical procedures can be used to derive scores for each candidate across the respondents. Scores with this procedure are usually quite similar to those from the paired comparison method. However, it is somewhat more difficult for respondents to rank order stimuli than paired comparisons.

Direct magnitude estimation is a method in which respondents are asked to provide a score on a dimension for each stimulus. This can be done most easily by having people choose a number from 1 to 100, where 1 represents the lowest score on the dimension and 100 the highest. Respondents could be asked, for example, to choose a number for each candidate. Another variation is to use a line to represent the dimension of interest. The extremes of the dimension are indicated, for example, 'Dislike very much' and 'Like very much'. The respondent is asked to make a mark representing his or her position on the dimension in question. A separate line can be used for each stimulus or one line can be used for all stimuli. Direct magnitude estimation has not been widely used, in part because it is not clear that people are able to provide the precision of judgement necessary.

Rating scales ask people to select one response choice from several that are ordered along a dimension. The choices are defined by an anchor, or statement that describes its position on the dimension. For example, for assessing liking of election candidates the anchors might be, 'Dislike very much', 'Dislike slightly', 'Like slightly' and 'Like very much'. Respondents give a rating for each candidate. Each stimulus is termed an item. This method is the most widely used, perhaps because of its

ease in quantifying responses. The response choices are numbered consecutively from lowest to highest, and overall stimulus values are computed as the mean of all respondent scores. It is also used to provide individual respondent scores for each stimulus as opposed to overall stimulus scores across all people.

The dimension underlying the rating scale can be almost anything, but most use one of a very small number of possible options. Perhaps the most popular is agreement. Respondents indicate how much they agree or disagree which each item, (for example, 'Disagree very much', 'Disagree slightly', 'Agree slightly', 'Agree very much'). Other popular dimensions are evaluation (for example, 'Poor', 'Fair', 'Good', 'Excellent'), frequency (for example, 'Never', 'Seldom', 'Frequently', 'Often'), and liking (see prior paragraph for example).

Hundreds of instruments to assess specific constructs have been developed using scaling methods. Most include multiple items to assess each construct of interest, and yield individual scores for each respondent. Such scales are called summated rating scales when they use the rating scale format for responses.

Evaluation

The scaling procedures mentioned so far have involved single dimensions on which stimuli are scaled, for example, liking. Stimuli are ordered along the single continuum from least to most liked. It is possible, however, to use more complex scaling methods in which multiple dimensions are dealt with simultaneously. Multidimensional scaling procedures allow one to identify two or more dimensions on which stimuli can differ. Graphical representations of the stimulus positions in multidimensional space can help interpret the ways in which individual stimuli differ from one another. These procedures are quite complex, requiring considerable statistical sophistication to use.

Paul E. Spector

Associate Concepts: composite measurement, indicator, Likert scale, semantic differential scale technique, summated rating scale, Thurstone scale, validity of measurement

Key Readings

Guilford, J. P. (1954) *Psychometric Methods*, 2nd edn. New York: McGraw–Hill.
Torgerson, W. S. (1958) *Theory and Methods of Scaling*. New York: Wiley.

SECONDARY ANALYSIS

Definition

The further analysis of an existing data set with the aim of addressing a research question distinct from that for which the data set was originally collected, and generating novel interpretations and conclusions.

Distinctive Features

The use of secondary analysis with large-scale survey data, using statistical analysis techniques, is most common, and has been well documented. A researcher may re-analyse a data set that he or she has collected earlier, or may use a data set collected by another researcher, or team of researchers. The technique can be distinguished from meta-analysis, which attempts to summarize the already interpreted results of a number of primary research studies; in contrast, secondary analysis attempts to re-interpret the original data set in relation to a new research question.

The first stage of secondary analysis is to obtain a suitable data set. Data sets are available from databases, which contain information about the context (time of collection, sampling techniques employed and so on) of each data set they offer. The data sets available are of high quality, often the result of years of data collection by a team of highly qualified experts. The main UK database is the UK National Data Archive, housed at Essex University (www.data-archive.ac.uk). Most developed countries have an equivalent national database. Both government data sets, and those gathered

by academics and social scientists are important resources for secondary analysis. Data sets can be continuous – that is, gathered on a number of occasions over a period of time – or ad hoc – carried out just once in response to a specific research request (Procter, 1993). An important example of a continuous data set is the UK government's General Household Survey (GHS), carried out every year since 1971. An example of an ad hoc survey is the Women and Employment survey carried out in 1984 by the UK government's Office of Population Censuses and Surveys (OPCS). Other data sets have been generated precisely for the purpose of providing a secondary analysis resource; an example is the General Social Survey collected by US academics at the National Research Centre at Chicago. While traditionally secondary analysis has been more widely used with quantitative data sets, the analysis of qualitative data sets has recently received increasing attention. A collection of qualitative data sets – 'Qualidata' – is now available at the UK data archive at Essex (www.qualidata.essex.ac.uk).

Having accessed a suitable data set the next step is to prepare this for re-analysis, which may involve recoding the original variables (which can be done using a statistical software package such as SPSS). Stewart (1984) has outlined a number of questions that should be answered prior to engaging in secondary analysis, including: What was the purpose of the original research? What sampling procedure was used? What information was collected? Is the original data set valid and reliable?

Evaluation

Secondary analysis is an important technique for certain types of research, in particular research requiring large-scale and longitudinal data sets. Using data that have been collected by a specialist team of experts not only maximizes data quality, but also proves efficient in terms of time and cost. Large data sets often contain a wealth of information that is not exhausted in relation to one particular research question. Secondary analysis both facilitates research where the data required would be too costly and time-consuming for the researcher to collect themselves, and can enable access to special populations due to the sheer size of the data sets often available (Procter, 1993). Longitudinal studies are also facilitated through access to continuous data sets such as the GHS. Instead of having to plan the collection of a primary data, the secondary analyst is freed up to focus on analysis and interpretation.

A number of drawbacks emerge when evaluating secondary analysis, however. The researcher is not able to make decisions concerning the way the data is collected, and therefore must be careful to assess the original data set on a number of key aspects (such as those identified by Stewart, 1984) in order to decide whether it is suitable for the new research question. There is always the danger in secondary research of tailoring the research question to fit the data (Procter, 1993). Lack of contact with the primary researchers can be a problem if further questions emerge about the context of data collection which are not addressed in the annotations provided in the relevant database. This issue of context of the original data collection procedures may be especially important in the re-analysis of qualitative data sets; indeed, the question of whether it is possible for a secondary analyst to properly engage with qualitative data which they were not involved in collecting has been raised as an issue. The researcher engaging in secondary analysis must also be aware of ethical requirements, and the extent to which the original ethical procedures (such as obtaining informed consent) extend to the new analysis being carried out.

Claire Hewson

Associated Concepts: data, data archives, ethics, informed consent, meta-analysis, official statistics, primary research, qualitative data archives, SPSS, validity

Key Readings

Dale, A., Arber, S. and Procter, M. (1988) *Doing Secondary Analysis*. London: Unwin Hyman.

Hakim, C. (1982) *Secondary Analysis in Social Research: A Guide to Data Sources and Methods with Examples*. London: Allen and Unwin.

Procter, M. (1993) 'Analysing other researchers' data', in N. Gilbert (ed.), *Researching Social Life*. London: Sage. pp. 255–69.

Stewart, D. W. (1984) *Secondary Research: Information Sources and Methods*. Beverly Hills, CA: Sage.

SELF-REPORT STUDY

Definition

A study in which respondents report their own behaviour. For example, in self-report studies of criminal behaviour, respondents are asked to declare if they have committed criminal offences. Self-report studies are often done for comparison with official records.

Distinctive Features

A self-report study is used where the point of interest is in comparing official or organizational records with alternative measures of behaviour. Examples include research on physical and mental health, and voting behaviour. Self-report studies are particularly prominent in research on crime.

The validity of official criminal statistics is limited by omissions and bias; a self-report study offers the promise of data free of these problems. For example, respondents may be asked if they have committed offences during a set period (often the past 12 months) and, if they have, how often. Self-report studies are conducted using self-completion questionnaires or by interview (Jupp, 1996). The research instrument is usually a list of offences (and sometimes other behaviours). Many self-report studies are conducted on juveniles, both because delinquency is an assumed indicator of crime trends, and self-report studies of adults can prompt demands to disclose respondent identities to the authorities.

Empey and Erikson's (1966) landmark study suggested that over 90 per cent of delinquency went undetected. Males aged 15–17 were interviewed about 22 offence types. The offence was defined, the respondent asked if he had participated, and, if so, how often, and whether he had been detected, arrested and appeared in court. As a validity check it was noted that none of those with a court record concealed it.

The sample of 180 boys admitted to enormous numbers of offences, including 24,199 thefts and 9026 assaults. They also admitted numerous instances of 'defying authority' and under-age drinking. Note that the former is not a crime, and the latter only a crime because of the respondent's age; self-report studies have been criticized for including behaviours that are not illegal. Empey and Erikson's other notable finding was the large proportion who had committed offences. For example, 93 per cent reported committing petty theft and 59 per cent, a serious theft or robbery.

These were important findings as official statistics gave no hint of such widespread delinquency. Subsequent studies tested if these findings applied generally; a particular concern was the implication that class differences were exaggerated. After reviewing 40 self-report studies, Box (1980) concluded that working class juveniles were not disproportionately delinquent. But self-report methods also encountered methodological criticisms. Researchers remain divided between those who see self-report as flawed and those who feel it is reliable. It remains much-used in criminological and other research, particularly social aspects of health, for example, in AIDS research where respondents are asked to report 'risky' sexual behaviours.

Evaluation

Self-report methods rely on respondents' honesty. If they regard researchers with suspicion as agents of authority they may downplay their involvement. But they might also 'talk up' their involvement in an effort to impress. To assess this, several studies followed completion of the offence list by telling respondents they would now take a polygraph test and inviting them to change any responses before doing so. Few took the opportunity.

However, this cannot detect respondents who believe they are telling the truth but whose recall is faulty, a particular problem where recall periods are long or the number of offences committed is large. Another validity check is to compare results with other sources. For example, Gold (1966) disclosed results to informants like teachers who knew respondents, asking if the findings rang true, and estimated that up to 72 per cent were truthful. This still only controls concealment, not exaggeration, and is only as valid as informants' knowledge – after all, the method was devised to compensate the failings of other sources.

Non-response bias is also a threat, because refusers may be particularly active offenders. Sampling schoolchildren introduces lower-class and ethnic minority bias because of their higher drop-out and truancy rates (Kleck, 1982; Junger, 1989). Further, aggregating trivial behaviours with offences overstates the proportion involved in 'delinquency'; for example, Elliot and Ageton's (1980) otherwise sophisticated study included items like 'hitchhiked' and 'been loud, rowdy or unruly in a public place'.

Offending is not the only field where problems arise. Admitting involvement in socially disapproved behaviours is subject to cultural factors and can suggest false variance. Dohrenwend's (1964) study of mental illness in New York found that Puerto Ricans had a higher self-reported rate than Jewish-Americans, Irish-Americans or African-Americans. However, when Dohrenwend subjected the mental health inventory to a social desirability rating it emerged that Puerto Ricans regarded the items as less undesirable than did the other groups and were thus more willing to admit to them.

Once methodological, measurement and selection biases are accommodated there is considerable congruence between self-report and official statistics. Farrington's (1989) sample reported contacts with police accurately, and under 4 per cent who denied committing particular offences had actually been convicted of such offences. Some thus argue that official and self-report data are complementary and that researchers can have considerable confidence in truthful answers being given (Tarling, 1993).

Nigel G. Fielding

Associated Concepts: bias, indicator, interview, official statistics, social survey, triangulation, validity

Key Readings

Box, S. (1980) *Deviance, Reality and Society.* New York: Holt Saunders.

Dohrenwend, B. (1964) 'A use for leading questions in research interviewing', *Human Organization*, 23: 76–7.

Elliott, D. and Ageton, S. (1980) 'Reconciling race and class differences in self-reported and official estimates of delinquency', *American Sociological Review*, 45: 95–116.

Empey, E. and Erikson, M. (1966) 'Hidden delinquency and social status', *Social Forces*, 44: 546–54.

Farrington, D. (1989) 'Self reported and official offending from adolescence to adulthood', in M. Klein (ed.), *Cross-national Research in Self-reported Crime and Delinquency*. Dordrecht: Kluwer. pp. 399–423.

Gold, M. (1966) 'Undetected delinquent behaviour', *Journal of Research in Crime and Delinquency*, 3: 27–46.

Kleck, G. (1982) 'On the use of self-report data to determine the class distribution of criminal and delinquent behaviour', *American Sociological Review*, 47: 427–33.

Junger, M. (1989) 'Discrepancies between police and self report data for Dutch ethnic minorities', *British Journal of Criminology*, 29 (3): 273–84.

Jupp, V. (1996) *Methods of Criminological Research*. London: Routledge.

Tarling, R. (1993) *Analysing Offending*. London: Her Majesty's Stationery Office.

SEMANTIC DIFFERENTIAL SCALE

Definition

A method of attitude measurement in which respondents rate the object of interest (for example, the police) on several bipolar scales, the ends of which are defined by pairs of adjectives that are opposite in meaning (for example, honest/dishonest; hard/gentle).

Distinctive Features

The semantic differential rating scale was developed by Osgood in the late 1950s. The technique is very adaptable and easy to administer. It is concerned with respondents' perceptions or attitudes in relation to the object of the research. Respondents are presented with a number of items each of which is presented as opposites. For example, if the aim is to examine attitudes towards police officers, bipolar items such as kind/cruel, powerful/not powerful, weak/strong, honest/dishonest are offered. Such items can be developed from repertory grid techniques. Sometimes an assumption is made about equality of intervals so that each item can be scored 1–7 and by summation an overall score can be determined. In this way the image or profile of almost anything can be obtained.

Evaluation

As with other such techniques, the semantic differential runs the risk of *response sets,* which is a tendency to respond in a particular way irrespective of the context of the questions. For example, there is a risk that respondents choose all the positive adjectives or all the negative adjectives. Therefore, it is necessary to vary the ends or poles of the items to counteract such response sets.

Victor Jupp

Associated Concepts: repertory grid technique, scaling, summated rating scale, Thurstone scale

Key Readings

Moser, C. A. and Kalton, G. (1971) *Survey Methods in Social Investigation*. London: Heinemann.

Osgood, C. E., Suci, G. J. and Tannenbaum, P. H. (1957) *The Measurement of Meaning*. Urbana, IL: University of Illinois Press.

SEMIOTICS

See Textual Analysis

SENSITIVE RESEARCH

Definition

Sensitive research may be defined as that which addresses difficult areas such as sexual deviance, or that which is conducted with vulnerable groups of respondents such as children.

Distinctive Features

Primary qualitative methods of data collection (depth interviewing and observation for example) are frequently employed in sensitive research, particularly work that seeks to explore feelings and beliefs amongst vulnerable or difficult to access groups. The intrusiveness of these techniques can increase the sensitivity of such research and consequently care must be taken in designing and undertaking this type of work. Reference to a code of ethical conduct, such as that produced by the British Sociological Association, should always be made.

Researchers should not be deterred from conducting sensitive social research as this is frequently the only way that policy makers and social scientists can learn about socially excluded groups, for example, but plans should be made to safeguard both the researcher and the researched at the design stage. There may need to be a contractual agreement with the funder regarding the nature of the planned safeguards. This is best illustrated with an example from my own experience.

I conducted a longitudinal study with men who had been convicted for committing sexual offences against children; the research was conducted within the context of probation work and interviews held on probation service premises. There were several issues to consider at the outset: first, participation in all social research should be voluntary. The difficulty here was that potential respondents may have felt forced to participate as they were probationers, or may have felt that participation would have a positive effect upon their sentence. In order to overcome this the group were informed that participation was on an entirely voluntary basis and would not affect their sentence outcome. The second more problematic issue was that of *confidentiality*. This is extremely important given the nature of the research and the researcher's desire to protect the identity of respondents, whilst encouraging full participation. Assurances regarding confidentiality were compounded by the existence of a child protection policy within the organization. The policy required that any information divulged by this group of offenders regarding the commission of un-convicted offences against children be passed to the police. Respondents were informed about this policy before they agreed to participate in the study. Since the research aimed to explore previous offending, this may have impacted upon the extent to which respondents were willing to participate fully in interviews.

Evaluation

The effects of such research upon researchers is an important but largely neglected area and two issues were raised here: first the *physical safety of researchers* working with these offenders (some of whom had convictions for violent behaviour). It was agreed that one-to-one interviews with offenders would be conducted in a room with an adjacent observational room (using video equipment), observed by a second researcher. Fortunately, these facilities were available. This set-up allowed for observation of interviews, without the intrusive presence of another researcher in the interview room. Respondents' written permission to be observed in this way was sought prior to interviews and the presence of a video recorder in the room did not appear to interfere with the conversational flow of the interview. The second point relates to the *impact upon the researcher*. Accounts of this type of offending can be distressing and researchers are unable to share such disturbing information with others not involved in the research, particularly given confidentiality and anonymity issues. Such graphic material will have an impact upon the recipient, particularly in longitudinal work; there should be recognition of this and a strategy put in place during the research design phase. In this research regular de-briefing sessions were held between the researchers directly involved in this work, and the sponsor agreed to fund sessions with a therapist when requested. This is unusual but constitutes good research practice given the highly disturbing and sensitive nature of the work.

Julia Davidson

Associated Concepts: ethics, informed consent, interview, research bargain, volunteer sampling

Key Readings

Ethical Codes of Conduct:
http://www.britsoc.co.uk British Sociological Association
http://www.the-sra.org.uk/ethicals.htm Social Research Association
http://www.britsoccrim.org/ethics.htm British Society of Criminology

SENSITIZING CONCEPTS

Definition

A notion found in the methodological writings of the US sociologist Herbert Blumer, the founder of symbolic interactionism. By contrast with what he called 'definitive' concepts, sensitizing concepts do not involve using 'fixed and specific procedures' to identify a set of phenomena, but instead give 'a general sense of reference and guidance in approaching empirical instances'. So, whereas definitive concepts 'provide prescriptions of what to see, sensitizing concepts merely suggest directions along which to look' (Blumer, 1969: 148).

Distinctive Features

Blumer recognized that vagueness in theoretical concepts could be a problem. However, he denied that this can be solved in the social sciences by developing 'definitive' concepts – the solution put forward by some influential US sociologists in the 1930s, 40s and 50s, including advocates of operationism. Blumer's championing of sensitizing concepts reflected the pragmatist philosophy from which his own thinking about methodology grew. Many pragmatists argued that concepts are tools for use, and should be judged according to their instrumental value in enabling people to understand, and especially to act upon, the world. Also crucial to Blumer's argument is the idea that concepts have to be developed and refined over the course of inquiry, rather than set in stone at the beginning, if they are to capture the nature of phenomena. He insisted that beginning research by stating precise definitions of concepts, as advocated by many positivists, amounts to a spurious scientificity; and is likely to obstruct the task of gaining genuine knowledge about the social world.

Evaluation

There are suggestions within Blumer's work of the more radical view that, in an important sense, vagueness may be an inevitable feature of social scientific concepts. One reason for this is the difficulty of capturing the diverse, processual and contingent nature of social phenomena. Blumer argues that this seems to imply inevitable reliance on tacit cultural knowledge, in other words on *Verstehen*. Thus, he writes that only physical objects can be 'translated into a space–time framework or brought inside of what George Mead has called the touch–sight field', whereas the observation of social phenomena requires 'a judgment based on sensing the social relations of the situation in which the behavior occurs and on applying some social norm present in the experience of the observer' (Blumer, 1969: 178).

Blumer recognizes that most of the key concepts of sociology fulfil an important sensitizing role. However, he insists that they need to be clarified, as far as this is possible, through researchers enriching their first-hand experience of the social phenomena to which they relate. This is to be done, above all, by what he calls 'naturalistic research', which is close to what has come to be referred to as ethnography, in which empirical instances are subjected to 'careful flexible scrutiny' in their natural context, 'with an eye to disengaging the generic nature' of the concept (Blumer, 1969: 44).

Martyn Hammersley

Associated Concepts: ethnography, grounded theory, positivism, research design, *Verstehen*

Key Readings

Blumer, H. (1969) *Symbolic Interactionism.* Englewood Cliffs, NJ: Prentice Hall.
Hammersley, M. (1989a) *The Dilemma of Qualitative Method: Herbert Blumer and the Chicago School.* London: Routledge.
Hammersley, M. (1989b) 'The problem of the concept: Herbert Blumer on the relationship between concepts and data', *Journal of Contemporary Ethnography,* 18 (2): 133–60.

SIMULATION

Definition

An experiment performed on a model and aimed at imitating the operation of systems over time for the purpose of analysis or of creating virtual worlds.

Distinctive Features

The understanding, analysis, and design of complex dynamic systems are at the core of simulation employed for scientific and engineering research. Realistic animations are central for using simulation for entertainment, training and education.

Whereas modelling is primarily concerned with the relation between reality and model, simulation is concerned with the relation between model and simulator (Zeigler et al., 2000). The simulator is responsible for executing the model.

The simulation of a model comprises the following phases: simulation initialization, simulation run and interpretation of results.

The simulation experiment has to take into account the constraints that are inherent in a model. Simulation experiments are executed during the validation of the model but also for predicting and analysing the behaviour of the system under study. In the latter case experiments have to be consistent with the set of experimental conditions for which the model has been validated, that is, the model's experimental frame. The initialization of the simulation includes the estimation of parameters and the identification of distributions for the inputs of the model. Beginning, completion and number of simulation runs are defined.

Simulation is very similar to experimentation in the laboratory: many simulation runs are required for understanding a model's behaviour. This is true not only for the simulation of stochastic models but also for the simulation of deterministic models.

Verification and validation, although they are conceptually distinct, are conducted simultaneously by the researcher. Verification involves assuring that the conceptual model is adequately represented in the computerized representation, and that the simulation execution is correct with respect to the computerized representation of the model. For validation the model and the behaviour produced during simulation are compared to the real system and its behaviour. Validation involves checking face validity, that is, model and behaviour produced during simulation should appear reasonable. Sensitivity analysis is also used to check a model's face validity. Model assumptions, structural and data assumptions have to be validated the same as input–output transformations (Banks et al., 2001).

Simulation employed for analysis and design requires that simulation runs are reproducible and correct (Zeigler et al., 2000). Numerical integration algorithms have to be carefully selected to produce valid results during continuous simulation. In discrete event simulation specific strategies are defined to resolve uniformly potential conflicts between events and to prevent causal errors.

Virtual environments, in which simulation is used for entertainment, learning, or training, require a sufficiently realistic imitation of the system's behaviour. Whereas the simulation for analysis is executed as fast as possible, in virtual environments the progression of simulation time is related to the progression of wall clock time. In both cases an efficient and effective simulation may require the application of parallel, distributed simulation methods (Fujimoto, 2000).

Evaluation

Analytical techniques have generally a smaller domain of applicability than simulation. However, analytical techniques are more powerful, as they provide an understanding of the model's behaviour under arbitrary experimental conditions. Thus, they should be applied where possible. However, often they are not applicable and simulation is the only technique available for the analysis of the system's behaviour.

This generality and ease of applicability are the strengths of simulation but ironically its most serious drawbacks. All too fast, users fall prey to the easiness of developing models and letting them run. Model and simulation represent a system and its behaviour only under certain constraints, which have to be carefully observed.

Adelinde Uhrmacher

Associated Concepts: econometrics, experiment, modelling, validity

Key Readings

Banks, J., Carson, J. S., Nelson, B. L. and Nicol, D. M. (2001) *Discrete Event System Simulation.* New York: Prentice Hall.

Fujimoto, R. (2000) *Parallel and Distributed Simulation Systems.* Chichester: Wiley.

Zeigler, B. P., Praehofer, H. and Kim, T. K. (2000) *Theory of Modeling and Simulation.* New York: Academic Press.

SNOWBALL SAMPLING

Definition

A form of non-probability sampling in which the researcher begins by identifying an individual perceived to be an appropriate respondent. This respondent is then asked to identify another potential respondent. The process is repeated until the researcher has collected sufficient data. Sometimes called 'chain letter' sampling.

Distinctive Features

Snowball sampling can be a useful technique in research concerned with behaviour that is socially unacceptable or involves criminal activity. The nature of such activities may make it a virtually impossible task to identify all members of the research population; even identifying a few members can be very difficult. In the case of research on, say, shoplifting or car theft, the identification of a single willing respondent may be difficult. The first stage in the process usually involves a purposive sampling decision to identify one respondent who is willing to provide data. Once the data collection has been completed, the researcher asks the respondent to nominate another person who may be willing to provide the type of data required. The process continues until either the researcher fails to make any new contacts, or the new data do not appear to add anything substantial to existing understanding.

Snowball sampling can also be a relevant technique for groups of people who may feel lacking in confidence to participate in a research project. Such people could include the homeless, alcoholics, or those who have suffered illness or an assault. In such cases, they may have more confidence and be more likely to participate if they are approached by a person with similar experiences.

Evaluation

The advantage of snowball sampling is that it enables the researcher to identify potential participants when it would otherwise be extremely difficult to do so. It is also a sampling strategy that demonstrates a sensitivity to potential participants, in that they are identified by people with a similar experience.

The disadvantage of the approach is that it is dependent upon each participant sufficiently understanding the nature of the research in order to be able to identify another suitable participant. The next nominated participant may have a limited or biased understanding of the research issue. In addition, the members of the snowball sample may have certain features in common which are uncharacteristic of the research population as a whole. The very fact that they are all acquainted with each other is a source of potential bias.

Paul Oliver

Associated Concepts: non-probability (non-random) sampling, opportunity sampling, probability (random) sampling, purposive sampling, quota sampling, sampling

Key Readings

Bryman, A. (2001) *Social Research Methods.* Oxford: Oxford University Press.
Knight, P. T. (2002) *Small-scale Research: Pragmatic Inquiry in Social Science and the Caring Professions.* London: Sage.
Lee, R. M. (1993) *Doing Research on Sensitive Topics.* London: Sage.

SOCIAL INDICATORS

Definition

Social indicators, often combined into 'indices', are indirect empirical representations used to define or refer to concepts when no direct measurement is possible. They are a special sub-set of the more general problem of operationalization, which is how to formulate precise definitions of social phenomena in empirical terms, ready for data collection.

Distinctive Features

Many social science topics can only be researched indirectly. Abstract concepts have to be converted into separate, clearly specified components that can be studied empirically. We cannot tell whether a 'thing' is present or absent, how often it occurs, in what circumstances and what importance it has, without these intermediate constructions. However, whereas some phenomena can be relatively easy to operationalize, others are more difficult.

In Western societies, classification by age and gender can normally be achieved by straightforward measurement of years and biological sex. Of course, the cut-off points of age bands, or gender identification depend on the research focus. Other topics are more problematic. To take the topics covered in just one issue of a recent journal, 'refugee', 'community', 'forced migration', 'social integration', 'gypsy', 'inner city schooling' and 'governance' are all social phenomena requiring operationalization. If we consider the first of these, even the number of 'refugees' – a politically important question – cannot be accurately counted without defining who is, and who is not, a refugee. Can a person with a work permit also be a refugee? Can one be a refugee in one's own country, or only if officially listed by a government or non-governmental agency? If refused such official recognition, does a person immediately cease to be a refugee?

Concepts like 'poverty' and 'social exclusion' are even more complex. They are conventionally measured by social indicators, sets of variables which are known to be associated with the key concept. Local social deprivation has been identified using multiple-indicator combinations of scores for, among others, unemployment rates, overcrowding, lack of housing amenities, renting, residential turnover, car ownership, occupational profile, single parent and pensioner household structures, young children, qualification levels and illness, together with death rates, derelict land, benefit recipients and contents insurance premium levels (Payne et al., 1996).

No single indicator would be sufficient on its own, nor do scores precisely measure the underlying concept (Carley, 1981). Alternative social indicators of deprivation (the 'Carstairs Index', the 'Jarman Index', for example) have chosen different combinations to meet particular needs, like health resources allocation or determining local government grants. Social indicators of disadvantage can be seen as an alternative to dependence on social class; some, like Townsend et al. (1992) seeking to expand class' explanatory powers, while others like Carr-Hill (1990) wishing to escape class altogether. Social indicators may be about measurement, but they are embedded in theoretical perspectives.

Social indicators should achieve four goals. They must properly reflect the essential nature of the core concept, while also covering the whole of the concept (which is why they are usually based on multiple indicators). They must exclude other non-relevant concepts. They must produce evidence in a form appropriate to the level of study, either as a quantified form of measurement or contributing to a plausible narrative of meanings and interpretations.

Evaluation

Social indicators are sometimes chosen because they are effective rather than exact. Miners used to take canaries down the pits: when the canary collapsed, it was time to escape, because the air was bad. The bird was more susceptible to carbon monoxide than the men. The miners did not measure the gas;

they 'measured' the indicator, the canary's health.

In the social deprivation indicators listed above, the first dozen or so variables are conveniently available from the UK Census (albeit likely to be out-of-date because the Census is taken once a decade), while the remainder can be obtained from other pre-existing official statistics. They may not be the best possible indicators, but they have been chosen because the data are readily to hand, in some cases for local authority areas, and in others down to ward or enumeration district. While ready-made social indicators are therefore useful, this also should alert us to the fact that they may have been constructed for administrative convenience, or political expediency, rather than social scientific precision.

However, indicators may change independently of the original concept. Social class is about social groupings developing from ownership and control of production. Traditionally, this has been empirically represented by occupation. That worked tolerably well while most workers were men in full-time paid employment, in an unchanging labour market consisting of large blocks of similar occupations. However, the rise of female employment, part-time working, self-employment, second jobs, early retirement, high levels of unemployment, training-delayed entry into the labour market and new types of occupation have all complicated the scene. Nor are life style or social identity as neatly associated with occupation as they once were. It is impossible to tell if social class *per se* has changed, independent of the changes in the indicator. If we measure something indirectly, this must always be a risk.

This tendency for operational definitions to freeze concepts in a fixed way is one of the main reasons why qualitative researchers reject prior operationalization, preferring to retain flexibility of response to fieldwork encounters. Pre-conceptualization cannot cover the full complexity of a concept, and dependence on common sense is likely to result in the researcher's own ideas being imposed at the expense of the informants' subjective meanings. Exploratory studies are a good way of discovering and clarifying the components and variations in the empirical manifestations of a concept.

Geoff Payne

Associated Concepts: composite measurement, exploratory research, indicator, measurement, multiple indicators, positivism, realism, reliability, sensitizing concepts, validity of measurement

Key Readings

Carley, M. (1981) *Social Measurement and Social Indicators*. London: Allen & Unwin.

Carr-Hill, R. (1990) 'The measurement of inequalities in health', *Social Science and Medicine*, 31 (3): 393–404.

Payne, J., Payne, G. and Hyde, M. (1996) 'The refuse of all classes', *Sociological Research Online*, 1 (1).

Townsend, P., Davidson, N. and Whitehead, M. (1992) *Inequalities in Health: The Black Report and the Health Divide* (rev. edn). Harmondsworth: Penguin.

SOCIAL SURVEY

Definition

A method of social research with three defining characteristics – its type of content, its form of the data and the method of analysis employed (Marsh, 1982). Its content is social, the form of data is systematic, structured and based around variables and the method of analysis relies on comparisons across groups.

Distinctive Features

The content of a social survey is social – it deals with human behaviour, knowledge, attributes, beliefs and attitudes. Surveys produce a structured data set in the form of a variable-by-case grid. The grid consists of rows, representing cases, columns representing variables and cells that contain information about a case's attribute on the specific variable.

There are two broad types of social surveys – descriptive and explanatory. The descriptive survey seeks to describe the distribution of phenomena in a sample and population. The explanatory survey seeks to explain relationships between variables – to explain why things are as they are. Many surveys fulfil both functions.

Survey analysis is based on systematically comparing cases and examining variation and correlation between variables. Explanations are sought by examining variation in the dependent variable (presumed effect) and selecting an independent variable (presumed cause) that might be responsible for this variation. Analysis involves observing whether variation in the dependent variable (for example, income) is systematically linked to variation in the independent variable (such as gender). While any such covariation does not demonstrate causal relationships, such covariation is a prerequisite for causal relationships. More complex multivariate data analysis methods seek to untangle the complex relationships between the many factors that affect social behaviour and to control for the effects of extraneous variables that experiments achieve via random allocation to groups.

While survey research is often equated with questionnaire-based studies there is no necessary relationship between the survey method and the particular techniques by which data are collected. A critical and distinguishing characteristic of a survey is that it yields a structured data set that produces a variable-by-case data grid. The particular techniques by which the data are collected for this grid can vary widely.

Evaluation

Social surveys can provide a relatively efficient method for collecting information from a large number of cases. The data grid that is produced in a survey is well suited to statistical analysis and thus is amenable to the potential power of statistical methods. Where a survey collects data from large probability samples the extent to which patterns in the sample are likely to hold in the population at large can be estimated as such survey research results can be generalized to a wider population with a known degree of confidence.

There is general agreement that surveys provide an effective way of describing the more objective characteristics of a population. However, there is less agreement about whether survey research can produce data that enable the testing of causal relationships and understanding of behaviour in terms of its subjective meaning to actors. Some critics argue that the focus on variables ignores the context in which the behaviour occurs and the intentions of actors. They argue that surveys rely on imposing external explanations for behaviour and ignore the intentional and subjective component. In her book *The Survey Method* Catherine Marsh reviewed and countered these criticisms (Marsh, 1982).

David de Vaus

Associated Concepts: causality, correlation, data, inferential statistics, multivariate analysis, sampling, variable analysis

Key Readings

Marsh, C. (1982) *The Survey Method: The Contribution of Surveys to Sociological Explanation.* London: George Allen & Unwin.
Rosenberg, M. (1968) *The Logic of Survey Analysis.* New York: Basic Books.

SOCIOMETRY

Definition

A theoretical and methodological approach which seeks to analyse relations between individuals in small group situations. Sociometry is a form of network analysis.

Distinctive Features

Sociometry was developed in the 1930s by the social psychologist Jacob Moreno. Moreno introduced the idea of a sociogram, which is a diagram representing the relationships between individuals. The sociogram, now often called a directed graph, is a diagrammatic representation of a social network, with individuals represented by dots or points and social relationships represented by lines. Arrow heads can be added to the lines to indicate whether a relationship is one-way or reciprocal. Additionally, the strength of a relationship can be indicated by the thickness of a line.

The technique used to develop a sociogram requires each member of a group to indicate which other members he or she likes most. A limit is put on the number of choices (usually three) each member may make. Once the choices have been collected from each member, the data are used to draw a sociogram, which can then be analysed to make inferences about the structure of a group, its integration and connectedness, the existence of subgroups and about whether there are 'stars' (members selected by a large number of others) and 'isolates' (those not selected by anyone).

Evaluation

As with all such structured techniques, the wording of instructions is crucial to the validity of the inferences that are made. If the aim is to find out which other individuals group members would most like to spend time with, they should not be asked which individuals they most admire. The people we admire are not necessarily the people with whom we would want to spend most time.

Victor Jupp

Associated Concepts: community study method, network analysis, snowball sampling

Key Readings

Bott, E. (1957) *Family and Social Network*. London: Tavistock.

Mitchell, J. C. (ed.) (1969) *Social Networks in Urban Situations*. Manchester: Manchester University Press.

Moreno, J. L. (1953) *Who Shall Survive?* New York: Beacon.

Scott, J. P. (1991) *Social Network Analysis: A Handbook*. London: Sage.

SPATIAL RESEARCH

Definition

The exploration of physical and spatial features of a particular environment which are associated with certain social outcomes, such as social exclusion or crime, and are therefore seen as having a contributory or perhaps causal effect on social processes or social phenomena.

Distinctive Features

Spatial research has applications in subject areas with a specific interest in the built environment and its relationship with society, for example architecture and the way individual buildings and groups of buildings, conurbations and even entire cities are designed to reflect the culture of their users and inhabitants. Physical features are studied through various means, including observation of their use and detailed analysis of spatial configuration in terms of other data, such as land use, movement patterns or crime figures. For example, the spatial patterning of offence and offender rates can be analysed by physically locating where offences occur relative to where offenders live.

Another example of spatial research is *space syntax* (Hillier and Hanson, 1983), an approach that uses computer modelling of space to analyse factors such as patterns of human circulation in spaces ranging from individual rooms in buildings to specific public spaces or whole urban systems. Observational data reveal the intensity and direction of flow of people through an area over time and this can then be plotted in map form and linked to other geographical information systems (GIS) data to show, for example, why some areas flourish socially and economically while others decay, or why some areas suffer higher rates of crime than others. This type of analysis purports to allow problems in layouts to be diagnosed, emphasizing the particular application of spatial research in the evaluation of design strategies in both new-build and remedial developments.

This evaluative aspect of spatial research was evident in the research of Newman (1973), which has inspired a great deal of interest in the relationship of the built environment and crime, but has also influenced public policy in the designing of spaces and places, such as housing areas, to prevent crime. In his study of crime in high-rise housing in New York, Newman observed that predatory crimes of mugging, robbery and rape tended to occur in spaces such as stairwells, lift lobbies and deck accesses, which were least inhabited, watched over or 'owned' by residents. As a result of Newman's research, many of the problems with the UK high-rise developments of the 1950s and 1960s, which became notorious for crime and social and physical malaise, were attributed to the way they had been designed. Moreover, Newman set a precedent for a whole movement of research into the sorts of spatial factors that were thought to be criminogenic, such as unlimited access through housing areas, and which therefore should be designed out of schemes for new building development at the outset, and those thought to prevent crime by invoking a sense of community and territorial attitudes among residents, such as inwardly focusing, defensible cul-de-sacs.

Evaluation

The fundamental question relating to spatial research is to what extent the environment shapes human behaviour and response as opposed to merely reflecting the social conditions and aspirations of its inhabitants. Although there is some scope for environmental or spatial determinism, the environment's influence on the social context is part of a process of reciprocity (Hillier and Hanson, 1984) in an extremely complex interrelationship. Attributing causal powers to space can lead to the problem of over-determinism, which attributes human behaviour solely to the influence of particular environmental conditions and this leads to the questionable suggestion that environmental modification will therefore effect human behavioural change, a major criticism of Newman and his followers. For example, Coleman's (1985) study of deprived housing attempted to show that certain housing design features led to social malaise by simply quantifying the simultaneous occurrence of design features such as number of dwellings in a block and the number of storeys, and malaise indicators such as litter, graffiti, vandal damage and the number of households with children in care. However, Coleman's preoccupation with spatial indicators failed to account for the fact that social malaise could also have resulted from social factors such as the concentration of problem families through housing allocation policies.

Graham Steventon

Associated Concepts: causal model, GIS, prediction

Key Readings

Coleman, A. (1985) *Utopia on Trial: Vision and Reality in Planned Housing.* London: Hilary Shipman.

Hillier, B. and Hanson, J. (1984) *The Social Logic of Space.* Cambridge: Cambridge University Press.

Newman, O. (1973) *Defensible Space.* London: Architectural Press.

Steventon, G. J. (1996) 'Defensible space: a critical review of the theory and practice of a crime prevention strategy', *Urban Design International*, 1 (3): 235–45.

SPSS

Definition

One of the major computer packages for analysing quantitative data.

Distinctive Features

SPSS stands for Statistical Package for the Social Sciences, indicating its initial purpose; more recently, however, it has been developed for business use. Since its first appearance it has undergone considerable development and new versions appear regularly, providing additional facilities. The most significant development was when the package became available for desk-top computers.

SPSS comes as a series of modules; the Base module is the minimum needed, and Statistics, Advanced Statistics and other modules are required for anything other than simple analytic procedures.

To use SPSS the researcher needs access to a computer that has the package installed and then has to create a data file containing the figures to be analysed. This can be created in a spreadsheet and imported into SPSS. The data file consists of a table in which the data for one case or respondent are entered in one row, with each column containing the data for one variable. The analyses to be performed are selected from screen displays and the relevant commands can then be pasted into a syntax or command file. Alternatively, the syntax file can be prepared on a word processor, but this requires considerable familiarity with the SPSS command language. (It is not necessary to create a command file, but there are huge benefits in doing so.) When the commands are run, the package generates an output file containing the results of running those commands on the data in the data file. The contents can be transferred to a word processor for further editing.

The analyses available depend on the modules that have been installed, but include the common statistical tests of significance as well as more complex procedures such as factor analysis and multiple regression.

Evaluation

The printout from SPSS often includes a lot of material that is not needed, cannot be suppressed and has to be ignored. This means the user needs to know how to read the output to find the particular parts which are of interest. The SPSS manuals were exemplars of computer manuals that required readers to be experts before they could understand them, and this has led to a cottage industry in writing books to explain how to use the package (for example, Anthony, 1999; Foster, 2001; Kerr et al., 2002).

SPSS is used world wide and provides enormous data processing power. The dangers are that users can access complex procedures while having little understanding of what they are doing and too easily trawl the data to see what might be thrown up. It is important that the researcher should know what analyses are wanted before using the package.

Jeremy J. Foster

Associated Concepts: analysis of variance (ANOVA), causal model, correlation, discriminant function analysis, factor analysis, hunting (snooping and fishing), multivariate analysis, path analysis, quantitative research, regression analysis, social survey

Key Readings

Anthony, D. (1999) *Understanding Advanced Statistics: A Guide for Nurses and Health Care Professionals.* Edinburgh: Churchill Livingstone.
Foster, J. J. (2001) *Data Analysis using SPSS for Windows versions 8 to 10.* London: Sage.
Kerr, A. W., Hall, H. K. and Kozub, S. A. (2002) *Doing Statistics with SPSS.* London: Sage.

STANDPOINT RESEARCH

Definition

An approach that starts with a focus on experience, arguing that groups of individuals share distinct experiences and that the 'truth' of that experience can be uncovered. Researchers and theorists who support this approach include some feminists and some of those interested in the experience of disability, race and ethnicity, and childhood.

Distinctive Features

Standpoint research is founded on foundationalist perspectives based on an insistence that 'truth exists independently of the knower'. This approach is political in that experience is considered to be the starting point for any knowledge production.

Feminist Standpoint Epistemology, for example, begins from the view that 'masculine' science is bad science because it excludes women's experience and suggests the importance of developing a 'successor science' to existing dominant social science paradigms. Thus, Feminist Standpoint Epistemology starts from the position that the 'personal is political'. Some suggest that this perspective is a development of Marxist ideas about the role of the proletariat and argue that women are an oppressed class and as such have the ability not only to understand their own experiences of oppression but also to understand the experience of their oppressors. This implies that research based on women's experience provides a more valid basis for knowledge. It is not just that the oppressed see more – their own experience and that of the privileged – but also that their knowledge emerges through the struggle against oppression: in this instance the struggle against men. Supporters of this approach suggest that objectivity is possible but that the critical scrutiny of all aspects of the research process is necessary to achieve objectivity. This presents a challenge to traditional notions of objectivity, which Harding (1993) argues are weak because the researchers' own values, assumptions and so on are hidden.

Standpoint research is not the preserve of those concerned with women's experience. For example, some researchers working in the areas of disability, ethnicity, and race and childhood argue for a standpoint approach. When searching for an epistemology based on the experience of African American women, the values and ideas that African writers identify as being characteristically 'black' are often very similar to those claimed by white feminist scholars as being characteristically female. This suggests that the material conditions of oppression can vary dramatically and yet generate some uniformity in the epistemologies of subordinate groups (Hill Collins, 1989). Similarly, researchers working in the area of childhood have argued that as both women and children are subject to patriarchy, those in power regard both groups as social problems and both groups find it hard to have their points of view heard and respected (Mayall, 2002).

Evaluation

One problem with standpoint research is that it can imply that one group's perspective is more real, more accurate and better than that of others. But if we accept a position which implies that there is only one (real, accurate, best) experience, this can only be built upon the suppression of voices of persons with experiences unlike those who are in a position to define. Further, the view that the more oppressed or more disadvantaged groups have the greatest potential for knowledge implies that the greater the oppression the broader or more inclusive one's potential knowledge. This could lead to an unproductive discussion about hierarchies of oppression: that is, those who are more oppressed (and how do we prove this anyway?) are potentially more knowledgeable. Even if we find the most oppressed group of all, how do we know that their way of seeing is the 'most true': surely no one particular social location has the complete access to truth. With all of this in mind, once we acknowledge the existence of several standpoints it becomes impossible to talk about 'independent truth' and 'objectivity' as a means of establishing superior or 'better' knowledge because there will always be alternative knowledge claims arising from contextually grounded knowledge of different standpoints (Letherby, 2003).

A further problem specifically in relation to Feminist Standpoint Epistemology is the focus on biology that some supporters adopt. Some feminists leave traditional definitions of women unchallenged and resist instead the traditional value given to women and womanhood. However, many of the values ascribed to women in this analysis originated in the historical subordination of women – their association with nature, procreation, nurturance and so on lies at the very heart of traditional sexist conceptions of womanhood. Further, any standpoint position brings with it the danger of viewing a group of people as all the same. Not women, nor children, nor black people (and so on) are a homogeneous group. We all occupy multiple, combined and intersecting positions of gender, class, ethnicity, disability and sexuality.

Yet there are values of taking a standpoint approach. Feminist Standpoint Epistemology, for example, insists on viewing traditionally defined female characteristics in a different and much more positive way. In addition, taking a woman-centred approach, a child-centred approach, or an approach that foregrounds the standpoint of people with disabilities when undertaking research provides a way of looking beyond individual perspectives and enables us to challenge stereotypical definitions. Furthermore, Harding (1993) argues that the claim that the experience of an oppressed group provides a better starting point for thought is not about arguing for one position but enables us to consider the significance of the experiences of the powerful and the less powerful.

Recognizing the importance of difference and yet acknowledging the significance of each of the multiple identities that individuals occupy, it is possible to argue for, standpoints rather than a standpoint position. By doing this we acknowledge that gender, age, disability and so are significant identifiers of status and experience whilst acknowledging that none of these is the only defining feature in anyone's life.

Gayle Letherby

Associated Concepts: anti-racism research, critical research, disability research, emancipatory research, epistemology, feminist research, relativism

Key Readings

Harding, S. (1993) Rethinking standpoint epistemology: 'what is strong objectivity?', in L. Alcoff and E. Porter (eds), *Feminist Epistemologies*. New York: Routledge. pp. 49–82.

Hill Collins, P. (1989) 'Black feminist thought signs', *Journal of Women in Culture and Society*, 14 (4): 745–73.

Letherby, G. (2003) *Feminist Research in Theory and Practice*. Milton Keynes: Open University Press.

Mayall, B. (2002) *Towards a Sociology for Childhood*. Oxford: Blackwell.

STATISTICAL SIGNIFICANCE

See Inferential Statistics

STRATIFIED SAMPLING

Definition

A method of sampling designed to ensure that the sample has certain characteristics, usually that it is representative of the population on key variables.

Distinctive Features

As with all sampling methods, stratified sampling is used when there is insufficient time or resources to conduct a census (which collects information from every member of a population). One form of stratified sampling is quota sampling, where the population is divided into strata and the number of sample members in each stratum is predetermined. Quota samples can be representative of the population in terms of the stratifying variables but are not random because not every population member has an equal chance of being selected. This is due to the method of selecting respondents.

Stratified random sampling has some advantages over simple random sampling, where members of the population are numbered and then numbers chosen at random to determine which individuals are included in the sample. There is no guarantee that a simple random sample will be representative of the population – for example, from a population where there are 500 men and 500 women, a sample of 100 may consist of 70 women and 30 men.

In contrast, choosing a stratified random sample can ensure that the individuals selected are representative of the population in terms of certain variables. Using the above example again, an even gender balance in the sample of 100 could be ensured by taking a sample stratified by gender. The 1000 people in the population would be listed with the 500 women first, followed by the 500 men. Every tenth name would be chosen from the list, with a random form of selection used to determine whether the starting point was 1, 2, 3, 4, 5, 6, 7, 8, 9 or 10. If the randomly chosen starting point was 4 then the people included in the sample would be those number 4, 14, 24, through to number 994. This sample would include 50 women and 50 men.

It is possible to stratify in terms of more than one variable. In the above example, the sample could have been stratified by gender and employment status if the population was listed in the following order: women in employment; women not in employment; men in employment; men not in employment. It is important to note that a stratified sample is still a random sample because the researcher has no control over who is chosen. This method guarantees some characteristics of the sample but not which individuals appear in it.

Evaluation

Stratified random sampling requires accurate information about the key variables prior to the research being undertaken (for example, the researcher would need to know which members of the population were in employment and which were not). There is then considerable work involved in listing members of the population in the correct order. However, once this task is completed, the sample can be selected quickly.

Stratified sampling cannot guarantee that very small groups are represented: in the above example, if there were only four men who were not in employment, the likelihood is that none of them would be included in the sample. It is also important to stratify by the most appropriate variable(s) for the research study in question: in a study of attitudes to alcohol consumption, it may be more important to have a sample that is representative in terms of age than one that is representative in terms of employment status.

Jamie Harding

Associated Concepts: bias, census, cluster sampling, error, non-probability (non-random) sampling, probability (random) sampling, quantitative research, quota sampling, sampling

Key Readings

Mendenhall, W., Ott, L. and Scheaffer, R. L. (1971) *Elementary Survey Sampling.* Belmont, CA: Wadsworth Publishing.
de Vaus, D. (2002) *Surveys in Social Research,* 5th edn. London: Routledge.

STRUCTURED OBSERVATION

Definition

A systematic method of data collection, where there is considerable pre-coding and the observation takes the form of recording when, how often, or for how long the pre-coded behaviours occur. Observing usually means watching and listening, although it may entail just watching *or* listening. By contrast, informal or casual observation is unstructured, and may form the basis of future structured observation. Informal or casual observation methods are sometimes seen as less objective than structured observation, because the observer may be focusing on behaviours without a clear theoretical framework, and may not be coding the behaviours in a reliable, that is, repeatable way. The counter viewpoint is that a theoretical framework can act as a strait-jacket that distorts reality.

Distinctive Features

Structured observation is used widely in the social sciences, from working on the behaviour of children and animals in the development and use of play behaviours, to group decision making in adults, and the non-verbal behaviour of politicians (Gottman and Bakeman, 1998; Martin and Bateson, 1993). Precisely because these kinds of behaviours can be subject to bias in recording, it is considered important to pre-code the behaviours to be observed. All the observers deployed in the study will need to have a very clear understanding of the definitions of the behaviours to be coded, and to be sure of examples of those behaviours. This ensures that the observations are valid, that is, that they measure what it is intended to measure; and also that observation codings are reliable, that is, individuals coding at different times, or different observers at the same time, record the same behaviours as examples of the code in question. Where the behaviour being coded is laughter, or raising the right eyebrow, there tend to be few disagreements, but for other behaviours coding can be far more challenging. For example, when is an infant protruding its tongue, and when is it licking its lips? How still does the tongue have to be, and how far from the lips, to be a tongue protrusion? This is an important question when infancy researchers are asking questions about infants' abilities to mimic adult facial gestures.

Researchers using structured observation techniques often prefer to have a permanent or semi-permanent record of an observation session on film, videotape, or, now, digital recording. This allows observers to play samples of behaviours over and over again, in order to agree that a particular behaviour has occurred. This can be very time-consuming and therefore it is necessary to take this into account when planning and costing the investigation or study.

How do researchers measure behaviours? They may do this by counting and timing the incidence of a given behaviour. How researchers classify their observations will influence how they can analyse their data later. There are four ways of classifying: nominal or categorical measures, ordinal measures, interval measures and ratio measures. An example of nominal measures would be indicating qualitative differences, such as 'walking' or 'standing'; they would be counted as incidents. Ordinal measures require that the behaviour being observed can be classified in some sort of order, for example, level of positive facial expression, or level of aggression displayed; it too, illustrates qualitative differences. Interval measures in observation tend to be time duration, for example, length of time spent talking, two minutes being twice as long as one minute. Ratio measures are used within observation when a time period is sampled, and the whole period is divided into the times in which the observed behaviours occur, or do not occur.

Narrative accounts of observations can also be produced, but these are more difficult to analyse, and tend to be analysed in a far more qualitative fashion. A narrative record is similar to a transcript but differs in that it requires more rigorous detail and information about the setting, time and participant under study; it also requires that the observer be uninvolved in the action, which is not the case when interviews are undertaken (Wilkinson, 1995).

Evaluation

Observation has the advantage of being direct, and of allowing researchers to see what happens at first hand, rather than relying on what people say they do. It allows researchers, under the appropriate conditions, to find out what happens 'in the real world'. It is seen as an uncontaminated technique, provided that those being observed are ceasing to be aware of this.

Apart from being very time consuming, structured observation suffers from the problem that it may exclude behaviours that could be of importance but are not catered for in the coding frame. Thus nothing new can be reported in the findings, because by definition structured observation requires all behaviours of interest to be coded before observation begins. It is in this way that a theoretical framework can act as a distorting mechanism. There are other issues, for example, those being observed have no say in the interpretation or coding of their behaviours. There is also the problem of inter-rater reliability: if different observers cannot agree on examples of behaviours, then what does this mean for research purposes: that the behaviours do not exist, or that some observers are much better at seeing examples than are others?

Jeanette Garwood

Associated Concepts: coding, interview, measurement, participant observation, reliability, videography

Key Readings

Gottman, J. M. and Bakeman, R. (1998) 'Systematic observation techniques or building life as an observational researcher', in Gilbert, D. T., Fiske, S. T. and Gardner, L. (eds), *Handbook of Social Psychology*, 4th edn. Oxford: Oxford University Press.

Martin, P. and Bateson, P. (1993) *Measuring Behaviour: An Introductory Guide*, 2nd edn. Cambridge: Cambridge University Press.

Wilkinson, J. (1995) 'Direct observation', in G. M. Breakwell, S. Hammond and C. Fife-Schaw (eds), *Research Methods in Psychology*. London: Sage. pp. 224–38.

SUBJECTIVITY

Definition

The inner state of the self constituted by thinking, experience, emotion, belief, intentionality, self-awareness and the awareness of others.

Distinctive Features

Speculation by philosophers on the nature of consciousness has a history stretching back at least to Aristotle (Plato did not really recognize a distinction between subjective and objective), who thought that the forms of our consciousness are derived in some way from the objective world, but also recognized the uniqueness of human consciousness to be able to receive or even create in some way these forms and use them for the development of scientific and moral understanding. The coming importance of the inner self is clear in the fourth-century Christian teachings of St Augustine, whose recognition, recorded in Book 7 of his *Confessions*, that the cause of evil resides in free will, occurs just prior to his conversion from Manichaeism to Christianity. Descartes increased the weight to be placed on inner life, in his *First Meditation* of 1641, when he declared *cogito ergo sum* at the end of an inquiry that declared the only certainty available to humankind was to be found in subjective experience. A century and a half later, Kant's argument – summarized in the *Prolegomena* – that the idea of pure subjectivity makes no sense, reaffirmed that subjective experience has to be *of* something, and must be, if it is to go beyond mere perception, framed by a general structure of understanding. From this point, the scope of subjectivity was effectively widened to include the structures of understanding, and this is the key move that enables us to begin to understand the complexities of the philosophies of *Verstehen* through nineteenth-century German thinking, and Edmund Husserl's notion of transcendental subjectivity as a basic component of twentieth-century phenomenology.

The clear lines of development in the understanding of subjectivity, from its Greek foundations forward, were broken in the second half of the twentieth century as a result of the debates that arose from developments in the philosophy of mind, and from programmes of neuropsychological empirical research into the nature of consciousness. Gilbert Ryle's timely argument was that subjectivity, understood particularly as self-awareness, is an illusion, since the observing self aware of the experiencing self is not itself observable. His work suggested that the broad understanding of subjectivity that had been developed over centuries was basically incoherent, and others, like Daniel Dennett, came along to develop the basic theme. The neuroscientific research programme had come to be, at least in part, about demystifying subjectivity by re-describing states of mind in terms of physically recordable states of the central nervous system. Thomas Nagel's famous discussion of how we cannot know what it is like to be a bat because we do not have access to a bat's subjective experience, was responded to by Paul Churchland, a die-hard physicalist, who pointed out that all that means is that we lack the appropriate synaptic connections. Probably the clearest statement from a physicalist position, and by no means the entirely reductive one that might be feared, is from David Chalmers, who thinks it now possible that we are moving to a genuinely scientific understanding of conscious experience, and regards the primary empirical data for this science as first person accounts of subjective states, for example of hunger, memory, anger, the perception of colour, and so on. For Chalmers, a science of consciousness will not reduce first-person data to statements about physical systems like brain states, but it will explore the connections. A scientific theory of subjectivity would, he thinks, explain the relationships between the subjective and the physical.

Within the domain of late twentieth-century social theory, the key discourses connected to subjectivity connect to the topics of identity and the self. There is a structural reluctance here even to conceive of a non-social subjective condition. Some historic examples are to be found in Durkheim's notions of anomie and egoism, and in the Hegelian notion of alienation, but these are far from perfect examples of subjective conditions uninflected by society. In general the debates on self and identity within sociology are concerned with the social component of subjective experience and self-understanding. Freudian developments here are not an exception to this. From a strict sociological point of view the removal of the social from the subjective leaves behind an empty chasm.

The place of subjectivity with respect to sociological method is much more important. The general issue concerns the relevance of the researcher's subjective position. In the fictional ideal situation the researcher should have no presence in the research findings. However, the increasingly strong position of qualitative research in sociology means that some account of the researcher's assumptions, preferences, experiences and decisions during the research process may be indispensable. If this can be provided in a succinct manner, then it can enable the meaning and performance of the research to come into focus. Breaking down the process into stages shows the importance of taking account of subjective variables, especially in qualitative research. The opening stage requires choice of research topic, and this emerges out of an engagement between research possibilities and discipline, beliefs, value commitments. The complex process leading to choice segues into questions of method and data collection and it would be mistaken to think that subjective factors play no part here. Most importantly, the decision about the form of data and their collection will substantially determine the form of the interactions that will take place between the researcher and his or her subjects. Following the research engagement, the production of research outcomes will fix the range of subjective and intersubjective meanings that the whole process will come to have for a range of related actors including the researcher, research subjects and sponsoring organization. At each stage of the research, the question of the inner experience of the researcher, and its translation into the outer context of the research, may become a complex area requiring careful analysis and public response – again leading us back to the paradox of subjectivity and social research, that it should not figure, but that it must be ventilated.

Evaluation

The topic of subjectivity is controversial. Two thousand years of philosophical development may seem to be coming to an end with the neuropsychologists' promise of a science of consciousness, but, as can be seen with the fundamental importance of questions of subjectivity in qualitative research, the notion of subjectivity is multi-faceted. The theoretical engagement of sociology with the concept of subjectivity is underdeveloped, but this is compensated for by the increasingly well highlighted issues around subjectivity and qualitative research.

Roy Boyne

Associated Concepts: constructionism, epistemology, inter-subjective understanding, methodology, ontology, phenomenology, positivism, realism, *Verstehen*

Key Readings

Boyne, R. (2001) *Subject, Society and Culture.* London: Sage.
Breuer, F. and Mruck, F. (2003) *Subjectivity and Reflexivity in Qualitative Research.* Deutsche Forschungsgemeinschaft.
Shear, J. (ed.) (1997) *Explaining Consciousness.* Cambridge, MA: MIT Press.
Taylor, C. (1989) *Sources of the Self.* Cambridge: Cambridge University Press.

SUMMATED RATING SCALE

Definition

One of the most frequently used methods for assessment of people's characteristics, especially attitudes, in the social sciences. Hundreds of summated rating scales have been developed for the measurement of attitudes, beliefs, emotions, feelings, perceptions and personality. They are widely used in both social science applications and research. One of the most popular is the Likert scale.

Distinctive Features

There are four characteristics of a summated rating scale. First, the scale must contain two or more items. Second, the format of each item must be a rating scale. Third, the scale must be designed to assess an underlying construct that is quantifiable. Fourth, the items do not have correct answers. Summated rating scales are preferred to single rating scales because they tend to have better reliability.

As with a single rating scale, each item in a summated rating scale yields a numerical score. These are combined by adding the items to give a total scale score. There are four steps to developing a summated rating scale. First, the construct is defined as carefully as possible. Second, an initial pool of items is written. Third, the scale is administered to a development sample so that an item analysis can be conducted. Fourth, the scale is validated by conducting research to support the interpretation of what scores on the scale represent.

Defining the construct carefully and completely is a vital first step in scale construction. It forms the foundation upon which subsequent activities are based. This step is a conceptual/theoretical task of delineating exactly the nature of the construct of interest. A clear and specific definition is necessary in order for items to be written that will assess what is intended. A clear definition can be derived from prior research and theory in the domain of interest. Part of this effort should include the formulation of hypotheses about how the construct should relate to other constructs.

Once the nature of the construct is clearly delineated, an initial test version of the scale can be written. This requires first choosing a format for the scale. The number of response choices, the anchors for the response choices, the underlying continuum for the rating scales (for example, agreement), and the number of items and number of subscales must be decided. An initial pool of items is written that is larger in number than is needed for the final scale, because some items might not survive the item analysis conducted in the next step.

A good item is a concise and unambiguous statement that reflects the intended construct. There are four rules to good item writing. First, each item should express a single idea. Multiple ideas cause confusion as the respondent might agree with one part and disagree with the other. Second, avoid colloquialisms and jargon. This is particularly important if the scale is to be used with multiple populations. An expression that is clear to people in one country, for example, might not be to someone in another, even if they all speak the same language. Furthermore, word meanings can change over time. Third, consider the reading level of potential respondents. Fourth, avoid the use of negatives to reverse the meaning of an item. For example, the item 'I do not like to eat in fast food restaurants' can be misread to mean the opposite if the respondent fails to see the word 'not'.

Once the items are written, the scale should be administered to a developmental sample of at least 100–200 people. This step's purpose is to select items that are related to one another so that the scale has internal consistency and reliability. We assume that an internally consistent scale has items that assess the same construct. A statistical procedure termed an item analysis will help select the best items from an internal consistency standpoint. Each item is correlated with a score computed as the sum of all other items minus the one being evaluated. This item-remainder coefficient is used to select items for the final scale. The most frequently chosen measure of internal consistency is coefficient alpha. A standard of 0.70 or higher for acceptable reliability is widely used (Nunnally, 1978).

The final step in scale development is to collect construct validity evidence to support the interpretation of the scale's meaning. This step is the most difficult as many social science constructs are abstract and hypothetical with no objective manifestation. Validation relies on testing hypotheses about how the scale should relate to other variables. With many scales, particularly those that assess attitudes, we often rely on face validity assuming that respondents interpret items in the same way as the scale developers. Validity is not as much a characteristic of a scale as it is the interpretation of the meaning of a scale. Thus, a scale can be found useful as a measure of one construct but not another.

Evaluation

For many scales it is important to collect normative data from various populations. Ideally, the scale would be administered to representative samples to yield reasonable estimates of population mean scores. More commonly, convenience samples are used for norms as researchers who develop scales rarely have access to representative samples. International norms are available for some scales, but translation equivalence problems and cultural differences in language interpretation make comparisons difficult.

Paul E. Spector

Associated Concepts: composite measurement, indicator, Likert scale, reliability, scaling, semantic differential technique, Thurstone scale, validity of measurement

Key Readings

DeVellis, R. F. (1991) *Scale Development: Theory and Applications*. Newbury Park, CA: Sage.
Nunnally, J. C. (1978) *Psychometric Theory*, 2nd edn. New York: McGraw–Hill.
Spector, P. E. (1992) *Summated Rating Scale Construction: An Introduction*. Newbury Park, CA: Sage.

T

TEXTUAL ANALYSIS

Definition

In social research the term refers to a method of analysing the contents of documents that uses qualitative procedures for assessing the significance of particular ideas or meanings in the document. It contrasts with content analysis.

Distinctive Features

Textual analysis is rooted in the hermeneutic tradition of textual interpretation and has most recently been organized around the particular procedures implied by work in semiotics. Hermeneutic philosophy stresses that the interpretation of a text must always be undertaken from the reader's particular standpoint. The inference of meaning is possible only by relating the text to some other frame of reference and entering into a dialogue with the text. We must comprehend a text by understanding the frame of reference from which it was produced, and the researcher's own frame of reference becomes the springboard from which this becomes possible. Semiotics (or semiology) adds to this the claim that this dialogue involves a 'decoding' of the categories used by those who produced the text.

As formulated by Saussure, semiotics is the study of cultural signs in terms of the cultural codes through which they are organized. Linguistic signs (letters and words) are organized by grammatical and semantic codes into meaningful sentences, so all other cultural signs – including those that are linguistically formulated – must be seen as organized by their specific codes into narrative accounts and forms of discourse. From this standpoint, the interpretation of the text contained within a document involves a decoding of the signs that were encoded in its construction.

The most influential semiotic writer in recent years has been Barthes, and his particular methods have been those that are most widely used in textual analysis. Barthes distinguished the denotative meaning of a sign from its connotative meaning. The former refers to the meaning that a sign has by virtue of describing and interpreting the world by pointing to something and labelling it: the sign *denotes* a cultural object. The connotative meaning of a sign consists of the range of associated meanings that it triggers in the mind of the reader or audience: any particular denotation also has certain connotations. A message that goes beyond mere denotation and is structured around connotative meanings to convey a particular message is, for Barthes, a 'myth', a term that he uses in preference to the Marxian term 'ideology'. A myth is a form of communication in which cultural meanings are structured in such a way as to convey a particular message to those who see, hear, or read it. It is 'distorted' by the demands of the underlying power relations. Barthes's analysis of myth is extended to non-linguistic forms of discourse, such as paintings, films, photographs and objects of consumption. Any cultural object that conveys a message can, therefore, be subjected to a textual analysis.

A principal task of textual analysis, therefore, is to uncover power relations through disclosing these distortions, demonstrating whether any particular myth reflects the position of the oppressor or the oppressed. In this respect, Barthes's work has a similar intention to that of Mannheim, also rooted in hermeneutics, whose sociology of knowledge contrasted the ideological knowledge of the powerful and the utopian knowledge of the powerless.

Evaluation

Because of its sensitivity to cultural context, textual analysis overcomes many of the limitations of content analysis. However, it does involve distinct problems of its own. Any reading of a text reflects the standpoint of the reader, and semiotics has provided no clear basis on which the validity of a particular reading can be demonstrated. Barthes's solution was to stress the criterion of coherence: if a reading of a text produces a coherent and systematic account, then it is, other things being equal, to be preferred. It is not clear, however, why coherence should serve as such a criterion. Indeed, Derrida and other poststructuralist writers have stressed that texts tend to be incoherent, to a greater or lesser extent, and they see the interpretative task as involving the uncovering of such inconsistencies and incoherencies.

John Scott

Associated Concepts: content analysis, cultural research, discourse analysis, document analysis, epistemology, hermeneutics, historical analysis, inter-subjective understanding, narrative analysis

Key Readings

Barthes, R. ([1957] 1973) *Mythologies*. London: Paladin.
Barthes, R. ([1964] 1967) *Elements of Semiology*. London: Cape.

Barthes, R. ([1961–73] 1977) *Images–Music–Text*. London: Fontana.
Mannheim, K. ([1929] 1936) *Ideology and Utopia*. London: Routledge & Kegan Paul.
Rose, G. (2001) 'Semiology', in *Visual Methodologies*. London: Sage.

THEORETICAL SAMPLING

Definition

Theoretical sampling is a central part of the grounded theorizing advocated by Glaser and Strauss (1967). Grounded theorizing is usually regarded as a form of qualitative inquiry, though in fact its originators saw it as applicable to quantitative data too. In this context, theoretical sampling is tied to the purpose of generating and developing theoretical ideas, rather than being aimed either at producing findings that are representative of a population or at testing hypotheses.

Distinctive Features

This form of sampling does not take place at a single point in the inquiry process but is a recurrent feature: at various times the researcher must ask what settings, events, people etc. it would be worthwhile investigating next in order to develop aspects of the emerging theory. In this way, theoretical sampling is guided by, and helps to generate, the 'theoretical sensitivity' that is necessary in grounded theorizing, and indeed in qualitative and ethnographic work generally (Glaser, 1978; Strauss and Corbin, 1998).

There is no fixed terminus to the sampling of cases for theoretical purposes. Glaser and Strauss suggest that it should be stopped when what they call 'theoretical saturation' is reached; in other words, when looking at new cases is no longer contributing to development of the theory. Judgement is involved here, but only in the same way that those engaged in hypothesis-testing must decide when to stop their work and conclude that a hypothesis is either true or false.

Theoretical sampling is a form of the comparative method, aimed at discovering significant dimensions of variation in categories of social phenomena and their relations with one another. At different times it will be designed either to minimize or to maximize the differences on particular theoretical dimensions that have emerged as important in the course of inquiry. Minimization of differences allows core features of theoretical categories to emerge more clearly. By contrast, maximizing the contrast on a particular dimension displays the heterogeneity within the theoretical category, but also enables researchers to recognize what is common across key categories.

Evaluation

It is indisputable that there are useful forms of sampling that are different in character and purpose from representative sampling based on statistical theory. And the idea that sampling can be carried out in such a way as to develop theory is surely a sound one. However, the concept of theoretical sampling is associated with a view about the nature of inquiry that raises a number of questions (see Dey, 1999). One of these concerns the relationship between developing and testing theories, an issue over which the originators of grounded theorizing later disagreed (see Glaser, 1992). Sometimes in *The Discovery of Grounded Theory* Glaser and Strauss suggest that theoretical sampling is designed to test as well as to develop hypotheses. At other points, they insist that a concern with hypothesis testing, or 'verification', has no place in their approach or that it is a stage of inquiry that can come after grounded theorizing. Furthermore, theoretical sampling is very different from selecting a case, or cases, so as to subject some theoretical idea to the sharpest possible test – what is sometimes referred to as critical case analysis. Within grounded theorizing discrepant evidence is treated as indicating a need further to elaborate the theoretical categories, rather than as necessitating abandonment of a theoretical idea in favour of one of its competitors.

The development and testing of theories are closely related activities and it is wrong to see them as practically distinct even if they can be distinguished analytically. What *is* true is that there is usually a shift over the course of much inquiry from a preoccupation with theory development towards an emphasis on testing out ideas; though a concern with testing is not absent at the start, neither does interest in theory development usually completely disappear even by the end. For this and other reasons, it is important to recognize that theoretical sampling is not incompatible with other kinds of sampling, including that concerned with subjecting theoretical ideas to test; and representative sampling may play an important part even in qualitative forms of inquiry (see Schofield, 1990).

Martyn Hammersley

Associated Concepts: analytic induction, constant comparative method, grounded theory, hunting (snooping and fishing), hypothetico-deductive model, induction, probability (random) sampling, progressive focusing, sampling

Key Readings

Dey, I. (1999) *Grounding Grounded Theory: Guidelines for Qualitative Inquiry*. San Diego, CA: Academic Press.

Glaser, B. L. (1978) *Theoretical Sensitivity*. Mill Valley, CA: Sociology Press.

Glaser, B. L. (1992) *Emergence versus Forcing: Basics of Grounded Theory Analysis*. Mill Valley, CA: Sociology Press.

Glaser, B. L. and Strauss, A. L. (1967) *The Discovery of Grounded Theory*. Chicago: Aldine.

Schofield, J. W. (1990) 'Increasing the generalizability of qualitative research', in E. W. Eisner and A. Peshkin (eds), *Qualitative Inquiry in Education: The Continuing Debate*. New York: Teachers College Press. pp. 200–25.

Strauss, A. and Corbin, J. (1998) *Basics of Qualitative Research: Techniques and Procedures for Developing Grounded Theory* 2nd edn. Thousand Oaks, CA: Sage.

THICK DESCRIPTION

Definition

The notion of 'thick description' is outlined by Clifford Geertz in the *Interpretation of Culture,* which draws on the work of the philosopher Gilbert Ryle, and especially his winking analogy. Ryle directs us to distinguish between a boy whose eyelid twitches, a boy who is winking and a boy who is parodying another boy's clumsy attempt at a wink. Drawing on these seemingly silly examples, Ryle shows that these similar behaviours were different because winks and fake-winks, parodies of winks, rehearsals of parodies of winks and so on communicate meaning while the twitch does not. The point is that even such a seemingly simple form of communication – the rapid contraction of an eyelid – produces multiple possibilities; unravelling and identifying those contexts and meanings requires 'thick description'. According to Geertz (1973), Ryle's example presents an image of 'the sort of piled-up structures of inference and implication through which an ethnographer is continually trying to pick his way'. Raw field notes are readable, but to understand them requires thick description.

Distinctive Features

One avenue of approach to culture, related to but distinct from both the American cognitivist and continental structuralist approaches, has been to treat cultures as systems of shared symbols and meanings. Geertz has been one of the most notable pioneers of this view. Borrowing from Ricoeur a broader sense of 'text', Geertz has treated a culture as 'an assemblage of texts'.

> Doing ethnography is like trying to read (in the sense of 'construct a reading of') a manuscript – foreign, faded, full of ellipses, incoherencies, suspicious emendations, and tendentious commentaries, but written not in conventionalized graphs of sound but in transient examples of shaped behavior. (1973: 10)

Anthropology thus becomes a matter of interpretation, not decipherment (in this, Geertz contrasts his own approach with Lévi-Strauss), and interpretation becomes thick description that must be deeply embedded in the contextual richness of social life.

Evaluation

Geertz is at his best when he employs thick description to interpret ethnographic particulars; unlike the cognitivist approach which he sees as reductionistic and spuriously formalistic, he finds these particularities in the richness of real people in real life: a funeral, a cockfight, a sheep theft. His thick descriptions are not disembodied and decontextualized myths or customs, but humans engaging in symbolic action.

His critics argue that it is easy to write a text that is thick, but it is very difficult to write a text that is valid. The problem has not escaped Geertz (1973). He admits that it is difficult to fathom 'what our informants are up to and what it all means'. Moreover, they ask, is not thick description simply detailed documentation of events and circumstances? As such it is, and for long has been, the cornerstone of much anthropology whatever its theoretical framework. In spite of these and other critiques, Geertz's use of thick descriptions, his evocation of the metaphor of the interpretation of reading culture as a text, 'has led to the present dominant interest within interpretive anthropology about how interpretations are constructed by the anthropologist, who works in turn from the interpretations of his informants' (Marcus and Fischer, 1986: 26). That key point has brought about a sea change in the discipline.

Paul Valentine

Associated Concepts: cultural research, epistemology, ethnography, idiographic, ontology, subjectivity

Key Readings

Geertz, C. (1973) *The Interpretation of Culture: Selected Essays*. New York: Basic Books.

Inglis, F. (2000) *Clifford Geertz: Culture, Custom and Ethics*. Cambridge: Polity Press.

Marcus, G. and Fischer, M. (1986) *Anthropology as Cultural Critique: An Experimental Movement in the Human Sciences*. Chicago: University of Chicago Press.

Shankman, P. (1984) 'The thick and the thin: on the interpretive theoretical program of Clifford Geertz', *Current Anthropology*, 25 (3): 261–80.

THURSTONE SCALE

Definition

An attitude scale with equal-appearing intervals. It was developed by Thurstone in 1928 to measure attitudes towards the church in the United States.

Distinctive Features

Thurstone scaling starts by generating an item pool comprising approximately one hundred statements, for example in terms of Thurstone's research 'I think that the church represents everything that is good in society'. A group of 'judges' (not in a judicial sense) is selected on grounds of representativeness and typicality. Each judge is asked to sort the statements into a set number of piles (for example seven) according to their favourableness to the attitude in question (for example, attitude towards the church). The piles are sorted as if they are equally spaced, say from 1 to 7. The researcher retains those statements on which the judges agree regarding the allocation to piles. These are then embodied in a questionnaire, in random order, and respondents are asked to agree or disagree with them. The scale score for any individual is the average of all of the statements with which he or she agrees.

Evaluation

The advantage of a Thurstone scale is that the procedure is simple insofar as it requires no scoring or judging of distances. Respondents simply have to indicate with which statements they agree. The criticism of the use of the scale is that the characteristics of the judges and the underlying dimensions of their attitudes may be significantly different from those of the respondents and yet the former determine the construction of the scale which is used to measure the attitudes of the respondents.

Victor Jupp

Associated Concepts: composite measurement, indicator, Likert scale, scaling, semantic differential technique, summated rating scale

Key Readings

Anastasi, A. (1988) *Psychological Testing*, 6th edn. New York: Macmillan.

Guildford, J. P. (1956) *Psychometric Methods*. New York: McGraw-Hill.

Schuman, H. and Presser, S. (1996) *Questions and Answers in Attitude Surveys*. Thousand Oaks, CA: Sage.

Thurstone, L. L. (1928) 'Attitudes can be measured', *American Journal of Sociology*, 33: 529–54.

TIME SERIES DESIGN

Definition

A research design in which measurements of the same variables are taken at different points in time, often with a view to studying social trends. For this reason such designs are sometimes also known as trend designs and are distinguishable from 'one shot' cross-sectional designs in which measurements are taken only once.

Distinctive Features

Time series designs can be used in conjunction with official data, for example by plotting crime rates for the same area but for different point in time (monthly, quarterly, annually).

This acts as a basis for making statements about trends in levels of crime. It is possible to plot the trends for different variables at one and the same time with a view to making inferences about their relationship, for example, to map unemployment rates against crime rates for England and Wales, 1990–2000, to consider whether changes in one rate coincide with changes in the other. Although such analysis may provide evidence of association, that is, that changes in crime rates are correlated with changes in unemployment rates, it does not by itself provide a sufficient basis for making inferences about causality (that is, that changes in crime rates are caused by changes in unemployment rates).

The term time series is sometimes also used to refer to a form of survey design in which equivalent samples of the population are taken at different points of time and data collected about them, usually by interviewing sample members. The samples are equivalent because they are collected by the same principles and using the same criteria but that does not mean that the same individuals are selected (although in statistical terms that is a theoretical possibility). The British Crime Survey, carried out under the auspices of the Home Office, is an example of a time series sample survey. The first BCS was carried out in 1982 and has been repeated at regular (usually 4-year) intervals. Although there are variations, at each point in time sample members are asked to specify the type of crime and also asked to indicate whether the crime was reported to the police. Adjustments are made to the number of crimes reported by sample members to facilitate comparisons with crime officially recorded in the publication *Criminal Statistics*. In this way an estimate of the 'dark figure' of unrecorded crime is obtained.

The BCS also provides evidence of trends in crime levels and because of recognized deficiencies in official recorded data it is usually viewed as the more reliable indicator.

Evaluation

Time series designs are predominantly descriptive rather than explanatory. For example,

victim surveys such as the BCS are descriptive studies that measure crime at particular points in time, and look for trends, but have no great claims to providing explanations. There is the potential, as with all trend designs, to theorize about why changes in trends have occurred, but surveys do not by themselves provide sufficient evidence as to causality.

The value of time series surveys is that they can be used to map changes and trends in society (or a sub-section of it). However, as indicated earlier, they are based on equivalent not identical samples, in terms of including the same individuals. Therefore they should not be used as a basis for making inferences about individual development (for example, development of criminal careers). For this some variant of a longitudinal cohort survey is required.

Victor Jupp

Associated Concepts: causality, cohort study, cross-sectional survey, longitudinal study, one-shot design, panel study

Key Readings

Goldstein, H. (1979) *The Design and Analysis of Longitudinal Studies: Their Role in the Measurement of Change.* New York: Academic Press.

Magnussen, D. (ed.) (1991) *Problems and Methods in Longitudinal Research: Stability and Change.* Cambridge: Cambridge University Press.

Magnussen, D. and Bergman, L. R. eds (1990) *Data Quality in Longitudinal Research.* Cambridge: Cambridge University Press.

de Vaus, D. (2001) *Research Design in Social Research.* London: Sage.

TRACE MEASURES

Definition

Alternative methods by which social activities or phenomena can be examined and quantified in non-reactive or unobtrusive ways.

Distinctive Features

Trace measures are usually physical traces of past behaviour often synonymous with unobtrusive measures and non-reactive measures, all of which refer to alternative and often imaginative units of measurement. According to Webb et al. (1966), who first documented the use of unobtrusive measures and non-reactive research in the social sciences, these forms of data amount to proxies which 'are not specifically produced for the purposes of comparison and inference, but are available to be exploited opportunistically by the alert investigator' (Webb et al., 1966: 36). Trace measures are therefore approximations to knowledge and might include hidden observation, contrived observation, trace analysis and secondary records.

Distinctively, trace measures, as vestiges or remaining marks of the presence or existence of something, are often cheap and simple indices or signs that can be used as ways of closely monitoring social activities. There are two main types of physical traces of past behaviour, these being natural erosion measures and natural accretion measures. Where physical traces manifest themselves as wear and tear of materials, these are erosion measures. Where they are deposits of materials such as debris, inscriptions, marks, remnants or other indicators, these are natural accretion measures.

Unobtrusive measures, or trace measures, can be valuable sources of data and evidence in the social sciences. No matter how sophisticated and expensive the methods of measurements adopted by the researcher, they are often criticized for being insufficiently sensitive to measure with enough precision and detail, especially in terms of time, place and circumstance. Take, for example, the context of crime and disorder. Despite the 'data explosion' in terms of information derived from both police crime figures and victimization surveys, some critics claim that specific local patterns, trends and demographics of crime and disorder remain insufficiently detailed for focused action to be based upon them (Garwood et al., 2002). In order to generate this level of detail, these authors have suggested 'sneaky measurement of crime and disorder' and have discussed several examples from this area of social research. Some of their suggestions as regards modern measures or traces of crime and disorder represent the realities of the street, store and club. Thus signs of disorder and incivility might include an Alcopop bottle in a town centre litter bin, shards of glass outside a specific nightclub and used hypodermic syringes in a public park.

Evaluation

As they are not specifically produced as social scientific data, there are several key advantages of physical evidence data. They are not only relatively easy methods of determining long-term change at low cost but their very inconspicuousness as units of measurement ensures they are relatively free from bias; in other words they are 'free of reactive measurement effects' (Webb et al., 2000: 50). Furthermore, gathering data and evidence by means of physical traces often involves imaginative and unconventional approaches to research and can make available data in content areas where verbal reports are otherwise unavailable, invisible or unreliable. Thus they can be an asset in terms of accessing some hard-to-reach populations or groups.

Whilst there are clear advantages to the use of trace measures in the social sciences there are perhaps greater advantages in employing them alongside, or in consort with, more traditional methods. In most cases, trace measures are simply signs or indices of activity or behaviours, approximations to knowledge that cannot usually be taken alone as evidence of an actual state of affairs or as absolute evidence. In some contexts, and when used alone without triangulation of methods or combining with supplementary obtrusive and reactive techniques, physical evidence data may remain largely anecdotal. There are other specific reasons to be cautious of the use of trace measures, including the problem of selective survival of materials over time and across space affecting the ability to generalize findings as well as the risk of there being a high 'dross rate'. Finally, for some there remain significant ethical problems with the use of trace measures. These ethical dilemmas are similar to those that arise when conducting covert or hidden and unobtrusive research more generally, namely collecting data about individuals without their knowledge and consent.

Pamela Davies

Associated Concepts: covert research, indicator, spatial research, triangulation, unobtrusive measures, validity of measurement

Key Readings

Garwood, J., Rogerson, M. and Pease, K. (2002) 'Sneaky measurement of crime and disorder', in V. Jupp, P. Davies and P. Francis (eds), *Doing Criminological Research*. London: Sage. pp. 157–67.

Webb, E. J., Campbell, D. T., Schwartz, R. D. and Sechrest, L. (1966) *Unobtrusive Measures*. Chicago: Rand McNally.

Webb, E. J., Campbell, D. T., Schwartz, R. D. and Sechrest, L. (2000) *Unobtrusive Measures*, rev. edn. London: Sage.

TRANSCRIPTION

Definition

The rendering of recorded talk into a standard written form.

Distinctive Features

Transcription of recorded talk is done to facilitate analysis, where the choice of one system over another, or of a level of detail within a system, depends on the researcher's analytic perspective. In social research, talk is often transcribed non-technically, often by secretarial assistants, so that researchers can work through materials such as interviews, looking for 'content' (ideas, arguments, etc.) of various kinds. Technical transcripts include additional linguistic intonational and interactional features.

The most influential technical system for social (rather than linguistic) research has been developed by Gail Jefferson for Conversation Analysis (CA). It is designed to support the examination of talk as social interaction; to include the features that participants demonstrably use and treat as significant; and to display the grounds for analytical claims.

The system shows the precise onset and ending of overlapping talk, timed pauses, and intonational features including emphasis, elongation, cut-offs and pitch movement. Here is a short segment of a telephone conversation transcribed by Jefferson:

Emma:	uh HONEY I'LL PR<u>A</u>Y FOR EV'RYBOD<u>Y</u>=
Lottie:	[=Alri:̤ght,]
Emma:	[=I:- ̣l] don't kno:w,hh this: [uh w]orld goes o:̣:n=
Lottie:	[Yeh.]
Emma:	=we have to <u>keep</u> ↓goin' d<u>o</u>[n't we.]
Lottie:	[Ye:ah,]
	(.)
Lottie:	[U h h <u>u</u> h]
Emma:	[D'you feel h]a:ppy toda:y?
	(0.4)
Lottie:	↑Ye:ah.
Emma:	Good.

Square brackets mark overlaps; colons signal elongation; underlining shows emphasis; and the arrows mark pitch rise and fall. Familiar punctuation marks are re-defined to signify intonation or speech delivery rather than grammar. For example, periods (full stops) signal a falling, 'terminal contour', and question marks signal a rising 'questioning' contour, irrespective of grammatical criteria such as sentence boundaries and interrogative syntax. There are many other features in the system.

The initial difficulty of reading CA transcripts is largely due to our familiarity with conventional written text. But that familiarity should not be mistaken for neutrality; ordinary typescript is not a straightforward way of representing talk. Rather, it transforms a lived medium of social interaction into a form that was neither invented nor designed for transcription. There is a large literature on the history, social functions, uses and effects of written text that warns against its ostensible neutrality. Jefferson's system encourages and permits analysis of talk as situated social action rather than, say, a decontextualized record of someone's ideas.

Evaluation

Producing technical transcripts is time-consuming, and requires practice and training. It also goes with an approach to language materials, including interviews, that many researchers may not wish to adopt, which treats them as interaction prior to any status they might have as collections of facts, information and opinions. One general advantage is the attention that has to be paid to talk's details; conventional transcripts are often surprisingly inaccurate.

Although Jefferson's system reflects a keen interest in the precision of conversational turn-taking, it is wrong to imagine that the system is limited to that interest. Primarily, it renders talk as social action. Features such as pauses, overlaps and detailed self-corrections display the status of talk's content as sensitive to interactional considerations and to speakers' concurrent activities. It is not a matter of choosing whether to use a transcription system or not. Conventional typescript imposes alterations and omissions that are easily overlooked, but that transform talk into a form that distracts attention from its status as social activity.

No transcription system is perfect or all-purpose. But alterations have to be slow and gradual, because standardization is crucial. Contemporary work (for example, Goodwin, 2000) is extending the system for the kinds of non-linguistic features, captured in video recordings, that were less significant in the telephone conversations that provided much of the material for the system's initial development.

Derek Edwards

Associated Concepts: conversation analysis, discursive psychology, epistemology, ethnomethodology, narrative analysis, naturalistic data

Key Readings

Atkinson, J. M. and Heritage, J. (1999) 'Jefferson's transcript notation', in A. Jaworski and N. Coupland, (eds), *The Discourse Reader.* London: Routledge. pp. 158–66.

Edwards, J. A. and Lampert, M. D. (eds) (1993) *Talking Data: Transcription and Coding in Discourse Research.* Hillsdale, NJ: Lawrence Erlbaum.

Goodwin, C. (2000) 'Gesture, aphasia and interaction', in D. McNeill (ed.), *Language and Gesture.* Cambridge: Cambridge University Press. pp. 84–98.

Have, P. (1999) *Doing Conversation Analysis: A Practical Guide.* London: Sage.

Psathas, G. and Anderson, T. (1990) 'The "practices" of transcription in conversation analysis', *Semiotica,* 78: 75–99.

TRIANGULATION

Definition

In social research, the term is used to refer to the observation of the research issue from (at least) two different points. This understanding of the term is used in qualitative as well as quantitative research and in the context of combining both.

Distinctive Features

Triangulation is most often equated with applying different methodological approaches. Earlier discussions about non-reactive measurement and of the multi-trait–multi-method matrix were the starting points for developing this idea of triangulation. Initially, triangulation was understood as a validation strategy. But in a broader understanding, four different forms are distinguished. *Triangulation of data* combines data drawn from different sources and at different times, in different places or from different people. *Investigator triangulation* is characterized by the use of different observers or interviewers, to balance out the subjective influences of individuals. *Triangulation of theories* means to approach data from different theoretical angles, which are used side by side to assess their usefulness. Most often, triangulation is seen as *methodological triangulation,* either 'within-method' or 'between-method'. The intention here was originally to maximize the validity of research by playing the methods off against each other.

Examples of within-method triangulation are the use of different sub-scales within a questionnaire or the episodic interview (Flick, 2002). Here, some research issue is explored by means of invitations to narrate, focusing on experiences in concrete situations. These narratives are combined with questions that focus more on definitions and general answers. Thus an attempt is made in such an interview systematically to unite the methodological approaches of the semi-structured interview and the narrative, using their respective strengths.

Between-method triangulation is most strongly associated with the keyword triangulation. For example, combination of different (qualitative or quantitative) procedures is proposed in order to transcend the boundaries of both methodological approaches. Moreover, this makes it possible to capture different aspects of the research issue – such as concrete professional routines in observations and practitioners' knowledge of their own modes of action and routines via interviews.

The most consistent variant is to apply the triangulated methods to the same cases: the persons being observed in a particular field are (all) interviewed. This makes a case-related analysis of both types of data possible. In addition, comparisons can also be undertaken at a higher level: patterns that emerge from analysing one type of data can be set against patterns in the other type of data. However, this increases the load for an individual participant in a study and the danger of dropouts rises markedly. Everyone who refuses either to provide an interview or to be observed is 'lost' to the entire investigation. In such cases, triangulation should be implemented at the level of data sets. Each method is applied independently of any other. Both data sets resulting from this are analysed first. Triangulation then relates the results of both analyses and to each other.

Evaluation

Triangulation has been criticized for several reasons. The idea to use it as a simple form of validation has been questioned, as was the mere and simple combination of methods without taking differences in theoretical backgrounds and ways of constructing the issue under study into account.

The idea of a 'systematic triangulation of perspectives' (Flick, 1992) tries to address both points. Here different research perspectives within qualitative research are combined with one another in a targeted way, to complement their strong points and to illustrate their respective limitations. So the combination of methods is contextualized in the combination of theoretical and research perspectives.

Triangulation is currently also being used in the debate about the relationship between qualitative and quantitative research. If the concept of triangulation is taken seriously, it is characteristic of all of these variants that they see the procedures they combine as being of equal value and that they do not begin by regarding one procedure as central and the others as preliminary or illustrative. We therefore have three modes of application for triangulation: as a validation strategy, as an approach to the generalization of discoveries, and as a route to additional knowledge.

Uwe Flick

Associated Concepts: analytic induction, data, methodology, mixed-methods research, qualitative research, trace measures, validity

Key Readings

Denzin, N. K. (1978/1989) *The Research Act: A Theoretical Introduction to Sociological Methods*. New York: McGraw–Hill (2nd edn)/Englewood Cliffs, NJ: Prentice Hall (3rd edn).

Flick, Uwe (1992) 'Triangulation revisited– strategy of or alternative to validation of qualitative data', *Journal for the Theory of Social Behavior*, 22: 175–97.

Flick, Uwe (2002) *An Introduction to Qualitative Research,* 2nd edn. London: Sage.

Flick, Uwe (2004) 'Triangulation', in U. Flick, E. von Kardorff and I. Steinke (eds), *Qualitative Research – Paradigms, Theories, Methods, Practice and Contexts.* London: Sage.

TYPE 1 AND TYPE 2 ERRORS

Definition

The category of error associated with the incorrect retention of a hypothesis. Error results when inference testing of a sample population suggests the retention of the hypothesis, when the unobserved true value present in the universe from which the sample was drawn would call for the rejection of the hypothesis. A Type 1 error occurs when the null hypothesis is falsely rejected, while a Type 2 error occurs when the research hypothesis is falsely rejected (thus wrongly retaining the null hypothesis). Essentially, Type 1 errors are 'false-positive' findings, while Type 2 errors are 'false-negative' findings.

Distinctive Features

The logic behind Type 1 and 2 errors rests on the underlying nature of random probability sampling. As a sample is *at best* representative of the larger universe under study, the decision whether or not to retain a hypothesis is based on an estimation known as a test of significance. As sampling makes it impossible to know the precise nature of the universe population under study, significance testing is unable to offer absolute confirmation that a hypothesis should be retained or rejected, but rather only a probability that we have committed an error in retention or rejection. A significance test results in the probability that an association observed in the data results from chance in the sample rather than a revealed true relationship in the universe population.

Hypothesis testing is an inherently conservative practice. This results from the philosophical underpinnings of the social sciences and recognition that, under certain conditions, false-positive findings can be dangerous. Therefore, focus is placed upon the null hypothesis, which typically assumes that there is no relationship between two variables. The counter to the null hypothesis is the research hypothesis, which has some degree of theoretical justification in suggesting a relationship between two variables. In order to minimize the probability of committing a Type 1 error, we retain the null hypothesis unless the significance test of a relationship is typically at the level of 0.05 or below. This results in a probability of 95 per cent that the observed relationship between two variables represents a real relationship in the universe, and not a function of chance in the sample population. Over time, a social scientist employing a 0.05 significance level for the rejection of the null hypothesis will commit a Type 1 error 5 per cent of the time.

Evaluation

The probabilities of committing a Type 1 and Type 2 error are inversely related, although the exact probability of committing a Type 2 error is unknowable. The more conservative the approach in deciding whether or not to reject the null hypothesis necessarily results in a likely higher probability of committing a Type 2 error. While the level of significance used to determine retention or rejection of the null is necessarily arbitrary, convention in the social sciences suggests a minimum level of significance appropriate for the rejection of the null hypothesis at 0.05. It is also common to report significance levels of 0.01 and 0.001, which further reduces the probability of committing a Type 1 error to 1 per cent or 0.1 per cent, respectively, with the concomitant increased probability of resulting in a Type 2 error.

A common example used to illustrate the difference between Type 1 and 2 errors is the presumption of innocence in criminal trials. A defendant in a criminal trial enjoys the presumption of innocence, while the state prosecutor has the responsibility to prove 'beyond a shadow of doubt' that the defendant is guilty. If an innocent citizen is found guilty of a crime, a Type 1 false-positive error is committed. If a guilty person is found innocent, a Type 2 error is committed.

David Brockington

Associated Concepts: error, falsification, hypothesis, inferential statistics, probability (random) sampling

Key Readings

David, M. and Sutton, C. (2004) *Social Research: The Basics*. London: Sage.
Nachmias, C. F. and Nachmias, D. (1996) *Research Methods in the Social Sciences*, 5th edn. New York: St Martin's Press.

U

UNOBTRUSIVE MEASURES

Definition

Measures that concentrate on the traces of human action, on the evidence of human activity left in the environment. Traces need not be incidental, they can be intentionally created, such as graffiti.

Distinctive Features

Although some disciplines are reliant on these methods, such as archaeology, in the social sciences the methods were not given a framework until 1966 when Webb, Campbell, Schwartz and Sechrest (1966) published *Unobtrusive Measures: Nonreactive Research in the Social Sciences* (updated in 1981 as *Nonreactive Measures in the Social Sciences*).

Unobtrusive measures can be used within an experimental framework, for example, within the 'lost letters' paradigm. Merritt and Fowler (1948) wanted to know about public honesty, and to test this they put letters in envelopes with addresses, and in some they placed lead weights the size of 50 cents pieces. The independent measures were the numbers of letters of each kind mailed back.

Unobtrusive measures can also be used to investigate much more sensitive matters, such as drug use of certain kinds. The goal in all of these cases has been to study behaviours that are very likely to be subject to response bias under more direct forms of measurement, for example direct questioning, or where researchers might be put at risk. An example is that of an investigation of the levels and patterns of drug use in the community. Police data are severely limited as this constitutes arrest data, and arrests are subject to police activity and 'special' operations. Therefore the data will misrepresent certain types of people or drug types that are less likely to come to police attention. Data from drug treatment agencies represent only those whose use has become problematic and have accessed services. Further, it is widely documented now that few drug users can obtain services, or even try to obtain them, even when needed. A survey of drug users would be subject to response bias with respondents either playing down or exaggerating their substance use, according to their own motives. Unobtrusive measures of drug use, including disposed or discarded drug paraphernalia and hepatitis 'C' rates, can identify patterns, which may confirm or complement trends in administrative statistics, while at the same time avoiding the problems associated with reactivity, invasion of privacy and ethical principles.

It is possible to use other kinds of unobtrusive measures, such as minutes of public meetings, or management committee meetings in schools or other public organizations. Although this is commonly called archival or document-based research, it is also a type of unobtrusive measure. The main principle behind the method is that the data should already be in existence, or very easy to obtain. Our personal experience is that asking public authorities for copies of information they already hold can make information suddenly very sensitive. Therefore it is wise to find unobtrusive measures that researchers can observe or collect for themselves.

The kinds of unobtrusive data suggested here are all amenable to quantitative analysis, and with care, inferential statistics.

Evaluation

Unobtrusive measurement has several crucial advantages over the alternatives. It is normally cheap, it is not liable to response bias and is seldom attached to any single individual, reducing ethical problems associated with invasion of privacy. Such data cannot always be conclusive when taken alone, but will be suggestive and are best gathered using the principle of triangulation, where several kinds of data are collected in order to address the same question.

The advantages include the non-reactivity of the methods: since the performers are not aware of being part of an investigation, they do not behave as if they are being observed. They provide cross-validation of mainstream methods. They encourage researchers to look at their research questions afresh, and consider new ways of investigation. Therefore they provide a spur to ingenuity and creativity in research.

The disadvantages of the methods, some suggest, include the lack of identity of the person providing the data. Also, there are problems of making inferences about the level of incidence. For example, one person may be responsible for most of the graffiti in an area. Also, the apparent level of cause and effect may be mediated by other influences. For example, consumption of diet foods in a girls' dormitory may have less to do with eating problems or worries about weight control, and more to do with sales promotions and free gifts. It is important to eliminate the unlikely explanation, before assuming that unobtrusive measures are signs of particular kinds of behaviour. Finally, although unobtrusive measures research may avoid certain ethical problems it can also raise others. For example, analysing the contents of residents, garbage cans may indicate forms of lifestyle but can also contravene the principle of informed consent.

Jeanette Garwood and Michelle Rogerson

Associated Concepts: content analysis, diary, Internet research, naturalistic data, photography, trace measures, triangulation, validy of measurement

Key Readings

Lee, R. M. (2000) *Unobtrusive Measures in Social Research*. Milton Keynes: Open University Press.

Merritt, C. B. and Fowler, R. G. (1948) 'The pecuniary honesty of the public at large', *Journal of Abnormal and Social Psychology*, 43: 90–3.

Webb, E. J., Campbell, D. T., Schwartz, R. D. and Sechrest, L. (1966) *Unobtrusive Measures: Non-reactive Research in the Social Sciences*. Chicago: Rand McNally.

Webb, E. J., Campbell, D. T., Schwartz, R. D., Sechrest, L. and Grove, J. B. (1981) *Non-reactive Measures in the Social Sciences*. Boston, MA: Houghton Mifflin.

V

VALIDITY

Definition

The extent to which conclusions drawn from research provide an accurate description of what happened or a correct explanation of what happens and why.

Distinctive Features

The assessment of the overall validity of conclusions drawn from a research project can be made by addressing three aspects. First, validity of measurement involves asking whether a research instrument, for example a questionnaire, measures what it purports to. Second, validity of explanation (sometimes also known as internal validity) involves asking whether the explanations and conclusions derived from research are the correct ones for the specific subjects or contexts that have been studied. Third, validity of generalization (sometimes referred to as external validity) involves asking whether the conclusions drawn from a particular study can be generalized to other people (population validity) and other contexts (ecological validity).

Evaluation

Validity is associated with the notions of truth and of realism (the philosophical viewpoint that there is some social reality which can be studied, described and explained). However, validity does not sit easily within forms of relativism (the philosophical viewpoint that knowledge and truth are relative to time periods, cultural, social and political frameworks), including phenomenology, constructionism, hermeneutics, critical research and postmodernism.

Victor Jupp

Associated Concepts: realism, relativism, reliability, validity of explanation, validity of generalization, validity of measurement

Key Readings

Bryman, A. (2004) *Social Research Methods*, 2nd edn. Oxford: Oxford University Press.
Smith, H. W. (1975) *Strategies of Social Research: The Methodological Imagination*. Englewood Cliffs, NJ: Prentice Hall.

VALIDITY OF EXPLANATION

Definition

The extent to which an explanation of how and why some social phenomenon occurs is the correct one. It is sometimes known as internal validity.

Distinctive Features

Most social research involves studying a sample of cases (for example, individuals) in specific contexts, with a view to generalizing beyond these. Such generalization is only sound if the conclusions drawn from the study of particular cases in specific contexts can be shown to be internally valid. In experimental, survey and other quantitative, variable-based research this usually means assembling evidence that no variables other than those under consideration could have produced the outcome that has been observed. In experimental research this is done by ensuring that control and experimental groups are matched on key variables – which may offer alternative explanations – prior to administering the 'treatment' to one group and not to the other (the control group). Any subsequent and significant differences between the groups can be attributed to the treatment variable. In this way, the threats to the internal validity of the explanation which may have come from the 'matching' variables have been ruled out.

The direct manipulation of variables to reduce threats to validity is only feasible in controlled laboratory conditions. For this reason survey-based research relies on statistical methods to rule out possible alternative explanatory variables. Statistical techniques allow the data analyst to hold some variables constant whilst manipulating others to assess whether any variance in the dependent variable can be attributed to such manipulation. Multivariate analysis encompasses such techniques.

In addition to demonstrating that changes in one (dependent) variable are associated with changes in other (independent) variables and also that other variables have been ruled out (either by experimental design or statistical control), valid conclusions – especially in relation to causality – require evidence of temporal sequence. This is evidence that the changes in the dependent variable only occurred *after* changes in the independent variables. Outside of the laboratory it is often difficult to obtain direct evidence of temporal sequence. For this reason, the explanatory validity of surveys tends to be weaker than that for experimental research.

Evaluation

The notion of explanatory or internal validity is most usually associated with quantitative research and the search for causes. However,

qualitative researchers are also concerned with establishing validity. This is not in terms of controlling or ruling out alternative variables but in terms of providing assurances that the account that has been put forward (say, of interactions in the classroom) is the correct one. This is done by analytic induction (searching for conclusions that do not fit the conclusions) and reflexivity (reflecting on the possible effects of the researcher on the conclusions put forward).

Victor Jupp

Associated Concepts: analytic induction, causality, experiment, field experiment, qualitative research, reflexivity, social survey

Key Readings

Bryman, A. (2004) *Social Research Methods*, 2nd edn. Oxford: Oxford University Press.

Hague, J. and Meeker, B. F. (1988) *Social Causality*. London: Unwin Hyman.

McKim, V. R. and Turner, S. P. (eds) (1997) *Causality in Crisis: Statistical Methods and the Search for Causal Knowledge in the Social Sciences.* Notre Dame, IN: University of Notre Dame Press.

Smith, H. W. (1975) *Strategies of Social Research*: *The Methodological Imagination.* Englewood Cliffs, NJ: Prentice Hall.

VALIDITY OF GENERALIZATION

Definition

The extent to which information from a sample gives us information about a population, or the extent to which information about one setting tells us about others (which may be of more interest to us).

Distinctive Features

Two varieties of the term can be noted. First, *population validity* is the extent to which sample distributions mirror those of the population which the sample is supposed to represent. Given perfectly conducted random sampling, probability theory permits us to estimate population parameters from sample readings with a calculable error margin known as sampling error – if 30 per cent of the sample believe something or have a certain characteristic, our best estimate is that this will be true of 30 per cent of the population, plus or minus a calculable error margin, in a calculable proportion of the samples that could possibly have been drawn. To the extent that the sample is less than perfect (non-sampling error), this estimate is distorted. A common source of non-sampling error, for example, is the fact that a proportion of most preselected random samples will decline to take part, or we will fail to locate them, thereby changing the nature of the sample in ways that cannot be predicted reliably.

In ethnographic and other qualitative research, where samples are small, this kind of generalizability is seldom achievable. In these cases the researcher will generally attempt to establish population validity by arguing the typicality of the setting or institution that is being studied, or assessing the extent to which it may not be typical, and/or demonstrating that the cases investigated at least cover the range of what might have been expected, with no group obviously excluded from the study.

Second, *ecological validity* is the extent to which results from one setting can safely be generalized to others. More specifically, the concept is often used to criticize the more structured varieties of research which attempt to generalize from the artificial social situations of the survey or the social laboratory experiment to what people do or say or believe in their ordinary lives, outside the research situation. What is at stake here is *naturalism* – the need to study everyday life 'undisturbed' and free from the artefacts introduced by research structures and procedures. We should note that this is seldom entirely achievable even in qualitative research; virtually all research imposes some degree of structure or change on the natural circumstance.

Evaluation

A third sense of the term is *theoretical generalizability*, the extent to which the *interpretation* of the data can be generalized beyond the immediate research sample or setting to give information about a wider population. The term is used most commonly in qualitative research.

Theoretical generalizability is generally established in the first instance by looking at other, similar settings or samples that differ in some key respect, to see whether the original theorized interpretation will also fit the new data. Researchers may check, for example, that accounts of doctors' decision making in terms of UK gender stereotypes based on a sample from the north of England can be reproduced in samples of southerners or people from Scotland or Wales, and whether conclusions based on predominantly working-class areas hold true for doctors with middle-class practices. A next step might be to see whether it is just *doctors'* decision making which is being described, by carrying out similar work with school teachers, perhaps, or social workers; the results might mean that theory needs to be recast in terms of the decision making of 'social professionals' in general. Finally, we might look for situations where the model should definitely *not* fit; in this example, if we are talking about doctors' or professionals' decision making rather than generally shared cultural stereotypes, then data from the doctors' *patients* should not be describable in the same terms.

Roger Sapsford

Associated Concepts: inferential statistics, non-probability (non-random) sampling, probability (random) sampling, sampling, validity of explanation, validity of measurement

Key Readings

Sapsford, R. and Jupp, V. (eds) (1996) *Data Collection and Analysis*. London: Sage. chs 1 and 2.

Schofield, J. W. (1989) 'Increasing the generalisability of qualitative research', in M. Hammersley (ed.) (1993), *Social Research: Philosophy, Politics and Practice*. London: Sage.

VALIDITY OF MEASUREMENT

Definition

The extent to which an indicator or variable adequately measures the theoretical concept it purports to measure.

Distinctive Features

The major requirement of measurement is *validity*. For research to be conducted, theoretical concepts (and research questions and hypotheses of which they are part) must be *operationalized,* that is, cast in terms of information that can be collected and manipulated in the public domain. The theoretical concept may be social class or social capital or sociability, but the operationalized indicator or variable will be about current job or extent to which people are engaged in vertical social networks or their scores on a personality questionnaire. The validity of this operationalization is the extent to which the fitness of the operationalized indicator to measure the theoretical concept can be justified and demonstrated.

The main ways of warranting validity are: *face Validity* – that 'on the face of it' the test measures what it says it does; *concurrent validity* – that it gives the same answers as an already validated measure; *predictive* or *criterion- related* validity – that the test or measurement predicts an outcome or correctly identifies group membership. Face validity is obviously the weakest form of warrant – 'well, it looks as though this ought to measure that'. It may be sufficient in some circumstances – it may be a sufficient warrant for the validity of a test of arithmetic that the items are patently arithmetical problems. Even then, doubts may be cast; arguably, timed tests measure people's tolerance of stress as well as their arithmetical ability, in that those who can tolerate stress will tend to do better at them.

Concurrent validity is useful when proposing an alternative measure because the accepted one is not appropriate – showing, for example, that a short form of a test or one rewritten in language appropriate to young children gives much the same results as the existing form. It does not itself solve the problem of validity unless the validity of the comparison test can be demonstrated.

Predictive validity is quite a strong form of warranty – demonstrating that your test can predict performance on something agreed to be an expression of the construct to be measured. Tests of initial ability, for example, are validated by their prediction of eventual performance. For example, the use of car ownership in an area as a measure of affluence can be validated against average income in the area (and is used when employing census data, for example, where car ownership is measured but income is not). A personality scale of Machiavellianism (the tendency to achieve one's goals by manipulating other people) was validated against performance in a game where manipulation brought results.

All of these may be seen as aspects of the broader concept of *construct validation* – demonstration of the extent to which the underlying concept ('construct') coherently fulfils what is demanded of it, by demonstration that measures can be devised which do so. Within construct validation we speak of two varieties. First, *convergent validation* is where tests perform as theory demands of them. Many of the senses of validity above are concerned with demonstrating this – that a trait measurement, for example, is stable over time, performs similarly to other accepted measures and correctly predicts behaviour. *Unidimensionality* (generally demonstrated by factor analysis) would be another aspect of convergent validation – demonstrating that the test measured a single trait or characteristic and was not contaminated by confounded variables. Second, *discriminant validation*, equally important, is to demonstrate that a test does *not* do what it is supposed not to do. A test of arithmetical ability, for example, should not also measure anxiety, and it should give high scores only to those who subsequently perform well at arithmetic. A test that also picked out people good at English or Art might more properly be considered a test of *general* ability.

Evaluation

In the main, validity of operationalization and measurement relates to quantitative research. Qualitative research does not operationalize but attempts to work holistically. However, it still faces problems of validity in trying to demonstrate that the patterns it records are typical of the persons or settings and not products of the research situation. In other words, it needs to consider *reactivity* – personal reactivity (reaction to the person, role and actions of the researcher) and procedural reactivity (reaction to the way in which the research was conducted). One strategy for overcoming these kinds of doubts is *triangulation* – using more than one person or more than one procedure (for example, comparing oral interviews with text produced by or about the informants) to look for convergence. However, the major tool is *reflexivity* – careful and practised sensitivity about the extent to which personal characteristics and behaviour, the accidents of the research setting, the relationships involved and the biases and preconceptions of the researcher may have an effect on the nature of the data produced. The aim is to produce a research report that is transparent about how data are collected and interpretations made, so that the reader can form his or her own judgement of their validity. This kind of sensitivity is also present in the best quantitative work.

Roger Sapsford

Associated Concepts: indicator, measurement, reflexivity, reliability, social indicators, triangulation, validity of explanation, validity of generalization

Key Readings

Blalock, H. M. Jr (1968) 'The measurement problem: a gap between the language of theory and research', in H. M. Blalock Jr and A. B. Blalock (eds), *Methodology in Social Research*. New York: McGraw–Hill. pp. 5–27.

Moser, C. A. and Kalton, G. (1971) *Survey Methods in Social Investigation*. London: Heinemann.
Smith, H. W. (1975) *Strategies of Social Research*. Englewood Cliffs, NJ: Prentice Hall.

VALUE-FREE RESEARCH

Definition

Research that has been produced by a completely impartial and dispassionate researcher. The proposition is that if a researcher can conduct a study shorn of his or her own particular beliefs, values, prejudices and opinions, this impartiality will presumably be reflected in the end product of the research.

Distinctive Features

The proposition that a researcher can truly be 'value-free' is hotly contested in the social sciences. On one side of the equation, one could argue that a researcher may indeed be 'value-free'. This is most likely in studies that incorporate large-scale statistical analysis in which a respondent is only able to provide answers in a closed setting. Examples of this can be found in market research, or opinion polling. Value-free research is therefore more indicative of a quantitative or positivist research methodology. Defenders of the approach sometimes argue that researchers can be just as impartial as a scientist observing a laboratory experiment or some particular phenomenon in the natural world.

On the other hand, however, a large number of academics dispute that research can be value-free. The main thrust of this line of thinking is that whenever a researcher analyses a given social area, he or she will always bring his or her own belief system into the research. In addition, and by implication, when a researcher decides to analyse a specific area, they will have done so because they have an interest in the subject matter. And where an interest exists, the researcher will necessarily have opinions and values.

From the outset, therefore, the researcher simply cannot be value-free. This is largely recognized in many forms of interpretative and qualitative research, particularly those that involve interaction with the respondent.

Furthermore, quantitative research can be criticized for the type of questions that are put to respondents. In a closed setting, the researcher is only asking questions on areas that he or she has already deemed fit for inclusion. Hence, even though the questions may be neutral and value-free, the process of framing the questions has been affected by value judgements.

A counter-argument is that a researcher may stumble into an issue area by chance (for example, becoming a research associate in an already established project). In such circumstances, the researcher may not have any previous knowledge, or values for that matter, in the subject. One could then plausibly assume that the researcher is indeed value-free. Those coming from an interpretative standpoint, however, would assert that as the research progresses, the researcher will necessarily build up their own value-system, thereby prejudicing their work.

Evaluation

For some, value-free research is a goal that all researchers should aim for. Nevertheless, an increasing number of researchers now recognize that their own value systems will influence their fieldwork to a greater or lesser degree. For those who come from a critical, emancipatory or standpoint research tradition, value freedom is not even a desirable goal.

Craig McLean

Associated Concepts: anti-racism research, critical research, emancipatory research, feminist research, relativism, standpoint research

Key Readings

Keat, R. and Urry, J. (1982) *Social Theory as Science.* London: Routledge & Kegan Paul.
Phillips, D. C. (1987) *Philosophy, Science and Social Inquiry.* Oxford: Pergamon Press.
Scheffler, I. (1982) *Science and Subjectivity,* 2nd edn. Indianapolis: Hackett.

VARIABLE ANALYSIS

Definition

Variables are units of data that can change between different cases. The different values that a variable can take affect the type of analysis that is possible. Variables can be analysed on their own (univariate analysis), with one other variable (bivariate analysis) or with a number of others (multivariate analysis).

Distinctive Features

Variable analysis is a key characteristic of quantitative research. While qualitative analysis tends to be concerned more with themes, interpretation and the use of language, quantitative analysis examines variables, which are typically collected through surveys, although sometimes by other methods such as observation. Variables can represent a characteristic (for example, a person's age), factual matters (the number of times they have been a victim of crime) or opinions (the punishment for criminals that they think is most appropriate). The types of analysis that can be undertaken depend on the nature of the variable, so it is necessary to consider some distinctions.

Categorical variables – here any number that is applied to a value has no meaning, other than as a label. For example, it is common to code male as 1 and female as 2, but there is no reason why this should not be 1 for female and 2 for male.

Ordinal variables place data in a particular order – for example a respondent may be asked to number different leisure activities from the one that they most like to do to the one that they least like to do.

Cardinal variables represent a 'real' value, for example someone's height in centimetres or the number of children that they have. Cardinal variables are sometimes further divided between *discrete variables* (which can only have a limited number of values, for example number of children) and *continuous variables* (where it is not possible to specify all the possible values, for example height). They can also be divided between interval and ratio variables.

The type of univariate analysis that can be undertaken with categorical variables is restricted to identifying the frequency with which values occur or calculating the percentage of responses falling into one or more categories. In contrast, ordinal variables and cardinal variables can be discussed in terms of measures of central tendency – the mean, median and mode – and measures of dispersion, such as the range and standard deviation.

Bivariate and multivariate analyses for any type of data seek to establish relationships between variables, for example whether high income tends to be associated with voting for a particular political party. When a random (or probability) sample has been taken, inferential statistical tests can be used to measure the likelihood that a relationship between variables that appears in a sample will be reproduced in the population.

Examples of such inferential tests are the chi-square test of independence – which examines the relationship between two categorical variables – and the *t*-test, which can be used where there is one cardinal variable and one dichotomous categorical variable (that is, one that can take two possible values, such as gender).

Evaluation

Bivariate and multivariate analysis are often used to establish that one variable (the independent variable) has an effect on another (the dependent variable). However, care must be taken not to draw incorrect conclusions about causation. Common difficulties include the following. First, confusion over the dependent and the independent variables: for example, homeless people are more likely than the population as a whole to have mental health problems, but is this because the onset of mental illness makes it more difficult to remain in accommodation, or because the experience of homelessness is likely to be damaging to mental health? Second, failure to take account of other variables: for example, a programme of teaching in schools about the value of exercise may be followed by an increase in the number of children taking part in sport, but it is possible that the children were more influenced by watching the Olympic Games than by the teaching.

Jamie Harding

Associated Concepts: chi-square test, coding, data, descriptive statistics, factor analysis, inferential statistics, measurement, multivariate analysis, parametric tests, probability (random) sampling

Key Readings

Fielding, J. and Gilbert, N. (2000) *Understanding Social Statistics*. London: Sage.
de Vaus, D. (2002) *Analysing Social Science Data*. London: Sage.

VERSTEHEN

Definition

Verstehen is a German word meaning 'understanding'. *Verstehen* sociology emphasizes the necessity of understanding the meaning of human action.

Distinctive Features

Verstehen sociology is usually associated with the work of Max Weber (1864–1920), but he was not the first to use the term, which derives from the tradition of hermeneutics in nineteenth-century German thought. Writers in this tradition, such as Wilhelm Dilthey (1833–1911), argued that the subject matter of the human sciences differs from that of the natural sciences since human action is meaningful and purposive. Social events, therefore, are contingent upon subjective interpretations, motivations and choices. The methods of the natural sciences could not deal effectively with these dimensions and it was argued that a special method of understanding, *Verstehen*, is needed to interpret the subjective and cultural aspects of social phenomena. Drawing upon this tradition and applying it to social science, Weber was critical of positivism, and also of Marxism, which proposed the existence of general laws, the discovery of which would provide a causal explanation of human action and social events. In contrast, Weber emphasized the need to understand the values that shape people's actions, and to understand these values in a non-judgemental ('value-neutral') way (Weber, 1949).

However, he did not consider that social science should be concerned only with the interpretation of subjective worlds. For Weber, *Verstehen* includes explanation, an understanding of motive and its relationship to action. He maintained that subjective meanings could be studied objectively in a scientific manner, through the analysis of ideal types, particularly of human rationality. He also argued that social science should look for widespread regularities in subjective values over periods of time: such regularities become social facts and amenable to scientific analysis and empirical proof. A scientific analysis should also demonstrate a 'fit' between the subjective choices typically made by individuals and the actual occurrence of phenomena. (Weber's own work on the relationship between protestantism and the development of capitalism (Weber, 1930) illustrates his approach.) Thus, Weber did not see subjective interpretation and causal explanation as opposed: rather he argued that in social science, any adequate explanation of phenomena must include an understandable account of the subjective meanings of action. That is, *Verstehen*, the rational understanding of the subjective world-views of the actors involved in social events, is an essential component of explanation.

Evaluation

Many aspects of Weber's work remain controversial (see, for example, Bauman, 1978), including his emphasis on rationality in human action, the extent to which subjective meanings can be determined objectively and proved to have played a causal role in social events. Issues about the relationship between structure and agency remain a central concern of social theory and Weber's work, although criticized, remains relevant.

Weber's work on *Verstehen* is an important strand of interpretivism in social science and social research in itself as well as informing the development of phenomenology and ethnomethodology and symbolic interactionism.

Maggie Sumner

Associated Concepts: hermeneutics, intersubjective understanding, methodology, textual analysis

Key Readings

Bauman, Z. (1978) *Hermeneutics and Social Science: Approaches to Understanding*. London: Hutchison.
Parkin, F. (1982) *Max Weber*. London: Tavistock.
Swingewood, A. (1991) *A Short History of Sociological Thought*, (2nd edn.) London: Macmillan.
Weber, M. (1930) *The Protestant Ethic and the Spirit of Capitalism*. London: Allen & Unwin.
Weber, M. (1949) *The Methodology of the Social Sciences*. New York: Free Press.

VIDEOGRAPHY

Definition

A form of visual anthropology encompassing the collection, analysis and presentation of visual data; more specifically, an audiovisually based ethnography that is the product of a participant-observational research method that records interviews and observations of particular peoples, groups and their cultural artefacts, utilizes them as data, edits them into a format for presentation, and represents it in the form of a film.

Distinctive Features

Videography collects a distinctive form of data: audiovisual ('AV') cultural data. It uses distinct means to capture and analyse it: video cameras, film and other AV recording devices. It produces its research representation in a unique form: as an edited film. As digital technology has advanced over the past decade, the expenses associated with producing and distributing broadcast quality video have plummeted. These developments have led to a blossoming of possibilities for almost any ethnographic researcher to enter the domain of filmmaking once reserved for documentary journalists and only the most well financed social scientists.

The most basic use of video, and still the most common, is the videotaped individual or group interview, conducted either in a research facility or in a field setting. Videotaped interviews offer the powerful advantage of capturing body language, proxemics, kinesics and other temporal-spatial dimensions of human behaviour and social meaning. In this use, the researcher is interested in capturing information about what the cultural informants say about what they do. The second most common use of video in research is to record naturalistic observations. In recording naturalistic observations, the videographer is more interested in capturing what people do rather than what they say about what they do.

Variants of the videography based on naturalistic observation are common. One involved the attempt to understand the culture member's viewpoint by having them directly capture it on videotape or film. This autobiographical and autovideographical technique has the advantage over researcher-conducted observation of being less intrusive and less directed by researcher motives and needs. Collaborative

videographic research techniques offer a middle ground between unobtrusive researcher observation and autovideography, in which researcher and informants jointly negotiate the edited end product. As well, by interviewing and observing other culture members, informants can leverage their own status as cultural insiders in ways that would be difficult and time-consuming for ethnographers.

Retrospective applications are also possible, using, for instance, home movies which may be combined with subsequent elicitation of verbal informant data. The film footage, in this case, acts as a projective stimulus for eliciting other videographic data. Other film archives, such as those of commercial and promotional films, are also often used in conjunction with retrospective videographic techniques. Unobtrusive observations – which sometimes use concealed video equipment – also fit into the toolkit of videographic researchers. The use of concealed camera techniques raises the importance of research ethics protocols in videographic research.

Once videographic data are collected, a variety of analytic tools may be marshalled to code and categorize them. Videographic analysis follows the basic principles of interpretive analysis, from grounded theory-building to hermeneutic cycling. Video analysis can happen holistically, or occur through a very formalized frame-by-frame coding and classification procedure. Once the AV data are analysed, the edited production of the film is undertaken.

There are two basic formats for disseminating video material. The first we term local access, and this would include fixed, physical, media such as CD-ROM, DVD and videotape. The second is a more broadcast format, which we term distributed access, and includes television broadcasts and Internet streaming. Local access media usually offer higher quality, better control of access to material and its pace, order and sometimes language, view and content control. Web-based access can offer some of these options as well, in addition to updating and linking to related material. However, due to technological limitation on bandwidth there are currently compromises in quality (in terms of lower frame rates, lower resolution, and smaller screen size) in streamed video material.

Evaluation

Videography offers many compelling advantages over other forms of ethnographic research, which is why is has become an increasingly frequent accompaniment to traditional ethnography. By collecting AV data, researchers hope to capture more of the subtle temporal, social and spatial dimensions of human behaviour, including the intricacies of human body language. The resulting research representation on film can be resonant, emotional, vibrant and humanizing. It can give audiences a sense that they have actually experienced some of the cultural events being represented, deepening human understanding, and making the unfamiliar seem familiar.

There are some important drawbacks to the videographic method as well. First, filmmaking involves technique, and in a world filled with experienced screen watchers, audience expectations tend to be quite high. Talking head video, for example, fails to take full advantage of the medium. Second, the camera can prove an unwelcome hindrance to the formation of interviewer–interviewee rapport. Third, ethnographic film tends to be read by audiences using the same suspension of disbelief they learn to apply to commercial films and television. Prevalent techniques such as rich imagery, special effects, emotional swells of music, cuts and other editing flourishes tend to engage viewers, but potentially manipulate their emotions and exacerbate the impression of realism. Even more than other research representations, videography must deal with crisis of representation issues in the many decisions involved in creating the research product, and realize that videographic representation is capable of telling many 'truths'.

Robert V. Kozinets and Russell W. Belk

Associated Concepts: coding, ethics, ethnography, grounded theory, idiographic, interview,

naturalistic data, photography, qualitative data archives, validity of measurement, visual methods

Key Readings

Banks, M. (2001) *Visual Methods in Social Research*. London: Sage.
Belk, R. W. (1998) 'Multimedia consumer research', in B. Stern (ed.), *Representation in Consumer Research*. London: Routledge. pp. 308–38.
Evans, J. and Hall, S. (eds) (1999) *Visual Culture: The Reader*. London: Sage.
Pink, S. (2001) *Doing Visual Ethnography*. London: Sage.

VISUAL METHODS

Definition

The use of visual images and technologies such as video, film, photography, art, drawing and sculpture in qualitative social research to both produce and represent knowledge. This includes using the visual as a documenting tool to produce visual records, in interviews to elicit comments from informants, in participant observation to research ways of seeing and understanding, analysing visual and material culture and using visual media to represent the findings of such research.

Distinctive Features

Because visually we can communicate knowledge, experiences and ideas in ways that we cannot using only written or spoken words, the visual is gaining increasing importance as a social research method. A range of visual methods have been developed for social research, including visual documentation, photo elicitation, photographic and video interviewing, asking informants to produce images, participant observation with a camera, ethnographic film making and most recently ethnographic hypermedia. We may classify images used in visual research into two categories. First, images produced by the researcher, and second, images found or produced by informants.

Photography, video or drawings produced by the researcher might be used to visually document a place or event, providing a visual record of that context as seen by the researcher. Such images may also have further uses. First they might be used to establish relationships with informants, for example offering photographs one has taken of people to them as gifts. Second, they can be used in photo or video elicitation, a method that involves the researcher showing informant(s) images to elicit their response. It has been found that showing people images is likely to evoke a whole range of responses and information that it would not occur to them to offer in a verbal interview (see Harper, 2002). Other types of images are also used in elicitation interviews, for example images from informants' own photography, drawing or video collections, or other 'found' images.

Visual methods often involve collaboratively producing images with informants, for example in video or photographic interviews. Here researchers will interview a person using a video camera or stills camera to record the visual aspects of that interview. This allows informants to explicitly use the visual to communicate during the interview, and provides researchers with audiovisual records of that encounter. Recording video, taking photographs or making drawings as part of a participant observation project can also help researchers understand or 'see' their informants' points of view, or 'ways of seeing'. For example in Spain I photographed the bullfight and asked my informants to comment on my photographs as a means of learning about the way they saw the bullfight and an attempt to photograph the event the way they saw it. Grasseni similarly used video in Italy to learn to see cattle from the perspective of her local cattle-breeding informants (Grasseni, 2004). Finally, images produced by researchers are used to represent the findings of social research. This might be in the form of a documentary film, a photographic or art exhibition or book, a multimedia hypermedia project produced for the Internet, CD-ROM or DVD.

Images produced by informants are also used in social research. Social researchers analyse other people's existing image collections and images they have invited informants to produce for the research. For example, studies of family or personal photography might focus on individuals' existing photographic collections. These teach us much about ideal representations of family and other relationships and offer insights into the social history of family and personal life. Researchers also might analyse people's art collections, the images they display on their walls and their home movies.

Visual researchers also ask informants to produce images for them to analyse. For example, an informant might photograph, video or draw aspects of her or his own everyday life, keeping a photographic or video diary to hand in to the researcher for analysis. In a method called 'image work', that has parallels with some types of therapy (Edgar, 2004), people are asked to make drawings that express their feelings about particular issues or experiences. These can then be discussed by informants and analysed by the researcher. Such methods allow people to represent to researchers ideas, knowledge and experiences that cannot be represented using solely the written or spoken word.

Evaluation

Until recently there was much resistance to the use of the visual in social research. It was often considered to produce data, or research materials that were too subjective. However, if we accept that subjectivity is an essential element of any qualitative social research project then it becomes clear that visual materials are just as valid as written or verbal data. Understanding this subjectivity is key to analysing visual images. Therefore when social researchers analyse images they focus on three main issues: the processes by which the images were produced, the content of the images, and the context in which they are viewed and understood.

This emphasis on subjectivity is linked to the insistence amongst visual researchers on reflexivity. Visual researchers need to be aware of how their own subjective feelings and assumptions influence the images they produce and their understandings of other people's images. To be fully reflexive researchers should reveal these assumptions in the texts they produce about their research.

Visual methods are never purely visual. They usually combine the visual with words, whether this is in the form of asking questions or conversing with informants, or in written texts. The visual is also never totally isolated from other sensory experiences, such as touch, smell, and sound. For example, videos are not purely visual, but audiovisual, and printed photographs are also material objects that one touches, feels and talks about.

Using visual methods is clearly beneficial to social researchers; it adds a new dimension to qualitative research by introducing the possibility of knowledge and experience that cannot be communicated verbally or in written words.

Sarah Pink

Associated Concepts: ethnography, mixed methods research, photography, projective techniques, qualitative research, reflexivity, subjectivity, unobtrusive measures

Key Readings

Banks, M. (2001) *Visual Methods in Social Research*. London: Sage.
Edgar, I. (2004) 'Imagework in ethnographic research', in S. Pink, L. Kurti and A. I. Afonso (eds), *Working Images*. London: Routledge.
Grasseni, C. (2004) 'Video and ethnographic knowledge: skilled vision in the practice of breeding', in S. Pink, L. Kurti and A. I. Afonso (eds), *Working Images*. London: Routledge.
Harper, D. (2002) 'Talking about pictures: a case for photo-elicitation', *Visual Studies*, 17 (1): 13–26.

Pink, S. (2001) *Doing Visual Ethnography: Images, Media and Representation in Research*. London: Sage.
Pink, S., Kurti, L. and Afonso, A. I. (eds) (2004) *Working Images*. London: Routledge.
Rose, G. (2001) *Visual Methodologies*. London: Sage.

VOLUNTEER SAMPLING

Definition

A form of case selection which is purposive rather than based on the principles of random or probability sampling. It usually involves individuals who agree to participate in research, sometimes for payment. However, it can involve other units of analysis, for example when organizational heads volunteer their institutions as sites for research.

Distinctive Features

The basic principle of random or probability sampling is that every case in the population being studied has an equal and non-zero chance of being selected as a sample member. If random selection is used it is possible to use probability theory to make statistical inferences about the population from a sample selected from it. For example, it is possible to infer the extent to which an estimate of average age collected by surveying a sample is likely to be close to the true figure for the population as a whole.

Sometimes it is not possible or desirable to use random or probability techniques, in which case the sample members are chosen for a particular purpose. The reasons may be that a sampling frame (a complete list of everyone in the population) prevents random selection; there are not sufficient resources or time to contact all those selected for a random sample; the topic of research is so sensitive that few members of a sample would be willing to be sources of data.

Volunteer sampling is a form of purposive/non-random sampling for all such reasons. It is used especially in sensitive research when it is necessary to rely on those who are willing to answer requests to provide data. For example, research conducted in the UK by the London Metropolitan Police in 2004 contacted imprisoned serial killers to construct a pool of volunteer subjects. Detailed interviews were conducted in order to study the psychological profile of such killers with a view to identifying potential offenders in the future.

Volunteers are also used as subjects in psychological experiments in which some are allocated to a control group and others to an experimental group (which is given some stimulus or 'treatment' to see if being a member of the latter produces some predicted effect). Similar principles can apply in programme evaluation research whereby individuals volunteer to be the recipients of some policy initiative, the efficacy of which is subsequently evaluated. Finally, focus groups, which are used in a wide range of marketing and social research, are often constructed from individuals who volunteer to take part.

Evaluation

A key problem with volunteer sampling is representativeness insofar as it is difficult to establish the extent to which those who volunteer to participate are typical of the group to which findings are to be generalized. For this reason it is important to be cautious about the claims that are made about and from such research.

It is also important to pay attention to the 'research bargain'. It is possible that those who volunteer to take part in research do so in order to gain some benefit to themselves. It is important for a researcher to consider whether such benefits can, or indeed should be met.

Victor Jupp

Associated Concepts: ethnographic interviewing, focus group, non-probability (non-random) sampling, opportunity sampling, purposive sampling, research bargain, sensitive research, snowball sampling

Key Reading

Moser, C. A. and Kalton, G. (1971) *Survey Methods in Social Investigation.* London: Heinemann.

W

WRITING RESEARCH

Definition

The process and techniques of communicating significant information about a piece of research. Writing research serves two functions, both of which make it an essential ingredient of the overall research process. First, writing research enables findings to become publicly available and thus allows other researchers to use the findings and build upon them in the furtherance of knowledge. Second, writing research allows the methods of investigation to become open to scrutiny by peers. On the basis of written accounts of how the research was conducted and how the results were obtained other researchers can evaluate the research and judge the quality of the findings.

Distinctive Features

Despite the variety of disciplines and approaches that characterize the social sciences there are certain conventions associated with writing research that are widely accepted. These conventions cover both the style and the structure of the writing. The style of writing research tends to be formal. This involves writing in the 'third person' and adopting a style that is succinct, direct and clear. It also involves a meticulous attention to citing the sources from which ideas and findings have been derived, and doing so using a specific style of referencing (such as the Harvard style).

The structure generally follows a logical sequence that provides the reader with information about what was being studied, how it was studied and what was found as a result of the investigation. Conventionally, the research is reported in line with the following headings.

Title	This identifies the topic and scope of the research.
Abstract	A brief overview of the research summarizing its principal aims, methods and conclusions.
Key words	A small number (4–10) of words that facilitate bibliographic searches.
Acknowledgements	A statement noting the help provided by others in conducting the research or producing its findings.
Aims	A broad overview of what the research was attempting to achieve.
Introduction	A relatively short section that explains the background to the research.
Literature review	A critical evaluation of previous studies whose purpose is to demonstrate how the research will enhance what is already known about the particular subject.
Research questions	A list of specific points to be investigated. These can take the form of hypotheses, propositions, or questions.

Methods	A factual statement of how the research was conducted. The design of the research, the methods of data collection and the techniques of data analysis need to be described. They also need to be justified as appropriate in relation to the research questions and to broader social, ethical and resource issues.
Findings	A section presenting the main findings from the investigation. The emphasis is on describing what was found without delving into possible explanations of the findings or considerations of what their implications might be.
Discussion	A section that attempts to analyse the findings and to explain what factors lay behind the findings.
Conclusions	A relatively brief, but very important, section that considers the implications of findings from the research.
Appendices	Technical and other supporting material that readers might need to refer to but whose presence within the body of the text would unduly disrupt the flow of the discussion.
References	A list of the published works cited in the report. The details allow readers to search for the original sources.

Additionally, there are aspects of research that sometimes get subsumed under other headings but which can also appear as separate and distinct sections in their own right. Three important examples are:

Outcomes	A section that specifies the 'tangible' end-products of the investigation. These can take the form of contributions to the stock of knowledge, developments of theory, suggestions for future research, practical recommendations or guidelines for good practice.
Limitations	An acknowledgement of what can be justifiably concluded on the basis of the methods, findings and analysis and, importantly, the limits to what can be deduced.
Ethics	A consideration of the ethical issues involved in the topic of research, the methods of data collection and analysis, and the dissemination of findings.

Evaluation

The growth of qualitative research and the influence of the postmodernist critique have effectively removed any illusion that writing research simply involves 'reporting what actually happened'. Instead, it is recognized that writing research involves producing an 'account' of the research. Such accounts are, in the first instance, *edited highlights* of what happened. Inevitably, writing research entails reducing the huge amounts of material researchers accumulate as a record of what was done, why it was done and what outcomes resulted. The editing process calls on researchers to prioritize certain things in terms of their significance for the investigation and possibly omit altogether some other aspects of the research process from their report. The extent of reduction will vary depending on whether the research is written up in the format of a journal article, PhD thesis or practitioner report, but the parameters of space will guarantee that the researcher could never provide a full and exhaustive account of the research. Accounts of research also call for *creative writing skills* on the part of the researcher. As Van Maanen (1988) has shown, writing research entails the use of 'rhetorical devices' through which the researcher aims to persuade the reader of the genuineness and authoritativeness of the account. The style and amount of detail provided in an account of research will vary, as well, depending on the expertise of the audience and the extent to which the researcher can presume the readers have prior knowledge of the subject matter and methods of research. The skill of writing research, then, resides in knowing what elements of the investigation to focus upon and being able to present them in a way that adequately and honestly describes the investigation and also justifies the approach and decisions in terms of expected standards of good practice among peers, colleagues, fellow researchers and others such as policy makers and the public who might feel the need to assess the worth of the research.

The skill of writing research is to match the need for transparency with the expectations of the audience within the confines of the space allowed by the format of the publication.

Martyn Denscombe

Associated Concepts: ethics, literature review, postmodernism, reflexivity, research design, validity

Key Readings

Atkinson, P. (1990) *The Ethnographic Imagination: Textual Constructions of Reality.* London: Routledge.

Denscombe, M. (2002) *Ground Rules for Good Research.* Milton Keynes: Open University Press.

Hammersley, M. (1990) *Reading Ethnographic Research: A Critical Guide.* London: Longman.

Van Maanen, J. (1988) *Tales of the Field: On Writing Ethnography.* Chicago: University of Chicago Press.

Subject Index

Author Index